HANDING ON THE FAITH

HANDING ON THE FAITH

A Manual of Catechetics

BY JOSEF ANDREAS JUNGMANN

HERDER AND HERDER

THIS ENGLISH VERSION TRANSLATED AND REVISED
BY A. N. FUERST (WITH SUPPLEMENTARY MATERIAL FOR GREAT
BRITAIN BY J. D. CRICHTON) IS BASED ON THE SECOND
GERMAN EDITION OF "KATECHETIK"
PUBLISHED BY HERDER, FREIBURG, 1955

SECOND IMPRESSION PUBLISHED 1959 BY HERDER AND HERDER,
INC., 7 WEST 46th STREET, NEW YORK 36, N. Y.

NIHIL OBSTAT: CLARENCE E. ELWELL, PH. D.
CENSOR DEPUTATUS

IMPRIMATUR: CLEVELAND. THE 6th FEBRUARY 1957
EDWARD F. HOBAN, S. T. D., LL. D.,
ARCHBISHOP-BISHOP OF CLEVELAND

LIBRARY OF CONGRESS CATALOG CARD NUMBER: 59—10748

MADE AND PRINTED BY HERDER DRUCK
FREIBURG, WEST GERMANY

CONTENTS

ABBREVIATIONS

CSEL	*Corpus Scriptorum Ecclesiasticorum Latinorum*
ChPBl	*Christlich-Pädagogische Blätter* (Wien)
KBl	*Katechetische Blätter* (München)
LThK	*Lexikon für Theologie und Kirche*
PG	*Patrologia Graeca*
PL	*Patrologia Latina*
RW	*Religion und Weltanschauung*
ZkTh	*Zeitschrift für katholische Theologie* (Innsbruck)
Bopp	L. Bopp, *Katechetik. Geist und Form des katholischen Religionsunterrichts (Handbuch der Erziehungswissenschaft* IV, 1*)*, München, 1935.
Eggersdorfer	Fr. X. Eggersdorfer, *Jugendbildung. Allgemeine Theorie des Schulunterrichtes,* 4th ed. *(Handbuch der Erziehungswissenschaft* I, 3*)*, München, 1933.
Gatterer	M. Gatterer, S.J., *Katechetik oder Anleitung zur Kinderseelsorge,* 4th ed.; Innsbruck, 1931.
Heuser-Solzbacher	A. Heuser und J. Solzbacher, *Katholischer Religionsunterricht,* Hannover, 1949.
Hirscher	J. B. Hirscher, *Katechetik oder der Beruf des Seelsorgers, die ihm anvertraute Jugend im Christentum zu unterrichten und zu erziehen,* 3rd ed.; Tübingen, 1834.
Hofinger	J. Hofinger, S.J., *Geschichte des Katechismus in Österreich von Canisius bis zur Gegenwart. Mit besonderer Berücksichtigung der gleichzeitigen gesamtdeutschen Katechismusgeschichte,* Innsbruck, 1937.
Lentner	L. Lentner, *Religionsunterricht zwischen Methode und freier Gestaltung. Die elementare religiöse Unter-*

	weisung in Frankreich (Veröffentlichungen des erzbisch. Amtes f. Unterricht u. Erziehung, Wien, Vol. I), Innsbruck, 1953.
Mayer	Heinrich Mayer, *Katechetik. Theorie des Religionsunterrichtes für Volks-, Fortbildungs- und höhere Schulen,* 3rd ed.; Freiburg, 1939.
Pfliegler	M. Pfliegler, *Der Religionsunterricht. Seine Besinnung auf die psychologischen, pädagogischen und didaktischen Erkenntnisse seit der Bildungslehre Otto Willmanns,* 3 vols., Innsbruck, 1935.
Proceedings	*Proceedings of the National Catechetical Congress of the Confraternity of Christian Doctrine* (Paterson, N.J.). The tenth Congress was held in Buffalo, September 1956; the first in Rochester 1935.
Raab	K. Raab, *Das Katechismusproblem in der katholischen Kirche,* Freiburg, 1934.

PREFACE

This book is the result of lectures which, as the successor to Father Michael Gatterer, S.J., I gave at the University of Innsbruck from 1934 onward. The influence of his "Katechetik" which appeared in four different editions (the last in 1931) can still be recognized in certain sections of the book; his pastoral views and his pastoral principles should continue to serve as guides for the future.

I have tried, however, to bear in mind the problems raised and advances made in recent years and to incorporate them into a unified concept of my theme which would be adequate to the task of proclaiming the faith to a modern generation. The methodological formulation of various problems could not be passed over lightly. It is now possible to sift and evaluate—in the calm which the passage of time brings with it—what former decades have achieved at such great expense of labour and time. In this I think I am justified in dispensing, for the sake of greater simplicity and clarity, with the technical terminology which, in Germany, in the last phase of the movement towards a more suitable methodology, has often been borrowed from the philosophy and pedagogy of value.

More important to me, however, than methodological considerations was the task of increasing and clarifying the awareness of the mission with which the catechist is entrusted. Our age is filled with so much noise and is so pre-occupied with material things that voices from a higher world can hardly be heard, and it is not at all easy to convey the word of God effectively to children, although it is the "good news" which we are proclaiming. Religious knowledge without order will soon lose its hold. Only concentration on the most important points and greater awareness of life's problems can help us to fulfill our task. The emphasis has therefore deliberately been placed on essentials.

In addition to theoretical insight, practical experience is as indispensable for catechesis as it is for the catechist. Since the days of my own active and intensive pastoral work lie in the rather distant past (although they found some continuation from time to time), I have endeavoured all the more to remain in close contact with the experiences of others, particularly through reports of the various changing situations published in catechetical magazines. On the other hand, I have quoted only a few examples of the text-books which are now beginning to appear again; I did not intend to give a complete list.

I hope then that I have not remained a stranger to the problems facing the catechist today. May he who once so lovingly blessed the children gathered about him, bless this work also!

April 27th, 1953 JOSEF ANDREAS JUNGMANN

Innsbruck, on the Feast of St. Peter Canisius, Doctor of the Church

INTRODUCTION

CATECHESIS and preaching are the two chief ways in which the Church exercises her teaching office. Whereas the sermon is limited to certain definite occasions, takes up and evaluates certain definite points of doctrine, and through them seeks to keep alive and to develop Christian life, catechesis furnishes a basic introduction to the whole of Christian doctrine. Today in most Christian countries catechesis is concerned with the younger generation who, as infants, were adopted into the kingdom of grace by baptism. After their mental faculties have awakened and before the children go into the wider life of the world, it attempts to familiarize them with the doctrines of their faith and to show them the way of salvation.

From this it is evident that catechesis is one of the most rewarding tasks of pastoral work, and this for several reasons: firstly, because by it is made possible the teaching of the glad tidings of the Gospel as a whole, with all the power and beauty that is hidden in them; secondly, because it affords an opportunity of delivering to the children the news of the kingdom of God, which their Divine Master meant to be theirs in a very special way; and finally, because their expectant hearts need to be given that nourishment which they as children of God require.

In all this, the individual psychological differences manifest in the spiritual life of the children, and its gradual development, pose definite difficulties and requirements which do not decrease with the advent of adolescence.

The attempt to outline the task of catechetics, the choice of subject matter and its planned distribution over the years require careful deliberation. From such deliberation has arisen the science of catechesis, catechetics. Catechetics is the science that is sister to homiletics. Homiletics always considers its subject from the practical standpoint insofar as it teaches that the sermon should never be a purely theoretical instruction, but should propose a practical course for life. Catechetics also pursues the same objectives. Catechetics must never lose sight of the fact that catechesis means the transference of the content of Christian doctrine to those who are maturing and that, as a consequence, the task of education cannot be divorced from it. This is true especially in our own times, when the Christian education of youth is threatened on many fronts.

For this reason specialists have characterized catechetics also as the "pedagogy of religion and of morals" (Göttler).[1] This concept is, however, somewhat wider than the object of catechetics. In the current meaning of the word, and so we consider it here, catechetics has to do only with that religious and moral guidance of the younger generation, which is exercised directly by the official ministry of the Church; it is ecclesiastical pedagogy in religion and morals. Besides, there remain the religious and moral tasks of the parents which are outside catechetics, and the educational responsibilities of the Catholic school and, in certain instances, of the state.[2] These must share in the educative tasks as well as the educative responsibilities of the Church. In the following pages we shall deal with these duties only in passing.

Frequently the concept, catechesis, is made synonymous with the phrase "religious instruction", a designation which stems from the era of enlightenment.[3] In adopting such a definition,

[1] J. Göttler, *Religions- und Moralpädagogik* (2nd ed.; Münster i. W.: Aschendorffsche Verlagsbuchhandlung, 1931), p. 2.

[2] In certain countries, particularly in France, catechetics denotes also all those influences which are brought to bear on the children by the family, the school, etc. (Translator's note.)

[3] E. Leen, *What is Education?* (New York: Sheed and Ward, 1944), p. 163; J. D. Redden and F. A. Ryan, *A Catholic Philosophy of Education* (Milwaukee: Bruce, 1949), pp. 21–31.

we must avoid a possible misunderstanding, namely, that catechesis is concerned only with purely theoretical instruction; it also implies the task of educating. For this reason we may, in general, use with greater precision the expression "religious training". This term indicates that catechetics does indeed deal with instruction, but with instruction which not only inculcates correct doctrine but also makes possible a genuine religious education. And this religious education implies moral guidance as its natural correlative.

In what pertains to the development of this work on catechetics, we intend first of all to offer in an historical survey the catechetical experience of the Church and to give an overall view of the gradual development of present-day basic requirements. We shall then turn our attention to the individual factors of catechesis: those who present it, the catechists; those who receive it, the catechumens; and its purpose: the effective transfer of the catechetical subject matter by the catechist to the catechumen. Finally, we shall discuss the principles of catechetical method, first of all, in general terms, the most universally valid ones, and then, in detail, those which pertain to individual or special tasks and to work with different age groups.

Ever since its foundation catechesis has always been found in the Church. We encounter the word, κατηχεῖν, in the New Testament sometimes already in its modern sense as meaning a basic training in Christian doctrine (Gal. 6, 6; compare Lk. 1, 4). In profane Greek literature the word was seldom used.

In such works κατ-ηχεῖν appeared in its original meaning, "down, to sound" or "to resound" (Compare ἠχώ = sound). This meaning is the foundation for its ecclesiastical usage: the message of God resounds downward in the direction of men, according to the words contained in the Office of the Apostles taken from Psalm 18: "into all the earth their sound goes forth" (v. 5). The word was also used in a transitive sense—"to instruct someone", especially in the sense of "an instruction for beginners".

The word then became the technical term to designate the teaching given by the Church; this is the catechesis (κατήχησις); the catechist (ὁ κατηχῶν; ὁ κατηχήτης) is the one who imparts the training; the catechumen (ὁ κατηχούμενος) is the one to whom it is imparted, the one who receives it. A more recent form of the word is κατηχίζειν, in Latin, *catechizare*. From this is derived *catechismus* which originally denoted only the catechesis (just as the word *catéchisme* in French today). In English the word refers to the book, which offers the outlines of the training.

I

THE HISTORY OF CATECHESIS

1. *The Age of Baptismal Catechesis*

THE catechetical life of Christian antiquity differs from that of the present especially in that catechesis was not given in school, and that there was no special catechesis provided for children. In this period, however, there was a special catechesis which was addressed to adults.[1] This was because at that time Christianity was concerned with propagation, with missionary activity which naturally was directed to adults. In these early days this adult catechesis was identical with the mission sermon. Such sermons differed from one another, of course, depending on whether they were directed to the Jews or to the Gentiles. To the Jews the missionaries had to make clear that Christ was the promised Messiah. They had also to take into consideration

[1] G. Bardy, "L'enseignement religieux aux premiers siècles" in *Revue Apologétique,* Vol. 66 (1938, I), 641–655; Vol. 67 (1938, II), 5–18. Consult also the article of J. A. Jungmann and J. Schmidlin, "Katechumenat" in *Lexikon für Theologie und Kirche,* Vol. V (1933), cols. 844–888. There is no general exposition of the history of catechesis from ancient times down to the present based upon the present state of our knowledge. For the time after the beginning of the Middle Ages the work of Göbl (see below under footnote 25) is the last that has appeared. There are, however, the works of C. Hézard, *Histoire du Catéchisme* (2nd ed.; Paris: Librairie des Catéchismes, 1900); G. Bareille, "Catéchèse, Catéchuménat" in *Dictionnaire de Théologie Catholique,* Vol. II, part 2, cols. 1877ff.; Guy de Bretagne, *Pastorale Catéchétique* (Paris: Desclée de Brouwer, 1953); J. Schmidlin (M. Braun, trans.), *Catholic Mission History* (Techny, Ill.: Mission Press, 1933), especially pp. 2–122; A. Seage, *La Catequesis Antigua* (Rosario, Argentina: Apis, 1953); R. G. Bandas, *Catechetical Methods* (New York: J. F. Wagner, 1929).

the Jews themselves who had already been prepared by the Law, which for them was "a tutor, bringing (them) to Christ" (Gal. 3, 24). The sermon having been accepted with faith, Baptism could follow at once (compare Acts 2, 41; 8, 12f., etc.). To the Gentiles, on the contrary, the doctrine of one God and of the futility of polytheism had to be preached and Christian moral law accepted. Thus, we find that for them a longer preparation was necessary, this also meant a longer term of probation, with prayers and fasting.[2]

At the end of the second century, at the very latest, individual tutoring had been replaced by group instruction followed by group Baptism. There were special catechists and for their continued training catechetical schools were founded. Baptism was administered at Easter,[3] making the liturgy and catechesis mutually complementary. Baptism as participation in the resurrection of Christ was made visual. Thus there arose the catechumenate.

In the establishment of the catechumenate we must distinguish an earlier and a later period. In the earlier period (up to the time of Constantine) we become acquainted, around 215 A.D., with a complete order of the catechumenate in the *Apostolic Tradition* of Hippolytus of Rome. According to this, the catechumenate began with a rigorous examination for the purpose of determining whether the profession and the way of life of the candidate were compatible with the Christian moral law. This stage lasted as a rule for three years. It was not only a period of probation but also one devoted to the teaching of Christian doctrine. The catechist, who might also be a layman, concluded every instruction with prayer and the imposition of hands.

[2] Justin, *Apol.* I, c. 61. The rise of catechetical schools after this date would seem to indicate that a more systematic catechesis was given.

[3] Tertullian, *De baptismo,* c. 19.

As subject matter of these instructions Origen[4] mentioned the Books of Esther, Judith, Tobias, and the Sapiential Books, that is biblical texts which could illustrate Christian conduct. At the conclusion of these three years there followed another examination, this time concentrated less on knowledge but on the moral conduct of life. When this was successfully completed, the candidate was permitted "to listen to the Gospel", that is, he was given a daily instruction; this dealt with the teachings of faith, and was joined to a daily imposition of hands which was exorcistic in character. As early as the third century the instruction culminated in the "handing over" of the Apostles' Creed, which the baptismal candidate had to recite before he received Baptism.

The later period of the catechumenate (fourth-fifth centuries) was characterized by the conditions resulting from mass-conversions. Many contented themselves with entering the catechumenate only. By this act alone they were recognized as Christians. Some sought to delay Baptism, with its rigorous obligations, as long as possible, in any case until they were of a riper age. One of the more important reasons for deferring Baptism was the fact that if a grievous sin had been committed after Baptism, the Christian could, according to the severe penitential discipline of the times, obtain forgiveness only by undergoing public penance. In fact even in Christian families this practice of deferred Baptism was sometimes adopted. Ambrose, Augustine, Chrysostom and others were baptized only in adulthood. The order of the catechumenate had to be adapted to these conditions. The catechumenate in this period consisted of the following elements:

1. To the first examination was added an introductory

[4] Origenes in *Num. hom.* 27, 1; compare this with Athanasius, 39th Letter *(Epistola eortastika)* to which the *Didache* and *Pastor of Hermas* are appended.

catechesis which now took the place of a later instruction. This catechesis was designed to give a survey of the content of the Christian doctrine of salvation. Instructions for this are given by St. Augustine in his work: *De catechizandis rudibus*. After this, the catechist was supposed to present in the form of a narration *(narratio)* the entire doctrine of salvation, from the fall of our first parents down to the Last Judgement. By this process it was hoped that the candidate would be led from faith to hope and from hope to love. For this reason Augustine attached great value to the fact that during the catechesis an atmosphere of happiness *(hilaritas)* should prevail.

The reception into the catechumenate took place by signing the candidate with the sign of the Cross, which was generally followed by an imposition of hands. To this were often added the presentation of blessed salt and an insufflation. Through these ceremonies the candidate became a catechumen, and hence a Christian. For many years he remained such. In any event, through assisting at that part of the Mass which consisted in the reading of the word of God, the catechumen received a certain measure of further Christian teaching.[5]

2. The Fathers in their homilies, urged the catechumens to make known to the authorities that they were ready for Baptism before the beginning of that period which is now customarily known as Lent and serves as a preparation for Easter. *Ecce Pascha est, da nomen ad baptismum.*[6] Those who applied were called from then on φωτιζόμενοι, *competentes,* in Rome, *electi.*

Of the catecheses, which were given during this period and which were associated as before with exorcisms and the imposition of hands, we have models informative in the catecheses

[5] The first unmistakable evidence we have for the presence of catechumens at the first part of the Mass (the so-called Mass of the Catechumens) is a reference in the Homilies of Origen.

[6] Augustinus, *Serm.* 132, 1 (*PL* 38, 735).

of Cyril of Jerusalem, which he delivered in about 348. These contain nineteen catecheses to be given before Baptism. After a beautiful introduction, the first five treat of sin, Baptism and faith; the rest, of the Creed. In other places it was customary in these catecheses first to explain the history of salvation[7] and only then in the last or in one of the final catecheses to present the Creed.[8] The imparting, or handing-over, of the Creed usually took place, especially in the West, in a special ceremony, the *traditio symboli;* to this was added in Rome the *traditio orationis dominicae*. Both formulas, the Creed and the Lord's Prayer, were subject to the strict discipline of the secret; they could be communicated only orally and had to be learned by heart. Further memory work was not demanded of the neophytes.[9] To this double *traditio* was frequently joined also a symbolical imparting of the four Gospels (Rome) or of the Psalms (Naples).

On such occasions the catechesis was turned into a solemn

[7] *Peregrinatio Aetheriae* c. 46 (*CSEL* 39, 97f.); compare it with *Constitutiones Apostolicae* VII, 39. Since the time of St. Ambrose of Milan the catechumens took part in a reading of Sacred Scripture during Lent. In the course of these readings *Genesis, Proverbs and the Sermon on the Mount* were read through in their entirety. O. Heiming, "Altliturgische Fastenferien in Mailand" in *Archiv für Liturgiewissenschaft,* Vol. 2 (1952), 44–60, especially 55.

[8] Augustinus, *Serm.* 212–214 et passim.

[9] Augustinus, *De fide et symbolo,* c. 1 (*PL* 40, 181) warns the catechist not to expect the candidate for Baptism to learn his explanation of the Creed by heart. Compare this with the article, "Auswendiglernen" in *Reallexikon für Antike und Christentum,* Vol. I, pp. 1034–1037. If in connection with the *traditio,* a *scrutinium* is mentioned, what is meant by this is not an examination on Christian doctrine, nor a simple test of the person requesting baptism, but an exorcist "test" of Satan, whose power was to be broken. A. Dondeyne, "La discipline des scrutins dans l'Église latine avant Charlemagne" in *Revue d'Histoire Catholique,* Vol. XXVIII (Jan. 1932), pp. 5/34, and Vol. XXVIII (Oct. 1932), pp. 751–788.

ceremony held at the assembly of the community on Sunday.[10] Catechesis and liturgy were thus fused into one.

The communication of the four Gospels, for example, took place in Rome in the sixth century according to the Gelasian Sacramentary[11] in the following fashion. Out of the sacristy there emerged a procession of clerics, *thuriferarii* with censers, acolytes with lighted candles, then four deacons with the four Gospels, and finally the priest. The four deacons placed the four Gospel books on the four corners of the altar. Following this, the priest spoke about the Gospels. Then the first deacon stepped forward and read the beginning of the Gospel of St. Matthew; thereupon the priest gave a short talk in which he explained the symbolism of St. Matthew: *facies hominis*. The same thing was done by the other three deacons with the other three Gospels, each followed by a short sermon by the priest, who at the end gave a concise summary of the meaning of the ceremony as a preparation for Baptism.

In the Sunday Mass (which was probably joined to this ceremony) the godparents of the candidates for Baptism came to the fore. Their names were read at the Memento of the Living; the names of the baptismal aspirants, who because of the discipline of the secret were unable to be present, were announced in the Hanc Igitur; the sacrifice was offered especially for them.[12]

3. Baptism was administered on the vigil of Easter with great solemnity. The ceremonies began with a renunciation of Satan and a confession of faith. The newly baptized were then confirmed. Vested in white baptismal robes, they assisted, for the first time, at the celebration of the Mass, and received Holy Communion.

[10] In Rome it appears that the third, fourth and fifth Sundays of Lent were chosen. The intervening weeks still contain unmistakable references to Baptism.

[11] I, 34–36 (Wilson 50–60).

[12] *Ibid.* I, 26 (Wilson 34).

4. The newly baptized wore the white baptismal robe during the entire octave of the Paschal feast up to Low Sunday. In this festal week in which they appeared daily at Mass and received Holy Communion, they were also given the final catechesis on the Sacraments. Because the rites themselves were also included under the discipline of the secret, and because on the other hand, the language of the liturgy was the vernacular, all essential matters, insofar as they had not been previously anticipated, were now for the first time explained during the course of their actual reception.

Examples are preserved for us in the five "Mystagogical Catecheses" of Jerusalem, which have been handed down to us with the catecheses of Cyril, and also in the writings of St. Ambrose, *De Sacramentis* and *De Mysteriis*,[13] and in the catecheses of Theodore of Mopsuestia.[14]

From the sixth century onward the catechumenate began to decline, since the Baptism of adults in the Roman-Grecian world, which had become Christian, was more the exception than the rule.[15] With the conversion of the Germanic tribes, and with that of the Slavs—these were most generally mass conversions—the old custom was no longer employed. A preparation lasting only a few weeks was thought sufficient after which the whole tribe was baptized. In these mass Baptisms whole

[13] Consult among others J. Quasten, *Monumenta eucharistica et liturgica vetustissima* (Bonn: Peter Hanstein, 1935); *CSEL* 73, 15-116. For the style of the catecheses of Cyril and Ambrose, consult G. S. Sloyan, "Religious Education: From Early Christian to Medieval Times", in *Shaping the Christian Message* (New York: Macmillan, 1958), pp. 10-12, 16f.

[14] Edition of A. Rücker, *Ritus baptismi et missae quem descripsit Theodorus ep. Mopsuestiae* (Münster, 1933).

[15] A written testimonial which already shows signs of this trend may be found in Johannes Diaconus, *Ep. ad Sennarium* (c. 500) Nos. 2–6 (*PL* 59, 401–403), and still another in Fulgentius (d. 532) *Ep.* 12, 2 (*PL* 65, 380) who answers the question put to him by the Deacon, Ferrandus, concerning the Baptism of a negro slave.

tribes were sometimes baptized; their subsequent education being left to the community under the tutelage of the Church. Only later were certain customs of the ancient Christian catechumenate revived.[16]

The usages of the catechumenate in a more or less condensed form were, nevertheless, incorporated into the rite of Baptism for children. In it we can still recognize the principal phases of the ancient preparation for Baptism. From the introductory catechesis there remains the insufflation, the sign of the Cross, the salt blessed under exorcism; from the time of the catechumenate itself, an exorcism (including another signing with the Cross) and the oration; from the final preparation of the *electi,* the imparting (and at the same time the recital on the part of the godparents) of the Lord's Prayer and the profession of faith, the Creed. From early on the last exorcism as well as the renunciation of Satan, and the replies to the questions concerning faith which are expected of the godparents immediately before the act of Baptism itself were part of the Baptism of children.[17]

The ecclesiastical catechesis of Christian antiquity was therefore generally given as a means of preparing adults for Baptism. What steps were taken to provide for the Christian training of baptized children?

That in Christian families the Baptism of children was from a very early date considered as a matter of course is attested by an incident in North Africa during the lifetime of St.

[16] J. Schmidlin, "Die Katechumenatspraxis in der gegenwärtigen Heidenmission" in *Lexikon für Theologie und Kirche,* Vol. V, col. 887.

[17] Benedictine Fathers, *The Rites of Adult Baptism* (Philadelphia: Dolphin Press, 1937), especially pp. 1–19; Ph. Oppenheim, "De Fontibus et Historia Ritus Baptismalis" and also "Commentationes Ad Ritum Baptismalem" (Pars I. Ritus Antebaptismales); both of these are in *Institutiones Systematico-Historicae In Sacram Liturgiam* (Turin: Marietti, 1943).

Cyprian (d. 258). A certain bishop, Fidus, was of the opinion that the Baptism of newly born children should be deferred to the eighth day following the practice of circumcision among the Jews. At a Synod, which 67 bishops attended, the question was settled and the opinion of Fidus unanimously rejected.[18] We must remember that in this controversy it was a question not of infant Baptism but of the period within which the sacrament was to be administered. Only about the fourth century, during which individuals frequently deferred their Baptism until the approach of death do we meet with a passing hesitancy about the practice of infant Baptism. This reluctance was overcome to all intents and purposes before the advent of the Pelagian controversy at the beginning of the fifth century.

There can be found no trace of an ecclesiastical catechesis for baptized children. It was considered normal for parents to undertake the further religious training of their children.[19] The children grew into the religious life of the Church through assistance at Mass, at which they frequently formed a special group shouting the response *Kyrie eleison* in the litanies with special fervour.[20] In the homilies of St. John Chrysostom we find admonitions to parents on the Christian education of their children.[21] They were also reminded of their obligation at the Baptism ceremony itself; for either they or other close

[18] Cyprian, *Ep.* 64 (*CSEL* 3, 717–721). See also G. Bichlmair, *Urchristentum und katholische Kirche* (Innsbruck: Rauch, 1925), pp. 52–58.

[19] That such an instruction was given was mentioned by the father of the young Origen; Eusebius, *Hist. eccl.* vi, 2, 8f. Consult also Hieronymus, *Ep. ad Laetam* (Ep. 107).

[20] *Peregrinatio Aetheriae* c. 24, 5 (*CSEL* 39, 72); *Constitutiones Apostolicae* VIII, 6, 9; *Testamentum Domini* (ed. Rahmani, pp. 55, 135, 143); Chrysostomus, *In Mt. hom.* 71, 4 (*PG* 58, 666). H. Selhorst, "Das Kind im altchristlichen Gottesdienst" in *Trierer Theol. Zeitschrift,* Vol. 61 (1952), 328–333.

[21] Consult J. Göttler, *Geschichte der Pädagogik* (3rd ed.; Freiburg: Herder, 1935), p. 58f.

relatives of the children were as a rule entrusted with the task of renouncing Satan and of reciting the Creed in place of the child.[22] By so doing they agreed to act as guarantors, that the child would lead a Christian life; they were the *sponsores*.

Only at the end of Christian antiquity did it become customary for others outside the circle of the family to undertake the office of sponsor or *fidei iussor,* hence that of a guardian. This is what we call sponsorship or "acting as a sponsor". To it was linked the obligation of providing the child with a Christian training and of looking after his religious education.[23]

When, in retrospect, we ask ourselves what can be learned from the catechesis of Christian antiquity, the following points emerge:

1. We see that the early Christians were not satisfied merely with purveying knowledge, but that they also sought primarily to form true Christians; for this reason they required a long period of probation, examinations and prayer and fasting.

2. The teaching had to be comprehensive; the entire arrangement both of the catechesis and of the catechumenate draws its name from it. They demanded little, however, in the way of memory learning.

3. Catechesis was closely bound up with the liturgy: Easter as the time for Baptism, assistance at the Mass of the catechumens, special celebrations in the course of religious training. An active participation in the liturgy was on the whole the most desirable way in which the individual Christian and the Christian com-

[22] Hippolytus, *Apostolic Tradition* (G. Dix, *The Treatise on the Apostolic Tradition of St. Hippolytus of Rome*. Historical Introduction, etc. [London, 1937], p. 33); Augustinus, *Ep*. 98, 6f. (*CSEL* 34, 527) had to assure his correspondent that by way of exception another person too could take *(offerre)* a child to Baptism, as for instance, the master in the case of child slaves.

[23] E. Dick, "Das Pateninstitut im altchristlichen Katechumenat" in *ZkTh,* Vol. 63 (1939), pp. 1–49, especially p. 46ff.

munity were able to acquire the necessary religious knowledge. The liturgy, the forms of which were clearly recognized and the language of which was understood, was in a certain sense the continuation of catechesis and a substitute for those who had already been baptized as infants.

4. For the children of Christian families the parents were the catechists in the true sense of the word.

2. Catechesis in the Middle Ages

A regular ecclesiastical catechesis for children did not exist in the Middle Ages. Even a catechesis for adults of the type that had been customary in the catechumenate of the ancient Christian communities, had passed out of existence, particularly after the medieval peoples had all entered the Church. The formative religious influence of the liturgy was, furthermore, essentially curtailed by reason of the increasing strangeness of its forms, and especially of its language. Christianity, nevertheless, flowered in the Middle Ages. This flowering of Christianity appears to be almost a puzzle to us. How did the people of that time receive the necessary religious training?

In the first place, parents, as well as the sponsor who was now distinct from them, were still bound to provide religious training for their children. In the Carolingian period this obligation fell on both in various ways.[24] They were reminded, that not only bishops, priests, deacons and religious superiors, but also married persons in their own home shared in the pastoral office *(pastoris officium)*; they were, as a consequence, expected to instruct their children in the mysteries of faith and in the

[24] Thus in can. 19 of the *Synod of Arles* (813) which was repeated frequently in subsequent synods: *Ut parentes filios suos et patrini eos quos de fonte lavacri suscipiunt, erudire summopere studeant; illi quia eos genuerunt... isti quia pro eis fideiussores existunt. Mansi*, Vol. XIV, Col. 62.

sacrament of Baptism.[25] The sponsors were specially selected.[26] Before anyone was permitted to assume the responsibility of godparent, he had first to undergo an examination to determine whether he knew the Creed and the Our Father by heart; for, in the absence of parents, the godparent had to undertake the task of teaching both these formulas; in addition he had to make the children understand the faith as he had promised on their behalf and lead them to a life worthy of their Baptism.[27] Since that time (it was first referred to at a Paris Synod in 829) a special godparent was required also for Confirmation; who could, if necessary, take on the same obligation.

Carolingian legislation also attempted to set up a school system in addition to the cloister and cathedral schools which were already in existence. This system, it was hoped, would serve as an active agent in the religious training of youth.[28] Here and there schools of this kind were actually opened in conjunction with rural parishes; but such schools as a rule never advanced beyond the training of acolytes and the preparation of candidates for the clerical state. Only after the crusades and the growth of trade was there an increase in the number of elementary schools, at first in the cities. Some religious training

[25] Thus, making his own the words of *Venerable Bede,* Jonas of Orléans, *De institutione laicali* II, 16 (*PL* 106, 197 199). Compare I, 8 (*ibid.,* p. 134ff.).—See P. Göbl, *Geschichte der Katechese im Abendlande vom Verfalle des Katechumenates bis zum Ende des Mittelalters* (Kempten: Kösel, 1880), p. 21ff., p. 51f.

[26] Göbl, pp. 35–60.

[27] *Ibid.,* p. 54ff. That this duty was taken seriously can be learned from the fact that confession formulas at that time often contained a reference to the godparent having failed in his duty to instruct his godchild; e. g., *Jh gihu, daz ih mîne funtdivillolâ (= fontis filiolos) sô ne lêrda, sose ih in dâr antheizo uuard:* Göbl, p. 59f.—J. T. McNeil and H. M. Gamer, *Medieval Handbooks of Penance* (New York: Columbia Univ. Press, 1938).

[28] Göbl, pp. 98–105.

was thus made possible for a small section of the youth. This training was given by a teacher and was (like the entire curriculum) merely supervised by the pastor. Only in isolated case did the synods (as for example in Béziers, 1246; 1254 in Albi) oblige those entrusted with the care of souls to give very simple instructions to the children.

Whatever was done directly in catechesis by the clergy and by those entrusted with the pastoral care of souls was directed first of all to adults. Episcopal and also civil ordinances of the Carolingian period urged that priests should teach the faithful in the vernacular about the faith and the moral law every Sunday or at least every second Sunday;[29] they were to acquaint the faithful with the Lord's Prayer and the Creed and cause them occasionally to be recited. The recitation of these formulas by clerics within hearing of the people, as well as their recital in common by the faithful, were customary throughout the whole of the Middle Ages. This took place generally in connection with the homily, which followed the Gospel of the Mass. From time to time, especially during Lent, it was required that an explanation of these formulas accompany their recitation. To the Lord's Prayer and Creed were added in the succeeding centuries, generally with the restricted obligation to go through them at least once a year, the Decalogue, the Hail Mary, as well as other incidental teaching upon, for example, the capital sins, ways of being accessory to another's sin, the works of mercy, the eight beatitudes and the like.[30]

In the later Middle Ages, that is, after the thirteenth century, regulations pertinent to religious education were issued by

[29] *Ibid.*, p. 76ff.

[30] *Ibid.*, pp. 90–105; P. Browe, "Der Beichtunterricht im Mittelalter" in *Theologie und Glaube*, Vol. 26 (1934), 427–442. The Synod of Brixen of 1511 demanded of clerics: *omni mense semel materna vulgarique lingua alta voce ac intelligibiliter summarie pronuncient Pater Noster, Ave Maria et*

many synods. In England catechesis for adults appears to have reached a very high stage of development during this period. Sometimes special instruction for children was also required.[31] As a rule, however, the children attended the catechesis for adults, and were supposed to be given fuller instructions by their parents at home; even the preparation to receive the sacraments continued to be the concern of parents.

A second means which the pastoral care of souls employed to some extent to promote the religious training of the faithful during the whole of the Middle Ages was the Sacrament of Penance. After the eighth century in France (but a whole century earlier in England) the rule was enforced that all the faithful should go at least once a year to confession. This confession was usually allied to an examination on faith. An outline of the questions which was used on these occasions ran as follows: "Dost thou believe in the Father, the Son and the Holy Ghost? Dost thou believe that these Three . . . are three Persons and one God? Dost thou believe that in this flesh in which thou now livest, thou wilt rise on the day of Judgement and wilt receive recompense for good and evil?"[32] Others demanded of the penitents the recitation of the Lord's Prayer and of the Creed. Later on, more matter was added, especially concerning sins.[33]

Towards the end of the Middle Ages this practice of question and answer gave birth to the so-called "confessional booklets": they were meant to serve as a preparation for confession and

Credo, hoc est Symbolum Apostolorum una cum decem praeceptis, quinque sensibus, septem peccatis mortalibus, septem sacramentis, novem alienis peccatis, octo circumstantii peccatorum et sex operibus misericordiae. J. Bauer, *Die Spendung der Taufe in der Brixner Diözese* (Innsbruck, 1938), p. 75f.

[31] Göbl, pp 89, 91, 94ff., 103.—The division of formulas into seven parts was especially beloved in the twelfth century, see Rudolf (below on p. 16) p. 72f.

[32] J. A. Jungmann, *Die lateinischen Bussriten* (Innsbruck, 1932), pp. 158, 170ff.

[33] Göbl, p. 107f.

generally contained a very exhaustive list of sins. After the invention of printing they found widespread acceptance among the people.[34] Some were intended for the use of priests. They may be considered forerunners of the catechism, except that the section devoted to the commandments dominated all others.

About this same time when reading had ceased to be a mysterious art, writings and books came to be part of religious instruction.[35] Some few written compilations of important catechetical texts, probably intended for the priest were published earlier. Thus we speak—in an anticipatory use of the title "catechism"—of a Weissenburger Catechism (end of the eighth century), which contained in addition to the German translation of the Lord's Prayer, the capital sins, both the Apostles' and the Athanasian Creed as well as the *Gloria in excelsis*.[36] A German explanation is appended to the Lord's Prayer. Latin expositions of these formulas often appeared from this time on.[37] After the invention of printing other works were published; these were intended for the reli-

[34] Before 1520 we can prove the existence of 50 printings of this penitential booklet. The oldest of these was published by F. Falk, *ZkTh*, Vol. 32 (1908), pp. 754–775; for other examples see *Lexikon für Theologie und Kirche*, Vol. II (1932), col. 102f.

[35] Göbl, pp. 281–292.

[36] E. v. Steinmeyer, *Die kleineren althochdeutschen Sprachdenkmäler* (Berlin, 1916), pp. 29–38.

[37] Of this kind is one chapter of the *Disputatio puerorum*, c. 11 f. ascribed to Alcuin (*PL* 101, 1136–1144) which is repeated in its entirety by Bruno of Würzburg (d. 1045), *Commentarius* (*PL* 142, 557–568), implicit proof that it was employed for centuries; see Probst (above 5), pp. 87–94. An excellent model for catechists was the Lenten sermons which St. Thomas preached in Naples in 1273. These are contained in the four *Opuscula* on the Creed (including the Sacraments), on the Lord's Prayer, on the Hail Mary and on the Commandments; consult the *Opuscula omnia* of Mandonnet IV, pp. 349–460.—They were translated into English by Laurence Shapcote in two volumes entitled: *The Three Greatest Prayers* (London: Burns, Oates & Washbourne, 1937) and *The*

gious instruction of the people and their content was far more extensive than that of the confessional book.[38] To this class of catechetical matter belongs the *Opus Tripartitum* of Gerson, Chancellor of Paris, and also a whole series of works which by their titles indicate that they could be used equally well as prayer books or books of devotion, as for instance, the *Christenspiegel,*[39] the *Seelenwurzgärtlein, Der Seele Trost, Die himmlische Fundgrube* and especially the *Himmelsstrasse* of the Viennese Dean, Stephen Landskron (d. 1477). Public posters were also pressed into use to further the instruction of the faithful.

In his German translation of Gerson's book, Geiler of Kaisersberg urged priests, parents, schoolmasters and masters of hospitals to see "that the teaching of this booklet be written upon placards and posted, whole or in part, in public places such as parish churches, schools, hospitals, and holy places".[40] In addition to the wall posters, we know of murals and in general of catechetical plastic arts being employed.[41] Throughout the Middle Ages the principle was maintained that pictures, stained glass windows, etc., were books for the unlettered. The principal statements of the Creed were also the main themes of ecclesiastical art.

Toward the end of the Middle Ages a more or less complete

Commandments of God (London: Burns, Oates & Washbourne, 1937).—Informative is R. Rudolf, *Thomas Peuntners Betrachtungen über das Vaterunser und das Ave Maria* (Wien, 1953), pp. 69–75.

[38] Göbl, p. 288ff. J. Janssen (M. A. Mitchell and A. M. Christie, translators), *History of the German People at the Close of the Middle Ages* (St. Louis: Herder, 1896), Vol. I, pp. 25–61.

[39] Composed by the renowned Franciscan, Dederich Kölde (Printed after 1480) and published by Moufang (see below in Footnote 46).

[40] Quoted by Janssen, I, 27 (I, 35 in the German).

[41] Göbl, pp. 268–278; J. T. Geffcken, *Der Bilderkatechismus des 15. Jahrhunderts.* I: *Die Gebote* (Leipzig, 1855); K. Künstle, *Ikonographie der christlichen Kunst,* Vol. I (Freiburg: Herder, 1928) (the "illustrated catechism"). The Biblia Pauperum is quite a different matter; see Künstle, Vol. I, pp. 90–92.

series of pictures was developed, which consciously sought to interpret the content of the catechetical. This is true of those representations in which the apostles were depicted, each with a scroll, upon which the article of the Creed that was attributed to him was inscribed: or when on church portals the works of mercy were depicted. For the Ten Commandments and the capital sins, too, artists also developed a set canon of symbols which frequently appear in frescoes and more often in wood carvings.

Finally, a distinctive factor in the religious formation of the faithful, especially in the later Middle Ages, was the communal life which was entirely pervaded by religion. People learned to speak a Christian language as soon as they learned to speak their own mother tongue—and this without the benefit of regular instruction. It was not doctrine couched in theoretical terms that was responsible for the religious life of the faithful; it was rather the hard and fast religious institutions. And besides everything else there was always the liturgy; even if it was only poorly understood, it still dominated the seasons of the year through the celebration of the ecclesiastical feasts and impressed the chief mysteries of faith upon the popular consciousness. How deeply the people were swayed by it, is shown by the mystery plays which after the tenth century had originated in and developed out of the celebration of Christmas (plays centring on the crib) and of Holy Week (Passion Plays) and which later incorporated the whole of the history of salvation in the plays for Corpus Christi. A formative force of tremendous effectiveness must have emanated from them.

Of great importance were the manifold religious customs and usages of the era.[42] They accompanied the course of the year;

[42] L. A. Veit, *Volksfrommes Brauchtum und Kirche im deutschen Mittelalter* (Freiburg: Herder, 1936); for a fuller development of the material in this section, consult the present writer's "Religious Education in Late Medieval Times" in Sloyan, *op. cit.*, pp. 38-62.

they accompanied the Christian from his birth to the grave; they pervaded all sections of the Christian community. By a religious consecration the Emperor was introduced to his office and the knight entered upon his knighthood. The guilds had their special patrons and their special ecclesiastical feasts. Hospitals were practically all dedicated to the Holy Ghost; pharmacies generally bore religious names. The names of inns derived from biblical sources; this usage pointing to the fact that men were accustomed to consider the lodging of travellers as a work of Christian charity.[43] Thus, the entire life of the faithful was spent in a religious atmosphere.

It is in accordance with this wealth of catechetical practice, as we have described it, that no important works on the theory of catechesis were published during this whole era.[44]

To summarize, we may say of the Middle Ages that formal catechesis was extremely sparse, to a great extent its deficiencies were remedied by the wealth of religious thoughts which were embodied in Christian community life. Youth grew up in a Christian environment and thus acquired the views and the religious knowledge of their elders.

We can therefore learn something from that epoch:

1. We can appreciate the great importance which was attached to catechesis in the home; in the waning years of the Middle Ages this must have become widely influential.[45] At no time can we dispense with it in our own catechetical work.

[43] Many names contain references to the Magi and the equipment which they took with them on their journey: others make use of the symbols of the four evangelists; K. Höber, *Der biblische Ursprung alter Wirtshausnamen* (Cologne, 1934); E. Weekley, *The Romance of Names* (London: John Murray, 1922), especially pp. 84–91; Ph. Oppenheim, *op. cit.*, "Commentationes, etc.", pp. 48–72.

[44] Anything touching on these points may be found in C. Krieg, *Katechetik* (Freiburg, 1907), p. 54f.

[45] The preacher of the Reformation, George of Anhalt, (*Predigten*, Wittenberg 1555, 298) points to the fact that in the Middle Ages mothers

2. We can see the formative influence of a life lived in a Christian community. If life today has been widely de-Christianized, we should for that very reason take every precaution that we provide the child at least with the atmosphere of a Christian family, with well-planned and beautifully executed religious ceremonies and, where possible, with a Catholic school. The importance of building up Catholic organizations for youth is obvious.

3. Throughout these centuries formal catechesis revolved around set formulas. This fact alone should vouch for the timeless value of such formulas, especially (besides the Lord's Prayer) of the Creed.

On the other hand we do not wish to be blind to the weaknesses which are manifest in the religious training imparted during the Middle Ages. This era contented itself too easily with religious usage and paid too little attention to the religious formation of the mind, knowledge and the understanding. Thus the people of the Middle Ages remained mentally immature. Only in such a way can we adequately explain the speedy collapse of religious thought which the Reformation caused in so many spheres and in such a widespread fashion.

3. The Tridentine Reform

Through the appearance and the success of Luther, it suddenly became evident, that the young as well as the old would have to be instructed in Catholic doctrine much more thoroughly than

were still "the noblest pastors and bishops in the family" by whom the articles of faith and the Commandments of God were preserved; this has been quoted by J. Baumgärtler, *Die Erstkommunion der Kinder* (München: Kösel u. Pustet, imp. 1929), p. 226.—Consult J. Janssen, *op. cit.*, (German edition, 25–28); Schrems, *ut infra* (under footnote, No. 55), p. 5ff., and p. 70ff. Catechesis within the family setting was still the general rule until the eighteenth century, cf. Hofinger, p. 21.

before. Thus the beginning of the new period is marked by a notable increase in efforts to promote catechesis, in particular the catechetical training of children. The Council of Trent obliged the bishops to provide for catechesis to be given to children in all parish churches at least on Sundays and holy days of obligation.

Admittedly all that was done must at first be considered a defensive measure. The Reformers zealously sought to propagate their teaching, not only among adults, but also among the children. In 1529 Luther himself published a catechism—the book received this title for the first time from him—in two different editions, one of which was intended for pastors and teachers, the other for the children. With regard to content Luther adhered fairly closely to the old formulas which he explained briefly; and his explanations, too, kept to the traditional lines. Only in its construction does the "new doctrine" betray itself: Luther begins with the main article of the Commandments—which man cannot observe and through which he recognizes himself to be a sinner. Only then follows the other main article: on Faith. Within forty years Luther's catechism achieved a distribution of well over 100,000 copies.

The Catholics then recognized that catechisms had to be written, but catechisms no longer in the sense of popular devotional booklets, which only incidentally offered some instruction, but in the sense of concise and clear summaries of Christian doctrine. Books thus came to dominate catechesis and to relegate to the background the community as a formative force. In fact, as early as 1530 a series of Catholic catechisms began to appear. In some instances their authors were eminent champions of the Church.[46] Among these we can list such names

[46] Chr. Moufang, *Katholische Katechismen des 16. Jahrhunderts in deutscher Sprache* (Mainz: Kirchheim, 1881) (complete texts of fourteen catechisms), also P. Bahlmann, *Deutschlands katholische Katechismen bis zum Ende des 16. Jahrhunderts* (Münster, 1894).

as Dietenberger, translator of the Bible, the theologians, Peter de Soto and Johannes Gropper, Bishop Maltiz of Meissen, and Bishop Helding of Merseburg. But their efforts were only moderately successful, since they retained the old devotional style, and lacked the necessary clarity and conciseness. Improvements came about in the catechisms written in the chief countries of Christendom by members of the newly founded Society of Jesus.

In Germany St. Peter Canisius published three catechisms which were constantly reprinted in ever new editions.[47] In 1555 his large Latin catechism appeared; it was called: *Summa doctrinae christianae, per quaestiones tradita et in usum christianae pueritiae nunc primum edita.* This was a catechism in the broad sense of the term; but the emphasis was on the word, *Summa.* If this book had originally been intended for youth at all, it could only have been meant for those who were studying theology. Numerous quotations from Sacred Scripture and the Fathers were printed in the margin. Between 1569 and 1570 these were added in their entirety to the *Summa* by Father Busaeus, S. J. and were published as a four volume commentary on the catechism. This commentary generally bore the title *Opus Catechisticum* and found widespread use among the clergy.

But Canisius also provided for the youth, and first of all for the children. In 1556 he published his "smallest catechism". This appeared at first in Latin as an appendix to a Latin grammar, and soon thereafter in German alone as an extremely small booklet with the title: *Der Klain Catechismus sampt kurtzen gebetlen für die ainfältigen.* In it we find the ancient formulas together with a few questions, in all only fifty-nine, to many of which it is true, very long answers were given.

[47] *S. Petri Canisii doct. Eccl. Catechismi latini et germanici,* ed. F. Streicher, S.J., 2 vols. (Romae: Pontificia Universitas Gregoriana, 1933/1936); O. Braunsberger, *Entstehung und erste Entwicklung der Katechismen des sel. Petrus Canisius* (Freiburg: Herder, 1893).

Finally, Canisius published a medium-sized catechism, which he intended for youths who attended school; it first appeared in Latin in 1559: *Parvus Catechismus Catholicorum,* afterwards, however, in German under the title *Kurtzer underricht vom Catholischen Glauben*. This medium-sized catechism is the one which, with only minor changes, dominated catechesis in Germany for more than two centuries. Already at the time of his death (1597) 134 editions of it had appeared, while the *Summa* at the same time had eighty-two, and the small catechism seventeen editions.

Canisius himself made many improvements and changes in his catechisms; he provided them with supplements and appendices, and sometimes changed the number and the order of the principal articles. The predominant arrangement which he ultimately retained consisted of five principal parts. They treated of: 1. Faith and the Creed; 2. Hope and Prayer; 3. Love and the Commandments; 4. The Sacraments; 5. Christian Justice.

Although his catechisms served primarily as a defence against heresy, we cannot detect any polemics in them. In fact in the *Summa* the opponents at which he aims are not even named. But the assailed doctrines were thoroughly explained. The atmosphere of the conflict suggests why the intellectual element predominated (in definitions and enumerations) in them. This element was, however, made palatable by his approximating as closely as possible to the language of Scripture and of the Fathers. The two smaller catechisms were, in many editions, richly illustrated with pictures.

In Italy Pope Clement VIII commissioned St. Robert Bellarmine to compose a catechism. This appeared in 1598 under the title: *Dottrina cristiana breve da impararsi a mente*.[48] An edition for catechists, which contained explanations, was also published. In this catechism, even more than catechisms of Cani-

[48] J. Brodrick, *Blessed Robert Bellarmine,* 2 vols. (London: Burns, Oates & Washbourne, 1928), Vol. I, p. 390.

sius, catechetical formulas and various enumerations which had been handed down from the Middle Ages were made the basis of explanation. The catechism of St. Robert Bellarmine was used for a long time in Italy and it achieved even greater prominence by reason of the fact that it was prescribed for the foreign missions by Propaganda. When during the sessions of the Vatican Council of 1870, a plan for a universal catechism was discussed in detail, the catechism of Bellarmine was held up to the Council as a model. But Bellarmine expressed his own mind on the matter in a letter as follows: "Had I, at that time known of the catechism of Peter Canisius, I would not have bestirred myself to compose a new catechism, but I would have translated his catechism from the Latin into Italian."[49]

In France a "Canisius" also appeared in the person of Father Edmund Auger (Augerius) S.J. His two catechisms, published in 1563 and 1568, were designed to ward off the dangers of the heresies and were written in a spirit similar to that which characterized the German Doctor of the Church.[50]

In Spain, likewise, about this time two catechisms appeared, both written by Jesuits; one by Father Astete, the other by Father Ripalda. Both remain in use up to the present.

Of another kind, but of the greatest importance, is the catechism which was drawn up at the request of the Council of Trent. This appeared during the reign of Pope Pius V, 1566, under the title: *Catechismus ex decretis Concilii Tridentini ad parochos,* or generally more concisely, *Catechismus Romanus.* This catechism, as the title indicates, was not intended for children, but for pastors. Through it the Council sought to help the

[49] J. Brodrick, *Saint Peter Canisius, S.J. (1521–1597)* (London: Sheed & Ward, 1935), p. 250, footnote 2.

[50] J. Dutilleuil, "Auger, Edmond" in *Dictionnaire d'Histoire et de Géographie Ecclésiastique* (Paris: Letouzey et Ané), Fasc. V (1931), cols. 380–383; F. J. Brand, *Die Katechismen des Edmundus Augerius, S.J.* (Freiburg: Herder, 1917).

clergy in their task of giving religious instruction both to adults and to youth. Its authors were four theologians, three of whom were members of the Order of Preachers; St. Charles Borromeo was entrusted with its supervision. Of the various English translations of this catechism two are worthy of note: the older work of J. J. Donovan and the more recent effort of John A. McHugh, O.P. and Charles P. Callan, O.P.[51]

The old basic principles form the basis of this catechism, but in such a way, that the entire teaching of the faith is presented in one piece. The first section devoted to the Creed is immediately followed by a second on the sacraments. Christian practice is dealt with in the third section on the Ten Commandments and in the fourth there is an explanation of the Lord's Prayer. Down to the present day the *Catechismus Romanus* has been constantly recommended by the Popes for use by the clergy, the last time was by Pius XI; it is indeed "the Church's book of religion".

The further progress of catechesis was promoted by the Council of Trent, which demanded that the people[52], and especially the children, be zealously instructed.[53] Diocesan statutes provided more detailed instructions. The difference between adults and children was not especially stressed in the ordinances and still less observed in practice. The principal form of instruction was intended first of all for adults and included church

[51] J. Donovan, *Catechism of the Council of Trent* (Dublin: J. Duffy and Co., 1908). The preface to this translation written by the translator himself carries the date-line, June 10, 1829. J. A. McHugh and C. J. Callan, *Catechism of the Council of Trent for Parish Priests* (2nd rev. ed.; New York: J. F. Wagner, c. 1923).

[52] *Sess. V. de ref.,* c. 2; H. J. Schröder (trans.), *Canons and Decrees of the Council of Trent* (St. Louis: Herder, 1941), p. 26.

[53] *Sess. XXIV de ref.,* c. 4: "at least on Sundays and other festival days the children in every parish (should) be carefully taught the rudiments of the faith and obedience toward God and their parents by those whose duty it is", Schröder, *op. cit.,* p. 196.

catechesis on "Christian teaching", which was frequently given on Sunday afternoon. In many Catholic countries, in addition to this, teaching of religion was made obligatory and supported by the civil authorities; it included all adults or at least the servants. This tradition, limited in application to certain groups of school-leavers, is still in existence today in certain dioceses of the Rhineland and Switzerland.[54]

The introduction of a special catechesis especially for children, planned to fit within the framework of ordinary parish work, was successful only on a small scale in the sixteenth and seventeenth centuries.[55] A certain additional teaching was provided by the catechetical work carried on by some of the ıeligious orders. The colleges of the Jesuits especially became centres of catechetical activity. The students themselves took an active part in it. Thus, for example, regular catechesis was given by the college at Fulda in nearly forty neighbouring villages. In Vienna and its outlying districts the Jesuit novices alone were entrusted with the catechesis in more than twenty places.[56]

An improvement in catechesis was noticeable in those places into which the *Confraternity of Christian Doctrine* was introduced. This Confraternity was founded in Milan in 1560 and was approved by Pope St. Pius V in 1571. Naturally it became especially widespread in Italy. After the middle of the seventeenth century it began to appear in Germany,

[54] R. Hindringer, "Christenlehre" in *LThK,* Vol. II, p. 905f.

[55] A concrete view of conditions is sketched by K. Schrems, *Die religiöse Volks- und Jugendunterweisung in der Diözese Regensburg vom Ausgang des 15. Jahrhunderts bis gegen Ende des 18. Jahrhunderts* (München, 1929). The regulations of the Diocese of Regensburg of 1588 prescribed a special catechesis for children on Sunday afternoons; this same regulation was renewed after the disturbances of the Thirty Years' War had subsided (pp. 88, 179ff.).

[56] B. Duhr, *Geschichte der Jesuiten in den Ländern deutscher Zunge,* Vol. I (1907), p. 458f.; Vol. II, 2 (1913), p. 9ff.; J. Brodrick, *St. Peter Canisius,* pp. 168–203.

where it frequently found ready reception due to missions which had been preached to the people. Its members undertook personally to attend instructions on Christian doctrine and especially to pass these on to members of their families and to their servants. This broadening of catechetical activity redounded especially to the benefit of the children.

The divison of the children according to age groups became an accepted practice in the cities, and catechisms were written for them. A booklet of questions as well as many other teaching aids were designed to ease the burden of the lay catechists.[57] The method employed, however, was very artless: nothing more than an explanation of the text. The questions and answers were first recited or read out by the teacher. The text was then analyzed and expressed in different words by the teacher and wherever possible, illustrated by examples; it was concluded by an admonition or by a practical application. The main emphasis was on brain work and questioning; a certain mechanical procedure was inevitable especially in the case of the less educated lay teachers. But even clerical catechists were taught little as far as method was concerned, their ecclesiastical superiors failing to provide them with any specific hints on procedure. What was offered in the way of catechetical theory centred on the obligation and on the proper sentiments of the catechists, on books and prayer formulas to be used, and suggestions on how the catechist might help the children to understand the questions, and how he might avoid thoughtless memorizing of texts which they did not understand.[58]

[57] Hofinger, pp. 14ff., 25ff.

[58] The attempts which were made from the 16th to the 18th centuries to formulate some kind of catechetical theory are treated thoroughly by F. J. Knecht, "Katechetik" in *Kirchenlexikon,* Vol. VII (1891), cols. 268–281. Among these attempts the work of several French clergymen is outstanding, e. g., Francis de Sales, Boudon, Fleury. For reproductions of their

4. *School Catechesis*

A new phase in the catechesis of children began with the introduction, by civil authorities, of universal compulsory school attendance toward the end of the eighteenth century. Religious instruction had always been linked with the elementary school and was now introduced in public elementary schools, which at first remained everywhere under ecclesiastical supervision. The era of catechesis in school had begun.

This had undeniable advantages. For the first time all children could be included. In the school curriculum catechesis was accorded a definite place. A greater amount of religious instruction was made possible. This had long been desired, firstly, because after the Reformation the defence against heresy had become necessary, and secondly, because the formative religious influence which had emanated from the community was becoming constantly weaker. By incorporating the period for religion into the other formative work of the school, a certain harmony in the total formation of the child was assured.

True, corresponding to these advantages we also encounter certain disadvantages. The secular classroom was substituted for the church or chapel. The danger of intellectualism increased. Religion became just another subject taught in school, and one might think that all that mattered was to learn and to memorize.

The danger of intellectualism became especially acute immediately after the general introduction of catechesis into the curriculum. It was the age of enlightenment and of rationalism. The spirit of enlightenment did not, in the form of genuine rationalism, enter into Catholic catechesis to any appreciable extent although its presence was felt in the circles gathered around certain leading figures of the new movement, among

efforts, cf. M. Dupanloup, *Méthode Générale de Catéchisme,* 3 vols. (Paris: Charles Duniol, 1862).

whom Vitus Anton Winter, Canon of Eichstätt, was perhaps the most outstanding.[59] Winter, author of *Religiös-sittlichen Katechetik* (1811), sought to suppress, as far as possible, the supernatural in the subject matter of instruction. Religious instruction was to be restricted chiefly to moral teaching. The catechist was to treat of the Sacraments, "omitting all useless disputes, for example, concerning the Real Presence of the Body and Blood of Jesus Christ"; he should content himself with explaining their purpose and their correct use. He championed the unqualified adoption of the "Socratic method" by which the pupil should be led to draw out those religious and moral notions which are contained in his own head . . . "and gradually raise himself to the highest possible level of moral culture." It never occurred to him that Christian doctrine is based essentially on revelation and for that reason can never, least of all in children, be "drawn out" by natural reasoning.

Yet this Socratic method, which was advocated by the educationalists of the enlightenment, contained a healthy thought, namely, the recognition that catechesis should be linked to the child's world of experience and from this starting point, should gradually lead him on, especially with the help of questions. It would not, however, impose upon his memory concepts which he could not understand. Up to that time the "acroamatic" method had been used in which the catechist gave a lecture, and the children were only listeners (ἀκροᾶσθαι). It was then replaced by the "erotematic" method. Here the children are induced to cooperate in the learning process by means of questions (ἐρωτᾶν).

The wish to consider the child's mental capacity is also connected with the fact that, in addition to the catechism, "Bible History" begins to occupy a more prominent place,

[59] F. J. Knecht, *op. cit.,* cols. 282–284.

and this not only as an independent part of the subject matter of catechesis but also as a primer in the schools. This innovation traces its origin to the organizer of the elementary school system in Austria, Abbot Johann Ignaz Felbiger (d. 1788).

In the period which followed the age of enlightenment and which attempted to overcome the harm that had been done by it, some priests emerged, who dissociated themselves from the rationalistic spirit of the age, but were concerned with deepening and developing the valuable suggestions and impulses which it had started.

One of them, although belonging chronologically to an earlier period, was Bernhard Heinrich Overberg (1754–1826) from Westphalia.[60] He worked first as a parish priest and earned a reputation for himself by his success as a catechist. He was then appointed by the Bishop of Münster, who was also a civil ruler, to run his *Normalschule,* a training institute for teachers, and eventually to supervise the entire school system in the episcopal domain. With especial zeal he turned his attention to catechesis. He advocated the system of developing the teaching matter by questioning, and emphasized the value for children of presentation in the form of a narrative. In order to promote this method of teaching Christian doctrine, he wrote *Biblische Geschichte des Alten und Neuen Testamentes zur Belehrung und Erbauung für Lehrer, grössere Schüler und Hausväter* (1799), which in various revisions appeared in almost a hundred editions and as a private manual is still used today. He also wrote a catechism (1804) which was in vogue in the dioceses of North Germany as late as the end of the nineteenth century.

Similar principles were advocated somewhat later by J. B. Hirscher (1788–1865), who was professor of Moral and Pastoral Theology first at Tübingen and later at Freiburg im Breisgau.[61]

[60] *Bernhard Overberg als pädagogischer Führer seiner Zeit. Festschrift,* ed. by R. Stapper (Münster, 1926).

[61] H. F. Schiel, *Joh. B. v. Hirscher* (Freiburg: Herder, 1926).

In his *Katechetik,* he emphasized against the current moralism that Christian doctrine should be presented as doctrine of salvation and as the teaching of the kingdom of God, but not by means of definitions but as far as possible in historical form. Religious education, not great learning, should be the goal of catechesis. In his *Katechismus* (1842) he attempted to give a concrete form to his ideas, but he found little response since his plan was too unusual, and the presentation too heavy, so that his catechism sank into oblivion after only a few years, although a popular Catholic writer, Stolz, published a commentary on it. What also impeded the success of his ideas was his opposition to scholasticism, which he regarded as responsible for over-intellectual and hence sterile catechesis, while in reality the unjustifiable use to which it was put by the catechists was to blame.[62]

Of another type, but more firmly rooted in Catholic tradition, was Augustin Gruber (1763–1835), from 1823 Archbishop of Salzburg.[63] As Archbishop he gave "catechetical lectures" to his clergy. These appeared in print between 1830 and 1834. In opposition to enlightened "Socraticism" he stressed that the catechist should stand before the children as a messenger of God, that the basic teaching form should be one of communication. He quoted from St. Augustine's, *De catechizandis rudibus* that there should be a *narratio,* and emphasized the importance of the narrative presentation which, according to him, should be employed especially with younger children.[64] Even in instruc-

[62] F. X. Arnold, *Dienst am Glauben* (*Untersuchungen zur Theologie der Seelsorge* 1) (Freiburg: Herder, 1948), p. 39ff.; F. Bläcker, *Joh. B. v. Hirscher und seine Katechismen* (*Untersuchungen zur Theologie der Seelsorge* 6) (Freiburg: Herder, 1953); T. Filthaut, *Das Reich Gottes in der katechetischen Unterweisung* (*Untersuchungen zur Theologie der Seelsorge* 12) (Freiburg: Herder, 1958), pp. 71-102.

[63] F. Ranft, *Fürsterzbischof Augustin Gruber. Ein Beitrag zur Geschichte der katholischen Religionspädagogik* (Innsbruck, 1938).

[64] A complete course of catecheses for beginners is appended to his

tions on the catechism he insisted that the catechist first present the subject matter and only then attempt to formulate its content. Over and above mere knowledge the catechist should aim at fostering faith hope and love in the children.

The valuable ideas which these men[65] developed and in which they sought to make use of the positive results of the preceding period did not meet with complete success. Bible History, however, came to be generally included in catechesis, but the attempts to give a new form to catechesis, one better adapted to the mental capacity of the children, never achieved their objective. The catechisms that were authorized in the age of enlightenment gave the impression of subjective drafts which seemed to offer no permanent solution to the problem. In the rising Catholic restoration, moreover, anything that had originated in the age of reason was suspect. When, thus, in 1847 the catechism of Jos. Deharbe, S.J. appeared, which again took up along the traditional line and which in addition was exceptional in its completeness, correctness of teaching, and clarity of expression, it soon prevailed over all previous catechism attempts and became the predominant catechism in Germany.

Also in regard to method, there was a return to the simple explanation of the catechism text, to which were added practical applications. Even the smallest children were instructed by means of a catechism-catechesis of this type as soon as they could read.[66]

Lectures; these catecheses were edited and published by M. Gatterer, *A. Gruber's Elementarkatechesen* (Innsbruck: Rauch, 1922).

[65] Allied with Gruber as the opponent of Socraticism and akin to Hirscher in his emphasis on the idea of the kingdom of God, but less balanced was B. Galura (1764–1856) who was a guiding light of the catechetical movement in Austria and finally became Bishop of Brixen; see J. Hemlein, *Bernhard Galuras Beitrag zur Erneuerung der Kerygmatik* (*Freiburger Theol. Studien* 65) (Freiburg: Herder, 1952); Filthaut, *op. cit.,* pp. 46-71, 164-167.

[66] Gustav Mey was an exception. His *Vollständige Katechesen für die*

Certain changes came about before the end of the century. The de-Christianization of the masses was growing in the big cities despite the intensive catechesis instructions which children had received over the years. It had to be recognized that it no longer sufficed in school catechesis to foster knowledge and particularly merely memorized knowledge since the family evidently no longer supplemented the work of the catechist as it generally had in earlier times. A second factor was that in the secular subjects psychology had helped to develop methods during the last decades of the nineteenth century which convinced teachers that they must more than hitherto consider the child's mental capacities. Catechesis could not very well fail to avail itself of these advances.

There arose around 1900 the Catechetical Movement,[67] almost simultaneously in Munich and Vienna. In both cities there had been, for some years previously, catechetical societies and reviews in which the state of catechesis was eagerly discussed as well as suggestions for reforms. These magazines, in Munich the *Katechetische Blätter* and in Vienna *Christlich-Pädagogische Blätter,* had a wide influence also outside the German-speaking countries. After 1903 catechetical courses were held in various places: Salzburg, Vienna, Munich, Lucerne, Agram, Aschaffen-

untere Klasse der katholischen Volksschule appeared for the first time in 1871 and have since been reprinted or re-edited many times (the last was by Th. Hoch, Freiburg: Herder, 1952). These instructions use the biblical narrative as their starting point and are very concrete both in presentation and application. Cf. A. Barth, "Wer ist Gustav Mey?" in *KBl,* Vol. 77 (1952), pp. 212–216.—In the catechetical theory which he propounded in *Theorie der geistlichen Beredsamkeit* (4th ed., 1908; first edition, 1877/78), J. Jungmann (d. 1885) refers to the principles set forth by Gruber on this as well as on other points. Outside of him these principles were practically forgotten.

[67] F. X. Eggersdorfer, "Die Kurve katechetischer Bewegung in Deutschland in einem halben Jahrhundert" in *KBl,* Vol. 76 (1951), pp. 10 to 16, 55–61.

burg, Aaarau, Budapest, Innsbruck, and Klagenfurt. The first success of the movement and, at the same time, a preliminary conclusion, was reached at the Catechetical Congress held in Vienna in 1912.

What the movement had aimed at was an improved method of catechesis, through which the subject matter of catechesis should not only be imprinted on the child's memory but also be grasped by the understanding. The catechist was warned not to begin with the catechism text and then to explain it question by question, but he was advised to use as his starting point an example which appealed to the children and from it to develop the text of the catechism. The text-explanatory was to be replaced by the text-developing method, which was then called the "Munich Method". At the first Catechetical Congress the relevant suggestions received their final and definite formulation. The theoretical objections which had been previously raised were heard no more. The first objective had been reached, although it would take a long time before the majority of catechists accepted these new ideas.

The Catechetical Movement, however, went on, especially after the First World War. The conviction grew that it was not sufficient merely to make catechesis understandable for the child; it had to produce a lasting educative effect upon him, and all the more so as the family provided less and less in the way of religious education for its members.

Again the methods used in teaching secular subjects provided new ideas and above all inspired the active or "learn by doing" school. This involved a teaching method based on the knowledge that children learn not only by hearing, but also by doing; that they are formed not only by words, but also by life itself. Life in the community had lost the formative religious power which it had possessed to such a degree during the Middle Ages. It thus became necessary to capture as much of religious life in the school as possible by catechesis, by pastoral care as well as by oral instruction. The connection with the liturgy, the entire religious activity of the children, had now to be fostered more strongly than ever before.

These findings and requirements were drawn up at the second Catechetical Congress which was held in Munich in 1928. The questions concerning method were to a great extent settled at this Congress.

The revival of method, however, influenced the arrangement of textbooks, especially the catechism. Existing catechisms proved to be hindrances to catechesis based on the new principles, because of their all too abstract language and, still more, because they contained too much matter. Thus at the turn of the century in various places attempts were made to emend the catechisms. These resulted finally in extensive revisions. Within Germany the so-called German uniform catechism of 1925 was finally substituted for the Deharbe catechisms. In 1930 in Austria a new catechism was introduced. In both these works passages to be memorized were reduced and the language simplified. At the same time in Austria a still further step was taken; the authorities restricted the use of the catechisms, which had always been couched in abstract terms, to the upper grades of the elementary school; for the lower grades a special book was designed, namely, the *Religionsbüchlein*. This booklet opens with a narration of biblical events and by means of them explains the most important doctrines.

In the United States the *Catechism of the Third Council of Baltimore* approved by Archbishop, later Cardinal, Gibbons, in 1885, was used almost exclusively by English-language teachers of religion, although it has been said that the last half of the nineteenth century was the "era of the Deharbe Catechism".[68]

[68] T. B. Scannell, "Doctrine, Christian" in *Catholic Encyclopedia*, Vol. V, p. 82.

In the first third of the twentieth century objections were raised against the Baltimore Catechism on the score of its scientific terminology, its wordy definitions, its size, and its abstractness, and attempts were made to improve upon it.[69] Several private studies gained some recognition, for example, Roderick MacEachen, M. V. Kelly, J. H. Heuser, E. H. Deck and J. H. Burbach, *et al.*, but their acceptance was limited. Their appearance did, however, hasten the day of official recognition of the discontent by making visual the shortcomings inherent in the official text. It was at Rochester during the National Congress of the Confraternity of Christian Doctrine that the first announcement was made by Father Francis J. Connell, C.SS.R. of the prospective work.[70] The plans initiated by the Episcopal Committee of the Confraternity of Christian Doctrine in 1934 were then implemented for the revision of the book. More than a hundred theologians, a number of bishops, and scores of teachers in the field collaborated in the work. After several thoroughgoing emendations of "trial" texts had been made, the resultant revision was submitted to the Congregation of the Council for approval. A few changes were suggested. When these had been made, the final text, based on the text of The Third Council of Baltimore, was finally sanctioned by the Holy See in 1941.[71]

[69] M. V. Kelly, "Catechism Teaching" in *American Ecclesiastical Review*, Vol. LX (Jan., 1919), pp. 36–44; (Feb., 1919), pp. 157–166; (March, 1919), pp. 281–287.

[70] In the various sessions over which he presided the professional teachers and priests who were in attendance were asked for their suggestions and recommendations. F. J. Connell, "The Forthcoming Revision of the Baltimore Catechism" in *Journal of Religious Instruction*, Vol. X (1940), pp. 638–650.

[71] A. G. Cicognani, "Two Great Scholarly Achievements of the Confraternity of Christian Doctrine" in *Proceedings*, Philadelphia 1941 (Paterson: St. Anthony Guild Press, 1944), pp. 7–14; F. J. Connell, "Special Features and Uses for the Revised Baltimore Catechism in

In England the catechism of Bishop Challoner underwent extensive revisions (1836, 1855, before 1879 and again in 1883) and through these revisions increased considerably in size (from 290 to 370 questions). In its revised form it has become the catechism of present-day England.[72]

The continental reforms were dictated by the needs of catechetical method. Soon religious pedagogues awakened to the fact that, to insure a proper religious training in which the powers inherent in Christian doctrines would become activitated in the children, still other requirements would have to be met. The manner in which the subject matter was presented in the catechism, had been determined in an all too biased fashion by the laws of the theological sciences and as a consequence by concern for clear definitions even in those catechisms in which the material had been reduced to a minimum and the language greatly simplified. An effective preaching of the Gospel and especially an effective catechesis must be bent on producing in the listeners a striking picture of the entire content of Christian doctrine and on making them aware that Christian doctrine is truly a joyful message. It is not sufficient that the content of faith be precisely presented in full detail; it must be imparted so that it appears in all its forcefulness as a synthesis and is appreciated as "a message" (as a kerygma) in all its beauty and in all its supernatural sublimity. After the efforts of the Catechetical Movement at the beginning of the century to bring about a formal methodological renewal had ebbed, a new movement for reform was set in motion. This new effort has for its objective a material-kerygmatic re-examination of catechesis and the

Religious Instruction" in *Journal of Religious Instruction,* Vol. XII (Dec., 1941), pp. 297–304; F. J. Connell, "Catechism Revision" in *The Confraternity Comes of Age* (Paterson: Confraternity Publications, 1956), pp. 189–201.

[72] J. S. Marron, "On the History of the Penny Catechism" in *The Sower,* No. 125 (Oct.–Dec., 1937), pp. 199–201.

catechetical problem. This new movement for reform is at the moment in the process of being further expanded.

5. Survey of the Present

Our survey of the history of catechesis considered chiefly the development that had taken place in Central Europe. But just as general cultural life, so also catechetical life has travelled its own road in different countries. The present phase of international development, in which national boundaries are gradually losing their meaning, impels us to cast an appraising look at the activities in the field of catechetics and to attempt to learn from them whatever of value they have to offer. This has been made possible for us through the literary output of the past few years.[73]

In order to obtain a satisfactory picture of the catechetical situation of the present day by surveying its progress in other countries, we must single out only a few typical examples.

In France the status of catechesis[74] has been conditioned by the fact, that the great mass of children, baptized Catholics,

[73] We must mention, first of all, the work which was put out by G. Delcuve, S.J., *Où en est l'enseignement religieux?* (Tournai, Belgium: Editions Casterman, imp. 1937) with a conspectus and bibliography for catechesis embracing France, Germany, England, Spain, Italy, Holland, the United States. This is a compilation of articles that had previously appeared in the *Nouvelle Revue Théologique,* No. 10 (Sept.–Dec., 1936). In a certain sense a continuation of this ambitious project is the international magazine *Lumen Vitae* which appeared for the first time in Brussels in 1946. At first this magazine contained articles in different languages, but since 1950 it has appeared in distinct French and English editions with contributions from all over the world. — A similar undertaking was begun in Vienna, but only one volume has appeared thus far: *Der elementare katholische Religionsunterricht in den Ländern Europas in monographischen Darstellungen. I: Die Länder des germanischen Sprachgebietes,* edited by L. Krebs (Vienna, 1938).

[74] A. Boyer, *Pédagogie chrétienne* (Paris, 1947), pp. 236–304; A. Elchinger, "Moderne katholische Erziehung in Frankreich" in *KBL,* Vol.

and especially those who are deprived of an effective religious education in the family, are forced to attend irreligious state schools. Only a fifth of the children, namely, those who attend Catholic private schools *(écoles libres)*, receive a suitable religious training. The efforts which are expended on catechesis, however, are very intense; they are concerned chiefly with establishing teaching centres outside the schools themselves. At an early age the children are regularly brought to these centres by lay-helpers, especially by women and girls. There they are tended in a religious atmosphere and are trained in the practice of their religion *(formation chrétienne des touts-petits)*.

Organizations of this kind are also entrusted with the task of eventually interesting the children in attending weekly catechesis in the parish. For those of nine, ten and eleven years of age who attend the State schools, catecheses are given by a priest in the parish church, as a rule once a week, usually on Thursdays which is not a school day. Regular attendance at these catecheses for a period of three years is required in most dioceses as a condition for admittance to *communion solennelle* (until just recently called *première communion*). In this custom the practice of receiving First Communion in a body for children of twelve years of age still survives—a practice which even religiously indifferent families still treasure highly. In a majority of dioceses authorities have actually succeeded in bringing over approximately ninety per cent of the children to attend such catecheses regularly for three years. Only six dioceses report an attendance as low as forty to fifty per cent. Aware that this one hour which is necessarily over-rich in

75 (1950), pp. 285–290 and 333–338: L. Lentner, *Religionsunterricht zwischen Methode und freier Gestaltung. Die elementare religiöse Unterweisung in Frankreich* (Innsbruck, 1953); C. Houle, "The Catechetical Movement in France as shown in Recent Pastoral Letters" in *Journal of Religious Instruction* (March, 1937), pp. 592–594; G. Delcuve, "Religious Pedagogy in France; Some Present Trends" in *Lumen Vitae*, Vol. 11 (1956), pp. 205–230.

instruction does not suffice to induce the children, who often are strongly influenced by their irreligious surroundings, to lead a truly Catholic life, those concerned have tried for some years now to lengthen the time devoted to the catechesis given on Thursdays, making it last the entire morning, and to embellish it with all types of child-like Christian activities: games, songs, occasional solemnizations of feast days, self-improvised recreation; in addition activities to foster Catholic charities as well as attendance at Mass, were eventually included in the programme. The children are required to spend at least a half day in a Christian atmosphere and in this way they are enabled to experience personally their religion.

Ever since the Decree of Pope St. Pius X, ecclesiastics charged with the care of children have attempted to prepare the children for an earlier "private first Communion", by means of an elementary catechesis, so that the *communion solennelle* later on would have only the character of a communion Mass to which a solemn profession of faith was added.[75] But their efforts have met with only partial success. Attempts have also been made, with results only fairly satisfactory, to bring children to attend voluntarily the *catéchisme de persévérance;* that is to say, the catechesis which is given to the older children as a continuation of compulsory catechesis.

Approximately since 1908, and especially since the appearance of the pastoral letter of Bishop Landrieux (1922), efforts have been made in France to do away with the simple explanation of the catechism and in its place to substitute, and to gain acceptance for, the concrete element, the *méthode historique* and *méthode intuitive*. Ever greater emphasis is, moreover, being placed

[75] For a discussion of the problems which have been broached here consult the special number of *La Maison-Dieu,* Vol. 28 (1951, IV): "Le problème pastoral de la Communion solennelle"; Lentner, *op. cit.,* pp. 155–166.

upon the active cooperation of the children *(méthode active)* on all levels, and the liturgy is accorded an especially prominent place. In the last few years, all these efforts have found significant expression in a new French edition of the uniform catechism (of 1938, resp. 1947) composed by Quinet and Boyer. This is an innovation in several respects, and we shall speak of it again. Of importance also is the formation of children's organizations whose members have been grouped together under definite watchwords; such as the Eucharistic Crusade, Catholic Boy Scouts, and for some years on a rather broad basis, the movement *Coeurs vaillants* and (for girls), *Âmes vaillantes.*[76] These are the preliminary stages for the *mouvements spécialisés* (*Jocist—Jeunesse ouvrière chrétienne* etc.) which blossomed so portentously in France and serve the purpose of both complementing and of enriching the doctrinal content of catechesis by a life lived in accord with the tenets of the Catholic faith.

In the United States the Catholic Church possesses its own school system, for which it alone is responsible and which it alone supervises.[77] There is no educational level on which it does not exist. This school system has its own complement of offices, school buildings, recreational facilities, and means of transportation. It has its own normal training schools, diocesan teachers' colleges, seminaries and observation schools. Its staffs

[76] A. Boyer, *Catéchétique* (Paris: P. Lethielleux, 1947), pp. 208–214.

[77] L. J. O'Connell, "Religious Education in the Elementary Schools of the United States" in *Lumen Vitae,* Vol. 4 (1949), pp. 749–766; J. Hofinger, "Catechesis in the United States Today" in *Lumen Vitae,* Vol. 2 (1956), pp. 246–267. See also the special number of the *KBl* devoted to the United States and particularly the report of J. Goldbrunner, *KBl,* Vol. 76 (1951), pp. 137–184; W. J. McGucken, "The Renascence of Religion Teaching in American Catholic Schools" in *Essays on Catholic Education in the United States* (Washington: Catholic University of America Press, 1942), pp. 329–351; F. G. Hochwalt, "Catholic Education in the U.S.A. in 1953" in *Religious Education,* Vol. 48 (Sept.-Oct., 1953), pp. 3–19.

rank with the best in the country: they are frequently graduates of other colleges and they are qualified and accredited teachers. What makes it most unique is that it has been inaugurated and has been able to carry on solely by means of the voluntary offerings of the faithful. During 1955 there were 4,423,200 students attending 12,241 schools staffed by 136,850 teachers. Elementary schools account for the majority of Catholic pupils with an enrolment of 3,325,251. High schools have 623,751; colleges and universities 281,999. These figures supplied by the National Catholic Welfare Conference represent a gain of 39 per cent since 1920, teachers by 142 per cent, and students by 110 per cent.[78]

Despite its size and its mushrooming possibilities the system takes care actually of only 50-60 per cent of the possible total Catholic pupil enrollment at the elementary level; 30 per cent at the secondary level and only 15 per cent at the college and university levels.[79] The hierarchy, the clergy and the faithful who conceived and help to keep in existence the Catholic school system rose to this challenge. Chiefly due to the inspiration and the zeal of the Most Rev. Archbishop Edward V. O'Hara of Kansas City, the *Confraternity of Christian Doctrine* (and the *Catholic Instruction League* in several dioceses before its merger with the Confraternity[80]) became a positive educative force for certain segments of the Catholic Church in the United

[78] A biennal summary of Catholic education carried out by the Department of Education of the *NCWC,* April, 1956 (The Register, July 29, 1956).

[79] These percentages are based on a national average, and do not represent the actual percentage in any individual dioceses, where totals may be either higher or lower.

[80] T. L. Bouscaren, *Canon Law Digest* (Milwaukee: Bruce, 1949), in which a résumé of the Letter of Pius, 5 August, 1925, is given; for further details consult: J. V. Brownson, *Stopping the Leak* (St. Louis: Central Bureau of the Central Verein, 1933); J. Lyons, "The Origin of the League" in *Catholic Mind,* Vol. 23 (Dec., 1925).

States.[81] In those sections which are too far removed from Catholic schools, or in which transportation difficulties present insurmountable problems, or in which Catholic schools are unable to cope with enrollment problems, or in which negligence or laxity on the part of parents make attendance impossible, Confraternities have been set up as the solution. These are complete with the active members: Fishers (home visitors), Helpers, Teachers, Discussion Club Leaders and Members, Parent Educators and Apostles to non-Catholics.[82] The Teachers are drawn for the most part from the ranks of Catholic public school teachers or from religious orders and congregations, chiefly women (who give unstintingly of their strength and their free time). Where such competent personnel is not available, training centres for future lay teachers have been founded. To facilitate their teaching and to supplement their doctrinal deficiencies manuals have been written by authorities in the various fields: *School Year Religious Instruction Manual,*[83] *Religious*

[81] St. Meinrad, *Essays and Documents on the Confraternity of Christian Doctrine* (St. Meinrad Essays, Vol. 11, No. 4, 1956); Confraternity Center, *The Confraternity Comes of Age* (Paterson: Confraternity Publications, 1956); Anonymous, *Mid-Century Survey.* Confraternity of Christian Doctrine in the U. S. A.—1950 (Washington: CCD, NCWC, 1951).

[82] CCD Center, *Manual of the Parish Confraternity of Christian Doctrine* (9th ed.; Washington: CCD, 1955); J. S. Middleton, *A Handbook of the Confraternity of Christian Doctrine* (New York: Benziger, 1950).

[83] There is a series of three booklets for the teacher arranged according to the various school levels: primary, intermediate and the upper grades, viz., Grades I and II; Grades III, IV and V; Grades VI, VII and VIII. These groupings also represent class groupings in those places where such apportioning is necessary. Actually what is preferred is every class a grade. When that is neither possible nor feasible, at least a five-fold break-up for class grading would be preferred. Cf. Sr. M. Rosalia, *The Adaptive Way,* p. 4 (see footnote 85). All this material may be obtained from *Confraternity Publications* (Paterson, New Jersey).

Vacation School Manual[84] and *The Adaptive Way*[85] as a methodological aid for the young lay teachers. Teaching centres have been set up wherever the Helpers are able to find suitable quarters or wherever the clergy provide parochial buildings for their use. The time at which this instruction is given varies: in some localities the teachers employ the released time offered by the various public school boards (either on the school grounds, or off them; either for the usual school year, or for special occasions such as preparation for First Holy Communion and Confirmation), free time (usually after school or on Saturdays, etc.) or the old Catholic Sunday School (after Mass, etc.).[86]

[84] E. V. O'Hara, *Religious Vacation Schools,* reprint from *The Ecclesiastical Review,* May 1930 (Philadelphia: Dolphin Press, 1938); W. T. Mulloy "Religious Vacation Schools and the National Catholic Rural Life Conference" in *The Confraternity Comes of Age,* loc. cit., pp. 27–40. E. Schmiedler, *The Religiously Underprivileged Child* (Washington: NCWC, 1933). For these schools the manuals are also arranged according to the same class grouping as for the *School Year Religious Program.* This material in its latest revision (1954) is built up according to *The Adaptive Way.* The booklets may be obtained (in their latest revision) from *Confraternity Publications* (Paterson, New Jersey).

[85] Sr. M. Rosalia, *The Adaptive Way of Teaching Confraternity Classes* (St. Paul: Catechetical Guild, 1955); id., *Teaching Confraternity Classes (The Adaptive Way)* (Chicago: Loyola University, 1944); *ibid.,* a series of four booklets called the *Adaptive Way* (Towson, Md.: Mission Helpers, 1941–1942) in which the principles that are embodied in the *Adaptive Way* are incorporated into an actual text for teachers.

[86] W. W. Keesecker, *Law Relating to the Releasing of Pupils from Public Schools for Religious Instruction,* Office of Education, No. 39 (Washington: U. S. Printing Office, 1933); M. D. Davis, *Weekday Classes in Religious Education* (Washington: U. S. Office of Education, 1941), Bulletin 1941, No. 3; J. P. Archdeacon, *The Week-Day Religious School,* Dissertation (Washington: Catholic Univ., 1927); J. M. O'Neill, *Religion and Education Under the Constitution* (New York: Harper & Bros., 1949); W. G. Torpey, *Judicial Doctrines of Religious Rights in America* (Chapel Hill: Univ. of N. Carolina Press, 1948), especially pp. 233–276; James J. Burke, "Burses, Released Time and the Political Process" *in Marquette Law Review,* Vol. 32, 3 (December, 1948), pp. 179–187; W. Parsons, "No Religion in the

No class of possible educators or of special pupils is neglected: for mothers at home, the special series of *Parent Educator*[87] pamphlets is available; for children who are unable to visit any Catholic school, or Confraternity school, *Correspondence School Classes*[88] are inaugurated, as, for example, in Montana. For adults whose early religious education has been neglected or who seek to deepen their scanty knowledge, *Discussion Clubs* are formed.[89] For these clubs special material is required.

Schools" in *The Sign,* Vol. 27 (May, 1948), pp. 12–14; R. F. Drinan, "The Lawyers and Religion" in *America,* Vol. 80 (March 5, 1949), pp. 593–595; Godfrey P. Schmidt, "Religious Liberty and the Supreme Court of the United States" in *Fordham Law Review,* Vol. 17 (November, 1948), pp. 173–199; J. H. Brady, *Confusion Twice Confounded* (South Orange, Seton Hall, 1954); N. Edwards, *The Courts and the Public Schools,* rev. ed. (Chicago: Univ. of Chicago, 1955), pp. 47–52, 350–360, 550–558; James M. O'Neill, *The Catholic in Secular Education* (New York: Longmans, Green, 1956), pp. 107–138.

[87] Mrs. J. J. Daly, "Parent-Educator Program of the CCD" in *The Confraternity Comes of Age*. A series of articles in the *Journal of Religious Instruction,* Vol. II (1931). *Parent Educator* (original series), Vol. I (Paterson, N. J.: St. Anthony Guild Press, 1931), especially pp. 5–8. In addition to these publications there are the two other series that contain some of the material that was projected for the parent-educators, e.g., the first of these called *The Parent Educator* (New Series); I. *Parental Responsibility*; II. *Teaching Prayer in the Home;* etc. (This series, five in all, may be obtained from St. Anthony Guild Press, Paterson, N.J.) The other group of publications is entitled: *The Parent-Educator Section* (Confraternity of Christian Doctrine). The first is a series of leaflets, *Teaching Religion in the Home,* Nos. 1–12 (Ages 1–3); Nos. 13–24 (At Home From 3 to 6) (Paterson, N.J.: St. Anthony Guild Press, 1945). There is also: M. L. Healey, *Heaven, Home and the School* (Paterson, N.J.: Confraternity Publications, 1948).

[88] L. S. Hauber, "Religion by Mail" in *Proceedings,* Boston, 1946 (NCWC; CCD, St. Anthony Guild Press, 1947); "Gaining Good Will Through the Mails" in *Proceedings,* Chicago, 1951 (CCD; NCWC, 1952); V. Day, "Correspondence Course in Christian Doctrine" in *Journal of Religious Instruction,* Vol. III (November, 1932), pp. 251–256; CCD, *Manual of the Confraternity of Christian Doctrine* (9th ed.; Washington, CCD, 1955), pp. 109–114.

[89] CCD, "The Religious Discussion Club" (Paterson, N. J.:

This is supplied to them, and whole series, for example, the pamphlets for the New Testament, have appeared. Special pleas were made to Catholic students attending non-Catholic colleges and universities to join *Newman Clubs*[90] to supplement their religious training and to have a corrective for possible errors taught in the classes they attended. To the non-Catholic who has never heard about the Church or her doctrines the Confraternity sends her street preachers.[91] To take care that the Confraternity would not be lost sight of, an office *(National Center)*[92] was set up at Washington. This office keeps its members

Confraternity Publications, 1942), Pamphlet No. 5; CCD, *Manual of the Confraternity of Christian Doctrine* (9th ed.; Paterson, N. J.: Confraternity Publications, 1944), pp. 61–67. For additional information see the Proceedings of the various National Catechetical Congresses in which various articles are grouped under the heading, *Religious Discussion Club.* The National Center of the Confraternity will supply suggestions and will recommend texts to be used in the course of these discussions. Cf. also J. Clendenin, "Religious Discussion Clubs" in *The Confraternity Comes of Age* (Paterson, N. J.: Confraternity Publications, 1956), pp. 71 to 84; R. S. Shea, *Discussion Action Clubs Challenge Adults,* CCD 115 (Paterson, N. J.: Confraternity Publications, 1952) pp. 1–8.

[90] D. M. Cleary, "The Confraternity of Christian Doctrine and Newman Clubs" in *The Confraternity Comes of Age* (Paterson, N. J.: Confraternity Publications, 1956), pp. 252–256; M. A. Pleasants, "The CCD Committee of the National Newman Club Federation" *op. cit.,* pp. 256–258; J. C. Richaud, "How to Organize Junior Newman Clubs" and A. E. Crawford, "Activity Program for Junior Newman Clubs": both of these papers appear in *Proceedings,* Chicago, 1951 (CCD; NCWC, 1952), pp. 273–278, 279–287.

[91] V. F. Kilborn, "Gaining Good Will Through Street Preaching" in *Proceedings,* Chicago, 1951 (CCD; NCWC, 1952); CCD, *Manual of the Confraternity of Christian Doctrine* (9th ed.; Paterson, N. J.: Confraternity Publications, 1955), pp. 74–80; A. J. Korioth, "The Apostolate of Good Will" in *The Confraternity Comes of Age* (Paterson, N. J.: Confraternity Publications, 1956), pp. 259–268.

[92] F. A. Walsh, "The National Center of the Confraternity of Christian Doctrine" in *Proceedings,* Rochester, 1935 (Paterson, N. J.: St. Anthony Guild Press, 1936), pp. 24–32; R. C. Rock, "The National

posted through *Our Parish Confraternity*[93] on developments in the field and serves as a clearing house for information that has been gained over the years. Priests are made acquainted with the need for and the special problems of the Confraternity not only after but even before their ordination by special classes devoted to these topics in the seminary. Perhaps one of the crowning achievements of the Confraternity movement has been the fostering of a Catholic paper for children who attend these Confraternity classes: The *Catholic Messenger* (*Confraternity Edition* for three different levels).[94]

Another remarkable achievement is the *National Catechetical Congress of the Confraternity of Christian Doctrine* which began holding its session in Rochester in 1935.[95] Sectional meetings have also assembled, and even diocesan groups have come together for the purpose of exchanging views and of swapping experiences to which actual practice has given birth.

In regard to methodology not only for the Confraternity Classes but also for the Catholic school system itself, the first book to appear was the translation of Archbishop Messmer,

Center of the CCD" in *The Confraternity Comes of Age* (Paterson, N. J.: Confraternity Publications, 1956), pp. 148–169.

[93] *Our Parish Confraternity,* a monthly messenger devoted exclusively to Confraternity of Christian Doctrine activities. Confraternity of Christian Doctrine, 1312 Massachusetts Ave., N.W., Washington 5, D.C. Write also to this address of the Confraternity for information.

[94] These are graded: *Our Little Catholic Messenger, Junior Catholic Messenger* and *Young Catholic Messenger,* with the by-line *Confraternity Edition.* Each of the numbers has a *Teacher's Study Guide.* This material is published by Geo. A. Pflaum, Publishers, Inc., 38 West Fifth St., Dayton 2, Ohio. The *Treasure Chest* by the same publisher is also used by the Confraternity.

[95] In the beginning these Congresses which were a part of the Catholic Rural Life Conference (National Rural Life Conference, Proceedings Twelfth Annual Convention [St. Paul, 1934], pp. 118–166) were held annually from 1936 to 1941. Since then they have been convoked every five years.

Spirago's Method of Christian Doctrine.[96] In this the author espouses three different forms of instruction: the lecture form, the question form, the object form. In other respects it incorporates at least in embryonic form latter developments, which have been much lauded, for example, visual aids, and special chapters on the various types of subject matter such as Bible History. His book was followed by another on the Munich Method in the form in which Father M. Gatterer, S.J. proposed it.[97] This Munich Method was given added support by a series of textbooks which Monsignor J. J. Baierl brought out; these were orientated on Stieglitz's catecheses.[98] The first exponent perhaps of the textbook for religion classes in the U. S. A., other than the catechism or Bible History, was Father Peter Yorke of San Francisco.[99] Although his works never succeeded in gaining a foothold, they did give impetus to the Catholic catechetical revival. Into this fermenting progressivism were added the contributions of Fathers Shields and Pace.[100] Father Shields banished the catechism and Bible History from the first three grades, and insisted on the principle of correlation. Father Pace collaborated with Father

[96] S. G. Messmer, *Spirago's Method of Christian Doctrine* (New York: Benziger, 1901).

[97] M. Gatterer (J. B. Culemans, trans.), *Theory and Practice of the Catechism* (New York: F. Pustet, 1914).

[98] The last edition of these complete catecheses of Stieglitz according to the Munich Method (psychological method); *The Creed Explained* (5th ed.; St. Paul: Catechetical Guild, 1943); *The Grace and the Sacraments Explained* (5th ed.; St. Paul: Catechetical Guild, 1949); *The Commandments Explained* (6th ed.; Rochester: St. Bernard Seminary, 1954).

[99] *Educational Lectures* (San Francisco: Textbook Publ., 1933); *Guide to the "Textbooks of Religion" and "Hints to Teachers"* (San Francisco: Textbook Publ., 1932). To these we should add his textbooks for the eight grades of the elementary school. They bear the title: *Text Book of Religion for Parochial and Sunday Schools* (17th ed., rev. ed., 1931).

[100] R. J. Deferrari, *Essays on Catholic Education* (Washington, D.C., 1943), pp. 336–337; J. Ward, *Thomas Edward Shields* (New York: Charles Scribner's Sons, 1947), pp. 217–258; E. A. Pace, *On Methods of*

Shields, but his untimely death cut off his further development of Shield's catechetical method. Father Roderick MacEachen also tried his hand at the problem. His book on method, *The Teaching of Religion,* contains much provocative material, especially his chapters on "The Child and Religion", "Character Building" and "The Rule of the Positive" (which contains an impressive rule for the teaching of the Commandments).[101]

In her desire to furnish the child with the best method possible the Church in the United States turned to Europe. There it acquired ideas from Madame Montessori[102] and from Fr. Drinkwater, whose system has been called *The Sower Scheme* because of the magazine of the same name in which his theories are broached.[103] He inveighs particularly against the "parrot-system of learning by heart" and grows angry at the too early introduction of the catechism into the teaching procedure ("It is definitely not for the children of the primary grades"). He thinks modern Catechisms are too large, have too many questions, are too theoretical (law of adaptation). He personally favours frequent use of dramatization at the children's level and adapted to their capacities.[104] Madame Montessori was of course a specialist

Teaching Religion (Wilmington, Del.: Oblates of St. Francis de Sales). These are the stenographic notes of Lawrence W. McCarthy.

[101] R. MacEachen, *The Teaching of Religion* (New York: Macmillan, 1921).

[102] Maria Montessori (Mortimer Standing, trans.), *Child in the Church* (St. Louis: Herder, 1930); id. (A. E. George, trans.), *The Montessori Method* (New York: Stokes, 1914); P. J. McCormick, "Montessori and Religious Instruction" in *Thought,* Vol. II (1927), pp. 56–71.

[103] His theory is contained principally in the following books: *The Givers* (London: Burns, Oates, 1926), *Religion in School Again* (London: Burns, Oates & Washbourne, 1936), and *Educational Essays* (London: Burns, Oates, 1951). The magazine of which he is the editor is called simply: *The Sower,* Lower Gornal, Dudley, England.

[104] F. H. Drinkwater, *Gabriel's Ave* (London: Burns, Oates & Washbourne, 1936); id., *Fourteen Catechism Plays* (London: Burns, Oates, 1950).

for the primary grades, and her approach to the child through the senses and through his personal activity have left their imprint on theorists for this grade level. Father John T. McMahon, weighing all the contributions that had been up to his time made, plunges for the project method, and favours the *Perth Plan*.[105]

American Catholics, acquainted with the contributions (or errors?) of John Dewey, early began to introduce the "learn by doing" principle into their schools. The unit was studied not only in its European progenitors but also in its American representatives.[106] The social educators were consulted on problems which began to take on a new meaning in connection with education. Other European methodological contributions, stressing the importance of emotional as distinct from intellectual factors, were also adapted for the American public (state) school system. Thus, from all possible sources the present methodology of the Catholic school system and of the organization which it had originated, the Confraternity of Christian Doctrine, have at their disposal the best that didactics, pedagogy and catechetics can offer.

The catechetical situation in Italy[107] is entirely different. In 1870 catechesis was suppressed in all public schools. Only in 1923 was it again permitted and then only in the elementary schools. In Italy, however, no attempt has been made to set up a Catholic school system such as exists in the U.S.A., and with certain

[105] J. T. McMahon, *Some Methods of Teaching Religion* (London: Burns, Oates & Washbourne, 1928), pp. 191–265.

[106] R. B. Raup, "The Unit of Instruction and Study" in *Journal of Educational Method,* Vol. VII (Dec., 1927), pp. 112–120; W. H. Burton, "The Unit Concept in Learning" in *Educational Outlook,* Vol. VII (May, 1933), pp. 206–213; J. G. Umstattd, *Secondary School Teaching* (new ed.; Boston: Ginn & Co., 1944), pp. 135–181; A. H. Jones, *et al., Principles of Unit Construction* (New York: McGraw-Hill, 1939).

[107] M. Barbera, "L'insegnamento religioso elementare in Italia" in *La Civiltà Cattolica,* Vol. 89 (1938) III, pp. 1–18; P. Moretta, "L'enseignement de la religion en Italie" in *Lumen Vitae,* Vol. 4 (1949), pp. 137–160.

exceptions in Northern Italy, even after 1923 no effort has been made to improve catechesis in the public schools. In these schools, however, Bible History is generally taught to the children. Catechesis on the catechism is also given generally in the parish, and usually in church, but only in the time-honoured way. This type of catechesis is trying to procure for itself to a much greater extent the advantages which are inherent in a formal school system, and which are obtained by the methods employed in the schools themselves. For several decades now, competent authorities have developed fixed courses of study with progressive programmes and in ever increasing amounts literary aids of prime value. The training of the catechists has been sponsored by numerous catechetical Congresses. In more recent years Catholic Action has especially busied itself with catechetical work. Through its agencies it has enlisted and trained a great number of lay catechists as well as turned out publications of its own (for example, several volumes of catechetical drawings, etc.). In Italy, in order to awaken the interest of the children, catechetical contests have been held and prizes awarded. Both are held in high esteem. These contests ordinarily take place on the parish level, but also on the deanery and diocesan levels, and have been elaborated into a Feast of the Catechism.

The attempts which had been made to exchange information on experience gained in catechetical work beyond the limits of national boundaries, reached their zenith in the "World Catechetical Congress", held in Rome, under the chairmanship of the Cardinal Prefect of the Congregation of the Council, in 1950.[108] This Congress afforded a survey in which the participants examined the goals which are everywhere the same and discussed the tasks at every age-level, from infants to adults, shared the

[108] "Report of the International Catechetic Congress held at Rome 10–14th October, 1950" in *Lumen Vitae,* Vol. 5 (1950), pp. 639–644; J. D. Crichton, "The Church's Mind and Catechetics" in *The Sower,* No. 189

methodological advances which have been made, sketched present needs and also noted the great differences in the circumstances for, and in the possibilities of, catechetical work. The following countries were mentioned as having school systems favourable to catechetical methods: Ireland, Spain, Austria and Germany.

The special nature of catechetical activity, which must be closely allied to given circumstances, suggests that only the most general ordinances can emanate from the highest ecclesiastical authorities; whereas the more concrete particularizations must come either from individual bishops or from national conferences of bishops.

With the advent of compulsory school attendance it has become the duty of bishops to prescribe textbooks and curricula, as well as to watch with a critical eye the efforts at reform. The Council of Trent, as we have seen, gave important directives for the catechesis of children, and the Popes of the succeeding centuries have expressed their concern in practical ways for the same objective. Recent attempts to fashion a universal catechism have not been successful. Whatever has been done since Trent in the way of achieving uniformity, and whatever enactments have been framed for the fostering of catechesis were compiled and condensed in the Code of Canon Law (1917). In three different sections the Code deals with the problem of catechesis: in a section concerning the duties of the parish priest (can. 467, cf. can. 336), in a special section devoted to catechetical training (can. 1329-1336), and in the portion dealing with the school system, in which the demands for a competent catechesis are raised and precisely described for those schools which are attended by Catholic children (can. 1373, 1381 f.).

(Oct., 1953), pp. 91–98; SCC, *Summa Relationum* (Rome: Cancelleria Apostolica, 1950).

In 1923 in Rome by order of Pope Pius XI the *officium catechisticum* was set up as a department of the Congregation of the Council and as the court of final appeal for catechetical problems. A whole series of guiding principles was drawn up by this office in the decree *Provido sane* in 1935.[109] These principles were formulated chiefly for those countries which are without regular catechesis in their schools. They deal with those organizations of laymen cooperating in the work of the Confraternity of Christian Doctrine, with parochial catechesis for children, with the Feast of the Catechism, with religious instruction for adults, with catechetical offices and departments in the various dioceses, with the inspection of catechesis, and with the formation of catechists.[110]

6. The Catechetical Movement in England

The course followed by religious instruction in England from the Reformation onwards was not substantially different from that of the Continent and may be followed chiefly, though not exclusively, through the various catechisms that were published from the sixteenth century to the middle of the nineteenth. The first of these, written by Dr. Vaux of Manchester, was entitled *A Catechisme or Christian Doctrine necessarie for Children and ignorante people . . .*,[111] and the author, who was already a refugee, says that it owes something to the Catechism of St. Peter Canisius. It is closer to the medieval scheme than the subsequent ones, keeping the lists of items so much beloved of medieval catechists: for example, "The Five Senses: How they are to be

[109] AAS, Vol. 27 (1935), pp. 145–154; cf. C. Louis (Editor), *Essays and Documents on the Confraternity of Christian Doctrine*. St. Meinrad Essays, Vol. 11, No. 4 (May, 1956), pp. 42–56.

[110] G. Götzel, "Zeitgemäße Wertung der Katechese" in *KBl*, Vol. 62 (1936), pp. 193–198.

[111] Ed. T. Law, *Chetham Soc., New Series*, 4, 1885.

used." There is very little reflexion of the current controversies. The book that spanned centuries was the so-called *Douai Catechism* (its connexion with the college is doubtful) which, with its *Abridgement,* went on being published until the end of the Penal Days. It was based on the catechisms of St. Peter Canisius and St. Robert Bellarmine. The immediate ancestor of the present catechism was the little book attributed to Bishop Richard Challoner which everyone agrees was his. It is called *An Abridgement of Christian Doctrine*. Revised and Enlarged by R. C., St. Omer, 1772.[112]

It will be seen that religious instruction was dominated by the question-and-answer catechism and when we examine the content of the instruction we see that it was strongly flavoured by the controversial exigencies of the time. The rigours of this kind of instruction were mitigated by the intense religious life of the small Catholic communities scattered over England and the Continent and by the books of devotion that appeared all through the period. Of these Challoner's *Garden of the Soul* and *Meditations* were the best known, and both contained solid instruction which parents will have passed on to their children. The piety of Catholics during the Penal times could be described as solid, both because it was based on doctrine and because it was markedly scriptural. The biblical flavour of the *Meditations* and the many psalms and "sentences" in the *Garden of the Soul* are evidence of this.

Yet even so Challoner's little book, perhaps because he too intended it for "Children and ignorante people", was not so

[112] It is a very rare book and will be found only at Oscott College and St. Edmund's Ware. The Oscott copy (Pamphlet Section, post-1620) is a small book, bound in vellum, of 32 pages. I was able to consult it thanks to the courtesy of the college authorities. For a fuller treatment of Vaux and Challoner, consult J.D. Crichton, "Religious Education in England in the Penal Days" in Sloyan, *op. cit.,* pp. 72-90.

abstract as its nineteenth successor became. The answer to the question (which may be regarded as a key question in any catechism) "What is God", was "He is the Maker and Lord of Heaven and Earth". In the manuscript another hand has added "God is a spirit the Creator and Sovereign Lord of all things", and thus prepared the way for the difficult answer which still stands in the English catechism: "God is the supreme spirit who alone exists of himself and is infinite in all his perfections."

This catechism, which came to be known as the Penny Catechism, and which is the one still in use, was revised in the nineteenth century after the National Synods and gradually brought up to date (for example, the answers on the Immaculate Conception and the Infallibility of the Pope which does not figure in Challoner's catechism). It was then, it would seem, that the catechism acquired its rather abstract tone and the sometimes tiresome rhetorical jingles that have since become so familiar to English Catholics.

All during the latter part of the nineteenth century the sociological and educational picture was changing. Large numbers of Catholics, mostly Irish immigrants, were moving into the large towns, compulsory education was introduced in 1870 and great numbers of Catholic children had to attend school. The old domestic bond was broken, the small "Sunday School" or their equivalent classes came to an end—except perhaps in the dwindling parishes of the countryside—and children from the age of five were confronted with a catechism which for the most part was adult in language and too abstract for their grasp. Still, Catholic parishes remained remarkably homogeneous and rather shut in on themselves, so that there was a strong community life that helped the child to live his religion. The system seemed to work. Schools belonged to the parish who had to pay the teachers salaries, often infinitesimal, and the priest played a big part in the running of the school. With the Education Act of 1902 and the raising of the teachers' status and a greater control by public bodies, there came a certain change which laid the foundations for the existing system. Since 1902 there has been a revolution in educational outlook and method that was bound to affect the teaching of religion in Catholic schools.

7. *The Beginnings of Reform in England*

The state of religious instruction in England at the beginning of this century was very much what it was elsewhere in the Church. The printed catechism was supreme and the only teaching method was learning by heart. The more gifted teacher made some attempt at explanation but the system was vitiated by the imposition of difficult and abstract answers on small children. Educationally speaking, the cart was very effectively being put before the horse. What was peculiar to the English situation was that at that time Catholics were a very small minority in the country, very conscious of the influence of Protestantism everywhere in public life. This gave a certain rigidity of outlook in the field of catechetics, and the need for fixed and very clear statements of doctrine was felt to be all-important in the face of the vague yet dissolvent heretical teaching that permeated the atmosphere.

It is not surprising that change came slowly. As teaching methods in secular subjects improved, many teachers and some priests felt the need for a more adequate way of presenting the faith to children. The first signs of a change were to have been observed after the decree of Pope St. Pius X *(Quam singulari)* which admitted young children to holy Communion. Although once a change of emphasis had been made, and many, both teachers and priests, collaborated, it must be set down as a matter of historical fact that catechetical reform in England began with the work of one priest. Francis H. Drinkwater (now Canon) was ordained in that year and he himself has recorded the beginnings of his work: "In 1910, when I began work in my first parish (as an assistant priest), Pope Pius X had just issued his decree admitting the seven-year-olds to first communion, and we were all busy trying to prepare these little boys and girls so that their first confession and first holy communion should be a spiritual and psychological reality. In this task, and with those children, the catechism was evidently not going to be any help, so we left it aside and learned how to teach them what was necessary in their own simple language. I always look back to this decree of Pius X as the real beginning of catechetical reform, for it forced us all back on the psychological realities of childhood. There were none of those helpful little handbooks to make everything easy for us in those days. Moreover, although we did not realize it at the time, Pius X's decree made suitable provision for the later stages of childhood also. After first communion (said the Pope) the whole catechism was to be learned, but 'gradually, step by step, in the measure of the capacity' of the learners."[113]

This testimony is important since it shows clearly the origin of the reform—the child, his needs and capacity—and the lines it was to follow. There was the constant effort for reality, one might almost say realism, in the presentation of truths to be learned, a persevering search into the psychological needs of the child and a determination to link instruction with the organic growth of the child. "Little and often" has been the slogan of the work of Canon Drinkwater which came to be known as the "Sower Scheme".

The war of 1914 brought all this work to an end, except that

[113] F. H. Drinkwater, *Educational Essays* (London, 1951), pp. 95–96. In a footnote he continues: "The present Holy Father has echoed the same requirement of Pius X, when he said to priests instructing children, 'See that what you say to them is solid, clear, interesting, alive, warm, and adjusted to their capacity, and their spiritual needs'."

it gave Father Drinkwater, who became a chaplain in the army, an opportunity to observe at first hand the effects of the traditional system when put to the supreme test. He found that what the soldiers had learned of the abstract formulas had been forgotten for the most part, but that the practical things like the sacraments, were still familiar even to those who had lapsed.[114] This influenced the next stage. Religion is not only something to learn but something to be lived, and every effort must be made to insert religious instruction into life, into the life of the Church (hence the liturgy), into the life of the family, and so far as possible it must be a preparation for life in the world. Writing in 1933 in answer to questioners who wanted to know what the "Sower Scheme" stood for, Father Drinkwater said, "The *Aim* is to help the schools to produce good practising Catholics in after life."[115] A simple aim, not a very exalted aim it may be said, but a fundamental one.

With his return to civilian life he determined to do what he could to change the existing system which, he was convinced, was inadequate to the needs of ordinary Catholic men and women living the hard life of industrial England.

His first act in 1921 was to found a small monthly review called *The Sower,* which by 1925 had been reduced to a quarterly. Always completely independent financially, it was able to give expression to views that were not always popular. In an early issue Father Drinkwater gave a sketch of what became known as the "Sower Scheme", in which he assigned the catechism to the Juniors with the easiest answers to be learned first. This scheme was given a trial when in 1922 Father Drinkwater was appointed diocesan inspector of religious instruction in the archdiocese of Birmingham.

At this point it is convenient to abandon a purely chronological account and to take a different perspective.

[114] *Ibid.,* p. 96. [115] *Ibid.,* p. 68.

The first thing that needs saying is that what for so long was known as "The Sower Scheme" was not an imposed system, itself the result of merely theoretical planning in some educational laboratory. It was not all thought out first and then tried out on unfortunate children. Its point of departure was, as we have seen, the child and his needs and his nature, and this original intuition has controlled and guided all the development that has come since. The "Scheme" (which is far too rigid a word to describe it) has undergone a growth that can only be described as a natural one. As the needs and psychology of the child have been progressively better understood, so has the scheme grown. And although one man was at the origin of the whole thing, he rapidly attracted a whole group of workers of various sorts who made valuable contributions in the course of years. The compilers of the international survey of religious instruction, *Où en est l'enseignement religieux?*, describing the Sower Scheme in 1937, wrote as follows: "It is not the work of one man but of a group. It is a real family, wide open to life, in which skilled collaborators work together in complete sincerity, frankness and courage" (p. 286). Again, in another place, they remark that it moves gradually and that it refuses to offer either to teachers or pupils the predigested or the ready-made. Father Drinkwater and his collaborators, they say, have created an entirely new atmosphere in which fresh air and optimism abound (p. 276).

From the beginning it was seen that religious instruction is a good deal more than the imparting of a certain amount of doctrine. First, the child is a living, growing creature and demands activity. Hence the emphasis on life, not only in the sense that the child takes in knowledge through living but in the sense that the whole purpose of instruction is to form him for life after he has left school. Hence, say the same writers, in the "Sower Scheme" the child is not considered as an end but as a middle term, a "growing thing" whose completed form is the adult.

Further, the child is meant to live the life of the Church both at school and afterwards. Hence the need to make the liturgy a living thing to him, and it is in this way that instruction in the liturgy and so far as circumstances allow, the practice of it in the parish church, has come to play so large a part in the scheme.

With all this there was the constant effort to infuse life into the instruction itself, and this in two directions. First, it was realized that words are of paramount importance. It was not just a matter of avoiding "hard" words or "big" words but of finding life-bearing words, words that would match the concrete thought-processes of young children, words that would appeal to their imagination. For this reason there was a strong emphasis on Scripture which, as the aid books which were written subsequently show, was used as one of the principal means for conveying doctrine. Hymns too and rhymed verses have all played their part in the same effort. Secondly, since children themselves are active, lively creatures, their activity was harnessed in various ways: drama, and classroom dramatization, have played a big part in the scheme; and what was early recognized as an original invention was the activity eventually known as "Home-made catechisms", in which children collected phrases, sentences, and prayers and illustrated the whole either with their own or ready-made pictures. This was the contribution of Miss A. M. Scarre and has been described as follows: "The idea was simple but of infinite application. Each child literally makes his own book; he composes it, writes it, illustrates it, according to the capacity of his age, with cut-out pictures or his own drawings, or with his personal reflexions. This book is his own, and the religion he finds there is his own also."[116]

It was these and similar ideas that were propagated in *The*

[116] *Où en est l'enseignement religieux?*, p. 286.

Sower year after year and it was thus that the scheme gradually attracted followers long before it became official. It was through the review that the scheme became known far and wide, and the reactions to what appeared in it aroused a good deal of opposition, especially in the early days. Indeed, it must be stated that there has always been and still is a certain amount of opposition, and by no means all are convinced of the truth of its basic assumptions or of its methods. Yet there has been a steady advance, and in the change of climate in these matters that has come about in the last thirty years the *Sower* has played a leading part.

The Sower, which circulates over the whole Catholic world, has undoubtedly been the main means for making known the aims, principles and ideals of the "Sower Scheme". This, with Father Drinkwater's innumerable books, brought his ideas to the knowledge of all engaged in Catholic education. There was a peaceful penetration of the Training Colleges, many of which have become the most convinced and active supporters of the Scheme. A reform in the examinations for teachers met with no opposition. In 1928 the system of religious examinations in grammar and convent schools was overhauled and Father Drinkwater played his part in this. Two courses corresponding to the Higher Certificate and the School Certificate were arranged, the latter based on Christ and the Church and the former on the traditional apologetics, with, in the second year, some treatment of Catholic sociology. Both these schemes are again under review, as the years have revealed certain defects.

But undoubtedly the main sphere of Father Drinkwater's work has been in what used to be called elementary schools which are now divided into Primary and Secondary Modern. Here the need was greatest and here the reform has been most beneficial.

When Father Drinkwater became a diocesan inspector in 1922 he put his ideas into practice throughout the diocese with what he called the "Optional Scheme"—teachers were left free to adopt it or not as they pleased. The learning by heart of the catechism was retained in the junior school but every effort was made to see that it was done intelligently and well. Eight years experience showed that the catechism for juniors was premature and when in 1929, with the active and whole-hearted support of Archbishop Williams, the Sower Scheme became the official scheme of religious instruction in the archdiocese, the learning of the printed catechism was allocated to the senior children. This apparently small change was in fact revolutionary (and one not accepted without protest) since it freed the junior school from a task that was beyond its capacity and left the field open for new methods and a fresh approach to the teaching of small children. In addition, the senior children came to the printed catechism for the first time and were able to look upon it with fresh eyes. The catechism course could be more thorough as well as more adult. With this change came the provision of aid-books for teachers, of which the best known are *Teaching the Catechism,* a commentary on the whole catechism, and *Doctrine for the Juniors* which provides lesson-material, with an emphasis on the practical side, on the whole of Christian doctrine for children below the age of eleven. Later, *Religious Teaching for Young Children* by S.N.D. was adopted for the infant's school.

With all this there was a steady development of all the other features of the Scheme, an increasing realization of the possibilities and limits of drama in teaching religion, of the importance of the liturgy and of Holy Scripture. A little book like *Twelve and After* intended for children over twelve, showed that Father Drinkwater had anticipated by many years the importance of presenting the faith as the continuing story of God's dealings with man, or what they call on the continent, Sacred History, in which Old and New Testaments are viewed in one perspective, and into which are inserted Christ and his saving acts, the Church and her life and liturgy.

The further stages of the development of the Scheme can be traced in the following publications. By 1935 the full catechism had been found to be unwieldy even for the senior children and in 1936 the *Abbreviated Catechism* was introduced with official approval of the Archbishop. This telescoped some answers and omitted a section of the catechism which has to do with Christian living. It was envisaged that this material should be linked to lessons that dealt with doctrine. More recently, to meet the needs of children who stay at school until they are fifteen, an *Abbreviated Catechism with Explanations* was introduced (1950) in which the explanations really explain in simple language the main truths of the Faith. It is completed with a brief view of Christian history and an appendix on the liturgical year.

A long-standing complaint had been that the scheme for juniors was too vague and that the teachers did not know quite what was required of them. To meet this a series of questions which were to be used by the teachers and intended to guide them was devised for both infants and juniors. More recently still, the scheme for juniors has been worked out in greater detail so that the head-teacher has less difficulty in working out a syllabus for the whole school. Now a term-by-term syllabus is provided, with continual references to the aid-books. It follows the liturgical year and within each year the three terms bear some relation to the actions of the Three Persons of the Trinity. The Primary syllabus thus seems to be complete and it is not envisaged that any great changes will have to be made in it.

The situation regarding the Secondary Modern syllabus is not so satisfactory and Canon Drinkwater notes as follows: "This (the syllabus for children from 11 to 15) never pretended to be anything but an arrangement for coping with the existing national catechism. It is an 'end-on' syllabus (the first year Creed, the second Commandments, the third Sacraments) which has many disadvantages; and the *Abbreviated Catechism,* shortened as it is from the national, is just as technical, abstract, definition seeking and unscriptural. However, the Secondary Modern schools have now come into existence, and the bishops are revising the national catechism, and thus there is an opportunity to revise this part of the syllabus. One would hope for a short catechism in more scriptural language, a catechism which might be all covered every year and welded with scripture and history. Thus an ideal syllabus might go something like this:

First Year: Jewish preparation for the Saviour; along with the whole catechism studied in the light of the Old Testament.

Second Year: Life of Christ, from the Gospels; along with the whole catechism again, but this time viewed as flowing from our Lord's teaching.

Third Year: History of the Church, from Pentecost until now; and again the whole catechism, studied as the summary of the Church's mission and community-life.

Fourth Year: the Christ-life (both communal and personal) for the twentieth century; once more the whole catechism, considered as a guide-book to spiritual life and conduct."

It cannot be disguised that though the so-called Sower Scheme has influenced educational thinking and practice, it has never been wholly endorsed by any other diocese in England. There is a very general measure of agreement that the catechism-answers should be explained before being memorized, though it is a matter of dispute when this process should start. So far no other diocese except Birmingham has postponed it until after the age of eleven. In 1944 the Westminster archdiocese produced a scheme which has been widely adopted. In this the bulk of the catechism has to be learnt from eight years onwards. The archdiocese of Liverpool has its own scheme and both these schemes are at present under review. Both these dioceses have issued good handbooks of *Suggestions to Teachers,* though the aid-books of the Birmingham scheme are widely used throughout the country.

Although the above account of catechetical reform in England has concentrated on the work of Canon Drinkwater, it would give a false impression if one did not add that many have been concerned in that reform. Innumerable teachers and the heads and lecturers in training colleges have made their contribution in one way or another, and if there is a great awareness in England at the moment of the urgency of religious teaching, it must be attributed to them as well as to the pioneer work of the Sower Scheme. This concern for the right kind of teaching was reflected among other places in the special number of the *Downside Review* (Autumn, 1955) which considered the whole matter. One point of special interest was the emphasis on the instruction of adult Catholics which normally should be done at Mass and for which a national catechism should be the principal means. This is but one small indication in this country of the union between catechetics and liturgy which existed in the early Church and which is having such fruitful results on the continent. With the rapid development of a Catholic middle-class and the ever increasing number who are attending universities, this matter of the continued instruction of lay-people at a level equal to that of their professional studies, will be one that will occupy the minds of Church authorities in the years to come.[117]

[117] See also Appendix IV.

II

THE CATECHIST

In this chapter we shall discuss two questions: Who should be a catechist? How should the catechist be trained?

1. As the historical review has shown, it was not always a priest who gave the children their religious training. What principles should as a consequence be enforced in connection with the person of the catechist?

Whenever there has been a question of perfecting the initiation into religion, which the family gave, by more profound instruction, the need has always been met by the clergy. And this is generally the case today for the sole reason that religious instruction must be given within the framework of the general formation which is the goal of compulsory education. Thus, it devolves upon the Church to appoint her ministers for this task; for she has received the commission to preach the Gospel to all nations from generation to generation (Mt. 28, 19 f.); this also includes and implies the training of children. The Church baptized the child; she ought also to provide for the unfolding of the life of grace which originated in Baptism. Just as long as the parents, the primary educators of the children by virtue of the natural law, are able to perform their task of imparting a religious education to their offspring, just so long does the Church avail herself of them as her ministers. They do not need any special commission; the office of parent based on Christian marriage enshrines this commission.[1] Whenever the parents can no longer discharge this

[1] CIC can. 1113 (On the duties of parents towards their children) and can. 1020 (Bridal examination).

task, the Church must send her ambassadors. The ambassadors ought to be priests, primarily the pastor together with the parochial clergy who are assigned to him for the care of souls.

This is the viewpoint which is expressed in the Code of Canon Law: "The pastor is obliged . . . to employ the greatest diligence in training the children in the Catholic religion" (can. 467; cf. can. 1330f.). This task is also incumbent upon the priest catechists of the kind who, for example, in Austria, are nominated and appointed to serve in the larger and more important schools by the civil authorities along with other members of the teaching personnel. At the high school level and beyond this task is confided to professors of religion. Both these and the others are ministers of the Church (at least in a wide sense), and as such ought not only to feel but also to assume responsibility for at least the children who are entrusted to their care. It is certainly significant that for some time now they have been assigned to parishes. By such an arrangement they are enabled to preserve the correct notion of their vocation to teach; and they avoid the danger not only of becoming secularized personally but also of fulfilling the obligations of their teaching office in a purely intellectual and theoretical fashion by concentrating their efforts on instruction.

This double danger is the reason why ecclesiastical authorities have frequently adopted a sceptical attitude toward catechists *ex professo*. We must, however, not overlook the great advantages which are implied in the fact that a priest can devote himself entirely to the care of children and to catechesis: he is better able to prepare for his classes undisturbed, to master the literature of his profession and in this way better to enter into the spirit of his office. The improvement in catechetical method effected at the beginning of this century would never have been possible without the contribution which was made by these catechists *ex professo*.

In addition to the parochial or diocesan clergy who devote themselves to the work of catechesis, members of religious orders can also be called upon by the bishop. He may, if necessary, invite them to become teachers of Christian doctrine to adults (can. 1333f.).

Canons 1333 and 1334 permit the pastor to employ clerics, religious, both brothers and priests, and laymen and women, to assist in the work of religious instruction. The assistance which they give may be either as teachers in the schools or as catechists in the parish classes. Before engaging in this work the Ordinary may prescribe that they undergo an examination and receive his approval. This seems to be indicated by can. 1336 and by recent decrees of the Holy See.[2] In the United States the majority of teachers in the Catholic elementary schools, and to a large extent also in Confraternity Centers are religious, nuns or sisters. Without their assistance pastors would be almost powerless to fulfill their duty toward their children, and without them the Catholic school system could not long continue in existence.

The Church may also commission the laity for the work of catechesis (can. 1333). They are baptized and confirmed and should give testimony of Christ. To preach in church is forbidden them (can. 1342), but not to give catechesis. On the level of catechesis in the school, teachers, both men and women, may be entrusted with this task. In those Catholic schools which correspond most precisely to Church legislation, it is considered to be a natural arrangement in cases of necessity to permit lay teachers to take over the teaching of religion. In many dioceses in Germany it is an old tradition that the lay teacher be entrusted with teaching Bible History and the Bible itself, and the priest with instructions on the catechism.

Especially in the lower grades, Church authorities gladly

[2] R. J. Jansen, *Canonical Provisions for Catechetical Instruction,* Dissertation (Washington: Catholic University of America Press, 1937), p. 44.

make use of lay personnel whenever there is a shortage of priest catechists or whenever the priests must be relieved of such teaching to enable them to assume more pressing duties (e. g., pastoral care of youth). In such instances it is chiefly women instructresses and educators who are called upon, because psychologically they are closer to the children. If the entire instruction of these younger children, religion included, is confided to one person in this way, this represents a distinct advantage which more than outweighs any eventual disadvantages in those classes in which the instruction should shun all fragmentation (which is tantamount to departmentalization) in order to be as all-embracing as possible (themes drawn from their areas of interest, in which their knowledge is enhanced and their skills exercised, for example, school, Church). Lay personnel is also pressed into service sometimes for smaller groups which require special catechesis: for children who are prevented from attending class because of sickness, for children whose First Communion has been delayed, and for converts. In big cities, especially where the number of priests is all too small in proportion to the population the full use of lay catechists has become a "must" for well-planned and well-executed pastoral work.[3] The need for lay catechists is at its greatest naturally in those countries in which a majority of the children attend neutral (or interdenominational) state schools (called "public schools" in the United States). In such places the children can to all intents and purposes be brought together only by means of laymen who either look after their welfare or who at least see to it that they attend catecheses in their respective parishes.

[3] In Vienna (1949/50) of a total 7,200 weekly instructions given to children, 1977 were given by laymen, *ChPBl,* Vol. 63 (1950), p. 193. About the same time, of the 1,100 catechists who were in active service, 268 were laymen, for twenty-four of whom this was a full-time activity.

For this reason the Confraternity of Christian Doctrine, an organization of lay catechists, is strongly developed in countries such as France and the United States.[4]

A well-planned mobilization of the laity presupposes, as a matter of course, a suitable training. To achieve this the Chancery of the Archdiocese of Vienna, for example, has, since 1926, offered a two year theological course. The graduates from this course receive a *missio canonica* for catechesis, after they have passed a prescribed examination. In other centres of Catholicism the ancient Christian ideal of a catechetical school has again been revived. In the U.S.A. the Confraternity of Christian Doctrine as well as certain religious orders and congregations have established such schools for the training of lay teachers.[5] The

[4] In the archdiocese of Paris, for example, 8,000 lay catechists were at work, *Orbis catholicus,* Vol. 3 (1949/50), p. 297. In Mexico City it is reported that 2,143 lay catechists gave instructions to 48,000 children every Saturday and Sunday, *Klerusblatt,* Vol. 84 (Salzburg, 1951), p. 123; E. V. O'Hara, "The Parish Confraternity of Christian Doctrine in the United States" in *Lumen Vitae,* Vol. 6 (1951), pp. 363–376. But in the U.S.A. a distinction must be made between the preparation of Catholic teachers for the Catholic school system and of teachers for Confraternity work. In 1955 the Catholic school system was staffed by 135,406 teachers and professors, e. g., 93,518 Sisters, 27,819 lay teachers, 8,995 priests (full time), 4,168 Brothers; cf. *Official Catholic Directory* (New York: P. J. Kenedy, 1956), see Appendix. For Confraternity schools, e. g., in the diocese of Detroit, 517 lay teachers took part in the programme for 1950: J. C. Ryan, "Preparation of Lay Teachers of Religion: A Survey" in *Proceedings,* 1951, pp. 99–105; cf. also Ellamay Horan, "Developing Lay Catechists" in *The Confraternity Comes of Age,* pp. 41–56; T. Frain, "A Survey of the Lay Catechists Teaching Public School Religion" in *The Catholic Educational Review* (April, 1955), pp. 238–254; A. N. Fuerst, *Systematic Teaching of Religion,* 2 vols. (New York: Benziger Brothers), Vol. I (c. 1939), pp. 115–130.

[5] Among others, e. g., *Mission Helpers of the Sacred Heart,* Towson, Maryland, *The Society of Missionary Catechists of Our Lady of Victory, The Religious of the Cenacle, The Sisters of Our Lady of Christian Doctrine,* and *Sisters of the Holy Family;* cf. also: Sr. M. Borromeo, "Religious Communities Prepare Prospective Lay Teachers" in *Proceedings,* 1951, pp. 432–437.

length of time varies with the dioceses and with the institutes to which the training is allied. In some instances a course lasting three years has been prescribed.[6] Methodology is represented by the current practices in the schools of the community where the teacher training centre is located or by the methods with which the teaching staff of these schools are best acquainted by their own preparatory work, for example, in a Catholic university. This *missio canonica* (canonical mission) which is accorded by the bishops is usually demanded wherever and whenever there is a question of planned religious instruction for children outside the family.[7] Through this *missio* such religious teaching becomes official ecclesiastical catechesis. Those who have earned such a *missio* should occupy the most prominent posts among those who help in this most important task of the cure of souls; they share in the teaching office of the Church. In those instances in which the teachers lack such an official commission, the religious instructions or religious exhortations which are given to the children remain a purely private activity, despite the fact that it is one of the noblest works of Christian charity.

The normal solution, that is, the normal catechetical situation insofar as conditions permit, is and remains the priest catechist. Granted equal pedagogical ability, the priest catechist will

[6] George Johnson, Director, "Religious Instruction" (Washington: NCWC, Dept. of Ed., 1931), pp.16–17; Ellamay Horan, *op. cit.*, pp. 51–53; E. V. O'Hara, *Mid-Century Survey, Confraternity of Christian Doctrine in the U.S.A.* (Washington: Confraternity of Christian Doctrine, 1951).

[7] R. J. Jansen, *op. cit.*, p. 44; C. Augustine, *A Commentary on Canon Law* (St. Louis: Herder, 1921), pp. 341–342, commenting on can. 1328; cf. also *Council of Trent,* sess. XXIII, *de sacr. ordinis,* can. 7; C. H. Boffa, *Canonical Provisions for Catholic Schools* (Washington: Catholic Univ. of America Press, 1939), pp. 165–166; Marg. Schmid, "Theologische Kurse für Laien" in *KBl,* Vol. 72 (1947), pp. 265–271; J. Colomb, "Une école de formation de catéchistes à Lyon" in *Lumen Vitae,* Vol. 2 (1947), pp. 343–349.

always be more highly esteemed than other catechists. In addition he is able, simply by the fact that he is a priest, to effect a union between the school and Church, between catechesis and divine worship which will facilitate in the future a living contact between priest and his pastoral work. A priest should take care of the special instructions for First Confession and First Holy Communion and of the catechesis before graduation, if possible, but in general, of catechesis in the upper grades.[8]

2. In pedagogical literature we read a great deal about the ideal type or the prototype of the teacher and educator. From this we are enabled to sketch a portrait of an ideal catechist as the end product toward which our efforts should be bent to achieve. Innate talent and acquired proficiency mutually complement each other. Just as there is such a thing as innate talent, so there is also an innate gift for catechesis, catechetical charism, such as was bestowed upon the great pioneers of catechetics, men, for example, like Augustin Gruber or Gustav Mey. But such a gift is truly a rarity. Ordinarily a person must work hard to acquire the skills and the knowledge of a good catechist. As we know, the catechist is entrusted with the task of forming children in the image of Christ, and of awakening within them the kingdom of God. This is ultimately a matter of divine grace, but it must employ human resources.

Just as in general we differentiate between two components of the pedagogical eros, love of the object upon which pedagogical activity focuses and love of the pupil (Eduard Spranger), so on a still higher plane the ideal catechist ought to have two characteristics which are fundamental: he must be filled with holy zeal for the kingdom of God in which he collaborates;

[8] G. Götzel, *KBl,* Vol. 63 (1937), p. 324; cf. W. H. Russell, "Who May Teach Religion?" in *The Catholic Educational Review,* Vol. 44 (Feb., 1946), pp. 78–86.

and he must be filled with a selfless and reverential love for the child upon whose salvation he is commissioned to labour. He ought to be, as has been said, to the youngest a mother; a father to the elder; a friend of the adolescent. Only in this way will the other desirable and more technical abilities be made fruitful for catechesis: a certain nimbleness of the imagination and a certain gift for oral presentation as well as an ability for keeping under surveillance all that takes place in the class during the course of the instruction (the distributive attention in contrast to the concentrated attention of the scientist.)

In a priestly vocation the aspirant will have, at least to a certain extent, both of these fundamental endowments, especially the first. Anyone who is not inflamed with this love of the kingdom of God should not become a priest.

The second characteristic, too should be inherent in the priestly vocation: the aspirant resolves to labour for the salvation of souls. We are thus enabled to affirm that every genuine priest (and every genuine religious) possesses the basic talents required for catechesis. It is with this in mind that Hirscher wrote: "A genuine enthusiasm is an ample substitute for what thou mayest have received from nature only to a limited degree."[9] But this original endowment must be strengthened and increased by personal effort, by a truly pious life, by study and practice.

It should be self-evident that the catechist be well-versed in theology, and also to a certain extent in kindred subjects, with which schools are concerned. This should hold true especially in the case of religion teachers in secondary schools and beyond. It is important that the future catechist (priest, nun or layman) keep alive a definite and lively interest in theology.

[9] Hirscher, *Katechetik* (3rd ed.), p. 724.

Only by so doing will he be able to give his catechesis a personal touch and to offer it in various and interesting forms. Besides scientific works on theology, the catechist can find many valuable hints in those popular books on theology which are written for purposes of apologetics. The reading of catecheses in printed form will also prove useful for him; even their direct use in the classroom is not forbidden him. Whereas theorists in general warn preachers not to employ printed sermons verbatim, because the sermon should be to a great extent the product of their own personal effort and should reflect their prayerful reactions to conditions here and now, printed catecheses can, however, serve very well as models. In them the catechist may find perhaps the best development of some precise and limited topic for the special group which he is instructing. The catechist should not, however, be satisfied simply with such "ready-made goods". In fact, he should not be content even with some happy formulations of his own, otherwise he would soon become repetitious and the pupils, especially in the upper grades, would quickly sense his strict adherence to stock phrases and their interest would soon falter.

Theoretical preparation for the work of catechesis takes for granted the study of catechetics which, as a pedagogy of religion, summarizes pertinent chapters both of secular pedagogy, and current secular didactics, offers an introduction to the nature of the catechetical task, and furnishes the results of catechetical experience gathered over past generations. Such a thoroughgoing formation is necessary, because today catechesis is practically synonymous with compulsory catechesis given in school. The catechist must not be found wanting in methodology when compared to his well-trained colleagues in the secular branches. The reading of some good catechetical magazine will also contribute greatly to his further development; it will keep him abreast of the best achievements that have been made in this field, and will be a link with the theological studies which lie behind him.

That he may be fully fitted for the task which he will assume, the catechist ought to avail himself of any practice teaching which might come his way. Under this category belong: assistance at catecheses given by a talented catechist; one or two trial catecheses, by which he could not only overcome his first shyness but also could become acquainted with any deficiencies which might become apparent either in the method he uses or in his training as such. In any case, during the years in the seminary it is well nigh impossible to acquire that deftness and sureness which are so necessary and so sought after in catechetical work. The first years of teaching should be for the catechist his most important years of apprenticeship. These they can become, if he carefully prepares for each and every catechesis, if he subjects himself to a subsequent self-examination, and, most important, if he accepts graciously and acts sanely upon the critical hints which he requests from his more experienced colleagues in catechetical work. In many dioceses the catechetical training of the young priests is regulated by special diocesan statutes.[10] These sometimes require that the catechetical student should assist at model catecheses given by able catechists for a certain number of periods. It is further required that his own work be inspected and supervised several times a year, without

[10] F. Coudreau, "Admission to the Higher Catechetic Institute" in *Lumen Vitae,* Vol. 7 (1952), pp. 478–479; ibid., "The Activities of the Higher Catechetical Institute" *op. cit.,* Vol. 8 (1953), 507–508; R. G. Bandas in *Catechetics in the Seminary* (Paterson, N.J.: Confraternity Publications); *AAS,* Vol. 38 (1945), pp. 173–176: *Apostolic Instruction; On the Importance of the Study of Pedagogy in Seminaries* (Paterson, N.J.: Confraternity Publications, 1945); R. J. Ryder, *Canonical Provisions for Catechetics in the Seminary* (Paterson, N.J.: Confraternity Publications, 1945); Johannes Hofinger, "The Training Our Catechists Need" in Sloyan, *op. cit.,* pp. 238—242.

advance notice being given, by the school superintendent or by a regional supervisor appointed for just such a task. It is finally required if possible that at clergy conferences catecheses on moral themes are given. All these aids should only be too welcome to any young catechist.[11]

The most important contributing factor to the success of catechesis is and will always remain the personality of the catechist himself, as this is revealed in his attitude and in his public behaviour. Of the small children particularly it has been said, with justice, that they learn more with their eyes than with their ears. This holds also for the older children who are more critical in their appraisals and who can detect instinctively any discrepancy between the instruction and the conduct of the catechist. The priestly personality wields a special influence over the adolescent. At this age level even priestly virtue in the strict sense of the term no longer suffices—youth hungers for an ideal, a well-rounded personality, in whom are embodied religion, nature and supernature, harmoniously combined. Here we may quote what Michael Pfliegler, an able judge of the student, has said: "The religion teacher will succeed in teaching to that extent to which he himself has advanced as a personality . . . This requires first of all free and even development—that firmness which shirks from nothing because it has the secure centre of gravity within itself . . . which manifests no nervousness when confronted by any problem whatsoever, because it has always faced every problem squarely and consequently permits others to voice their queries with the same honesty. Such personalities are the result of self-education, which has its origins back in the days of childhood."[12]

The perfect example for all catechetical and pastoral activity

[11] The Regulations of the Apostolic Administrator of Innsbruck-Feldkirch, *ChPBl,* Vol. 65 (1952), pp. 120–121.

[12] M. Pfliegler, *Der Religionsunterricht,* Vol. II, p. 219.

is ultimately the person of Christ Himself: in the zeal with which He preached the word of God, in the love with which He chose to pour Himself out for all and by which He drew especially children to himself.

The catechist is, however, only one educator among many, who busy themselves with one and the same child. He must try to be on a friendly footing with these others, even though their educational activities contribute little to his own efforts. In the school there are in addition to himself other teachers. He should, as a consequence, try to establish favourable contacts with them and to cultivate friendly relationships which will serve to promote the objectives they have in common. The catechist should also try to keep in touch with the families of the children. In the country this contact will gradually evolve of itself. In the city parishes provision should be made for specific office hours, during which the parents can talk to the catechists about their children in the school building itself.[13] Meetings (socials, study clubs, etc.) which could be organized for the parents by one or other of the Catholic school organizations (e. g. P. T. A.) can serve the same purpose. The catechist should try to keep as closely as possible in contact with the parents of the First Communicants and of those who are about to graduate. He could, for example, hold special meetings to which they could be invited.

While parents, teachers and catechists actually carry out the programme of a planned education, actual success in religious education depends upon a whole series of elements, which are called educative factors, that is, everything that the children see and hear on the way to and from school, on the playground,

[13] More effective is the procedure recommended by a zealous catechist: "Every time I am assigned a new class, I visit the families of all the children in it" *KBl,* Vol. 62 (1936), p. 386. In this way the catechist learns to know the environment from which his charges come.

placards and bulletin boards, the example of adults and of their school companions, and especially the influence of their own class. As Pfliegler has remarked:[14] "Education is not a duet of two voices, those of the educator and the pupil; the more or less discordant orchestra of environment keeps intermingling its tones with those of the duet." As a result the catechist and the educator must resist the influence of a hostile world; they must create in the true sense of the word, another kind of world, out of the school class itself and out of the liturgical life which is so essential to the school. In a school that is pervaded by a truly Catholic spirit such a task should not be too difficult. When the catechist is, however, called upon to teach in a so-called interdenominational or neutral school, in which the religion period is regarded as an alien subject, his catechetical activity can from the very start be compared to the sowing of seed in hard stony ground from which only a scanty harvest can be expected,—but the personality of a Catholic teacher may render ineffective the false principle upon which such a school is based.

The situation in England is very much the same as that described for the United States. Most of the instruction of children is in the hands of lay-teachers who are properly trained for the task in the many Catholic training colleges throughout the country. In addition to this the pastoral clergy are required to visit their parochial schools to teach and they will usually take a considerable part in preparing children for First Confession and Communion. Many young priests are taking a special interest in the school-leavers. It should be observed that the American term "graduation" means in England "school-leaving age" which in the secondary-modern schools is fifteen and in the grammar schools anything over sixteen.

[14] M. Pfliegler, *op. cit.*, II, 238.

On the subject of cooperation with the family, parent-teacher associations are established in various parts of the country and here and there are to be found fruitful experiments to make the First Communion a family-parish event rather than a merely parish-school event. A description will be found in *The Sower,* Jan. 1949, p. 170.

For the training of lay-catechists—apart from teachers—there is the organization known as Our Lady's Catechists (Waterfall Cottage, Shoreham, Sevenoaks, Kent) who confine their attentions to the teaching of children and produce some very acceptable booklets on First Confession and Communion that can be used by children. In the Birmingham Archdiocese, there is a Guild of Catechists who, after examination, are licensed by the Ordinary to teach all categories of people.

III

THE CHILD AND CATECHESIS

UNDER present day circumstances, catechesis deals primarily with children. As catechists, we must as a consequence present Christian doctrine in such a way that it is grasped by the child. To this end we must take into account their psychological differences, especially those special peculiarities of disposition, which are relevant to their religious training. In this respect both child and adolescent psychology can offer us valuable insights. The growing understanding of, and appreciation for, the psyche of the child with the conclusions which flow from it are the most valuable contributions through which the scientific studies of preceding generations can enrich catechesis. Of course we do not forget that in the baptized child we are not dealing with a merely natural being, but with a creature that belongs to the supernatural order through grace. This life of grace by its very nature remains as yet in the realm of the unconscious, but it is a seed that urges to be developed and to be developed into the conscious life of the soul. This development should take place in such a way that in the process the child becomes acquainted with the kingdom of God, assents and adheres to it in faith, and subordinates all his activities ever more and more to it in hope and charity. The life of grace in the soul of the child clamours for protection. If during childhood this life has been left undisturbed, and in peaceful and undisputed possession, the situation will basically change in adolescence. We should as a consequence strive to aid the child to anchor his conscious soul-life to God so strongly that during the stormy years of adolescence it may not be torn loose from such a mooring.

In catechesis we are concerned chiefly with the years of the elementary school, that is, with children from their sixth to their fourteenth year, but we are also equally interested in children in their later years, in adolescence. They too should not be left without religious training. Differential psychology—which among other things determines the psychological differences at the various age-levels—has arrived at a division of psychical development similar in arrangement to the sevenfold division which was formulated by Aristotle, and which finds expression in Canon Law (can. 88) from time immemorial. Of a child of seven years it is assumed that he is not master of himself, not *sui compos*. Children up to the age of 14 (girls to the age of 12) are called *impuberes;* they are not as yet subject to the ecclesiastical penal laws. Youths up to the age of 21 are termed *minores, minorennes;* they are exempted from certain laws.

At the age of five or six a child begins to attend school and to take part in religious instruction. At this point we are faced with the difficulty: to what extent is the child capable of understanding religion, taken in the full Catholic sense, namely, as a relationship to God based upon knowledge (apart from the especially favourable or especially unfavourable formation received from the environment)? Child psychology supplies the catechist with an encouraging answer.[1] The psychological stage through

[1] Rudolph Allers (E. B. Strauss, trans.), *The Psychology of Character* (New York: Sheed & Ward, 1939); Alvena Burnite, *Your Teen-Agers: How to Survive Them* (Milwaukee: Bruce, 1952); C. L. Burns, *Mental Health in Childhood* (Chicago: Fides, 1956); Charles Curran, *Counseling in Catholic Life and Education* (New York: Macmillan, 1952); Daniel Dougherty, *Catholic Child Guidance* (New York: Paulist Press, 1941); Urban Fleege, *Self-Revelation of the Adolescent Boy* (Milwaukee: Bruce, 1945); Paul Furfey, *The Growing Boy* (New York: Macmillan, 1930); id., *Social Problems of Childhood* (New York: Macmillan, 1929); Ursula Gerty, *The Adaptive Behavior of Adolescent Children* (Washington, D. C.: Catholic University Press, 1955); Arnold Gesell *et al., The Child from*

which the child from 4–7 passes is called the second age of questioning. He has for some time previously learned how to reduce the objects in his surroundings to general concepts and to acquire mastery over them through speech.

The child then begins to delve deeper into the relationships which lie beneath outer appearances. He has already discovered the principles of causality and has arrived at the use of his own ability to think causally which he must exercise immediately.

Five to Ten (New York: Harper, 1946); id. *et. al., Youth: The Years from Ten to Sixteen* (New York: Harper, 1956); William & Margaret Kelly, *Introductory Child Psychology* (Milwaukee: Bruce, 1938); Joseph Kempf, *Helping Youth to Grow* (Milwaukee: Bruce, 1941); Charles Leahy, *Teen: A Book for Parents* (Milwaukee: Bruce, 1950); Daniel Lord, *Questions People Ask about Their Children, with Answers* (St. Louis: Queen's Work, 1948); Raphael McCarthy, *Training the Adolescent* (New York: Bruce, 1934); Vincent McCorry, *Those Terrible Teens* (New York: McMullen, 1947); Mary Michael, *Why Blame the Adolescent?* (New York: McMullen, 1956); Thomas Verner Moore, *The Driving Forces of Human Nature and Their Adjustment* (New York: Grune & Stratton, 1948); Carl Murchison, Ed., *A Handbook of Child Psychology* (2nd ed.; Worcester: Clark University, 1933); James Royce, *Personality and Mental Health* (Milwaukee: Bruce, 1955); Mary Scharlieb, *The Psychology of Childhood, Normal and Abnormal* (New York: Smith, 1930); Alexander Schneiders, *Psychology of Adolescence* (New York: Rinehart, 1954); Louis Sherill, *Understanding Children* (New York: Abingdon, 1939); U. S. Department of Labor, *Your Child from One to Six* (Washington, D.C.: Department of Labor Children's Bureau, 1945); Theodore Vittoria, Ed., *Adolescent Conflicts* (Derby, N.Y.: Society of St. Paul, 1951); Lilly Zarncke, *Kindheit und Gewissen* (Freiburg i. Br.: Lambertus Verlag, 1951); C. W. Valentine, *Psychology and its Bearing on Education* (London: Methuen, 1950); Charles L. C. Burns, *Maladjusted Children* (London: Hollis & Carter); Gilbert Highet, *The Art of Teaching* (London: Methuen, 1952); David L. Greenstock, *Christopher's Talks to Catholic Teachers* (London: Burns, Oates, 1953); Vera Barclay, *The Way into the Kingdom.* With an Introduction by the Editor of *The Sower* (2nd ed.; London: Burns, Oates, 1947). This little book, of some eighty pages, contains all the essentials of sound teaching. Chapter-headings like "The Imagination in Religion", "The 'Interior life' of Children" and "The Psychology of Charity" will give some indication of its approach.

As a consequence he begins to ask endless questions: why is this so? who made it? The child is not critical of the answers he receives. His mental activity is limited to a provisional concept of the world and to a philosophy of life which needs to correspond to actual reality only in the broadest sense of the word and for which the fairy-tale with very few figures and its simplified natural laws is the typical expression. But to this broad general outline belongs also knowledge of God. The child returns constantly to those questions which we can answer only by offering him the Ultimate Cause (Why is it raining today? Why does the water run away so fast?). "From this logical standpoint the child of his own accord arrives, compelled as it were, at the concept of God or at least at an elementary notion of Him" who is to him "the ultimate agent behind all things".[2] The idea thereby arising spontaneously in the heart of the child is that of a personal being. The child has in fact experienced the notion of causality first of all in himself when, for example, he started something rolling or made a noise. In this way he is inclined *a priori* to conceive as personal beings all other things which cause something to happen and to humanize them. For example, the sun, the stars and the wind. All the more, then, is He, who created all things, regarded as a personal being.

In such a process, the notion of God which the child forms is necessarily anthropomorphic. He represents God to himself after the same fashion in which he envisages his own parents, whose capacities and whose care are, for his mental horizon, unlimited. This opens a second, and very natural approach, to the formation

[2] Ch. Bühler, *Kindheit und Jugend* (3rd ed.; Leipzig, 1931), p. 342; consult also Pfliegler, Vol. II, pp. 85–86; Vol. III, pp. 28–29; Sr. M. Mary, "Religious Concepts of Catholic Children of Pre-School Age" in *The Parent Educator*, Vol. II (Paterson, N.J.: Confraternity Publications, 1932), p. 9.

of the notion of God. If the child sees that his parents are resigned to the will of God, he becomes aware that God is greater than his parents; he is given an inkling of a Father in heaven. God is then that one to whom a person speaks, without seeing him, but who, nevertheless, hears us.[3] The affective ties by which he is bound to his parents determine the nature of the sentiments which he entertains toward God. The concept which the child has, especially of his human father, is largely decisive in the formation of the impression which the child has of God. The love and reverence, which he shows his father, or in unfortunate circumstances, the fear and anxiety, in which he trembles before him, are unwittingly transferred to his idea of God.

Of extreme importance is the way in which the notion of God is first presented to the child. If a parent constantly threatens the child with God and with hell fire for only simple, childlike faults and failings, God Himself can become for him an object of fear during his whole life. "Perhaps the child has previously been afraid only of a dangerous black dog or a vicious bull. He is threatened now with God. And so God takes on the unlovable qualities of the animals he had feared. And this impression remains."[4]

The child comes to us to be catechized endowed with this psychological foundation, to which the Christian family, or the Catholic kindergarten, will add, without any special order, certain other basic concepts drawn from revealed religion, viz., the Christ Child, the Mother of God, and the Angels, together with a few nursery rhymes and some prayers learned at his

[3] L. Barbey, "La notion de Dieu chez l'enfant" in *Lumen Vitae,* Vol. 2 (1947), pp. 117–128; M. Hutard, "La Prière de l'enfant, appel filial au Père tout puissant" in *Lumen Vitae,* Vol. 2 (1947), pp. 325–332; W. Roche, *The Child At Prayer* (London: Catholic Truth Society, 1933), especially pp. 15–16; A. G. Cicognani, *et al., The Parent Educator,* New Series Vol. II (Washington: Confraternity of Christian Doctrine, 1943), p. 22.

[4] Pfliegler, Vol. II, p. 76.

mother's knees. Upon such a foundation the catechist must build by inducing order into the concepts, by teaching new truths and by educating. The first year of the elementary school which is still part of the first septenary, can, in keeping with the psychological level of this age group, still have a transitional character unless the child is already to be admitted to First Communion. The existing psychic world of the child can be consolidated, enlarged upon and clarified through the discussion of those realities with which the child is confronted in nature, in the Church and in the ecclesiastical year. The catechist must, however, be reconciled to the fact that today he will very often have to deal with children who fail to bring with them from the family that foundation upon which he can build. We shall return to this later.

What is the spiritual make-up of the children in the subsequent years of the elementary school not only in regard to the task of teaching but of educating which is incumbent upon the catechist? In regard to the didactic role of catechesis, he will find the same favourable bent: the children at this age level retain their yearning for knowledge until toward the end of the elementary school. In these years the reasoning of the children is dominated by a great thirst for knowledge, for which, viewed in their essential aspects, the school and especially the religion period furnish the most appropriate and most satisfactory answers. The child seeks ever more eagerly to become acquainted with the real world; he wants it freed ever more fully from the fairy-tale elements which, at first, had captured his imagination. But this appetite for knowledge has its own peculiar characteristics.

1. This longing is restricted to the particular, to detail. Whereas previously the child was content to gather only a rough view of the world, his interest is now directed to particulars, not to their ordered arrangement, and certainly

not to any system. When children of this age level undertake to describe an incident or a picture, they recount single details without troubling much about the relationship between them.

2. Their interest is directed to externals: to phenomena in nature, to incidents in their external features, to tangible facts. Contrariwise they show little capacity for phenomena of the interior life despite their great sensitiveness. They are furthermore incapable of reviving their own personal experiences by means of reflection. This is forcibly brought to our attention by the way in which they report in compositions things which have exercised considerable influence over their own soul-life, for example, a feast, a trip, an accident in which they were involved. In such reports all we are given is a sober recital of external facts.

3. It is, moreover, a fact that the child's thinking is still very much attached to visual things and achieves mastery of abstract matter only with difficulty. We must, however, make a distinction here between the lower and the upper grades. In the lower grades, that is, up to the age of ten, general ideas, which the child has used for some time, still require the support of images; it is usually an individual image upon which the child regularly relies. For example, the notion of a "well" is always connected with the image of a particular well existing in the world of the child. Even for notions drawn from the realm of inner experience (faith, love, sin, contrition) the child must as a rule lean upon some concrete precise experience. Here, too, he still deals with individual images.

From these facts we can realize that it is indispensible for catechesis at this age level to present Christian doctrine in such a way that notions are joined as far as possible to concrete images, preferably and most effectively in the form of a narrative. The catechist can meet this need simply by recounting to the children in simple terms the history of redemption and basing further instructions upon this.

From the tenth year on, the child is able more easily to dispense with the assistance of concrete images. At the same time, he begins to feel that he can rely more readily upon his own understanding. At this stage he experiences within himself a powerful urge to differentiate sharply between phantasy and reality, between the world of fairies, which has continued to affect him, and the real world which he now perceives with ever greater clarity. In this sense Charlotte Bühler says of the ten year old child, that he is "truly a fanatic for reality".[5] From this time on the catechist can draw more frequently and to greater advantage upon abstract notions, definitions, general laws; instruction on the catechism can now begin. The sentences of the catechism, as we shall see, must, however, still be developed from the seen image.[6]

[5] Ch. Bühler, *Das Seelenleben des Jugendlichen* (5th ed.; Jena, 1929), p. 195. Children of this age begin to lose those concepts which still have something of the aura of fairies about them, namely, the idea of *Santa Claus* who enters the home at Christmas, admonishing, rewarding and punishing, as well as that idea of the *Christ Child* personally bringing presents into the home and placing them under the tree before the children are permitted to enter the room. It may, however, happen that parents may try to keep artificially these concepts (phantasies we might be tempted to say) from disappearing, because of the joy they experience in the childlike simplicity and naivety of their offspring. During the fairy age such concepts cause the children no harm, especially if parents try to give an understanding of them in language which does not over-tax their capacity. (The catechist should not himself, however, embark upon such a course in the classroom.) These concepts can be disastrous, if they are kept alive beyond this stage, because they will of necessity result in deception being practised, and because their rejection later on will bring with it the rejection of that ideal religious world which had been inculcated in them. P. O'Donnell and Msgr. Mendelis, *The Truth About Santa Claus* (Baltimore: St. Alphonsus).

[6] The transition to abstract thought which takes place during the final years of compulsory school attendance is graphically depicted by A. Burgardsmeier, *Gott und Himmel in der psychischen Welt der Jugend* (Düsseldorf, 1952).

In regard to the educative role of catechesis the tenth year also constitutes a line of demarcation. Up to this year educative influence is exerted upon the child by means of habit, by outward influences; inward perception as yet plays scarcely any part in his life. The teacher must still decide what the youngsters should do, show them how to do it, practise it with them, admonish and encourage them. To this we may add, that in these years the children are still easily influenced; by nature they are still disposed to be guided by their elders. We cannot, however, rely too greatly on the virtues and piety which they acquire in these years. Whatever they may have amassed, should be considered only as a kind of a preparation; it will be either consolidated and strengthened or dissipated in this now dawning period of growing independence and maturity.

At this point we must consider a weighty observation made by experienced catechists. Whereas up to the tenth year scarcely any difference in conduct can be detected in children from religious and religiously indifferent families, now a definite divergence can be discerned: children from religiously indifferent homes begin to sense the dissonance between school and their home. Their intellectual development has progressed to such an extent that they begin to seek a solution for it. They have, however, not advanced far enough to be able to make a definite personal decision themselves; the stronger environment settles the issue. If the child is happy in the circle of the family, the family will retain its grip. But the catechist should not think that his work has been in vain. In adolescence the question will again be raised and at least in the case of the more talented pupils the insight which has been gained, and which in the interim should have been deepened and vitalized, should tip the scales decisively. This will surely be the case, if the catechist succeeds in fitting such young folk into suitable youth groups.[7] But even

[7] Pfliegler, Vol. II, p. 95; compare with p. 229.

if a complete estrangement from religion should result, there would still remain the hope that at least at life's end the religious truths which the child had learned in his youth might still become the plank of salvation.[8] A majority of the children may have come from environments estranged from God, a condition that ought to be considered in the kind of catechesis which is given. In such circumstances the abstract sentences of the catechism will scarcely find echo. Practically, at least, only a biblical training and contact with religious practice hold out some hope of success.[9]

[8] In this respect the experiences which Barbara Lerchenfeld had while caring for the sick and dying in the tenement districts of both Paris and Vienna are very enlightening. She often said when reminiscing: "The religious instruction which these people, even the most abandoned, had received in Vienna, produced amazing results in their last hour, in contrast to what I saw in Paris . . . where the broad masses of people, who had grown up without any religious instruction, were left untouched by death and in that fatal hour failed to find their way back to the Church." Reported in the *ChPBl,* Vol. 63 (1950), p. 162. In this connection we might cite a passage from *The American Freemason,* an organ of Freemasonry, printed in the U. S. A., "let death come into their (i. e., those who claim to be Catholics and retain Masonic membership) homes, or let them face death themselves, and ten to one they will go back to the Church and abjure the fraternity" (*Catholic Mind* [March, 1945], p. 190)—an undoubted tribute to the kind of instruction in their faith that they have received.

[9] F. Jantsch, "Seelsorge am Arbeiterkind" in *ChPBl,* Vol. 62 (1949), pp. 68–71; L. Rétif, "La formation religieuse des enfants de milieu populaire déchristianisé" in *Lumen Vitae,* Vol. 1 (1946), pp. 471–498; L. Rétif, *Catéchisme et mission ouvrière. Du Catéchisme au catéchuménat* (Rencontres 31), Paris, 1950. The Rev. L. Rétif found meeting places for groups of children in Christian families in the neighbourhood. These families took upon themselves the task of acting like guardians for their respective group. In these families the children had time not only for happy, carefree life in common, but also for religious guidance; in other words, they came together not solely for instructions, but to experience personally the value of a Christian way of life. For further literature on efforts in this direction being made in France, consult Lentner, pp. 162–165 and 174–178. Some

The last years of the elementary school are, at least for boys, characterized as the teen-age. It is not wickedness, but inner unrest, the need to do something spectacular, which is responsible for all kinds of pranks. The suggestibility of former years has vanished. Discipline in the class may well become a problem for the catechist. In these years the children need a strong hand to hold them in check, but the hand must "be united to a clear head and a good heart."[10]

The maturing years, adolescence, are for the young people who are pursuing higher studies a time to be devoted to regular and somewhat more intensive religious training. The youths who have gone to work are exempted from attendance at school. They can no longer be considered as regular recipients of catechesis. They may continue their formation only within the limited framework of evening classes, vocational training or Sunday school. For this reason it is of the greatest importance that in such circumstances their religious care be not neglected. A cursory glance at the psychology of this age level will provide justification for such a demand and will permit us an insight into the kind of religious guidance which is required.

A new situation is created for these teen-agers by their sexual development which begins at this time. This process, which is primarily physical, actually affects the soul by reason of the demands which it makes. But the spiritual condition of adolescence is thereby no more than partly touched upon. For along with bodily development there also takes place, and to

attempts that have been made in the U. S. A.: Sr. of St. Francis, "The Peoria-Aledo Plan" in *The Catholic Educational Review,* Vol. 46 (1948), pp. 148–152; Eva J. Ross, "The Leakage and a Dutch Experiment" in *The Catholic Educational Review,* Vol. 39 (1941), pp. 84–88; E. Schmiedeler, "Rural Education in Action" in *The Catholic Educational Review,* Vol. 41 (1943), pp. 202–207; C. J. Nuesse and T. J. Harte, *The Sociology of the Parish* (Milwaukee: Bruce, 1951), especially pp. 285–322.

[10] Pfliegler, Vol. II, p. 109.

a great extent independently, a spiritual process of awakening whose beginnings are manifest in a tendency to introspection, in the discovery of the self, which may take up practically the entire third septenary.

The youngster whose attention has up to this time been directed to the mastery of the external world and who has known and has appreciated the fact that he has been guided and protected by adults, becomes aware that every person must ultimately discover for himself his own way of life and must forge his own happiness. This knowledge results in an inner detachment from the home and from all that recalls his childhood, a strong antipathy for authority and for tradition, an impatience with restrictions of every kind, those of religion not excepted, an ardent desire to taste the freedom of the wide world (wanderlust), and the "felt need" to establish relationships outside the family.

This first negative phase of development, which imparts to the beginning of the adolescent period its distinctive character, is gradually transformed into a positive phase. There begins a searching and yearning, a pursuit of ideals, after which a person can fashion his own life, a longing for friends in whom these ideals are embodied, a confidential adviser, who is capable of leading and showing the way. Under these conditions it is evident how important religious ideals are at this stage, ideals, which must be offered not by means of instruction, but in a friendly and informal fashion (social gatherings, discussion groups), in any case, however, as an answer to the questions which seethe within them and torment them. Up to this point their religious world had of necessity remained limited to concepts which were childish and inadequate; it must now be rebuilt if it is to be integrated into the image of the world which youngsters entertain. Knowledge carried over from the elementary school years supplies invaluable material for this task, if it has not entirely disappeared. But the great outlines into which religion and life, nature and supernature, must be fitted harmoniously, can be rightly appreciated and effectively accepted as a map of life only now when life presses upon them from all sides.

In England the school-leaving age varies from fifteen (secondary modern) to eighteen (grammar and boarding schools). It is for the former of these categories that most work needs to be done. Various experiments are made by different schools, and Canon Drinkwater has provided a book to assist priests and teachers in the task entitled *Talks to Teenagers* (Burns, Oates). Material of a rather different kind will be found in the same author's *Twelve and After* (Samuel Walker). Finally, his *Abbreviated Catechism with Explanations* (Burns, Oates) was compiled with school-leavers in view. All these books will, in one way or another, provide a lively revision course of the whole of Christian doctrine and practice.

The youth movement in England cannot be said to be highly developed. There is an active Catholic Scout Organization which works in conjunction with Imperial Headquarters, and makes provision for the training of Catholic Scouts. The Young Christian Workers' movement is active in certain areas and publishes a splendid review, *The New Life,* intended for chaplains and leaders as well as other kinds of literature for younger members. The archdiocese of Birmingham runs a Youth Hostel at Stratford-on-Avon where, among other activities, courses for school-leavers and youth leaders are held.

IV

THE TASK OF THE CATECHIST

1. Teaching and Education

In conformity with the concept and the phraseology we have inherited from the past, it would seem that the task of the catechist was nothing more than to impart religious instruction. This impression is deepened if one looks at present-day catechesis. It has become catechesis in school. By that fact emphasis is placed on religious knowledge.

When catechesis was first given to children, knowledge, since it was knowledge of doctrinal differences, possessed an importance all its own and could hold the centre of the stage, as long as in other respects religious education was provided for sufficiently through other channels. Considered, however, in its essence catechesis cannot be restricted solely to religious instruction, to doctrine, to something that need only be "known".

Christian doctrine can never be an end in itself; it must direct us to God. Knowledge is necessary, but it is a knowledge of that way, which we must traverse. Catechesis must be religious-moral direction; it must be a part of pastoral work. The life of grace as a seed, which is implanted in the soul of the child at Baptism, must ultimately unfold into a well-rounded Christian life. The power of faith, the *virtus infusa fidei* must be channeled into action; it must be fostered into a believing acceptance of the divine message of "good news". From faith, hope must spring up, and from hope, love, the wholehearted and ardent turning to God, the Supreme Good. Through the moral virtues the right attitude towards earthly things must be found: a conviction, a resolution, a holy resolve. This objective may sometimes be also a sentiment, a joy about God's might and God's ways, a prayer, a hymn, in any case not simply knowledge.

A year of catechesis should produce much the same effect in the children as a retreat does. In such a retreat knowledge is inculcated: the gracious plans of God for humanity are brought to our attention not simply to be affirmed consciously and theoretically, but to furnish us with a map for life and with convincing motives for our future course of action. The fact that in catechesis the classes follow one upon another at greater or lesser intervals is scarcely a disadvantage in view of the limited powers of concentration of the child's psyche. By means of judicious repetition the view of the whole will gradually grow more rounded and will be ever more deeply imprinted on the receptive souls of the children. Frequently, by devoting several religious instruction periods to subordinate partial topics, the catechist can offer much instructive and formational material. From time to time, however, especially on the great feasts of the liturgical year, he can reach certain desired objectives incidentally; perhaps during a religious hour in which the children forget for a while the task of learning. The world of faith which up to that moment had been inaccessible to them will suddenly appear in a transfigured form in all its elevating and sanctifying beauty.

Plainly there exists a tension between the ideal of religious *education* which we have just outlined and the task of catechetical *instruction* which has already been mentioned and which is inseparable from the task of the catechist. How can we effect a reconciliation between these two?

This reconciliation is posited by the fact that according to the wisdom of education[1] first formulated by Aristotle, teaching

[1] Consult, for example: O. Willmann, "Erziehung" in *Lexikon der Pädagogik,* Vol. I (Freiburg: Herder, 1913), pp. 1156ff.; J. A. Jungmann,

represents the most essential part of education; for education is perfected in three stages: in the cultivation of those natural dispositions which in the child as in every other human being clamour for fuller development; in the regulation of the child's conduct from without by means of discipline (by training him to acquire habits, he can be brought to observe the law externally and to integrate himself into the existent order) finally, in the formation or the instruction by which his mind is prepared to grasp the idea of law, the ideal, and to assimilate it and to conform his interior life to it.

As a teacher the catechist must always bear in mind that his task is not simply to imprint upon the minds of the children a great number of theoretical statements without paying any heed to their meaning or connection with one another. He must rather introduce the children to the supernatural world of faith in such a way that the momentous thoughts that are embraced by it become those ideals by which they can orientate themselves and by which they can be guided on life's highway, and that these ideals evolve into powerful virtues which will propel them along the ways of Christian living.

These principles require, however, some explanatory observations:

1. We should point out that especially in the early grades of the elementary school, the catechist cannot educate the child by means of an insight into the truths themselves, but almost exclusively by training him to acquire habits and by imposing

"Die idealen Güter im Erziehungsbegriff Otto Willmanns" in *Internationale Zeitschrift f. Erziehungswissenschaft,* Vol. 6 (1950), pp. 25–36; F. De Hovre (E. B. Jordan, trans.), *Catholicism in Education* (New York: Benziger Brothers, 1934), pp. 461–493; H. E. Mayer, *The Philosophy of Teaching of St. Thomas Aquinas* (Milwaukee: Bruce, c. 1929), especially pp. 50–53; F. De Hovre et L. Breck, *Les Maîtres de la Pédagogie Contemporaine* (Bruges: Charles Beyaert), pp. 307–318; Edward Leen, *What is Education?* (New York: Sheed & Ward, 1943).

on him external discipline. This insight can only supplement the words of authority and will do so increasingly as the years roll on. Does this mean, then, that we cannot achieve anything lasting, anything essential in education by means of instruction?

We have established that the child does not yet possess any sense of the cohesion and of the unity of a system; his mind is still entirely orientated by the particular. Nevertheless, our efforts are not entirely without fruit; for whatever we accomplish in these years in the elementary school will serve as a preparation and as a foundation for later life, in fact a very important preparation and foundation. Later on, when the young man has perfected the change from the exterior to the interior life he should find this inner world in essentials within himself or at least he will see the plans for and the constituent element of it so that he will need only a few more suggestions to bring it into contact with the new psychological situation in which he now finds himself. But in childhood there will be at least the beneficial influence of that joyful mood contained in our catechesis if it realizes its own basic characteristic as the message of good news.

2. The concept of religious instruction as directive teaching, as landmarks on the road to God, offers still another advantage: it permits us to assign precisely its relationship to other subjects, because for these as well as for religion the same basic notions hold true. Whereas the religion period gives us access to the highest sphere of reality, secular subjects introduce us to the other realms. It is thereby shown that, and in which way, the many points of contact between the two sectors of instruction combine in one single world of ideal values. It should be the task of the school to impart to the child a concept of this world which finds its finest expression in religion, a concept which reaches its culmination and enfolds its blessing during the years of adolescence.

3. The question is how to distinguish this apostolic and educative perspective in the teaching of religion from that instruction in which religious knowledge is imparted solely for its own sake. In its ultimate analysis it is a problem which centres on the relationship between the message of faith and theology. In theological science revealed doctrine is taught primarily from the standpoint of truth, without considering its value for life. Theology determines what is contained in revelation, and what can, in the way of knowledge, be deduced from it by means of logical reasoning. The results are compared with the knowledge acquired in the light of natural reason, obscurities are dispelled, apparent contradictions are resolved. As a consequence, the periphery of revealed truths constitutes the chosen ground of theological speculation.

In the preaching of the word of God, and consequently also in catechesis, we treat, it is true, of the same revealed doctrine, but of this doctrine considered from the viewpoint of the good, from the standpoint of value. We deal with this doctrine, insofar as it includes and offers the treasure of the kingdom of God, insofar as it is a doctrine of salvation. This preaching is, therefore, concerned not with marginal zones or with the borderlines of revelation but with the very centre of Christian truth. From those materials which theology has proved durable must be built the house in which one can live or, at least, the road upon which one can travel. Christianity must, as in the time of the Apostles, be proclaimed as "the good news". The basic facts of salvation must as a consequence stand in the foreground: Christ as the apex of the divine economy of salvation, as the Redeemer and Dispenser of grace, living and continuing his mission in his Church and in his sacraments; in the sphere of moral law, the principles of Christian conduct must be presented as the generous responses of man to God's merciful love.

Christian doctrine may thus be presented in three different aspects:

1. In an outward form that is both religious and practical. In the spiritual life with its set expressions which have been derived from usage and tradition, especially in the Church's liturgy.

2. In its historical form: as the history of redemption as it is contained, above all, in the Scriptures.

3. In its systematic form: as a structure of dogmas, which are arranged logically into a system as presented in the catechism.

It is according to this division that catechetical matter was considered and evaluated in ancient Christian catechesis. This is evident, for example, in the threefold teaching of the Christian mysteries in the Roman regulations regarding the catechumenate: Lord's Prayer, Gospels and the Creed.[2]

2. Liturgy and the Spiritual Life

If for centuries it was possible for Christian youth to grow into Christian doctrine and Christian life without any special catechesis being apportioned them, this was possible only because of a Christian environment in which Christianity was lived and preached in the home and in the church. The child saw himself drawn into a religious environment which was sanctified by daily prayers, by pious practices and by Christian symbols. He was taken to Mass and to liturgical functions; he celebrated Church festivals with the community. In these he absorbed both the doctrine and the practice of his religion, without being able to understand clearly, it is true, its single details. The religious instruction in schools of the present day, in which the notional (the intellect) is accorded pre-eminence, must not neglect this element of Christian formation. On the contrary, it must avail itself of its advantages more conscientiously and explicitly the

[2] See above, p. 4 ff.

less the spontaneous effect of these educational forces is available in a religiously frozen atmosphere. The liturgy forms an imperishable treasury; its pedagogical possibilities have frequently been extolled by the authorities of recent times.[3] In what do these possibilities consist?

The entire teaching of the Church is contained in the liturgy. Liturgy is dogma that is prayed. Although liturgy is full of life and religious vitality, it is not dominated by unrestrained feeling but by "the primacy of the Logos" (Guardini). The chief events of the "good news" parade in an impressive fashion before our eyes in the ecclesiastical year. For this reason St. Thomas was able to say: the faithful must know and must believe expressly those truths of the faith which are the object of a feast.[4] This offers the explanation for the ancient axiom: *lex orandi—lex credendi.*

In the liturgy (as generally in prayer) we approach the truths and the facts of religion with the proper dispositions. In the liturgy we do not philosophize about God, but we adore him. In the liturgy we do not attempt to analyse faith, hope and charity, but we practise them. In the liturgy we avail ourselves

[3] Guardini (Ada Lane, trans.), *The Spirit of the Liturgy* (New York: Sheed and Ward, 1930); L. Bopp (A. P. Schimberg, trans.), *Liturgical Education* (Milwaukee: Bruce, 1937); D. v. Hildebrand, *Liturgy and Personality* (New York: Longmans, Green and Co., 1943); A. Beil, "Die Formkräfte der Liturgie in der Erziehung" in *Bibel u. Liturgie,* Vol. 19 (1951/52), pp. 120–125; V. Michel, *The Liturgy of the Church* (New York: Macmillan, 1937); G. Ellard, *Christian Life and Worship* (Milwaukee: Bruce, 1955); J. A. Jungmann, *Public Worship,* Eng. trans. (Challoner Publications) *Lumen Vitae,* Vol. 10, nos. 2 and 3, special issue on "Liturgy, the Re-presentation of Salvation" (International Centre for Studies in Religious Education, rue Washington, Brussels, Belgium); *Liturgy,* Vol. 23, no. 4, special issue on "Liturgy and Education" (Publ. from 14 Priest Lane, Pershore, Worcs., England).

[4] *De ver.* q. 14, a. 11; J. V. McGlynn, *Truth: St. Thomas Aquinas,* 3 vols. Chicago: Henry Regnery, Vol. II (1953), p. 262.

of the Sacraments with holy reverence, and we live as children of the Church. Although liturgy is not primarily concerned with educating us, but only with bringing us into union with God, it, nevertheless, tends to communicate to us those dispositions which are required by the whole of reality which gravitates around God and in this way forms Christian character so profoundly. All its values cast their rays harmoniously upon us. Order enters into the soul; humility, reverence, esteem for everything holy and sublime pervade those who have surrendered themselves to God.

If in catechesis we should succeed in introducing children to the content of the liturgy, we would open up a well which could supply the adult Christian with "waters of eternal life" his whole life through. Whereas doctrine, assimilated as theoretical knowledge, may fade from memory, and often no new knowledge is added to what one already knows, the liturgy accompanies the Christian through life, at least at Mass on Sundays and holy days. The liturgy, consequently, as has been rightly said, is the catechism of adults. There is the further advantage that the liturgy with its wide view and virile serenity is not exposed to the danger of being discarded by adolescents and adults as a part of a childish world of phantasy. In the liturgy religion is built to last a lifetime.

A glance at the essential points in the field of liturgical practice confirms what we have said. A fruitful symbol of a Christian concept of life is the church, especially when, as is so often the case in the country, it forms the centre of a town or village at the point where all roads converge, its tower a symbol of strength. In this church, where the living come together and in the encircling cemetery the dead await the resurrection, thoughts of eternity must surely be imprinted upon the Christian soul. At the same time by its monuments and by its treasures upon which men have perhaps laboured for centuries and which are adorned with love as much as skill, the Church builds a bridge to the sublime achievements of the past and so strengthens the meaning of tradition and gives substance to sane perseverance. To many statues of the saints there may be attached memories which are mirrored in the celebration of the feasts and in the lives of the faithful. The altar with the tabernacle before which the vigil light flickers displays most forcibly the living heart of Christian dogma. The costliness of the vessels and the preciousness of the vestments used at daily Mass offer the faithful more than faint intimations of the all-Holy whom they serve. There is no need for many words to call attention to these and other details and to centre the powers of observation upon them.

In the beginning the Mass itself is in its innermost essence not easily accessible to the children because of the strangeness not only of its language, but also of the formulation of the thoughts contained in it. But its very inaccessibility is an all important expression of the sublimity of the mystery itself. Moreover, in every living parish the catechist should avail himself of those parts, which are readily understandable, in High Mass and in the children's Mass, in vernacular prayers and hymns, in order to explain and to make clear the mysteries of the Mass in a manner adapted to their capacity. If he chooses these parts well, he can bring the children by their participation in them to experience what it means to be a Christian and to belong to the Church. In fact by such a participation the child will appreciate these truths incomparably more efficaciously than if he had learned a long and difficult definition of the Church by heart. To the teaching of the liturgy the catechist should add a proper evaluation of the diocesan prayerbook and the diocesan hymnal with their treasuries of prayer and hymns in which are contained that living portion of the liturgy so dear to the people, and which may be described as diocesan liturgy.

The liturgical or ecclesiastical year permits us to delve more deeply into the thought-structure of Christian dogma. The mystery of Christ is its basic theme; its two essential elements have each its cycle of feasts: the Person of Him, who became man for us, and His work of redemption. The teaching of these festal cycles will be so much more deeply anchored, the more the rhythm of the catechetical course is synchronized with these two major feasts, incorporating their mysteries in the themes to be taught. Such objective can be attained not only in biblical catechesis when the school year begins in autumn, but also generally in a syllabus that is arranged systematically. The culmination of the liturgy should also be the culmination of the catechesis. In the ancient Christian catechumenate, Easter was the goal towards which Christian training was aimed. Even the minor feasts in the course of the year should not be passed over unnoticed; by making allusions to them in prayers and hymns, they, too, can be employed to advantage.

Of importance are also religious usages with which the liturgical year is usually surrounded and by which it is usually accompanied both in the home and in the family. The children should become aware of these early in life and take part in them, decorating the family altar, the Christmas crib and, in May, the image of Mary. Even clothes for special feast days and a more luxurious meal on Sundays and holy days are not without religious significance. The prayer-life of the family may also be an educative factor of decisive value. Such family prayers are: grace at meal-time, night prayers, the parents' blessing, fortified with which the children betake themselves to bed. It is a great misfortune, that in the wide areas of our industrial population such religious traditions have been lost. Precisely for the sake of the children pastoral work should aim at the creation of new religious customs which will be apparent in the decoration of the homes, in the selection of prayers and in the celebration of the Church's feasts.[5]

As we have already noted, in this practical concept of the Christian liturgical heritage, there would be only a small part—the sacrifice of the Mass alone excepted—which would require special courses of instruction. This principle we would enunciate as follows: not much liturgics, but much liturgy, many practical examples of religion, in the home, in the school and in the church. What must be explained can usually take the form of incidental instruction. At the conclusion of, and in conjunction with, a given topic in the religion period, pertinent material relating to liturgical life can be taught the children. The new French catechism of Quinet and Boyer (1947) supplies us with helps pertaining to the liturgy at the end of every lesson. The new uniform catechism for Germany, wherever possible, offers the same kind of hints. The catechist is only too glad to take up and to develop such suggestions. In addition there will always be opportunities for independent liturgical instructions before the advent of one feast or the passing of another.

Bibliography

An attempt to be comprehensive is made in the present writer's *Public Worship* (Collegeville, Minn.: The Liturgical Press).

The following will be useful to teachers in the preparation of lessons:
H. Chéry, O.P., *What is the Mass?* Eng. trans.
A. M. Roguet, O.P., *Holy Mass, Approaches to the Mystery*
—, *The Sacraments, Signs of Life* (London: all Blackfriars Publications)
C. W. Howell, S.J., *The Work of Our Redemption* (Oxford: C. S. G.)
Denys Rutledge, O.S.B., *Catechism through the Liturgy,* Four parts (London: Douglas Organ).

See also the Appendix in *Abbreviated Catechism with Explanations* (Burns, Oates), and the section of *Catechism at Early Mass* called "The Christian Life" (2nd ed.; Burns, Oates and Macmillan, 1957). Finally,

[5] Cf. for example: M. R. Newland, *The Year and Our Children* (New York: P. J. Kenedy, 1956) and T. Mueller, *The Living Parish* quoted in *The Sower:* "Family Feast Days" No. 192 (July, 1954), pp. 83–85.

the special number of *Lumen Vitae*, Vol. 11, No. 4, which contains the first part of the proceedings of the International Congress on Religious Education held at Antwerp in 1956. The general orientation of all the papers in this first part of the Congress was liturgical and scriptural, the paper by Father Stenzel, S.J. on the liturgy and that by Rev. J. D. Crichton on "The Role of Gesture and Chant in Religious Education" may be referred to.

3. Bible History

Liturgy and religious life permit us to become acquainted with the deposit of faith by giving us ever new glimpses, but only partly its inner connection. But this is also important for religious training which tries to be thorough and profound. Whereas in the catechism we are presented with truths in a systematic logical form, in Bible History we are offered these same truths in historical dress.

The possibility of an historical presentation is postulated by the very nature of Christian revelation. Christianity saw the light of day not as a philosophical system, but as an historical fact; the divine plan was disclosed gradually over periods of time. The historical sequence of events is a genetic development; for in it we can detect the gradual growth of the kingdom of God. We see how God himself gradually makes real the Christian economy of salvation—in the Old Testament preparing and laying the foundation; in the New Testament building up and perfecting it. As a consequence this method of viewing events has been held in high esteem from the very beginning. The Old Testament supplies us with historical psalms; the New Testament constantly refers to incidents in the Old Testament, frequently narrates them with a wealth of detail (for example, the speech of St. Stephen, Acts, 7, 2–50): the missionary sermons of the Apostles are for the most part historical reports of facts, of things they themselves had seen and heard. And this factual narrative has been laid down in the Gospels. In fact, it was the biblical narrative which, in the first decades of Christianity, dominated the presentation of the Christian faith. The Fathers of the Church, by preference, preached Christian doctrine in a biblical guise. Frequently they expounded whole books of Sacred Scripture in the form of homilies, and by explaining the New Testament they also dealt with some books of the Old Testament (Origen, Chrysostom, Augustine). For catechesis Augustine favoured the *narratio* as an essential form of presentation.[6]

The medieval catechesis restricted itself chiefly to the liturgical pericopes, to the events surrounding the Birth and the Passion of Christ. As a consequence it treated those topics with greater intensity. Especially remarkable is the narrative and teaching character of medieval church paintings dealing with these matters. The Christmas and Passion plays also prove how widely biblical knowledge was diffused and avidly absorbed. But at this point we must make the surprising observation that biblical subjects played scarcely any part in the catechesis started for children in the sixteenth century. This fact can be explained by the apologetic character of the catecheses which were then being given. These were concerned with the clarity of the notions presented and there was reluctance, due to Protestant abuses, to spread the use of the Bible, even in excerpt form among the people. Despite this, the older catechisms in general contain a great deal of biblical material.

An extensive instruction on the Bible, which was at the same time a book to help the catechist, appeared in France[7] in 1683. This was *Catéchisme Historique* by Claude Fleury. In Germany, after indifferent beginnings, Johann Ignaz Felbiger (1767)

[6] See above, p. 4; J. P. Christopher, "The First Catechetical Instruction" in *Ancient Christian Writers* (Westminster: Newman, 1946), especially p. 116.

[7] J. Hofinger, *Geschichte des Katechismus,* pp. 81 f. Further information on the beginnings of Bible History, cf. Bopp, p. 237; A. N. Fuerst, *op. cit.,* Vol. II, pp. 47–48.

produced a work of merit. The effort of Bernhard Overberg, *Biblische Geschichte des Alten und Neuen Testamentes* (1797) brought an awakening. The pedagogical knowledge of the "age of enlightenment" enabled this branch of catechesis to achieve its notable triumph.

What was envisaged was an abridgement of Sacred Scripture for the use of children; in this the narrative episodes were to predominate. The principles by which this project were to be realized received definite formulation only gradually.[8] Felbiger, and, in his footsteps even more logically, Christoph von Schmid, the renowned teller of children's stories, chose texts on the basis of their fitness to be understood and to awaken devotion in the children, without paying too much attention to their intrinsic coherence. The latter entitled his book, concisely: *Biblische Geschichten für Kinder* (1801). In it he permitted himself great latitude in the method of presentation and in the use of biblical vocabulary.[9] The outline sketched by Felbiger was adopted by Ignaz Schuster and has been followed continuously down to the present by Schuster-Mey, and later by Schuster-Mey-Knecht (1921). According to him, Bible History should be the servant of the catechism; it should offer the catechist illustrations for his catechesis by putting at his disposal suitable pictures and moral examples. In opposition to this interpretation Overberg championed another viewpoint: Bible History should be first of all a history of redemption. Bernhard Galura, later bishop of Brixen (d. 1856), expressed the same idea in the title of his textbook: *Biblische Geschichte der Welterlösung* (1806).

The catechetical movement of our century almost unanimously adopted this last mentioned solution, and for a good

[8] P. Bergmann, *Lexikon der Pädagogik der Gegenwart,* Vol. I (1930), pp. 322–325.

[9] Pictures of this kind existed in France: M. Noirleau, *Bible de l'Enfance. Lectures amusantes sur l'Ancien et le Nouveau Testament* (Tournai, 1854).

reason. Today every effort must be made to reinforce the understanding of the basic facts of Christianity. A presentation of a history of redemption, which reaches its culmination in Christ, makes it abundantly clear that he is the chief element of Christian doctrine. It also demonstrates in a very emphatic fashion that the Christian message is rooted in the course of world history. At the same time the grandiose plan inherent in universal history is unfolded. Every event that takes place in the world is connected in some way or another with the kingdom of God, to which all men have been called. Especially today, when even the most remote peoples enter into the all-embracing purview of the child, such an all-embracing interpretation is of tremendous importance.

In this way we can treat only of the most outstanding events of redemption: paradise, the fall, the promise of the Redeemer, the election of Abraham and Israel, the guidance of the Chosen People, the prophetic messages, and finally the coming of the Saviour, his work for the whole of mankind which is continued in and through the Church. By laying stress upon the chief happenings the catechist will overcome the difficulty which the child has in understanding an historical course of events. Children cannot as a rule reason historically, but in Bible History the catechist deals with stories which, as experience proves, are as easy to narrate to, and as easy to be grasped by, the children as any other children's story. It is with this in mind that the new textbooks of biblical history have been written. Of those which in the last decades have been used in German countries, the following are the most important: Jakob Ecker, Michael Buchberger, and the Leo Society of Vienna. Other attempts, such as the *Schulbibel* of Heinrich Stieglitz (1910), and the *Katholische Schulbibel* of Paul Bergmann (1927), have had a stimulating effect, but none of them has achieved widespread acceptance; they remain private attempts by individuals.

It is entirely within the scope of the history of redemption to offer in biblical textbooks, such as the above-mentioned *Leo-Bible* and the *Herder-Bible,* a short résumé of Church History. Of course this is not history in the strict sense of the term; that is, a true relationship which exists between cause and effect, but rather history in the sense of offering individual biographies and of presenting the outlines of the various eras and of tracing the fate of leading personalities who have shaped the course of events. In any case the children are enabled to obtain an inkling of how the Church has fulfilled her mission with the help of God, even though she has been exposed to untold dangers; they are also enabled to find an explanation for the many extraordinary phenomena of the present day with which they will soon be confronted (for example, the variety and multiplicity both of religions, sects and of confessions).

By stressing the history of redemption the problem of the choice of subject matter is solved only in one respect. Still another question remains: how should non-narrative passages of an instructional character from Sacred Scripture, be included in the text? The biblical textbooks which originated during the age of enlightenment did contain a large amount of non-narrative material. This was due to the fact that in that age preference was shown for moral instruction, and to the fact that in the elementary schools of that period readers as such were unknown. Bible History was pressed into service in much the same way as during the Middle Ages reading was taught and practised from the psalms (*psalmos discere* = to learn to read).[10] Once this function was dropped, the principle of selection which is contained in the name, "Bible History", has predominated. Since the beginning of the biblical movement, the

[10] B. Smalley, *The Study of the Bible in the Middle Ages* (rev. ed.; New York: Philosophical Library, 1952); J. W. Thompson, *The Literacy of the Laity in the Middle Ages* (Berkeley, Calif.: U. C. Press, 1939).

question has been phrased anew: whether or not it suffices to give to children only narrative material from Sacred Scripture? In answering this query it should be fairly evident that the leaders of the movement never intended to put the entire Bible in the hands of the children. Even the Protestants, who regard the Bible as the sole rule of faith, have tended to discard this practice and to substitute "Bible Readers". Holy Scripture was not written for children (for example, note the freedom with which sex is treated). At graduation, however, every boy and girl should be given a New Testament.[11] The intention, manifest in the biblical textbooks written for the children, to include more than mere narrative material is evident in the very titles of a number of books that have recently appeared. In this respect the Bible Histories of Ecker and Kastner should take precedence because they were among the first to incorporate such material in their books. Extracts, in some cases very brief, are culled from every single book of the Bible. Even the illustrations in the *School Bible* of Ecker are for the most part (initial letters, paragraph headings, etc.) devoted to instruction or in any event to an evaluation, for didactic reasons, of the narrative elements.

An important principle of selection, which may be employed for the narrative, as well as for the instructional, parts of Sacred Scripture, is the liturgical use of biblical excerpts, of biblical ideas and thoughts. The liturgy often employs biblical texts in an applied sense which for their better understanding presuppose a certain knowledge of the literal sense or of the original context (for example, readings taken from the Book of Wisdom on Mary's feasts). As a consequence, the more important pericopes of the liturgy for Sundays or holy days, important prophecies of the prophets etc., should find a place in Bible

[11] This was recommended by a Synod of the Diocese of Klagenfurt, 1933.

Histories, as they do in the Bible History published by Herder. The same holds true also of the choice of psalms and of extracts from them (Ps. 42, 50, 129, etc.), with some of which the faithful ought to be more familiar (a task that can be done by means of a diocesan prayerbook).[12]

A final criterion to be used in choosing texts from the Bible, and one to be preferred above all the others, is the point of view of pedagogy, a criterion which was employed from the very beginning in the development of the children's Bible: "pedagogy" in the sense that the mental capacity of the child is not gauged too narrowly, and conversely, that it be not overtaxed inconsiderately; "pedagogy" especially in the sense that it is a pedagogy of morality, offering training in virtue. At this age, the child has very little experience of life. Consequently, in the Bible History, typical situations to be met with in life should be put before him, examples of goodness as well as of wickedness, but in either case they should be accompanied by the judgement which God has pronounced on them. With this in mind, it will be found worthwhile to retain certain episodes, as for example, the story of the Egyptian Joseph, which although they contribute little to the history of redemption, do illustrate moral conduct.

For pedagogical reasons as well as for motives derived from child psychology, it has been found useful to grade Bible Histories; for example, one for primary, and another for the intermediate grades and a third for the junior high level. This was done in the older textbooks and more recently in the *School Bible* of Ecker. This presupposes, however, that graded catechisms are available. For the children on the primary level

[12] Some stimulating suggestions have been offered by Richard Beron, *With the Bible through the Church Year* (New York: Pantheon, 1953). Recommendations much more developed were offered by Kl. Tilmann, "Eine zeitgemäße Schulbibel" in *KBl*, Vol. 75 (1950), pp. 156–162.

this cannot be done. Moreover, a special book for the intermediate grades is superfluous. School Bibles should, therefore, generally be edited for the junior high level. And this is justifiable even on the assumption that the time available is not sufficient for an exhaustive treatment in the course of the instructions. A Bible text book, however, may and should serve as reading matter in the home.

For the youngsters in the primary grades, this biblical textbook should take the form of a Religion Book. To the single excerpts of the biblical narrative should be appended at appropriate places as many of the doctrines of the catechism as are deemed necessary for the children to know at this age level. Indeed, at this stage, all the basic teachings relating to God and to the world, to the body and to the soul, to good and to evil, to the fall and the economy of redemption, can be presented in a much more effective way through the first chapters of the Old Testament, than through an abstract presentation. The same is true of the mystery of redemption in the New Testament. The idea for a book of this kind was first suggested by Wilhelm Pichler at the Catechetical Congress in Vienna in 1912. This able catechist showed how this suggestion could be incorporated into a book by offering his own text as a model.[13] His example was imitated elsewhere very quickly.[14]

[13] *Referate des Kongresses für Katechetik* (Vienna, 1912): Part I (Vienna, 1912), pp. 54–172. This draft corresponds in substance with the book which appeared first in 1913 and then later in many different printings and languages. This work was especially welcomed in mission countries and according to *Orbis Catholicus,* Vol. 4 (1950/51), it has been translated into 54 languages. Consult F. Jachym, "Wilhelm Pichler. Sein Leben und Werk" in *Katechetische Besinnung* (Vienna, 1951), pp. 19–22.

[14] The *Katholische Religionsbüchlein für die Grundschule* of Karl Raab was adopted by Bavaria in 1927. Under the title, *Katholisches Gottlehrbüchlein,* it was accepted by the Archdiocese of Freiburg, but only after it had been revised. L. Grimm wrote a practical handbook to be used in conjunction with it: *Praktisches Handbuch zum Katholischen Gottlehrbüch-*

In what concerns the language of the Bible History, in the selection of excerpts there should be no departure from the wording of a good translation except when these are likely to be understood only with difficulty by the children. Such difficulties may be encountered as a result of the great disparity in the culture which is described and in the incidents which are narrated. These discrepancies become less important when we remember that the great majority of the events took place in a "patriarchal" environment, hence generally under conditions which are common to all mankind and can be easily understood.

For a long time now it has been taken for granted that the biblical narrative should be accompanied by pictures. On this point, however, it is necessary to formulate certain demands which must be fulfilled. Choosing great masterpieces does not answer the requirements. Why not? Because the pictures in the School Bible should be uniform, that is to say, the same person should always be represented by the same face. Furthermore, the pictures should lend substance to the story. As the psychology of the school child demands, these pictures should supply many supplementary details with great distinctness; unusual notions (a tent, palm branches, sepulchres hewn out of rock) should be clarified through them. To achieve these objectives, that sober realism which singles out and employs only pictures which are archaeologically true must be avoided. Particularly in the likenesses of holy personages in particular, the mystery of their lives which is inaccessible to historical empiricism, should in some fashion or another filter through to

lein (Freiburg: Herder, 1950). In the U. S. A. the adoption of books in general for school use, and especially a Bible History, is left to the individual Ordinary, who usually acts through his superintendent of schools. As a consequence, many different Bible Histories and religion series are in use at the present time. Of the great number of such Bible Histories cf. A. N. Fuerst, *op. cit.,* Vol. II (1946), pp. 49–58.

the reader. From the standpoint of technique, a lineal method of drawing rather than paintings which are conceived solely for their colour schemes, best meets the condition which we have laid down. Colour, which as a matter of fact greatly enhances the pleasure children derive from pictures, should be striking. As products, which fit all the requirements, and are prized at the same time as works of art, we may mention the pictures of Philip Schumacher, and for more advanced tastes, those of Gebhard Fugel.

The history and development of Bible History in the United States is both interesting and involved. In the nineteenth century the various dioceses used translations of those histories which had been well received in the Old World. Among the earliest of this kind was M. Fleury's, *Catéchisme Historique* which was either translated outright or cleverly adapted (Bishop Cheverus, Gahan). In addition some school systems used versions of the more popular German works, some of which have already been mentioned, for example, Mey, Ecker, Walther, and Knecht. Of English and American origin the works of Milner, Noethen, Sadlier and Reeve achieved some degree of recognition and acceptance.

In the twentieth century due to the growth of the Church and its school system, as well as to the fact that the various diocesan school systems usually adopt textbooks which best fit their syllabuses, a goodly number of Bible Histories are currently being used. Chronologically of an earlier date, but still unusually (and for good reason) popular is Bishop Gilmour's little volume. Enjoying public favour are the works of: Newton-Horan, G. Johnson and J. Hannan and Sr. Dominica, McDonald and Jackson, S. A. Raemers.

Some of these texts incorporate very little of the exact wording of Sacred Scriptures in their composition, for example, Johnson, Hannan *et al.* In this respect they differ from the attempt made by Mother Eaton and J. Hart who, in giving the children an abridged edition of the Bible, have conscientiously retained the terminology and the flavour of both Testaments; they differ also from such compositions as for example, Newton-Horan.

The purposes which these histories serve actually varies a great deal. Some are designed to be simply readers (Jennings); others have as their objective the unity of the plan of redemption and its fulfillment in the Testaments which have been given us (Martindale, Sidney); still others are scarcely more than biographies of scriptural characters (Petersham, Williams).

Most of these books are richly and in most instances correctly illustrated. Both in the drawings and in the use of colour all of the acceptable canons for children's interests and tastes have been observed. Garishness has been avoided, but the advance which may be noted on the continent in regard to the conception of figures and the sketching of events is still lacking for better or worse.[15]

Bibliography

Since the publication of *A Catholic Commentary on Holy Scripture* in 1953 (London: Thomas Nelson and Sons) Catholic teachers have a source to go to for fundamental information. Articles such as "The Place of the Bible in the Church", "The Interpretation of Holy Scripture" and "The History of Israel" for the O.T. and "The Person and Teaching of our Lord Jesus Christ" and "Christianity in Apostolic Times" for the N.T. will give them much useful material.

The series of Scripture Textbooks edited by Mgr. J. M. T. Barton is intended to cover the whole ground for children from the age of eleven to seventeen:

P. J. Crean, *A Short Life of our Lord*
Hubert van Zeller, O.S.B., *Old Testament Stories*
T. E. Bird, *A Study of the Gospels*
S. Bullough, O.P., *The Church in the New Testament*
R. A. Dyson, S.J., and A. Jones, *The Kingdom of Promise* (O.T.)

[15] As other pictures worthy of special consideration we can name those of A. and E. Seeger in Beron (see footnote No. 12). Further considerations on this subject: Bopp, pp. 241 f.

S. Bullough, O.P., *Christian Teaching in St. Paul and the Apostolic Age* (London: all Burns, Oates)

General introduction to N.T.:

Maisie Ward, *They Saw his Glory* (Sheed & Ward)

Helps to reading the Bible:

Guide to the Bible, by the Monks of Maredsous (Sands, Eng. trans.)

How to Read the Bible, by R. Poelman (Longmans, Eng. trans.)

Lives of our Lord for young children (apart from Crean above):

Marigold Hunt, *Life of Our Lord for Children* (Sheed & Ward)

A. Boyer, *The Story of Jesus* (Longmans, Eng. trans.)

Lumen Vitae, special number on the Bible, Vol. 10, 1 (1955): The Bible, History of Salvation.

See also *Lumen Vitae,* Vol. 11, 4: "Religious Education Today", papers by Dr. Arnold, Father Poelman, and Father Tilmann.

The Sower, Nos. 170, 171, "How shall we teach the Old Testament?" by J. D. Crichton.

Heinisch, Paul, *Christ in Prophecy*

—, *History of the Old Testament*

—, *Theology of the Old Testament* (Collegeville, Minn. all: The Liturgical Press, 1950-56)

Charlier, Celestin, *The Christian Approach to the Bible* (Westminster, Md.: Newman Press, 1958)

Sullivan, Kathryn, *God's Word and Work* (Collegeville, Minn.: The Liturgical Press, 1958)

Bible in the Church (New York: Sheed & Ward, 1959).

4. *The Catechism*

In logical sequence and in well-rounded systematic form the catechism presents to us the doctrine of redemption. Such a presentation is possible and after a fashion is also necessary, because the essence of Christian doctrine demands it. If Christianity was only an incident in the past, an historical narrative of its origin, a tale of its successes or failures, would suffice. If conversely it is looked upon as a phenomenon of the present, but intended to satisfy religious edification only, in addition to a narrative all that would be required would be a study of customs and liturgy. Christianity must, however, lay the foundation for life and be a rule of conduct. As a consequence of the successes and failures, of the zeniths and the nadirs of the narrative, and of the variety of usages, we must draw those facets which embrace everything to which we hold fast, everything which supplies our life with its essential meanings and its moral norms. From facts in the history of redemption and from the relationships with God that result from them, there emerges a method of presentation which is arranged according to themes, a presentation which is at the same time determined by the fundamental plan of redemption itself. This leads to systematic summary whose extent and characteristics vary according to need.

A certain systematization cannot be divorced from Christianity. Even in the liturgy and still more in the history of redemption there are indications of an inner world. For this reason we can combine for the children systematic teaching with an historical narrative. This systematic aspect reveals the great superiority of the Christian religion. Nothing similar to it can be found in ancient religions. These on examination dissolve into a myriad of myths. This synthesis is missing, for example, also in Buddhism, which at most leads only to a negation. In Christianity ecclesiastical writers began very early to phrase the essential outlines of revealed truth in set formulas, in short dogmatic statements. These formulations appear from the very outset, for example, in the epistles of the Apostles. In the formulas of greetings, which appear in the prefaces of these letters, we recognize a God-Christ confrontation and are made aware of the Passion and Resurrection of Christ as the source of redemption. Here and there, as, for example, in 1 Cor. 15, 3f., a synthesis of this kind is presented to the readers as an already existing tradition. In connection with the moral law, we can discern in the *Doctrine of the Two Ways* its primitive Christian formulation. It is an exaggeration, when the Protestant theologian Alfred Seeberg, in daring contrast to the older explanations that had been offered, tried to show that, "soon after the death of Christ there appeared a catechism which was composed from the words of Our Lord".[16] Perhaps, by such a statement he wished only to show that the Gospels themselves reveal such a synopsis, whose concise outlines are sketched in the preaching of the Apostles.[17]

With good reason we may designate the Apostles' Creed as the first catechism. Just as this presents us with a synopsis of the early Christian catechesis on our faith, so also the catechumenate and catechesis eventually hastened the formulation of still further summaries, some rigid, others more flexible.[18] In this sense we can speak of a Christian kerygma or of a kerygmatic synthesis.[19]

A more novel type of summary or of systematization is given to us in the polemico-scientific dogmatic treatises which deal with articles of faith that had been called into question by the various controversies with the heretics. Whatever the Fathers wrote in connection with these controversial subjects, especially, concerning the Trinity and grace, but also whatever they developed in their exegesis of Holy Scripture, has been woven into the fabric of Catholic thought in the *Libri Sententiarum* at the dawn of Scholasticism and eventually into the *Summas*. With these begins the golden era of theology or the age of scientific compilations. In them stands not only the solution to the problems connected with the foundation and

[16] A. Seeberg, *Der Katechismus der Urchristenheit* (Leipzig: A. Deichert, 1903). The question was taken up anew by N. A. Dahl, "Anamnesis" in *Studia theologica,* Vol. I (Lund, 1948), pp. 69–95, especially p. 77, footnote 3, where literature on the subject may be found. P. Carrington, *The Primitive Christian Catechism* (Cambridge: University Press, 1940).

[17] Acts 2, 22–36; 4, 8–12; 5, 30–32; 10, 34–43; 13, 16–41.

[18] See above, pp. 4-13.

[19] Further particulars on the notion of *kerygma* will be found at the end of the book in Appendix II.

with the norms of Christian life, but also everything that, by the aid of reason, both regular and deductive, could be gathered from the sources of revelation. This preoccupation with a systematic presentation of revealed truth is no longer so important for the layman as it is for priests. Through this means he can make himself independent of the more fortuitous and imaginative formulations of revealed truth. He should be in a position to adapt the formulated doctrine to the conditions in which he finds himself so as to be able to help the faithful more effectively.

For the simple faithful, and consequently for the catechism, what is necessary is the kerygmatic synthesis which has a practical life-value because it indicates the way which the Christian must follow to reach God. In the actual history of the catechisms, by force of circumstances, it has not been possible to bring about a complete separation between the scientific and kerygmatic synopsis. The catechisms which saw the light of day during the Reformation were forced by necessity to erect barriers against heresy. These were emergency structures, for which their authors had to requisition material ready at hand, for example, in the numerous enumerations found in the catecheses of the preceding centuries, in the definitions of scholastic theology. Diamond-sharp concepts and strict emphasis on the doctrinal differences were of utmost importance. Biblical phraseology softened the harshness and lessened the rigidity of the formulas, especially in Canisius' catechisms.

But even in the subsequent periods a well-ordered systematization was not created out of these emergency synopses.[20]

[20] The history of the various catechisms in Germany has been almost completed in the course of the last few decades, at least in all that concerns its external development. F. X. Thalhofer, *Entwicklung des katholischen Katechismus in Deutschland von Canisius bis Deharbe* (Freiburg: Herder, 1899); W. Busch, *Der Weg des deutschen Katechismus von Deharbe bis zum*

In the following centuries theological material began to increase more and more—since these centuries witnessed a renewed interest in theology—first of all in the commentaries on the catechism, and later on in the catechisms themselves. Definitions from theology, and casuistry taken from moral theology, were injected into the catechisms.[21]

The religious pedagogy of the age of enlightenment, conversely, made a definite stand against such practices; the authorities in the field demanded that more attention be paid to the mental capacity of the children *(captum)*. There appeared, as a consequence, various attempts to offer a catechism which presented doctrine not in the form of abstract notions, but more in the form of induction and narration.[22] None of these experiments succeeded in gaining wide acceptance. Even the catechism of Hirscher was used only in his own diocese of Freiburg, and even there only for a short time. The pedagogues of the period suffered more and more from the confusion that had been occasioned by the new catechisms. Consequently they deviated more drastically from them, especially when they detected in them those evil tendencies of the "age of enlight-

Einheitskatechismus (Freiburg: Herder, 1936); J. Schmitt, *Der Kampf um den Katechismus in der Aufklärungsperiode Deutschlands* (München: R. Oldenbourg, 1935); J. Hofinger, *Geschichte des Katechismus in Österreich von Canisius bis zur Gegenwart* (Innsbruck: F. Rauch, 1937); F. Weber, *Geschichte des Katechismus in der Diözese Rottenburg* (Freiburg: Herder, 1939).

[21] Hofinger, pp. 7f.; Thalhofer, *op. cit.,* pp. 24ff. and pp. 55f.

[22] To this category belong the catechisms of B. Overberg (2nd ed., 1804), B. Galura (1806), J. Weber (1814). Most successful was the historico-inductive form employed in the catechism of J. B. Hirscher (1842), who made the divine economy of redemption the focal point of his development. Consult the theoretical considerations which moved him to adopt such a plan: Hirscher, *Katechetik,* pp. 120ff. and pp. 167f. The start of the movement to formulate a catechism on historical principles was made in France: Cl. Fleury, *Catéchisme Historique* (1683). Compare Thalhofer, *op. cit.,* pp. 102ff.

enment" which had wreaked such devastation among the faithful.

From the year 1847 onward the catechisms of Josef Deharbe, S.J. appeared. They soon found ready acceptance in a majority of the dioceses in Germany. They excelled by reason of their clear logical arrangement and by reason of the completeness and the correctness of their doctrine, which was presented in simple, concise language. In these was effected the return to the earlier "theologizing" kind of a catechesis, it is true, but with many improvements. It is, however, worthy of note, that the Deharbe Catechisms never were able to infiltrate into the Austro-Hungarian Empire. There the Catechism of 1777, which had originated in the circle which gathered around Abbot Felbiger, and combined the traditional theological content with certain didactic improvements, was retained during the decades of the age of enlightenment. What Deharbe had brought back from the past was still in essentials to be found in Felbiger's effort. Thus it was that in Austria this Catechism of 1777 was employed for as long as that of Deharbe was able to retain its popularity on German soil. At the turn of the century a reform took place in Austria as well as in Germany which, however, was concerned only with minor improvements within the old pattern.[23]

[23] In 1894 a new catechism was approved for Austria; it was a revision of an older catechism for which Deharbe had been used as a model. Its object was greater theological clarity; Hofinger, pp. 273ff. A revision of the Deharbe catechism undertaken by J. Linden was introduced into various dioceses of Southern Germany after 1900. This catechism attempted to simplify language to meet the requirements of the children; Busch, *op. cit.*, pp. 56ff. Linden was of the opinion, however, that the catechism must of necessity be "dry in content and of only limited interest to the children". In the U.S.A. the attempts made by Fander, Kelly, Deck, Newman and others were in the same direction. The new revision of the Baltimore Catechism is an attempt to meet the demands that were made in as satisfactory a manner as

A solution of grandiose proportion, which in the interim formed the topic of much discussion, was never realized. At the Vatican Council of 1870 a plan was suggested to create a uniform catechism for the whole of Christendom, a universal catechism, for which the Catechism of Robert Bellarmine would serve as basis. In this sense there was presented a *schema constitutionis de parvo Catechismo,* for and against which 41 different speeches were delivered. In general the plan found a favourable reception, but it was decided, that the bishops of the various countries should be permitted a certain latitude in translating the Latin basic text and in adding an appendix, if they saw fit. A definitive decision, however, was not reached.[24]

Later attempts of the same kind to produce a universal catechism (namely, the two catechisms which were drawn up at the request of Pius X,[25] and the catechism of Cardinal Gasparri[26])

possible. German catechisms have also appeared in English: J. Linden, *Catechism of Christian Doctrine* (6th ed.; Catechism of Christian Doctrine, 1934); J. Deharbe (translated by J. Fander), *A Catechism of Christian Doctrine*. Revised and adapted to the New Code of Canon Law (New York: F. Pustet, n. d.).

[24] C. Butler, *The Vatican Council,* 2 vols. (Longmans, Green, 1930), Vol. I, pp. 228–232; Busch, *op. cit.,* pp. 114–116.

[25] His first catechism which was prescribed for the ecclesiastical province of Rome appeared in 1905. A second and thoroughly revised edition was in 1912 again prescribed for the province of Rome and recommended for use by the other dioceses of Italy. An English translation was made by J. Hagen under the title: *Catechism of Christian Doctrine* (Dublin: M. H. Gill, 1914). His monumental work: *Compendium of Catechetical Instruction,* 4 vols. (New York: Benziger Bros., 1928); see Vol. I, pp. lv-lviii for mention of St. Pope Pius X's catechism.

[26] *Catechismus Catholicus,* Rome, 1930. A translation appeared in English (exclusive translation by H. Pope), *The Catholic Catechism* (New York: P. J. Kenedy, 1932). A graded catechism in three volumes based on this catechism was written by Fr. Kirsch and Sr. Brendan, *The Catholic Faith Explained* (New York: P. J. Kenedy). This catechism of Gasparri is the work of a commission which was set up by Pope Benedict XV for the purpose of composing a universal (uniform) catechism. The

were never intended to be obligatory for the entire Church. These attempts were designed to furnish knowledge of religious truth as broadly and as clearly as possible in language that children could understand.

At the turn of the century the "Catechetical Movement" gained momentum. This movement brought in its wake a very vocal criticism of the catechisms then in use. They were deplored because they were too rich in content. It was contended that only the more gifted children could possibly learn them by heart, and even if they did, they would never be able to understand them. A second complaint was directed against the all too rational theological treatment of the subject matter; the "practical application" appended at the very end of each lesson could not be accepted as an adequate substitute for ethical and moral values which were lacking.

In addition the educative factor in the teaching of morality appeared to be lacking: too much attention was paid to the enumeration and description of sins and too little to the training of the spirit in Christian ideals.

To these objections the new catechism ventured solutions. This catechism appeared after several years (1925) and was called a uniform German catechism because of its acceptance by practically all the German dioceses—only Freiburg and Rottenburg[27] were exceptions. The Austrian dioceses, which at the outset had intended to accept the solution which the Germans

results of its labours were published, however, only under the name of Cardinal Gasparri who had presided over its sessions. As was reported in *Lumen Vitae,* Vol. 5 (1950), p. 522, this catechism was adopted by the Mexican Episcopacy. The trial was not over successful. As a consequence, the book itself was dropped in a majority of the dioceses.

[27] The catechism of the diocese of Rottenburg which was revised in 1920 represents a happy evolution of the work which Ignaz Schuster published in 1844; it was (at least in part) in use in the German cantons of Switzerland.

would offer, in the end attempted their own reform with the same ideas in mind, but on the basis of the Austrian catechetical tradition. The result of their efforts is the Austrian catechism of 1930.[28]

The change that meets the eye most forcefully in both these catechisms is the noticeable reduction in the amount of matter to be memorized; there remained only some 300 questions, that is practically only half of the earlier number. In place of these, explanations were inserted between the questions, more extensively than in the earlier Deharbe. This was not required to be learned by heart. Other criticisms that had been voiced were also accorded attention. In addition the liturgical movement exercised considerable influence on its composition. The Mass and the liturgical year were explained very fully; Holy Communion was treated in connection with the Sacrifice of the Mass as the sacrificial Meal.

From the very beginning this German uniform catechism was conceived only as a preliminary step to the full solution; it would have to be tested by experience, by daily use, and in this fashion pave the way for a definitive future text. Soon after its appearance criticism was voiced on practically all sides. These objections were collected by the German Catechetical Society[29]

[28] This catechism retains among other matters the order and the titles of the three chief sections which Canisius had introduced: Faith and Creed, Hope and Prayer, Charity and the Commandments, to which was added the further chief section, that of Grace and the means of Grace. This division is also basic to the Christian doctrine of St. Thomas (see above, p. 15). This goes back to the *Enchiridion, sive de fide, spe et caritate* of Saint Augustine. With the difference, however, that St. Augustine never developed the teaching of hope and of charity as main headings in his work, but introduced them as the fruits and the culmination of faith.

[29] The essentials published in *Katechetische Blätter,* mainly since 1933; a part of the criticism was put in the form of independent drafts of possible catechisms. A conspectus of all of them is offered in summary form in Bopp, pp. 261 ff.

and presented to various episcopal committees. It soon became evident that it would not suffice simply to emend the text. As a consequence the Bishops' Conference at Fulda in 1938 set up a commission which was to undertake the preliminary spadework on an entirely new catechism. In the previous criticisms which were evaluated as well as in the deliberations and discussions which ensued,[30] we can detect the outlines of an ideal catechism which went far beyond the kind of catechism that had been envisaged up to that point, and which necessitates a closer examination. In this examination we shall deal with the questions of external organization as well as with the questions of internal form.

Questions of External Organization

At the outset we are justified in proposing several questions. Is a catechism conceived as a systematic exposition of Christian doctrine in any way possible for children? Is it not a hindrance rather than an aid to their religious training? Children learn only words which they quickly forget. To these questions we answer with a distinction: for children up to approximately ten years of age a catechism should not even be considered. This desired objective has been realized in Canon Drinkwater's *Sower System*. ("For the Junior classes, ages 8–11, knowledge of the catechism text as such is not prescribed by the Scheme, and any systematic learning of the full catechism at this stage is entirely against the spirit of the Scheme.") A religious booklet of some kind, in which the elements of indispensable doctrines are contained, is more in conformity with their psychological ability to grasp truth. In such a booklet everything necessary in the way of doctrine could be interwoven into the

[30] Consult the brochure of G. Götzel, *Auf dem Weg zu einem neuen Katechismus* (Freiburg: Herder, 1944).

narrative presentation of the history of redemption.[31] For the upper-grades, that is to say, for children from 10–14 years of age, a catechism can and should be used. From a purely psychological viewpoint it would be desirable to defer its use for at least two more years, because actually it is only with the advent of adolescence that the ability to grasp larger relationships, the spirit of synthesis, develops and becomes evident.[32] But we cannot think of offering this solution, because the time necessary to give a thorough treatment of the catechism can no longer be found in the school years which remain—and it is only upon them that we can count.

If we admit that a child's catechism is possible, we must still ask a further question. Is it necessary? Isn't such a book of precisely formulated definitions justified only in times of controversy, such as was carried on during the sixteenth century and after? After all, there was no such book used during the previous centuries. To this we must reply that in less advanced societies it is quite possible to work without a systematic catechism and to base teaching purely on a book portraying the story of the redemption.[33] In a period, however, in which the general education of masses has been raised to such a high level as a result of compulsory schooling, we cannot dispense with a thorough and complete education, especially in religion; at the present time much less so, because all barriers have broken down. Even the most simple Catholic is incessantly exposed to

[31] See above, p. 85.

[32] Compare this with the brochure mentioned in the above: *Au, dem Wege zu einem neuen Katechismus,* p. 39.

[33] In mission countries it appears actually that the missionaries have turned to such a solution. Nothing else would explain the rapid diffusion of the religion book of W. Pichler: see above footnote p. 110. Consult also the judgement which J. Hofinger passes on it in *KBl,* Vol. 67 (1941), pp. 96f. The missionaries also seem to think that a book of this kind suffices for part-time students, cf. Bopp, pp. 388f.

all types of ideologies current in the world, especially when through a war, deportation or emigration—he is suddenly thrown into an entirely new and perhaps hostile environment. This need becomes still more imperative by reason of errors undermining the very foundations of civilization. To counteract such influences it is not necessary that all the details of the Christian religion should become the conscious possession of the pupils, but its broadest outlines should. To etch such outlines in their minds, there is scarcely any aid more suitable and any help more indispensable than the clear systematization of the catechism.[34]

[34] Another problem is to know whether this book ought to have the character of a text to be remembered. Raab, pp. 3–87, seeks to show that for a long time the catechism was a book intended for the teacher, as it had been in the days of Luther. In the era of enlightenment it became a reader for the pupils. Deharbe was the first to make it a manual. Raab refuses to admit that the catechism should be a book filled with texts to be memorized (pp. 144f.). Memorization should rather be required in the form of a profession of faith and of prayer as it was in antiquity. The text to be learned by heart (which should be uniform for the entire Church, and should in this way become a universal catechism) should be in the form of a Creed divided into articles and should be put into a prayerbook or a manual of devotion, as had been done in the catechisms of Canisius.—This idea, right in itself, is justified by the fact that catechesis itself—as we shall see later—turns the memory passages into prayer and aims at maintaining and strengthening faith. —The role of "reader" (for the home) is restored to the catechism by the "lesson-unit" catechism. Certain works destined for both young and old embody these points, e. g., F. M. Willam, *Unser Weg zu Gott* (Innsbruck: Tyrolia, 1951); A. Hildenbrand, *Hausbuch der christlichen Unterweisung* (Freiburg: Herder, 1951), both of which in their own way do justice to the principles of the inner structure of the catechism. In the U.S.A. the religion series, W. R. Kelly, *et al., Living My Religion,* 8 vols. (New York: Benziger Bros.) and E. Fitzpatrick (ed.), *Highway to Heaven,* 8 vols. (Milwaukee: Bruce) are readers that all can use, for they are adapted to the mental capacity of the children and to their vocabulary in the various grades. C. E. Elwell, *et al., Our Quest for Happiness* (Chicago: Mentzer, Bush) are meant to form the nucleus of a religion library in the home.

In so far as the didactic arrangement of the catechism is concerned, the question we should ask ourselves is: whether the traditional question and answer form of the catechism should be retained. Precisely because of this form, it frequently appears as if the catechism had become the handmaid of "parrot learning", which can answer questions only if they are formulated in a certain way. Moreover, if it is employed in connection with minor details of subject matter, the question destroys the inner coherence and cohesion of the thought. In the course of the centuries the plea has been made to drop the question form entirely. Sporadically one or the other catechism has attempted to eliminate it, especially during the age of enlightenment.[35] Hirscher himself was averse to the question form; but when he himself embarked on his own catechism, he clung to the question and answer. As an excuse for his action he gave the pointed reply:[36] "because only questions can fix the subject matter of the instruction on the mind and hold the attention of the children." A still further reason is simply: tradition has never jettisoned them. In the first centuries of her existence the Church required the prospective candidates for Baptism to make a profession of faith by answering certain questions—a custom she still preserves today: "Dost thou believe in God, the Father Almighty?" The question was taken for granted in the Middle Ages, when the pastor examined the godparent, or the confessor his penitent, on his knowledge of the faith.[37] Textbooks were written with this in mind. Thus, the very first catechisms stemming from Protestant as well as

[35] Thalhofer, *op. cit.,* p. 230, names the catechisms of Grill (1789), Stattler (1794), Schneider (1790), Rumpler (1802), as well as the one adopted for Freising (1812). The catechism of Galura should be included in this category.—In modern times the Czech catechism (1919) dispensed with the question and answer form.

[36] *Zur Verständigung über den . . . Katechismus* (Tübingen, 1842), II.

[37] Cf. above pp. 11–15.

from Catholic sources appeared in question and answer form. In them the question is frequently ascribed to the child as a query addressed to the teacher (Witzel, Bellarmine) or is made to appear as discussion carried on by pupils among themselves in the form of problems and rejoinders.[38] Question and answer served to imprint the sound of the word upon the mind by means of the memory, by which it was thought that faith itself would be made secure.

That this question and answer form, so much attacked during the age of enlightenment, should no longer predominate, was a conclusion arrived at gradually in the succeeding centuries. Deharbe repeatedly inserted texts from Sacred Scripture as well as other complementary matter between the various questions. In the German uniform catechism as well as in the Austrian Catechism of 1930 the interpolated matter formed practically half of the content of the entire catechism.

In the United States in addition to the catechisms translated from the German in which explanatory material from Scripture and other sources was interpolated, certain others, native in origin, inserted scriptural as well as explanatory material between the various questions and answers, for example, as early as Kinkead, and then in E. M. Deck and the works of Kirsch-Brendan. But even before the appearance of these catechisms, the foremost representatives of the "Catechetical Movement", who sought to improve catechetical method, proposed an even more radical solution: a catechism in "lesson units". And they were able at the same time to show how such a project could be realized by offering a finished product of such a catechism.[39]

[38] F. J. Peters, "Der 'fraglose' Katechismus" *KBl* (1941), pp. 177–184.

[39] H. Stieglitz, *Grösseres Religionsbüchlein* (Kempten: Kösel, 1916; 2nd ed. 1919); Stieglitz published a *Religionsbüchlein für die Kleinen* as early as 1915; W. Pichler, *Katechismus der katholischen Religion* (Vienna, 1928).

By such a proposal they meant a catechism in which the subject matter is divided into "lesson units" (which did not necessarily imply that each lesson of the catechism corresponds to such a unit) within which the matter is presented in a free but coherent fashion. In such a catechism it was never intended to suppress the question entirely, but merely to relegate it to the end of the lesson, either with or without the addition of the answer. In early times catechisms based on lesson units had actually appeared but only in isolated instances.[40] Today, in many respects it is gaining ground.[41] Its advantages are obvious: the catechism loses its earlier tediousness and dryness; acquiring a knowledge of its content becomes easier, and the cooperation of the parents in teaching religion at home is made lighter by not restricting it merely to asking the children to repeat the answer which they had first to memorize.

These advantages were already present in that undeveloped form which the "lesson units" had in their original version. The catechism is no longer merely a book to be known by heart; it is also a well-arranged and easily readable presentation of Christian doctrine in which emotive values are not wanting. But these definite advantages can be increased still more by

[40] The catechism of Fleury (1683) and Pouget, both of France (1702), may also be inserted here; in Germany, the large *Saganer Katechismus* of B. Strauch (1766).—Cf. Hofinger, pp. 48f. along with footnote 20.

[41] F. M. Willam, *Katechetische Erneuerung* (Innsbruck: Tyrolia, 1946); F. M. Willam, *Der Lehrstück-Katechismus als ein Träger der katechetischen Erneuerung* (Freiburg: Herder, 1949). Review of this work by C. J. Fuerst, *Theological Studies,* Vol. 12 (1951), pp. 134–136.—The first territory into which the lesson-unit catechism succeeded in gaining entry was the diocese of Brixen and the diocese of Trent in South Tyrol, which adopted the catechism of W. Pichler for the German speaking children there around 1933. There followed in turn the catechism of the French cantons in Switzerland, the uniform (national) French catechism and now the German catechism.—The Bishops of Austria authorized the preparation of a new catechism in lesson-unit format in 1950.

adapting its content to the psychology of the child and by making its purpose more practical. The catechism can and should become a book which by reason of its varied forms of presentation is able to reach the various psychological types among the children, and can and should be capable of being employed with profit in even the most difficult circumstances without assuming any special didactic gifts on the part of the teacher.

In France, Quinet and Boyer broke new ground along these lines when they published their version of the French uniform catechism in 1938–40. Their catechism is illustrated; in fact, each unit is preceded by a coloured picture, which not infrequently, anticipating the text, covers at least a third of the first page. The text begins with a narrative or descriptive account which is generally taken from Sacred Scripture, usually from the Gospels, but in isolated instances also from the life of the Church. After this there follow questions without answers. They serve to provoke reflection on the preceding text. In the lesson dealing with the forgiveness of sin, after the parable of the Good Shepherd, we find the following questions. To what does Christ compare the faithful? With what did the Pharisees reproach Jesus? What does the parable of the lost sheep prove? Then the true "leçon" with questions and answers (the latter in bold-faced print) follows as the second main section. The conclusion takes the form of a practical discussion embodying a series of hints, its outline reappears each time in exactly the same way: For my Life—Prayer (generally a short formula)—Liturgy—Exercise (in this lesson: search the Gospels for all those texts in which Our Saviour shows his mercy for sinners)—Applied Tasks (drawing: barren fig tree, lost sheep, lost drachma, prodigal son)—Word of God (a text of Sacred Scripture).

In the Adaptive Way[42] recommended for the use of the

[42] Sr. M. Rosalia, *The Adaptive Way of Teaching Confraternity Classes* (St. Paul: Catechetical Guild, 1955), pp. 16–17.

Teachers in the Confraternity of Christian Doctrine and also in its Manuals[43] the following points are stressed: story, picture, doctrine, practice, prayer. In the series of textbooks appearing under the title *Living My Religion,* we find positive presentation which may or may not begin with a scriptural passage; points for classroom discussion and then various suggestions such as the following (varying with the individual lesson): suggestions for a pageant, questions for thoughtful boys and girls, points for discussion, etc.; in other words, no fast and set arrangement for every lesson but "learning by doing" in a way calculated to emphasize the matter that has been treated in the lesson.

In the most recent series of texts, *Our Holy Faith* (8 vols., Bruce Co.), we have a definite schema for the conclusions of its various lessons. For example, in the volume intended for grade three, we find a short prayer at the end of each lesson. This prayer offers a summary or résumé of it, adapted to the child's mentality. Then there follow: *Things To Be Remembered* (in which the chief points of the lesson are repeated, key words emphasized, and the knowledge-content stressed) and *Things To Be Done* (here are listed the values to be gained, applications to be made, rules for conduct to be emphasized, etc.). At the end of each unit is appended a study of such problems as are vital for a child or important for his moral life.

An important advance was made by putting a story or a description at the beginning of the lesson, instead of a theoretical presentation which developed theoretical ideas in logical fashion. The authors of the new German catechism, who at first tried another theory, finally adopted this solution.[44]

[43] These may be obtained from the Confraternity Publications, Paterson, N.J.; they are graded for class groupings under three headings: primary, intermediate, and upper (VI–VII–VIII).

[44] Cf. the preliminary trial texts which were distributed for criticism to experts in the field.

This meant of course that they had to dispense with the uniform presentation of the subject, progressing from one thought to another, from one lesson to the next. The lessons therefore form a consecutive but independent pattern, like pieces of a mosaic, which when put together result in a clear picture. But what is lost in such a procedure is richly compensated for by the advantages which accrue. The lesson has a point of departure which is capable of impressing and capturing the child's imagination such as the proper catechesis requires.[45] This is actually the objective at which catechesis aims, and the teaching that is presented has more of a chance not only of being understood, but also of being retained. The work of the ordinary lay catechists and especially of parents, is essentially lightened. Indeed, the cooperation of the latter only thus becomes possible; for only few are capable of putting into different words something that is first taught in abstract terms. Anyone, however, can tell a story. Of course, the example chosen should not only be related to the instructive matter of the lesson but should contain at least its central theme which is not always true of the French Catechism, even in its revised version of 1947.

In general it is fitting that the example be drawn from scripture. The words of the Bible, as coming from God, are weightier than mere human words. But the nature of the subject-matter in the catechism, unlike that of the school Bible, will often necessitate that only a résumé, a synthesis of scripture be given, and not the full biblical version (for example, in the sections on Christology: Christ's testimony of himself, the miraculous cures); but the demand that a biblical example should be used cannot obviously, be a hard and fast rule. In treating the sacra-

[45] Without doubt a certain restraint is placed on the catechist. But whereas the book sketches a happening only in bold strokes, it is left to the catechist to develop and to make it vivid. Furthermore, he is free to choose another example, should he so desire.

ments, the external rites which of themselves are essentially symbolic, will offer the most natural means of illustration. In teaching the moral code the example of some saint canonized by the Church will have enough dignity to illustrate the Christian ideal in the catechism.

Of great importance is the final section of the "lesson unit" which deals with the practical application for life. In this the German Catechism contributes greatly to the religious education of the children. In connection with the model of the French catechism of 1938, with its hard and fast scheme—in the catechism of 1947 only the order is changed—we may ask whether all parts of the scheme need to be incorporated into every lesson. In a lesson devoted to the seventh commandment, we can surely dispense with a reference to the liturgy. Exercises and applied tasks can sometimes be merged into one without harm. A number of hints appropriate to the subject matter of each lesson would be preferable.

The repeated application to life which is contained in the conclusion of each lesson and especially the narrative at the beginning furnish us with a rich source of inspiration for the illustration of the catechism. In German-speaking countries the Austrian Catechism of 1930 was the first to make moderate use of pictures. Again, in Canisius, especially in his smaller catechisms, pictures were never entirely lacking.[46] Today the catechism cannot dispense with pictures for the simple reason that it would otherwise become inferior to the textbooks which are

[46] Consult the edition of the Canisius catechisms of Streicher, (see above p. 21), especially the survey of the pictures Vol. I, pp. 74f. In the same volume, Vol. I, pp. 273–298, the reproduction of the catechism printed at Antwerp in 1598 which on every page presents the reader with a picture and a few lines of text in explanation. From a pedagogical standpoint the illustration of these ancient catechisms is not always exemplary, especially if, when treating of the commandments, sins are graphically depicted, and the children are warned not to commit them.

used in the secular branches. Furthermore, intrinsic reasons both of a pedagogical and didactic nature demand the use of pictures in the elementary religious text books, and all the more so when the educational aspect must be stressed. It is difficult to understand why pictures should decorate the pages of Bible History, and not those of the catechism. On this point, however, we must make a distinction. In the catechism, even in those instances in which it treats of events related in the Bible, we are concerned not simply with recalling the historical scene but rather with stressing its supernatural character, or its meaning for the divine plan of redemption. A symbolical treatment in the design of catechism pictures can therefore be used to advantage.[47]

From what we have said it follows that the answers to be memorized form the backbone also in the "lesson unit" catechisms. They should, however, be as short and concise as possible. Insofar as it is compatible with clarity, the language of the Bible should be used in preference to the language of theology. Definitions should not as a rule be phrased in the form of a "What is" question, but should be worded in such a way that they represent a statement concerning an effect or a cause, that is to say, by a "What happened" question. Care should be taken to ensure that they flow rhythmically.[48]

By their nature the parts that are to be memorized are least subject to modifications. They form the most stable part of the catechism. Only improvements which are manifestly required justify the departure from traditional formulations. On the other hand, whatever precedes or follows in the text, the parts to be memorized can be changed more readily, precisely because

[47] In this respect the pictures in the catechism of Burkart furnish us with a solution.

[48] This point did not escape the attention of Marie Fargues. See "Catechism Recitatives" in *Lumen Vitae,* Vol. 5 (1950), pp. 605–609; E. Dubois, *Catechism in Verse* (St. Paul: Catechetical Guild, 1952).

they are drawn from life and must be applied to life in all its fullness. This implies that it is quite possible to have separate books for the parts to be memorized and for the other material without foregoing the advantages of the "lesson unit" catechism; these can be preserved to a great extent through recourse to equivalent forms. Countries which still adhere to question and answer catechisms have already created such forms. In the United States the Baltimore catechism, which in 1895 was adopted by a majority of dioceses, was revised and republished with only a few improvements and additions in content in 1941. This catechism consisted exclusively of question and answer in graded editions, adapted to the upper and lower levels of the elementary school. At the end of each edition is contained the following note: "These catechisms are doctrinal summaries of religion and a basis for pedagogic textbooks, which will be prepared as courses of religion by capable and experienced theologians or catechetical teachers."[49] Actually such textbooks have appeared (for example, McGuire-Horan); they were designed for the pupils. In them the matter required for the various grades is culled from the catechism and supplemented by a variety of additions, which enable the pupil to understand both the words and the content of the text, and ensure its retention by the memory through a variety of prescribed tasks. Bible stories and prayer formulas are employed as well as pictures.[50]

[49] The difficulties which are raised on this point have been anticipated and answered by Raab, III–26.—In addition to a stable catechism Raab demands a "work book" or a children's newspaper.

[50] F. M. Willam, *Der Lehrstück-Katechismus,* pp. 69–98 takes passages from the textbooks of McGuire (1941) and of Horan (1945); he claims that they are *Lehrstück-Katechismen.*—Holland has also embarked on this course. For the new question and answer catechism of 1948, portions are selected for the various classes. These extracts are then provided with explanations and with pictures if possible. *Lumen Vitae,* Vol. 4 (1949), p. 351.

Hence we can say that nothing stands in the way of developing these textbooks into "lesson unit" catechisms, understood in our sense of the word, even though in them attention is directed primarily to learning. But in that case they do not possess any official character as do the catechisms upon which they draw.

England also has held fast to its traditional question and answer catechism. But since (in its public, independent and state-subsidized Catholic schools) a religion period is provided for daily, and since great diligence is being shown in developing better methods for the catechists, and in a better training of them personally, it is possible to use almost every means to enliven the subject matter, and to permit a "lesson unit" catechism to be arranged by the children themselves. Whatever the catechist imparts in the way of clarifying, summarizing and of evaluating the instructional matter is written concisely on the blackboard. This is then entered by the children into their notebooks and is there enriched by their personal contributions varying according to their ability. In this notebook the matter entered is illustrated by drawings and by pictures which are pasted in at the appropriate places. In this respect the children's environmental heritage furnishes important data.[51] In England this takes the place of the "lesson unit" catechism.

A newspaper for children has also been suggested as possible for the performance of these functions.[52] This must, however, conform to the official syllabus and should, perhaps, in correlation with the chief divisions of the catechism, be graded for a three-year span. This would offer to the children everything that is calculated to enliven the content of the catechism and to

[51] F. H. Drinkwater, "Home-Made Catechisms" *Lumen Vitae,* Vol. 5 (1950), pp. 419–425.

[52] Raab, pp. 212–215. The U.S.A. has two newspapers of this kind at the present: *The Catholic Messenger* (Little, Young and Junior) (Dayton: Geo. A. Pflaum); *Mine* (Minneapolis, Minn.: Publications for Catholic Youth) (also in a similar three-fold division).

elevate the sentiments of the child to God: stories and descriptions, poetry and prose, pictures and symbols, prize essays and contests. Basically this proposal was realized in the newspapers published for first communicants in Germany at the turn of the 19th century. These, meant for children of the twelve to thirteen age group, enjoyed great popularity. Today they seem doomed because of early First Communion.[53]

In conclusion, we must ask whether a "lesson unit" catechism is superfluous. To this we may reply that such a catechism is not the only possible solution, but it is the best way of attaining the objective we have been discussing and have outlined. Without it, the less imaginative catechists would soon revert to a mere explanation of the texts to be memorized. As far as replacements for it are concerned, experience has shown that they have never been able to be used by all the children, nor in all the schools. On the other hand, place can always be found alongside the "lesson unit" catechism for the work-book and for newspapers. Finally, the book should not only serve to help the children to rediscover by means of repetition at home the skeleton of the catechesis; it should also bring to life the spiritual values and driving force which were contained in it.[54]

Questions of Internal Form

More important than the questions dealing with the external form of the catechism are those which are focused on its internal structure, on the choice and the arrangement of Chris-

[53] J. Solzbacher, "Zeitschriften für Erstkommunikanten?" in *KBl,* Vol. 76 (1951), pp. 489–492.—The religious newspapers for children which appear in connection with a definite weekly or diocesan paper, e. g., *Our Sunday Visitor,* and do not have any close ties with any definite catechism, may be pressed into service.

[54] In this sense read the final judgement of G. Delcuve and P. Ranwez on the new attempts to write a new catechism. *Lumen Vitae,* Vol. 5 (1950) "The Catechism Textbook - Conclusions", pp. 619–632.

tian doctrine, by which it can best fulfill its task of transmitting the "good news" of faith. The transformation of the traditional catechism into a "lesson unit" catechism leaves untouched the sequence and the wording of the matter to be learned by heart. We have actually become acquainted with "lesson unit" catechisms of a kind which simply modify the inherited question and answer form in consonance with norms both formal and methodological, and in this way succeed in vitalizing them educatively.

Increased knowledge and fuller experience, however, have awakened us to the realization that this reform in formal methodology hardly completes half the task. We must re-examine fundamentals and attempt a material-kerygmatic reformation.[55] In doing so we should not think it strange that only after a catechetical history embracing more than four centuries, our own age is the first to become fully aware of the need for this task. As long as the child was surrounded by a Christian atmosphere, not only in the family but also in the

[55] The terminology: a "formal methodological" reform and "material-kerygmatic" is taken from F. X. Arnold who in his two works: *Dienst am Glauben* (1948) and *Grundsätzliches und Geschichtliches zur Theologie der Seelsorge* (1949) highlights the importance of the reform in question from the viewpoint both of history and of theology. Compare this also to: Th. Kampmann, *Die Gegenwartsgestalt der Kirche und die christliche Erziehung* (Paderborn, 1951). In the same sense F. Weber concludes his *Geschichte des Katechismus in der Diözese Rottenburg* (1939) by calling attention to this task: "The catechism which we are looking for is a book which, within a framework that is essentially Christian, presents the mysteries of faith and the economy of redemption in its entirety, as the essential laws of the Christian 'message' demand."—The "Conclusions" which we have just mentioned in the above footnote (the number of the *Lumen Vitae* was devoted solely to the catechism) draws our attention to the danger which confronts us in a catechism which is based exclusively on the psychology of the child and his needs: it would be a catechism in which not only the doctrine of the sacraments but also dogma itself would be subordinated to moral (p. 626).

community, and received a Christian formation through his environment, it was sufficient for catechism and catechesis, no matter how indifferently employed, to communicate to the child the necessary knowledge. The lack of the educative factor was not noticeable. Since the auxiliary educative forces of former ages have disappeared, the defects of the old catechism became increasingly evident.[56] To these defects we must turn our attention.

The traditional catechism both in its choice of subject matter and in its construction was dominated by two factors, which were without any supernatural importance. The first was the medieval enthusiasm for enumerations and for formulas divided into numbered parts. Catechisms consequently betrayed a marked preference for divisions. In addition to the Apostles' Creed, which was made difficult to understand because earlier it had been divided into twelve articles, the pupils were compelled to learn up to twenty other formulas of which the majority belonged to the moral order, and in this way the emphasis was placed on morality rather than dogma.[57] The other determining factor was the continuous defensive against, and complete preoccupation with, heresy, which was understandable in the sixteenth century, but which has actually been retained in catechisms down to the present. The points of

[56] F. M. Willam, *Katechetische Erneuerung,* p. 83.

[57] Cf. above p. 12. In the *Christianae doctrinae latior explicatio* of Bellarmine (among others, 1711) the construction of the catechism is determined to a great extent by the catechetical formulas. Besides the Creed, the Lord's Prayer and the Hail Mary there appear as independent chapters: decalogue, commandments of the Church, evangelical counsels, sacraments, the theological virtues, the cardinal virtues, the gifts of the Holy Ghost, the eight beatitudes, the seven corporal and the seven spiritual works of mercy, the seven capital sins, the six sins against the Holy Ghost, the four sins that cry to heaven for vengeance, the four last things.—On the other hand the *Catechismus Romanus* of set purpose broke away from the servitude to these formulas.

doctrine which were assailed by the heretics were not only explained and defended, but they were accorded a prominent place in the book: faith as assent to truth,[58] the hierarchical concept of the Church,[59] the Real Presence of Christ in the Eucharist,[60] the meritoriousness of good works, etc. In general, the truths of faith were considered preponderantly from the viewpoint of human action and of duty. Edmund Auger is the forerunner of that arrangement of the catechism which by way of Deharbe has predominated in a majority of more modern catechisms. He begins with a question on the goal of man and develops from its answer the captions which serve as divisions of the book itself. In order to reach our goal, we must: 1. believe what God has revealed; 2. keep the commandments; 3. make use of the means of grace.[61] In such an arrangement Christianity appears to be nothing more than a number of obligations by which we are bound, whereas in reality it is characterized in Scripture itself as "good news of great joy". Christianity appears to consist of a series of actions, which we are called upon to perform, whereas in reality it is a great work of God's grace. Everything that is presented in this catechism

[58] F. X. Arnold, *Dienst am Glauben,* pp. 26f. and passim.

[59] M. Ramsauer, "Die Kirche in den Katechismen" in *ZkTh,* Vol. 73 (1951), pp. 129–169; 313–346; E. A. Ryan, "Three Early Treatises on the Church" in *Theological Studies,* Vol. 5 (1944), pp. 113–141.

[60] F. X. Arnold, *Vorgeschichte und Einfluss des Trienter Messopferdekretes auf die Behandlung des eucharistischen Geheimnisses in der Glaubensverkündigung der Neuzeit: Die Messe in der Glaubensverkündigung* (Freiburg: Herder, 1950), pp. 114–161.

[61] Cf. J. Hofinger, "Die rechte Gliederung des katechetischen Lehrstoffes" in *Lumen Vitae,* Vol. 2 (1947), pp. 719–746, especially p. 720. This article is a synopsis of a still greater study made by the author: *De apta divisione materiae catecheticae, Collectanea Commissionis Synodalis,* Vol. 13 (Peking, 1940), pp. 583–599; 729–749; 845–859; Vol. 14 (Peking, 1941), pp. 1–16; J. Hofinger, "Should the Customary Arrangement of the Catechism be Changed?" in *Catholic School Journal,* Vol. 55 (Jan., 1955), pp. 3–5.

is correct, but it only glances at man's needs, his searching and his endeavours; it is a subjective and narrow aspect of divine reality. By such an arrangement the pupil can never attain to a full and unbroken vista of the magnificent plan of man's redemption.[62] Because the true adversary of the Catholic Christian is today no longer any specific heresy but complete unbelief, it is important that upon the soul of the child be imprinted a clear and striking insight into the faith as a whole. To achieve this it will be found worthwhile to give an overall survey in the very beginning of the book, especially if it can be broached in fitting imagery and not in abstract statement. For this purpose the parables of the kingdom of God are especially suitable and in particular the comprehensive parable of the great banquet. The invitation of the heavenly Father extended, through his only-begotten Son and his ambassadors, to the whole of mankind which must decide whether it will foolishly seek excuses to absent itself or gratefully accept.[63]

More important than this introduction is the view of the

[62] W. Pichler (*Katechismus der katholischen Religion,* edition for catechists [Vienna, 1928], pp. XXI–XXII) does not advance beyond this position, since he uses as its basic thought the phrase: "Serve God".—The Austrian course of study, sad to say, adopted the recommendation of Pichler, because it uses for the graduating class the synopsis of the chief articles of faith under the headings: Profession of Faith (Why I should serve God), the Commandments (How God wishes us to serve Him), Sacraments and Prayer (Means of serving God).

[63] It is a justifiable demand that the "kingdom of God" and the "kingdom of Heaven" be employed in the full biblical sense in catechesis and hence also at the beginning of the catechism: as the manifestation of the sovereignty of Christ, as the state of perfection of the people of God at the end of the world. But we can and we ought to attach to this purely temporal view—or more exactly to this eschatological and universal view—and to use, as far as circumstances permit, the usual spatial representations of "heaven" as "the dwelling place of God" and as "the place of sentence which awaits all men" (Men can find this "door closed", Mt. 25, 11 sq.); in the parable of the Great

whole. If, as we have just attempted to make clear, we should not start with the subjective accomplishments which are demanded of us to obtain eternal salvation, it is equally incorrect to begin with the notion of faith and with the sources of revelation, no matter how well such themes seem to fit in with the logical order of the theological system. Figuratively speaking, we should not first of all draw the children's attention to the telescope with which they can search the heavens but to the magnificent world of God into which they are permitted to look with the eyes of faith.[64] What should be offered to the children in the catechism as a synopsis of Christian doctrine is, no the one hand, a presentation of all that God has done and is still doing for us, and on the other, a presentation of the reply which we should give to God by conforming our conduct to the Christian ideal.[65] That the Christian moral code, even in the catechism, should form a separate subject of instruction and as such should be separated from dogma has always been acknowledged; what is

Banquet both these views converge. Cf. R. Schnackenburg, "Zum Reich-Gottes-Begriff in der Katechese" in *KBl,* Vol. 72 (1947), pp. 33–39; F. J. Schierse, "Himmelsehnsucht und Reich-Gottes-Erwartung" in *Geist und Leben,* Vol. 26 (1953), pp. 189–210; Th. Filthaut. *op. cit.* (cf. p. 30 above); the more restrictive viewpoints are emphasized by H. Mayer, *KBl,* Vol. 72 (1947), pp. 322–323. R. A. Dyson and A. Jones, *The Kingdom of Promise* (London: Burns, Oates & Washbourne, 1947), pp. 174–180. St. Matthew's Gospel is sometimes called the Gospel of the Kingdom of God.

[64] The teaching on faith, on its importance and its conditions, are integrated in an organic fashion into the doctrine of the Church: we become members of the Church by our faith and by the reception of Baptism.—The Catechism of Gasparri does not speak at all about the sources of faith in his catechism for children; only in the catechism for adults is a chapter dedicated to "Divine Revelation" (QQ 12–29); in H. Pope (trans.), *The Catholic Catechism* (New York: P. J. Kenedy, 1932), pp. 12–29; 66–69.

[65] Cf. Hofinger, "Our Message" in *Lumen Vitae,* Vol. 5 (1950), pp. 277–294. These ideas are fully developed in the same author's *The Art of Teaching Christian Doctrine* (University of Notre Dame Press, 1957).

much more difficult is the division which must be made in both types of subject matter, especially in the doctrines of faith.

An arrangement which would be useful in catechesis can manifestly not be made simply by joining together doctrinal points in a purely arbitrary fashion; nor does a purely logical arrangement appear to be sufficient. A strictly scientific system also no longer suffices. The arrangement should rather afford a view of the whole, should be easily understandable, but at the same time it should be inspired by the nature of the subject matter itself.[66] These conditions would be fulfilled, and the chief chapters of belief would be joined together in an easily comprehended sequence, if the redemption of the world by Christ and ultimately the Person of Christ Himself were to become the focal point upon which everything converges.[67]

The Apostles, and especially St. Paul, presented the Christian message in just this way. St. Paul designated as the object of his "good news" "the mystery of Christ", or "the gospel of Christ" (2 Cor. 2, 12; 9, 13; 10, 14), and on all sides he makes all his lines of thought converge on this focal point. From all eternity the economy of redemption was based on the advent of Christ; in Him God wished "to re-establish all things" both those in heaven and those on earth (Eph. 1, 10). With Him the new creation begins: the life and activity of the Church, the sacraments, forgiveness of sins, the life of grace, final transfiguration are nothing more than effects of His redemptive act.

[66] J. Hofinger, "In what order should religious truths be presented?" in *Lumen Vitae,* Vol. 2 (1947), pp. 726f.

[67] *Ibid.,* pp. 738ff.—J. A. Jungmann, *Christus als Mittelpunkt religiöser Erziehung* (Freiburg: Herder, 1939); *ibid.,* "Die Stellung Christi in Katechese und Predigt" in *ChPBl,* Vol. 66 (1953), pp. 65–71; A. O'Connor, "Christocentrism, The Core of Integration" in *Catholic Educational Review,* Vol. 49 (1951), pp. 390–395; W. H. Russell, "Possibilities in Christo-centrism for Mental Health" in *The Catholic Educational Review,* Vol. 45 (1947), pp. 209–218; 279–287.

As a result of the careful ordering of these associated parts the good news character of the dogmatic structure will be made apparent. Through unswerving concentration on what is taught the chances are that the children will remember at least the basic facts of the Christian faith, even under the most unfavourable circumstances. Through the awe-inspiring Person of our Lord, who can be discerned behind each single doctrine, the act of faith will be made easier even when it encounters special obstacles; for every obscurity is ultimately only that mystery which surrounds His Person. On the other hand it is precisely the Person of our Saviour who not only towers above history but, in a very tangible way, dominates also the present, serving as a foundation for faith. Christian doctrine is not a human invention, but His own word. By stressing His personal character, by making clear that in Him we are dealing ultimately not with something but with someone, we meet the need of youth to follow someone. Such a need can be satisfied only by that one Person who is most worthy of youthful enthusiasm.

In doing this we should not stress Christ-centredness unnaturally. It would not only be absurd to deduce the entire content of moral teaching down to its subtlest ramification from the example and teaching of Christ; but also in Christian doctrine it would be impossible to evolve what is taught about God simply from Christology. It should rather precede it,[68] just as the preaching of Christ and the Apostles began with a reference to the eternal decree of God the Father. The various ways of arriving at a natural knowledge of God must be sketched and made understandable, even though the notion

[68] This holds true of a catechism for children. Eugen Fischer in his *Christenlehre* (Colmar, 1944), which is designed for adults, presents the whole of the dogmatic doctrine under the title "Listen to Jesus", and then follows it with his doctrine on the sacraments.

of God that is acquired by such a train of thought can only germinate from the words of our Lord Himself.

Christ-centredness will, however, have to be expressed throughout the entire content of revealed doctrine. To do this we must, at the very beginning, draw a striking picture of the Person of our Lord. It is not enough if in the catechism we speak only of two natures, of the facts of His birth in Bethlehem, His passion, death, burial, and resurrection, and then finally of the infinite merit of His death on the Cross. The historical course of Christ's life is delineated more vividly in Bible History. Through the catechism we must make the children conscious of the redemptive value of the Person and work of our Saviour. This can be accomplished to a certain extent by an explanation of the Names "Jesus", "Christ", "our Lord".[69] The traditional symbols for his Person may also be employed here with profit. It is permissible for the purposes of recapitulation to refer to the most important figures of the Old Testament as has been done in several catechisms. Comparison with the first Adam permits Christ to appear as the new Adam, as the founder of the new Chosen People of God. Furthermore, in this connection we can sketch summarily and in rough outlines the public life of Jesus, and at the same time illustrate briefly His teaching, His human nature, His passion and death, in the sacrifice of redemption, by which He exercises His priestly office. His resurrection must not be treated from the apologetic point of view only and as a guarantee of our own bodily resurrection, but rather as the crowning work of His redemption. In it we are shown the glory which He acquired for us and which is

[69] This expression which is both Pauline and biblical is used all too little in German, whereas in other modern languages it is employed frequently, e. g., "Our Lord", "Notre Seigneur", "Nostro Signore". This title expresses the dignity of κύριος as well as the fact that we belong to him.

implicit in that grace which embraces us all.[70] His transfiguration in the resurrection and the ascension will then also be the revelation of His royal nature.

Christ-centredness will need to be especially remembered in those chapters which deal with the Christian means of salvation: Church, grace and sacraments. For a true concept of the Church it is important that we present it as a community of those who belong to and share in the life of Christ,[71] before we explain its organizational and hierarchical character. If we should content ourselves with saying that Christ founded the Church, we would by that statement reduce the Church to simple earthly dimensions.[72] To understand the Church properly it is important to place Christ in the consciousness of the faithful as He who continues to live on in transfigured human-

[70] A layman expresses the importance of this theme in a striking fashion: "We must awaken in Christians, in fact in all men, the understanding that the transfiguration of the Redeemer is the symbol and the proclamation of the transfiguration of both man and nature." G. Papini, *The Letters of Pope Celestine VI to All Mankind* (New York; E. P. Dutton, 1948), p. 97.—The dominant position of the message of resurrection in the preaching of primitive Christianity is underlined by H. Schürmann, *Aufbau und Struktur der neutestamentlichen Verkündigung* (Paderborn: F. Schöningh, 1949).—That the resurrection of Christ must be considered to be at least the *causa exemplaris* of our justification is clear from a number of passages from the Epistles of St. Paul; it may also be looked upon as an efficient-cause relationship. L. Lercher, *Institutiones theol. dogm.,* Vol. III (3rd ed.; Innsbruck: Rauch, 1942), pp. 215ff. As a consequence quite logically he treats of the *momentum kerygmaticum* of the Paschal miracle in connection with it (pp. 218f.).

[71] Ramsauer, *op. cit.,* pp. 340ff.; cf. also the special number of *Lumen Vitae,* Vol. 8 (1953), "The Sense of the Church" and especially those articles which purpose "To develop the Sense of the Church at the Different Stages of Life." pp. 398–486.

[72] Cf. the fate of the notion of the Church in the era of enlightenment; Ramsauer, *op. cit.,* pp. 316ff; G. Weigel, "The Body of Christ and the City of God" in *Social Order,* Vol. 5 (1955), pp. 271–275; R. Hasseveldt, *The Church, A Divine Mystery* (Chicago: Fides, 1954).

ity; in this way, He appears as the Head of the Church and we are His Mystical Body, notions which today may be inserted into the catechism.

The ecclesiastical functions can be made much more understandable and be put in a more correct light, if they are described as continuations of the functions of Christ: in the teaching office of the Church, His teaching office lives on; in priestly activity, His own priesthood; in government, His own omnipotence.[73] Thus it will easily become evident that the fulness of divine power continues to be exercised by and in the Church.

In most catechisms of the past century the teaching on grace and the sacraments has always been treated in an independent section separated from the doctrine on faith by another section devoted to the commandments. This placing, coming as it does after the moral code, might create the impression that both grace and the sacraments were considered merely as helps to enable men to lead moral lives. This impression was further deepened by the fact that their presentation was prefaced by a lesson on actual grace. In this way the supernaturalness of the life of grace became obscured in the Christian consciousness; and this obscurity is in no sense changed by including the word "supernatural" in the definition of grace.

This can be remedied, however, by reverting to an earlier method: grace and the sacraments belong to that subject matter which centres on the creed. In them the work of redemption becomes fruitful for us. In Baptism the spark of divine life leaps from Christ to us. The Holy Ghost who indwells in Him, takes up His abode in us and sanctifies us.[74] We become (adopted) children of God alongside Him, who is the first-born.

[73] Cf. the presentation in the new German catechism and in addition that of F. Schreibmayr, "Organischer Aufbau im Katechismus" in *KBl*, Vol. 72 (1947), p. 261.

[74] Just as we speak of the sanctifying action of Christ and of the Holy

All these insights into the Christological structure of grace and of the sacraments will be guaranteed us naturally if the doctrine of grace and the sacraments follows upon that section which expounds the dogmatic teaching in accordance with the order of the Creed, as is done in the Tridentine catechism. This goal, however, would be attained much more readily, if the doctrine of grace and the sacraments in general should be treated within the framework of the Creed, as St. Thomas does it. The Angelic Doctor deals with the seven sacraments in connection with the article of faith: *sanctorum communionem.*[75] But such a sequence is not absolutely necessary; without it we can still indicate their relation to Christ. In any case, it is not sufficient when treating of the sacraments simply to attribute their institution to Christ. The theological proposition, that in the sacraments Christ acts through a human instrument, should not be neglected in the catechism; nor should the other thought be omitted, namely, that in the sacraments, especially Baptism, we are made to share in the sufferings and in the resurrection of Christ.[76]

To God's condescension in the work of redemption and of salvation, we, the redeemed, must give an apt answer in prayer and in a Christian conduct of life. Here, where we are no longer

Spirit, we might ask ourselves the question: how can these two notions be brought into accord in catechesis so that they can be understood by the children? On this subject, consult Kl. Tilmann, "Was ist 'organischer Aufbau' im Religions-Unterricht?" in *KBl,* Vol. 66 (1940), p. 4, where he suggests that we use the comparsion between a person and his hand: of both we are able to say the same thing: I grasp, or the hand grasps this book; M. J. Scheeben (C. Vollert, trans.), *Nature and Grace* (St. Louis: Herder, 1954), pp. 201–203.

[75] *Opusc. de expositione Symboli* (see above p. 15, footnote no. 37).

[76] R. Graber, *Christus in seinen heiligen Sakramenten* (München, 1937), p. 15: "The accusation of magic could never have been made against the sacraments, if in their exposition emphasis had been placed on their personal, living connection with Christ's death and resurrection."

concerned with gaining knowledge of the meaning of the works of God, where we are no longer preoccupied with obtaining a clarified picture of the world of faith, but with our actions, with our practical conduct, a definite order of topics is no longer of the same importance as it was before.[77] But here again we should not let order be a matter of indifference. Our first answer to God is prayer. Only when prayer is looked upon as an answer to God's call of grace does the meaning of the prayer of thanksgiving and of praise become apparent.[78] And the common prayer of the redeemed, the liturgy of the Church, must assume a place of primary importance. There are catechisms which devote a special chapter to the liturgy.[79] In any case it is not especially of advantage, if, as has been the case in the catechism tradition of Austria, prayer is appended, in the second section entitled "Of hope and prayer", to the virtue of hope. This means that only prayers of petition can be considered. We must say almost the same thing about the German catechisms since Deharbe, in which prayer is presented with the sacraments as a means of grace only. The classical model of all prayer, the Lord's Prayer, gives in a different order the things for which we are to pray.

The moral teaching of many catechisms has often been the target of criticism, namely that it has remained at the level of the Old Testament.[80] It goes without saying that this is due to

[77] Cf. Hofinger, "In What Order Should Religious Truths Be Presented?" in *Lumen Vitae,* Vol. 2 (1947), pp. 721 f.

[78] Cf. Hofinger, in *Lumen Vitae,* Vol. 2 (1947), p. 738.

[79] Among others in France, the catechism of Bossuet. Concerning the German catechisms which devote a special chapter to the liturgy (to ceremonies and the liturgical year), cf. Hofinger, *Geschichte des Katechismus in Österreich,* pp. 176 f.—Sailer wanted a catechism constructed on the basis of dogma, morals and liturgy.

[80] Consult especially the study of H. Woroniecki, "La place des préceptes de charité dans l'enseignement du catéchisme" in *Angelicum,* Vol.

joining the teaching of morality to the Decalogue. The ancient Church as well as that of the early Middle Ages did not use the Decalogue as a basis for their catecheses on morality.[81] In this respect the Tridentine catechism, too, betrayed a weakness: it restricted itself to an explanation of the Ten Commandments.[82] Admittedly, St. Thomas had done the same thing, but at least he had placed the double commandment of charity at the beginning of the Ten Commandments.[83] Canisius followed him in this respect. One cannot condemn outright the fact that Christian moral teaching is joined to a formula of such authority as the Decalogue. It offers only too many advantages for catechesis, not the least of which is a hard and fast written scheme for the examination of consciences. Such a jointure should, however, be expounded and deepened by relating it to the New Testament, as our Lord Himself did in His Sermon on the Mount (Mt. 5, 21 ff.).

25 (Rome, 1948), pp. 18–26; C. E. Elwell, "In Character Education What Habits Shall We Build?" in *Catholic Educational Review,* Vol. 40 (1942), pp. 523–528.

[81] In any case in the primitive Church besides the doctrine of the *Two Ways,* the Decalogue was also employed on occasion. R.M. Grant, "The Decalogue in Early Christianity" in *Harvard Theological Review,* Vol. 40 (1947), pp. 1–17. F. X. Eggersdorfer, *Der hl. Augustinus als Pädagoge* (Freiburg: Herder, 1907), pp. 164–168, shows that although Augustine valued the Decalogue highly, he did not use it as the basis of his instructions on morals.—For the subsequent centuries consult F. J. Peters, "Der Dekalog im katechetischen Unterricht" in *KBl,* Vol. 57 (1931), pp. 434–445; E. Kurz, "Pflichtenlehre und Dekalog" in *KBl,* Vol. 72 (1947), pp. 193–197; F. Bläker, *Joh. B. v. Hirscher und seine Katechismen* (*Untersuchungen zur Theologie der Seelsorge,* 6) (Freiburg: Herder, 1953), pp. 205–209. Only in the fifteenth century did the decalogue become the basic outline for morality and the confessions of sins, see J. Greving, "Zum vorreformatorischen Beichtunterricht" in *Festgabe A. Knöpfler zur Vollendung des 60. Lebensjahres* (Munich: J. J. Lentner'sche Buchhandlung, 1907), pp. 46–81.

[82] See Woroniecki, *op. cit.,* pp. 18 f.

[83] *Opusculum* 35: "De duobus praeceptis charitatis et decem legis praeceptis" (Mandonnet IV, 413–455) (Shapcoate, pp. 1–27).

Another complaint against a catechesis based on the Decalogue springs from the negative formulation of moral standards: "Thou shalt not." The expansion of such a formulation in many catechisms actually led to moral doctrine becoming a teaching on sin. The too intimate connection with moral theology, such as the confessor requires for the exercise of his office, has promoted this development. The negative formulation of the commandments need by no means confine moral teaching to negations. Thus it was not necessary for the German uniform catechism of 1925 to try to pass this difficulty by going to the opposite extreme of re-formulating the Decalogue in positive terms.[84] It is truly sublime to think that God bestowed upon us freedom and limited us in its use only by some distant boundary where a "Thou shalt not" warns us of transgression. In fact, in many domains He refrained entirely from revealing either command or prohibition; He simply gave us the light of reason by which we were to find our own way and were to deduce from the nature of things the order which we were to follow. In a simplified form the concept of an order based on creation as the foundation of morality can be evaluated in the catechism: God is the Lord of the world, but He has placed man over it as its steward; man has all creation at his disposal, but he must use it correctly, not abuse it.[85] Taught in this way, the moral order will be firmly enrooted

[84] By means of titles such as "Be subject to God", "Fulfill your vows", "Be truthful".—A morality based on the Christian virtues such as St. Thomas Aquinas presents differs greatly from this (cf. *Summa theol.* IIa, IIae).Today the writings of Josef Pieper are collected and appeared in abridgement in J. Pieper, "Über das christliche Menschenbild" in *Hochland,* Vol. 33 (1936), pp. 97–111. In this regard: R. MacEachen, *The Teaching of Religion* (New York: Macmillan, 1921), pp. 79–90; E. Reichert, "Taking the 'No' out of the Commandments" in *Catholic Educator,* Vol. 20 (1949/50), pp. 164–165.

[85] Cf. *Auf dem Wege zu einem neuen Katechismus,* p. 65. This idea

in the consciousness of the child and of the adolescent, because it becomes evident to them that the moral laws are not arbitrary commandments, which God has decreed because of his absolute omnipotence, as nominalism had asserted. Conversely, the notion of God, developed by this view, is full of warmth and acquires an appealing grandeur, because it makes clear that God demands only what is good and just. His holiness thus becomes a living concept. In addition, the children of God have an opportunity to find the answers for their questions: what is best? what belongs to the perfect service of God? There is room for an upsurge of love, for the asceticism which, in moral training, must undoubtedly supplement the negative moral law.[86]

has been incorporated very well into the catechism of F. M. Willam, *Unser Weg zu Gott* (Innsbruck, 1951), especially pp. 395 f.

[86] Concerning the Situation in England see Appendix IV.

V

THE TEACHING PLAN

1. *Principles for a Teaching Plan*

IF the task of catechetics is to be fulfilled correctly, the order in which the varied subjects of catechesis are to be taught to children during the time that is at the disposal of the teacher must not be left to caprice or chance. Under conditions prevailing in German-speaking countries, where regular catechesis is given within the framework of the denominational schools, the time allotted to children's catechesis coincides with the years of compulsory school attendance, hence, for a great number of children, with the eight years of the elementary school.[1] But the position within the frame-work of the school system varies. In practically all the German Länder the denominational state-schools allot up to four periods weekly to the religion teacher. In Austria the State school is an interdenominational school. This type of school, if it is not influenced by peculiarly local conditions, does not purpose to give anything more than a broad general moral and religious education. Religious instruction is, therefore, limited to two periods a week.[2]

[1] More precisely: in Austria there are four years of elementary school and four more years either of elementary school or "Hauptschule" (the latter with different teachers for different subjects); in Germany there are eight years of elementary school, of which the first four are of "the common foundation school" *(Grundschule)*: I. L. Kandel, *Comparative Education* (Boston: Houghton Mifflin Co., 1933), pp. 140–142.

[2] On the other hand in the Catholic schools of other countries such as the U.S.A., Belgium, Holland, England, Ireland, time is allotted for catechesis daily, lasting at least a half-hour.

The planning must take into consideration the degree of organization in the schools themselves. In the cities, because of the great number of children, it is usually possible to group the children in such a way that each class constitutes a definite grade. Educators speak of a school organized on these lines as a highly organized school.[3] On the other hand, in the country, the children of all eight grades must sometimes be crowded into one or two classes; these are called less highly organized schools. We must, furthermore, distinguish between the upper and the lower classes or grades. As a rule, educators describe the first four years as belonging to the lower grades. An intermediate grade, which would generally comprise the fourth and fifth years, is no longer considered practicable, and in some countries it is no longer taken into consideration.[4] Under German conditions the completion of the fourth grade regularly marks the time at which a majority of the pupils pass from a school of one type to a school of another type, such as High School or "Gymnasium" (Secondary Grammar Schools). Classes, which embrace more than one grade, are generally taken in the secular subjects in two separate groups. Catechetical training avoids as much as possible group instruction within a class. At the Catechetical Congress in Vienna there was general agreement that "If in one class several grades are mixed the rule to be followed is that the grades are to be instructed together on the same subject matter."[5] Only in a one-class school is the catechist forced, and

[3] W. C. Reavis *et al., The Elementary School* (Chicago: University Press, 1931), pp. 5–14.

[4] Down to the law of 1926 governing the *Hauptschule* in Austria, pupils were required to attend a municipal school consisting of three grades after they had completed five years in the elementary school, so that the fourth and the fifth classes may be looked upon as intermediate grades.

[5] *Bericht über die Verhandlungen des Kongresses für Katechetik II* (Vienna, 1913), p. 601.

then by necessity, to make a distinction between upper and lower grades, hence to divide the children into groups within the class (apart from occasionally giving, for a short time, separate attention to the infants of the first grade). While he instructs one group, the catechist usually occupies the other with some "silent activity".

The order in which the catechetical content is to be imparted to the children under various circumstances at any given time must also be specified in the teaching plan. By this name, teaching plan, we only want to emphasize the instructive element which should stand out prominently in the planning, but not to obscure the educative task inherent in catechesis. A teaching plan prescribed by competent authorities is necessary not only because of the number of children who change residence during their school life, but also because of the possible changes among the catechists. Moreover, the catechist is generally spared the time and trouble of doing his own planning. The task of preparing a teaching plan for catechesis was, even in the nineteenth century, considered to be the duty of episcopal authorities, as is natural in view of the task involved.[6]

Because of the numerous moves which a great many families are forced to undertake, it is desirable that a uniform teaching plan be prescribed not only for a single diocese but also on a national scale.[7] Sometimes such a teaching plan can be no

[6] For a broad survey of the basic problems as well as actual circumstances conditioning the course of studies at the turn of the century, consult J. E. Pichler and W. Pichler, *Lehrplan für den katholischen Religionsunterricht an den Volks- und Bürgerschulen Österreichs* (Vienna, 1904).

[7] Here are some of the programmes, official and semi-official for: France, Canada, Belgium, Switzerland, England and the U.S.A.: "Programme progressif d'enseignement religieux" *Documentation catéchistique* (Septembre, 1948): "Guide pour l'enseignement religieux et l'éducation chrétienne des enfants catholiques dans les écoles primaires d'Alsace" (Stras-

more than a framework into which the subject matter is roughly divided. These general divisions must be elaborated by the local teaching authority.

Teaching plans should not be absolutely immutable. They must be constantly adapted to circumstances, especially if a change is made in the school structure or in the choice of textbooks. These plans must, furthermore, be used with understanding as well as with discretion by the catechist. Precisely for these reasons it is necessary to throw some light on the principles which are employed in the construction of a teaching plan for catechesis.[7a] In planning and in creating a teaching plan several approaches are possible.

1. One method of preparing such a course considers the whole

bourg, *Direction diocésaine de l'enseignement*): "Programme d'études des écoles primaires élémentaires" (Montréal)—Programme et répartition de l'enseignement de la religion dans les écoles primaires communales du diocèse de Tournai (Tournai-Paris: Casterman, 1947). Le règlement pour l'enseignement religieux dans la Suisse romande (Dioceses of Lausanne, Geneva and Fribourg). "The Fulda 'Lehrplan'" in R. Bandas, *Catechetical Methods* (New York: J. F. Wagner, 1929), pp. 269–287; *Scheme of Religious Instruction* (a development of the *The Sower Scheme*), for the diocese of Birmingham (London: Burns, Oates & Washbourne, n. d.). In the U.S.A. there is no general scheme or course of study; the individual school system in the individual diocese makes its own choice or personally formulates its own course. For certain difficulties which beset the educator in the States as well as some of the principles to be followed, cf. W. McManus "Curriculum Building" in *Bulletin NCEA* (Feb., 1949), pp. 17–28; and also Sr. Maristella, "Basic Principles Permeating the Catholic Elementary Course of Study" in *NCEA-Proceedings and Addresses,* Vol. 47 (1950/51), pp. 419–426. A course of study which could be adapted generally for every diocese: E. A. Fitzpatrick, *A Curriculum in Religion* (Milwaukee: Bruce, 1931).

[7a] P. Hofer, "Die Technik des Religionslehrplanes für die Volksschule" in *Referate des Kongresses für Katechetik* (Vienna, 1912) pp. 29–53. In this study we can see the organization which existed at that time for the primary school in Austria (the fourth and fifth grades were considered to be intermediate).

of Christian doctrine as forming a unity which must be taught in every grade and in every year, a unity which grows with the mental capacity of the children, just as the rings in the trunk of a tree. This is the principle of concentric cycles. Earlie catechetics tended to divide the subject matter on the basis of this principle: the catechism of Felbiger (1777) appeared in a small, a medium and a large edition.[8] The same was done for other catechisms of this and subsequent periods. In these catechisms their authors set off by means of asterisks, or bold face letters, those questions which could be left out when the catechism was used for the first time. Teachers in those days expected even the smallest children to learn some of the catechism. From grade to grade and year to year, the amount of matter they were required to master grew apace. Up to the catechism reform of 1925–30 the catechisms continued to appear in two or three graded editions, as they still do in the United States.

With an increased understanding both of child psychology and of the pedagogical task which is involved in catechetical teaching, the judgement on the concentric cycle has undergone a change. True, for the learning of a set number of necessary questions or for a minimum of knowledge to be learned by heart, the concentric principle was of value. But there was always the danger that the doctrine presented always in the same way, and always in the same setting, would degenerate into a mere knowledge of words and of phrases. Besides, the reappearance of matter that had been taught several times before would inevitably dull the interest of the children, and the educative effect of the catechesis itself would be noticeably impeded. In addition the catechist, who is constantly forced to repeat matter that has already been treated, has scarcely any time at his disposal

[8] For further details, consult Hofinger, pp. 113–128.

to develop any one topic thoroughly or with it to appeal to the children's interest.

Thus, the principle of concentricity has even fallen into disrepute in the secular subjects. It served purely as a symbol of the authoritarian school, in opposition to the active school, which aims at true education. Only in certain subjects, as, for example, those in which a skill is to be exercised (languages) or in which a system of theorems is to be progressively taught, can we find justification for its use.[9] Taken in a broader sense, however, and applied in accordance with the psychological development of the children and with the subject matter, but not with a definite formula or with a specified series of topics, the concentric cycle is still of value both for the teaching of religion and for other subjects.[10] It permits us to take into account the actuality of what is being taught as well as the mental and spiritual make-up of each particular grade.

2. The successive method takes an exactly opposite course: the entire subject matter is treated only once in the time allotted. The matter is so divided that new topics are being dealt with all the time. This method has the advantage that it can properly evaluate the structure of the subject matter by an objective presentation and that it can hold the interest of the pupils.

But we may well ask whether or not the knowledge which the catechist imparts in this way actually endures. It would appear that the educative work that has been done lacks a firm foundation. Some kind of repetition is necessary if what the child has learnt is not to disappear as quickly as it came. A sane solution would be to combine these two methods. The progressive division could serve as the basis. If we keep before our minds the three different kinds of catechetical teaching material: religious

[9] Eggersdorfer, pp. 109ff.; J. K. Sharp, *Aims and Methods in Teaching Religion* (New York: Benziger Bros., 1929), pp. 66–68.

[10] Eggersdorfer, p. 111.

practice, Bible History, and systematic doctrine, it is clear that simply by arranging the teaching plan in such a way that they succeed one another, we do not achieve an actual progression but do effect an immanent repetition of the matter that has already been taught. All three are different aspects of one and the same subject matter, presented under different forms and in different guises. The mysteries surrounding Christ's birth, for example, are treated not only in the liturgy but also in Bible History and in the catechism. The distribution, moreover, can be made in such a way that it takes into account the psychological make-up of the children, corresponding to their actual age; so that the progressive arrangement becomes psychologically progressive.

For the children in the first grade, for whom a textbook is out of the question, but for whom possibly a picture book might be desirable, there is a choice of material that could easily be grasped. This material would be drawn from the practical sphere of Christian teaching, hence it would offer the children the beginnings of what we can call visual education or a religious interpretation of their environment. Much space will be given to the teaching of the natural revelation of God in creation. The subject matter of the catechism for these children will therefore be as follows: the creatures, which recall for us the goodness, wisdom and almighty power of the father in heaven; the fundamental forms of our conduct toward him; the first prayers; certain particulars of the external features of the Church and of divine worship along with liturgical feasts and certain incidents from the life and passion of Jesus.[11]

[11] Pfliegler, Vol. II, pp. 99f.—This viewpoint is taken into consideration in the *Fulda Lehrplan* (1925), pp. 11f. and also in the *Course of Study* for the diocese of Paderborn (1946), pp. 9ff. For the *Fulda Lehrplan,* consult R. Bandas, *op. cit.,* pp. 269–287.

During the remaining years in the lower grades religious instruction should be given in the form of Bible History. The catechist should, therefore, treat of the history of redemption for the first time. Bible stories are always concrete in character and fit in well with the perceptive faculties of this age. It is especially from the narratives of earlier history and from the New Testament that the catechist will to a great extent be able to draw the fundamental truths of Christianity. From them he will be able to extract many of those truths which later on will be deepened and developed in the catechism. At this age level the religious booklet is the most fitting textbook. In the second and third year the subject matter can be dealt with best in two concentric cycles. The first time it can be treated in broad general outlines, as befits seven year olds, perhaps stressing those things that are important for the first reception of the sacraments; the second time with the inclusion of other material which circumstances may dictate. If, as is the case in Austria, the school year begins in the autumn, it will be possible, while twice going through the story of salvation, to enter more deeply into the great feasts of the Church.

A definite difficulty, which is peculiar only to European countries, will be encountered in the fourth year. Since, according to civil laws, some children must pass on to other types of schools at the beginning of the fifth year, it is not advisable to begin with instructions on the catechism at this point unless a provisional systematic presentation be made of what has already been taught. The question still remains whether a complementary course in biblical catechesis using a school Bible as text, or a course that is mainly liturgical (Sacraments, Mass, Ecclesiastical Year), should be introduced?[12]

In the upper grades the catechism should come into its own

[12] Discussion on this subject was begun in the *ChPBl,* Vol. 64 (1951), pp. 289–294.

and should receive its just due. As a rule, the catechist will have to be content with covering the whole of the catechism once during this time. This can be accomplished by apportioning the various sections to the different years. In accordance with long tradition the catechist will, in these upper classes, use the school Bible in addition to the catechism; and he can try to take the children through Sacred Scripture to the extent of which they are capable. Naturally in those instances in which there are only two religion periods per week at his disposal, the catechist must be satisfied with expounding only a few extracts—but he should try to induce the children to read the Bible at home. In those cases in which four such periods are allotted to the teacher, as in the majority of German dioceses, the traditional solution would be: the teacher (other than the catechist) should take over the teaching of the biblical catechesis for two of these periods, while the catechist uses the other two exclusively for the catechism.

True, such a division of work has its pedagogical disadvantages, and so various attempts have been made to bring these two courses together or at least to eliminate their more obvious shortcomings. At the Munich Catechetical Congress this question was thoroughly discussed, but no solution was reached.[13] It would certainly be an underestimation of the importance of biblical catechesis if, with the older catechetics, it was accorded a position subordinate to the catechism.[14] We must remember

[13] See the reports of K. Raab and P. Bergmann, *Zweiter Katechetischer Kongreß München* 1928 (Donauwörth: Ludwig Auer, 1928), pp. 196-231.—A weighty argument raised against uniformity was the idea that school master and priest should each represent a self-contained subject in its entirety. Consult the discussion which was carried on about it in Eggersdorfer, *op. cit.*, pp. 227ff.

[14] F. J. Knecht, *Praktischer Kommentar zur Biblischen Geschichte,* Preface to the first edition (Freiburg: Herder, 1882), and was still repeated in the 19th edition (1903) but was suppressed in the twenty-third (1913); see

that the school Bible is as much a religion book of the Church as is the catechism, and that the same doctrines are contained in it as in the catechism, although written in a different manner.

The teaching plan can effect in outline a definite coordination, and bring about what theorists call a "symbiosis of subjects", in the sense that the Old Testament is treated in conjunction or side by side with the moral law; the life and passion of Jesus Christ with the doctrine of Christ and the Redemption; the history of the early Church and its continuation in Church history with the doctrine of the Church and the Sacraments.

Such a combination is all the easier if the catechism takes into account, more fully than formerly, the historical character of the Christian religion. On the other hand, a merger in one book and in one course of study cannot be carried out naturally and still be effective. Either Bible History is made the basis in such a course of study, in which case certain sections of the catechism will have to be interpolated into it. The systematic character of the catechism will then be destroyed unless these interpolations are few in number and in large sections, and we would have, as an end result, although in enlarged format, that which would suffice for the lower grades, namely, a religion booklet. Or, if the catechism is chosen as the basis, the chronological order of the biblical account must be discarded. In either case catechesis loses something that is valuable. The catechism arranged in lesson units, which usually start with a biblical passage, preserves valuable scriptural elements for catechesis, and by so doing supplements to a large extent instruction on the Bible, even in the most unfavourable circumstances.[15] It should

F. J. Knecht (M. F. Glancey, trans.), *Practical Commentary on the Holy Scripture* (Translated from the 16th edition) (5th ed.; St. Louis: Herder, 1930).

[15] F. Schreibmayr, "Bibel und Katechismus" in *KBl*, Vol. 71 (1946), pp. 73-81 and also pp. 116-118, which contain the remarks of J. Wiesheu

not, however, sacrifice the systematic character of the catechism or of catechesis, nor should it devote too much space to details, as can be done in biblical catechesis and is so very desirable in the interest of the educational result.

There is no need to provide especially in the plan, even in the upper grades, for the liturgy and the life of prayer. In as much as liturgy and prayer are concerned with the Sacrament of the Eucharist and the Mass, and with the intrinsic nature of prayer and divine worship, care must be taken that it be done within the framework of the catechism. Beyond this, religious subjects of a practical nature, especially the liturgy, should be part of every catechesis—by way of application and as incidental instruction—in which the teacher deals with materials that are actually outside the topics of the catecheses themselves but arise naturally. For example, a feast is to be celebrated in the near future, or a celebration in which the children love to take part. In general the value of incidental (informal) instruction must not be underrated. It can make use of subjects outside the normal course when a favourable opportunity arises. What is best learned is learned incidentally.

We must mention here that principle for the teaching plan which was championed by Josef Göttler (d. 1935) and which we can label "sacramental grading".[16] The course which we

who championed anew the combination of the two, and the answer of F. Schreibmayr; cf. J. Heeg, *Jesus and I* (Chicago: Loyola University, 1934) who teaches prayers and prepares children for First Confession and Communion through the use of the Bible narrative. F. Drinkwater, "The Ideal Catechism" in *Religion in School Again* (London: Burns, Oates, 1935), pp. 166–168; E. A. Fitzpatrick and P. F. Tanner, *Methods of Teaching Religion in Elementary Schools* (Milwaukee: Bruce, 1939), pp. 21–42; H. Borgmann, *Libica* (Baltimore: J. Murphy, 1930) who essays a threefold principle as the core of the religion period: Liturgy, Bible and the catechism.

[16] J. Göttler, *Religions- und Moralpädagogik* (2nd; Münster, 1931), pp. 11–118. Göttler has presented this idea in many different publications since he first broached it. In certain sections of the U.S.A. this plan,

have outlined thus far would be brought into harmony with this principle, necessarily modified so that the reception of one of the sacraments, first Confession, first Holy Communion and also Confirmation would be made the culminating point of the instructions of each year. Since, according to this usage, prevalent everywhere, Confession should precede the reception of Holy Communion, and since the maturity which would permit the child to receive the sacrament of Penance with the earnestness that is required is not generally reached before the third year, the following order would result. In the first year visual instructions on religious and moral topics; a two year course based on Bible History; then a "one or two year course on the Sacraments"; upon this a two or three year course on the catechism; finally a preparatory course for Confirmation, offering subject matter from apologetics carefully prepared with a view to encouraging further study in adulthood.

The obvious advantages of such a teaching plan cannot be denied. By it the reception of the sacraments is accorded a prominent place in that it conforms to certain religious and educational high lights which introduce in the children a sense of expectancy in regard to what they will be taught and what they will receive in the course of the year.

This idea was actually incorporated into the syllabus of the Bavarian dioceses as well as into the Fulda teaching plan. In these first Confession and first Communion were placed in the third and fourth grade (not in the fourth and fifth, as had been provided for by Göttler). This was, however, more feasible then, since in those German dioceses late first Communions were customary, and an earlier first Communion (that is, midway between early and late) appeared to be the only

although perhaps without all the refinements he proposes, has been used in connection with the *Year Round Instructions* and the *Vacation School,* and certainly in other religion classes for public school children.

possible solution. Göttler had, however, intended that his proposal should be a definitive solution. Such a late first Communion, however, can no longer be reconciled with the precept of the Church which sets the *anni discretionis* as the age at which first Holy Communion is to be administered. Even looking at the matter in itself, it appears to be unreasonable to make children, who have been ready for the reception of the sacrament so long and who are perhaps more worthy to receive it than their elders, wait for years simply for the sake of possible psychological and pedagogical benefit.

Objections may also be raised against such a plan, especially if an entire year would have to be spent treating of such a sombre theme as the sacrament of Penance. Children, out of reverence for the Eucharist, are required to make their confession before they receive first Holy Communion. For them this has a different meaning and not that importance that it has for adults. Instruction on Penance cannot be as profound in the lower grades as it ought to be.

On the other hand, first Confession and first Holy Communion do constitute important highlights of the catechesis in the lower grades. Appropriate time can, however, be devoted to them in the Bible History classes in the second year. The religion book could establish a link between the relevant passages in the Old and New Testaments and both sacraments, and thereby ensure that all the demands that are laid down for their reception are met. In many instances, moreover, special instructions for first Communion and first Confession are given in preparation for these sacraments, in addition to the ordinary catechesis which is imparted in school.[17]

So that the basic principles for the construction of the teaching plan might not be misunderstood, two further additions

[17] See below, pp. 300-329.

appear to be necessary: one of these is concerned with the *what*, and the other with the *how* of religious training.

2. *The Basic Catechism*

We can never realize our proposed objective, namely, that all the material provided for in the teaching plan will be mastered by all the children. We are as a consequence faced with the problem of a minimum of religious knowledge, which we must ensure that all children should acquire. This is the problem of a basic catechism.[18] By a basic catechism we mean the whole of knowledge and of moral dispositions which everyone ought to acquire in order to lead a Christian life and to work out his salvation. It is much more important as early as possible to provide each child with a minimum amount of religious equipment necessary for life than it is to explain an abundance of material which only a few can possibly assimilate. We must apply the ancient principle: *non multa sed multum*.

What are the essential points that must be taught? They are not to be identified with those six basic truths[19] which up to

[18] M. Gatterer, *Katechetik* (4th ed.; Innsbruck: Rauch, 1931), pp. 311 ff., pp. 486 ff.; G. B. Garrone, "What ought a catechism to contain?" in *Lumen Vitae*, Vol. 5 (1950), pp. 593–602.

[19] That the "six basic truths" were required from the beginning of the 18th century, we are able to prove. At that time they were grouped together for the purpose of showing what a Christian "had to know and believe expressly" *necessitate medii* as was still prescribed in the Austrian catechism of 1894. Besides the truths drawn from Heb. 11, 6, Trinity, Incarnation, and the immortality of the soul, a sixth basic truth was introduced, namely, "the grace of God is necessary to obtain eternal happiness", an addition that was necessitated by the Jansenistic controversy. Still other enumerations in other catechisms included those points of doctrine which had to be known *necessitate praecepti*. Hofinger, pp. 134–137. An *"acte de foi"* of the Belgian catechism of 1946 enumerates the first four of these fundamental truths, and drops the other two.

the present have at least in part been placed at the beginning of catechisms; for we are not dealing merely with the fulfilment of our obligation to believe, which theologians wished to define with these points, and for which the Apostles' Creed no longer seemed to suffice, but with what is necessary as a foundation for a Christian attitude and for a Christian conduct of life. We are concerned here with the minimum essentials of a Christian economy of salvation.[20]

To this belongs, first of all, the knowledge, or better still, the awareness of the immensity and the absolute dominion of God, the orientation of ourselves to life hereafter according to his will. To this pertains also the knowledge that Christ is God and man and also our Redeemer, that he has shown us the road to heaven, that the Catholic Church teaches and guides us because of her commission. To these we must add as a minimum for our religious life in the Church, a knowledge of the sacraments through which we are sanctified (especially of the Eucharist and the sacrament of Penance) and of the conditions which must be fulfilled to receive the sacrament of Penance; an understanding of the essentials of the Sacrifice of the Mass and of the manner in which we should assist at it; finally the prayers most important for Catholics.[21] Since these must be taught as set formulas, they should be learned by heart and, thus learnt, they will serve as memory aids to recall the doctrine contained in them (Our Father, Apostles' Creed).

The commandments of God confirm the natural moral law; they are made known to us by the voice of conscience. As a consequence, from the standpoint of the basic catechism it is not

[20] That a picture of the whole of Christianity should be given to the children and even to the smallest among them is a concern that lies close to the heart of Hirscher, *Katechetik* (3rd ed.), pp. 59f., 80ff. and *passim*.

[21] The points of doctrine which are listed here agree fairly closely with what Cardinal Gasparri offered in his *Catechismus Catholicus* as a catechism for First Communicants.

absolutely necessary to expend the same care on all the details of their explanation. The catechist would, however, do well always to come back to the basic law, that we must obey God, and to the moral senses which all Christians should possess and which are contained in the double commandment of love of God and neighbour.

From the first or at least from the second year on, these subjects should be repeated in different contexts and in different ways, and the catechist should treat them with special warmth. We need not fear that by such a repetition we might revert to the concentric cycle type of treatment; for we are dealing here with the centre itself, with the innermost core of Christian doctrine. We should, however, always try to approach these basic truths from a new angle perhaps starting from a biblical episode, or from the celebration of a feast, or from an aspect of the liturgy, or from a special division of the catechism.[22] Only little of this needs to be retained in literal formation. As Karl Raab has said: "What has been retained should be revived by repetition through reading and prayer, so that the pupil can make it his own."[23]

On the other hand it should be clear that under normal circumstances we must not be content with this basic catechism, but ought to provide the children with as thorough a religious instruction as possible, yet we should not be led astray by the idea that we may not teach the children anything they do not fully understand. In the teaching of faith we are constantly confronted with mysteries; even adults are not able to understand them. That is why it suffices if, with the help of a good

[22] The necessity of keeping alive in the hearts of the children a knowledge of the basic truths of faith is especially stressed by Hirscher, *Katechetik,* pp. 384–412. To them we can apply the words of Sacred Scripture, Deut. 11, 18–21.

[23] Raab, p. 149.

method, we succeed in partially explaining certain obscurities and imparting to the children some inkling of their content. We must not, for example, withhold from the children such doctrines as inspiration, original sin, a one true Church.

In moral teaching, too, everything essential should be mentioned. We must stress consequently the principle of actuality: that is to say, we must touch first of all upon those moral commands which the children are already observing and in which they are themselves interested. This should not lead us to neglect other teachings of the Christian moral law. It is by no means without value if the children learn to judge correctly those moral conditions with which they are not yet familiar, but with which they will be later confronted, and to associate, early on, the notions of good and evil with actions pertaining to the world of adults.[24] For example, the awfulness of perjury, the correct concept of work, the duties of one's state of life, and last but not least the obligations of parents. This is the task of forming the conscience which need not be limited to purely contemporary considerations.

3. Concentration

The second element which should help to form a correct concept of every teaching plan concerns the basic principle of concentration. Concentration of instruction is required by didactics in each and every subject.[25] We should not attempt to inculcate in the children a large number of details—details which are unrelated and have only a remote relationship; we should rather strive as far as possible to focus the particular upon a

[24] It is impossible to give the children of this age level in the elementary school a sufficiently detailed knowledge of matters that pertain to sex. But this is a point that will be discussed later.

[25] Eggersdorfer, pp. 121–133; A. N. Fuerst, *op. cit.*, Vol. II (1946), pp. 164–175.

common centre by which we can reduce the manifold to a unity and the parts to a whole. In this way we will succeed in instilling into the children a unified picture of the whole of reality. This is the objective which corresponds most closely with Christian ideology. It is also the purpose of the modern "education of the whole person" theory. The world which God created is not a chaos but a cosmos. The image of the world in our knowledge of truth should therefore be a cosmos.

The centre upon which theorists seek to concentrate the varied material offered in the secular subjects is the pupil's home or his native land.[26] The children are to be made aware of their environment and, to an ever greater degree, of the world which lies closest to them. This connection with their native soil is to increase their interest in the more technical subjects such as arithmetic and writing. As far as these subjects are concerned, the native land may suffice as a centre. For the whole of instruction and the whole of education such a focal point must be sought in something still more profound: in our ultimate home, heaven. In a Catholic environment and in a genuine Catholic school worthy of the name, such a deepening can be taken for granted. At the centre of the pupil's own interests should be the parish church and the religious practices which illuminate his life and give it cohesion.

Catholic education will thus constantly attempt to connect all points on the periphery with the centre, with God, his laws and his kingdom. But not only should there be links between the secular subjects and religion, the catechist too will strive to

[26] On this point, consult Eggersdorfer, pp. 205–223; and also pp. 118f., 26, where an extensive bibliography may also be found. In the U.S.A. the words that are used to express somewhat the same idea are the "field trip", and "school journey"; cf. E. Dale, *Audio-Visual Methods in Teaching* (New York: Dryden Press, 1946), pp. 42–43. R. de Kieffer and L. W. Cochran, *Manuel of Audio-Visual Techniques* (New York: Prentice-Hall, 1955), pp. 79–83.

bring religion into relation with the secular branches and thus to guide the children to God. He should be only too glad to avail himself of those aids which these other subjects offer him to realize this aim. The reader may sometimes offer valuable hints, knowledge of the natural sciences may help to illuminate the greatness and the wisdom of God. Geography may be enlisted, not only when the teacher speaks of the Holy Land, or of the Holy Father in Rome, but also in order to localize incidents taken from the lives of the saints or to give background to stories of the missions. Even arithmetic can serve to show how much money is wasted on drink or what the parents have to spend in the course of a year to provide food and clothing for the children.

The catechist should utilize to the full the principle of concentration within the framework of the subject matter which he teaches. This is not difficult, since the three great branches of catechetical instruction as we have seen are only three aspects of one and the same revealed truth and since the catechetical subject matter is ultimately nothing but the one message of the way of salvation.

The way of salvation is the way to God, which we follow in union with Christ. As a consequence, there will always be two thoughts which we must constantly stress: God and Christ, God-centredness and Christ-centredness. These two notions are closely associated; but they must not be confused. God-centredness denotes the complete orientation of our life as human beings; this is posited by creation and constitutes the basic law even of Christianity.[27] Christ-centredness, however, refers to the presentation of those doctrines, institutions, and aids, through which we attain to union with God in the Christian faith.

[27] We must avoid a "panchristism" which in zealous excess replaces God by Christ, and thus practically denies the mediation of Christ and along with it the whole structure of the Christian faith. Such expressions find their way frequently into Protestant piety, but they can sometimes also be found in Catholic devotional literature.

God-centredness demands that our teaching should always lead to thoughts of God, his right of dominion over us, our duty of obedience to his will. This obedience should be translated into the Christian terms of faith, hope and charity. According to the admonition of St. Augustine, we should so speak that "he, by hearing, may believe, and by believing hope, and by hoping love".[28] Christ-centredness concerns the ways and means of salvation, so that it becomes clear to the children that all these are ultimately focused on the person of Christ, that grace means participating in his life, that the sacraments at different stages in our life effect union with him and obtain from him justification, sanctification, and in certain instances divine powers; that the Catholic Church is the Church in which the work of salvation is continued; that we venerate Mary as His Mother and the saints as his friends, in whom the light of his holiness may be seen, as it were, under different forms.

Likewise in Bible History, which should retrace the ways of the history of salvation, Christ must be made the centre, even in the Old Testament, which is delineated by St. Paul himself as "our tutor unto Christ" (Gal. 3, 24). We should not be satisfied merely to explain to the children those Messianic prophecies and those prototypes of the Redeemer which God Himself has designated as such, but in the spirit of patristic theology and of the liturgy we should advance still farther and should point out the more notable parallels, or even better, we should permit the children themselves to discover and to establish those parallels which exist between Old Testament personages and the reality of the New; thus, for example, in Isaac who carried the wood of sacrifice up the mountain himself; in the angels of Jacob's Ladder, who ascended and descended; in the Egyptian Joseph, one of a group of twelve, who was sold into slavery, innocently condemned, thrown into a pit and then

[28] *De catechiz. rudibus,* c. 4; J. P. Christopher, *op. cit.,* p. 24.

into prison, and finally was made king; in Moses who as a child was persecuted, and ultimately rescued by God, and who led the Israelites into the Promised Land.[29] In this way the children will gradually awaken to the realization that Christ, who is the focal point of all history, possesses a grandeur that surpasses time and place.

In his efforts properly to evaluate the central facts of the Christian economy of redemption, the catechist will find an incomparable ally in the liturgy. He needs only to follow the course of the ecclesiastical year, to arrive along with his charges at the illuminating centre of the great mysteries of faith.[30] It is that core which that great German, Bishop Sailer, defined as: "God in Christ, the redemption of a sinful world."[31] From this we should realize that the catechist may not think that he has finished his task when he has offered corroboration for the fundamental notions of faith; he must move on, for he has to awaken that supernatural joy which blossoms so easily in the hearts of children, and he must make it efficacious for their lives and their aspirations.[32]

A concrete teaching plan, which is the standard and to be followed by the individual catechist, will as a rule, be issued by the diocesan authorities. Such a plan, however, cannot

[29] A collection of parallels which may be used with profit in catechesis may be seen in J. Dreyssen, "Verheissung im Alten Testament — Erfüllung im Neuen Testament" in *KBl,* Vol. 72, pp. 103–108. An extensive presentation of patristic materials can be consulted in J. Daniélou, *Bible and Liturgy* (University of Notre Dame Press, 1958). R. Beron, *With the Bible through the Church Year* (New York: Pantheon Books, 1953).

[30] M. Pfliegler, *Heilige Bildung* (Salzburg: A. Pustet, 1933), pp. 81–107; idem, *Der Religionsunterricht,* Vol. III, p. 85.—Th. Kampmann, *Mysterium und Gestalt des Kirchenjahres* (with wall-charts) (Paderborn: F. Schöningh, 1952); B. Strasser, *With Christ Through the Year* (Milwaukee: Bruce, 1947).

[31] F. X. Arnold, *Dienst am Glauben* (Freiburg: Herder, 1948), p. 37.

[32] The so-called "reflections" play a leading role in the educational

regulate down to the last detail the procedure employed in catechesis for the individual grades, otherwise it would prove to be a shackle for the catechist who has to work in different circumstances and under conditions which are constantly changing. A more precise division of the subject matter in accordance with the number of hours at his disposal must be made by the catechist himself.

The catechist should keep a "class record" of the subject matter that he treats. This "record" he either does for himself or—as is customary in Austrian schools—in conjunction with the other teachers for all branches in the same class. This weekly record permits a rapid survey of the state of catechesis. This record becomes even more important when there is a change of religious instruction. Through the weekly record the substitute (or successor) can quickly apprise himself of what has been done, and so is enabled to carry on the work of his predecessor without interruption.

practice of the Brothers of the Christian Schools, founded by St. John Baptist de la Salle. Since catechesis was conceived to be something more than a mere imparting of knowledge, the first five minutes at the beginning of every instruction were to be used for an explanation of one of the central truths of our religion. In the early years of this Congregation, the reflections dealt with the following points on the five days of the week: the salvation of the soul, the uncertainty of the hour of death, the service of God, to die rather than to commit a sin, safeguards against danger. At the present time these themes are allowed a wider interpretation. Consult W. Stein, *Anregende Ermahnungen zur Herzensbildung und Willensübung,* 2 vols. 3/4 (Kirnach-Villingen, 1921) (I, 4th ed.), pp. 15–23 give the historical sources; L. di Maria, "L'educazione religiosa dei fanciulli nelle scuole elementari rette in Italia dai Fratelli delle Scuole Cristiane" in *Lumen Vitae,* Vol. 1 (1946), pp. 665–676. Br. Philip, *Considerations for Christian Teachers* (2nd ed.; Baltimore: J. Murphy, 1922), pp. 177–182. From another angle very pertinent suggestions can be advanced to enable the children to acquire certain "leading thoughts". These thoughts, which are frequently repeated and are made the object of self-examination, e. g., "I am a soldier of Christ"; "We carry a torch". In this fashion: M. A. Gramlich, *Gehet hin und lehret* (Freiburg: Herder, 1949), pp. 11–15.

VI

GENERAL METHOD

1. Learning from Texts

AFTER having attempted to throw some light upon the task of catechesis, and also upon the material aspect of its content, we can now approach the question of its correct formal qualities, the problem of method.

Method (μέθοδος: μετά-ὁδός) means "the way to", or "after-way", that is, the procedure necessary to reach a goal. In the sphere of instruction it denotes "the procedure which the teacher adopts to enable the pupils to follow him" (Göttler).

Genuine method is always a realistic procedure, a process which is adjusted or adapted to the task to be done and to the actual means at our disposal. Now, the task of catechesis never remains the same period after period; and the resources which are available are constantly changing. As a consequence, method should not be rigid. Method should, furthermore, not be employed in a stereotyped or mechanical fashion; it must be flexible; it must be pliable enough to permit adaptation to definite objects and in accordance with concrete resources. To a certain extent, however, both the task and the resources are fixed. That is why we are able to discuss this task as well as the psychological make-up of the children. For the same reason we can formulate in broad general outline a universally valid and fixed method of catechesis.

It will be one method, although separate methodical instructions might be developed for a catechesis on the catechism, or for Bible catechesis, or for a catechesis on any other kind of subject. The differences between them, however, would not be so profound that we could not envisage a common stock of norms valid for all forms of instruction. These norms flow naturally from the task of training the children in their religion, a task which remains always the same. We can, therefore, discuss the chief problems of methodology in a general methodology.[1] But so as not to lose touch with concrete circumstances in the following considerations, we must constantly keep before us the classical exemplification of catechesis: namely, catechism-catechesis, because the difficulties connected with it are greatest and because from it we can obtain sufficient suggestions to permit us to make satisfactory adaptions to other subjects. The special difficulty of catechism-catechesis is to be found in the fact that as a rule it treats of abstract doctrines. These abstract doctrines have the advantage of being universally valid and possessing both clarity and conciseness. Their disadvantage, however, is that they can be understood only with difficulty by children; they are as it were kernels enclosed within hard shells which must be broken in order to extract the goodness inside. In contrast, subjects like Bible History, Church History, and liturgical catechesis, because of their concrete character, are at once close to the children's understanding. In fact, in most cases, they need only to be presented and to be made fruitful.

What we are looking for, therefore, is a way to construct the catechism-catechesis correctly and in particular the single

[1] J. Göttler, "Alte und neue Unterrichtsstilistik" in *Zweiter Katechetischer Kongress* (München: Ludwig Auer, 1929), pp. 106–120, and especially pp. 109f.—The special features of method for the different subjects: Bible History, Christian doctrine, Prayer, Liturgy, Church History, etc., are especially described in H. Mayer, *Katechetik,* pp. 113ff.; J. Baierl, R. G. Bandas, *et al., Religious Instruction and Education* (New York: Wagner, 1938); Sr. M. Agnesine, *Teaching Religion for Living* (Milwaukee: Bruce, 1952); J. B. Collins, *Teaching Religion* (Milwaukee: Bruce, 1953); A. N. Fuerst, *op. cit.,* vols. I and II.

religious instruction period. We shall not now consider the beginning of such a period which usually serves for recapitulating matters already treated in a previous lesson. Here we intend to develop the way in which *new* subject matter should be broached.

The correct construction of a catechesis in this sense is the key problem of catechetical methodology, just as it was also the key problem of the catechetical movement at the beginning of the present century. The state of the question will become clearer in the light of what, up to that time, had been considered to be proper catechetical method and its guiding principles. The text-explanatory method was practically universal at the time. The catechism questions were taken through one after another. Each question was read out aloud and then explained by the catechist in his own words. If illustrative material was needed, the catechist had recourse to the words and examples of the Bible. Occasionally he added a moral to be drawn before proceeding to the next question. Whatever he treated in this fashion in class was assigned to be learned by heart.[2] To what

[2] This method was not always employed in the same way. Often in the course of the first hour the catechist read or recited the text of the catechism and gave an explanation of its terms when the question and answer were difficult to understand. He then permitted the children to memorize the answer and after he had asked questions one by one, only in the following class did he attempt to offer an explanation of the matter. Thus, it was taught in former times, and in this form we can see it in the introduction to Fr. Schoberl's work in 1888. Cf. G. Kifinger, *KBl,* Vol. 63 (1937), p. 328; F. H. Drinkwater, *Religion in School Again* (London: Burns, Oates, 1935), pp. 87–91. One of the last defenders of this antiquated method, W. H. Meunier, *Die Lehrmethode im Katechismus-Unterricht* (Cologne, 1905), pp. 50ff., names five different parts of which every catechesis should be composed, in imitation of a didactic sermon: explanation, confirmation (corroboration), repetition, application to life, and paraenesis.—Other catechists refused to give up suggestions which they had gleaned from the era of enlightenment and added to the explanation a great number of questions for memorization by the children.

extremes and in what exclusive forms this exegesis-like method was still being propounded at the end of the nineteenth century may be seen from an official instruction addressed to Austrian teachers of religion at that time:[3]

"Although in the foregoing the principal conditions for a fruitful catechesis have been laid down, these are not the only ones. Moreover, it is important to understand that the procedure in catechesis be methodologically and pedagogically sound as well as adapted to its purpose. In this respect, we recommend the following points: 1. In the explanation, the catechist should keep exactly the wording of the catechism without adding other matter, for example, from other catechisms. The content of the prescribed catechism is in itself so rich that the catechist need not waste time searching for subject matter outside it. We would advise that the catechist either personally read the answer slowly and with the proper emphasis or permit it to be read by the pupils. Then when this has been done, he should divide the answer into its component parts, first by singling out the subject and predicate of the sentence and their modifiers, and then by stressing the relative clauses pertaining both to the subject and to the predicate. This simple analysis often suffices to make the matter sufficiently clear. Should a word, however, require explanation, the catechist should give it, but in so doing he should avoid verbosity, which instead of throwing light on the subject often renders it still more obscure or wastes precious time. . . . 5. The catechist should not forget occasionally to address a few words of admonition to the pupils without giving the impression of sermonizing. Should fitting thoughts prove difficult to find, the catechist may take these from the appended instructions."

Such a procedure was "good exegesis, but poor catechesis". To be sure it was a very easy method, but one which scarcely deserved the name. The priest catechist was able to give such an explanation of words and phrases without any special preparation, simply by relying on his theological training.[4] But even when he employed this method with care, he actually

[3] A passage of this kind is reproduced in W. Pichler, *Unser Religionsunterricht* (Vienna, 1907), pp. 129f.

[4] It is worthwhile noting that up to the turn of the century many commentaries on the catechism were published, but never any detailed catecheses, in which the authors showed how the matter should be treated and be given concrete form.

forced the children into a procedure which was at best suitable only for students working at a higher level. It was completely overlooked that a child's thought process depends wholly on sense data. Nor was it considered that the instruction in question should contain not only doctrine but also religious nourishment, and that this should be the decisive factor in the children's education.

It is true that this last consideration was less important in former times than it is today, since the family and life in the community had the effect of a religious education to an extent greater than they have now. Catechesis could thus confine itself, without too harmful results, to the teaching of purely religious knowledge. Indeed, for centuries, ever since there was a catechesis for children, this system had survived without upsetting anyone. The text-explanatory method in its extreme form coincided with the introduction of catechism instruction into the schools and with the enlarged catechism. In earlier times, when the catechisms were shorter, the catechist had sufficient time to extend the explanations as much as he liked.[5] In the meantime, due to changes in external circumstances, the educative effect of catechesis has become one of the most acute problems of pastoral work. As a first step there was the demand that the content of catechesis, should at least once be imparted

[5] The *Practica Catechismi* which appeared in the sixteenth century, probably the work of St. Peter Canisius, stressed very strongly the element of perceptibility in the instruction: "The catechist should speak slowly, and he should take care to have ready stories especially of holy persons who led good lives from infancy on. Also beautiful comparisons and parables . . . . Likewise at Christmas he should build for them a crib, with Mary and Joseph, angels, and ass and an ox, in such a way that the children can cradle the Christ Child to the tune of *Resonet puer natus, In dulci jubilo,* both in Latin and in German." And he adds: "The Jews know their Talmud, and the Turks the Koran, which is their dogma, better than we Christians know the catechism." F. J. Knecht, "Katechetik" in *Kirchenlexikon,* Vol. VII (1891), pp. 271f.

to the understanding of the children and that the purely logical instruction should be given with an eye to the psychological make-up of the child.

Above all it was necessary that the catechesis should be understandable. This was based on the fundamental psychological principle of Aristotelian-Scholastic philosophy, *Cognitio incipit a sensibus,* which means that everything that is not acquired from inner experience, that is absorbed from without—natural knowledge of God as well as revealed religion comes to us from without—gains entry into the soul through the senses, and must in some fashion or other be perceptible, so that the mind, abstracting from it, can arrive at an idea. This law is universally valid; it is of special importance, however, for the instruction of children. Adults have, during the course of years, formed many notions from originally perceptible material and it can be assumed that they have these notions. Children, however, are only at the beginning of their mental activity. That is why we must always begin with that with which they are acquainted and traverse with them the process of recognition from the beginning.

If we should neglect this, and in its stead offer the children ready-made notions, we would expose ourselves to the danger of giving the children only a knowledge of words and no more. "Notions cannot be received like presents, for notions, thus handed on are neither understood nor usable and they are without influence on life."[6]

That is why the Catechetical Movement took this demand for perceptibility as its starting point,[7] and from it developed the basic principles for the construction of catechesis. The Movement

[6] Pfliegler, Vol. III, p. 42.

[7] The demand for concreteness formed a chief topic of discussion during the first catechetical courses; 1905–1908; cf. Pfliegler, Vol. III, pp. 142 ff.

achieved a kind of graded catechesis based on various steps. These steps, which are borrowed from the laws of human psychology, give a definite form to the instruction. According to these laws the acquisition of knowledge begins with the perceptible object, proceeds to thought and finally to action in accordance with the powers of the senses, the understanding and the will. The system of steps has a long history, but, they were first formulated for teaching in the nineteenth century, and in their essential features, were defined by the German philosopher Johann Friedrich Herbart (d. 1841), and then in more detail by his pupil, Thuiskon Ziller (d. 1882).

Ziller required above all the division of the teaching matter into so-called methodical unities: each period of instruction should form a complete whole with a unified theme. It should then be developed according to the steps system. Ziller suggested six steps of which the first two are preliminary ones.[8]

[8] Ziller suggested these steps: 1. Statement of objective: this acquaints the pupils with what the period is to accomplish, and serves to arouse their interest.—2. Preparation or analysis (in the sense of opening up the spiritual world—the terminology of Ziller especially in the use of Greek terms is unfortunate). Drawing on the pupils' previous knowledge of this step helps apperception in such a way that they are enabled to understand the new matter. Previously acquired knowledge of the pupils is evoked and when necessary supplemented.—3. Presentation or synthesis: the new matter is propounded through the medium of clear and precise concepts.—4. Association: abstract and generally valid factors are seized upon.—5. Systematization: what has been taught and understood is integrated into the matter that is already known.—6. Method: the matter acquired in the process is brought to life and fruition by means of practice and application.—Cf. J. J. Wolfe, "Formalstufen" in *Lexikon der Pädagogik,* Vol. I (1913), pp. 1336–1342. One weakness of the formal steps of Ziller is that in the Herbartian philosophy which he followed a representation and a concept are not sufficiently differentiated; O. Willmann, *Aus Hörsaal und Schulstube* (Freiburg: Herder, 1904), pp. 32 f.; F. Eby, *The Development of Modern Education* (2nd ed.; New York: Prentice-Hall, 1953), pp. 471-495.—The steps became better understood and were used more frequently only much later, after the Catechetical Movement was already in full swing; the adaptation was made by W. Rein, *Pädagogik in systematischer Darstellung,*

Otto Willmann (d. 1920) was a pupil of Ziller and a leading Catholic pedagogue at the beginning of the century. He rendered a great service to the Catechetical Movement in Germany. He rid the steps theory of the influence of Herbart's philosophy and restored its essential outlines.[9]

He retained the primary assumption of methodical unity but suggested only three steps, corresponding to the faculties of the soul: memory, understanding and will. The resulting three steps are as follows:

1. Presentation: a perceptible basis is offered,
2. Explanation: notions are singled out,
3. Application: references to life are established.

Looked at from the standpoint of the children they are:

1. Perception,
2. Understanding,
3. Practical application.[10]

The catechists of the Munich Catechetical Society, among whom Heinrich Stieglitz played a prominent role, found in these three steps what they had been searching for for such a long time. They fought against the pure "test analysis" and the

3 vols. (2nd ed.; Langensalza, 1912), Vol. III, pp. 246 ff. Cf. Eggersdorfer, pp. 358 ff. Because Eggersdorfer in repeating the steps of Ziller failed to include the statement of purpose, we arrive already at the five steps which Rein proposed: 1. Preparation, 2. Presentation, 3. Association, 4. Synthesis, 5. Application; P. Monroe (editor), *A Cyclopedia of Education,* 5 vols. (New York: Macmillan, 1911–1913), Vol. V, pp. 419–420; P. J. Marique, *History of Christian Education,* 3 vols. (New York: Fordham Univ. 1932), Vol. III, pp. 117–127.

[9] Pfliegler, Vol. III, pp. 198–206.

[10] O. Willmann, *Didaktik* (6th ed.; Freiburg-Wien: Herder, 1957), pp. 442–452, and especially p. 444.— For the third step Willmann used the expressions, *Confirmation,* and eventually *Elaboration.* O. Willmann (F. Kirsch, trans.), *The Science of Education,* 2 vols. (Beatty, Pa.: Archabbey Press, 1922), Vol. II, pp. 210-222, and especially, p. 216; cf. L. Nolle, "The Formal Steps in Religious Education" *The Catholic Educational Review,* Vol. VII (1909), p. 7.

merely logical treatment of the subject as a kind of psychological procedure. Their aims are recorded in numerous articles and discussions in the *Katechetische Blätter* of the years 1896–1903. Their work resulted in the establishment of five steps:

1. Preparation,
2. Presentation,
3. Explanation,
4. Summary,
5. Application.

They recognized, however, (as early as 1900) that Willmann's three steps contained everything essential. Hence it was customary to recognize three major steps and two minor steps, preparation and summary, the latter generally today called "deepening".[11] The new method being completed, it became popular and was accepted. Because of the place of its origin it is generally called the "Munich Method". In opposition to the "text-explanatory" method it is described today as the "text-developing" method because the catechism text is not the starting point but has first to be developed.

The principles of this new method are actually so clear that it is not surprising that in their essential broad outlines they can also be met with in the past and under circumstances not specifically concerned with children.

Christ Himself was the precursor. He did not, like the Pharisees, take propositions from the Law or from the Prophets in order to rephrase their contents in different words. If the situation did not supply Him with a starting point, He spoke in parables or used examples taken from the world around Him. In these His audience quickly discerned a deeper meaning. He emphasized this meaning which usually concerned the invisible world of God's kingdom and concluded with a

[11] Pfliegler, Vol. III, pp. 206–210.

challenge: "Go and do likewise", "He who has ears to hear, let him hear."

In his *Liber Didascalicus,* Hugh of St. Victor (d. 1141) distinguishes three steps in the absorption of intellectual matter: *lectio, meditatio, operatio,* which correspond to the steps: perception, understanding, application. In the *Introductions* which he gives for meditative prayer, St. Ignatius frequently recommended a similar course. The retreatant should first of all try to picture to himself the event; he should then attempt with his understanding to fathom its purpose, its meaning, and its bearing; finally he should seek to draw from it something beneficial for his own spiritual life. For a long time similar directions have been given to preachers to observe the steps: *propositio, explicatio, applicatio.*

As a model for this method (somewhat condensed) a catechesis written by the leader of the Munich Catechetical Movement, Heinrich Stieglitz, may help to acquaint the catechist with its advantages as well as with certain disadvantages, chiefly the undue emphasis placed on understanding which in the development that followed had to be overcome.[12]

Sins against Faith

PREPARATION. Dear children, it is God's will that we all honour and adore God Almighty with body and soul. Let us review this important duty. (Question the children briefly on the preceding lesson)—You have already learned about faith. Is faith necessary for salvation? Christ says: "He that believeth not shall be condemned" (Mark 15, 16). Will any faith save a man? Which Church has the genuine faith that will save us? Why has the Catholic Church the true faith? How could the Catholic Church preserve the true faith pure and undefiled throughout the centuries? Where shall we find the chief truths which the Church teaches?

Faith is necessary. But between faith and faith there is a whole world

[12] J. J. Baierl, *The Commandments Explained* (2nd ed.; Rochester, N. Y.: Seminary Press, 1925), pp. 61–68.

of difference. Our faith must be a living faith. We must show our faith by our daily life and actions.

ALMS. The true faith is a great grace. To lose the faith is, therefore, a great misfortune. We shall see that today. I am going to tell you about a certain young man, who lost his faith. From this we shall learn how a Christian may sin grievously against holy faith, but also how careful you ought to be to preserve the grace of faith in your hearts.

PRESENTATION. Anthony was a good boy. His mother loved him and watched over him as the apple of her eye. But alas! she was obliged to leave this world all too soon. With her heart overflowing with motherly solicitude she spoke to Anthony as she lay upon her death bed: "My child! soon you will no longer have a mother. Listen to what I have to say to you. Fear God and keep His Commandments! Remain strong in the faith; be faithful to His Church! May Mary be your mother! She will protect you in all danger." Weeping, the boy kissed the hand of his dying mother and promised: "Mother, I promise to do all that you ask!" Soon afterwards his mother closed her eyes in death.

The boy remained faithful to his promise for a while. But soon he grew to be careless in studying his catechism. And when he became a young man he fell in with bad companions. Day after day he heard their wicked talk and their ridicule about prayer and attendance at church and everything that we Catholics hold sacred. At first he became angry at this sort of talk and at times spoke strong words in defence of his faith. However, he did not have the courage and the strength to separate himself from his false friends. That was unfortunate for him. Gradually he became hardened to their continual criticism and ridicule and in the end he even laughed with them and boldly took part in those conversations.

Henceforth matters continually went from bad to worse. He read bad books, that were filled with irreligion and infidelity; yes, he swallowed those writings most greedily. For hours at a time he would think about these things, until he was no longer able to find his way out of those difficulties. "What if all that I have hitherto believed were really not true?" Such doubts troubled him continually. It was not very long before he made up his mind, saying: "Oh, one faith is as good as another; every religion is good in God's sight." He ceased praying; he went to church only occasionally and he no longer received the holy sacraments even at Easter time. Religion became for him only a secondary concern.

One day there was a public meeting. Anthony and his companions, too, attended it. A false apostle made a malicious speech ridiculing the Church. Addressing himself to any Catholics present, he said, "The Roman Church is filled with superstition and idolatry. We Protestants have the pure gospel of Christ. Therefore separate yourselves from Rome!" Some foolish young people wrote their names in a list as a sign of their apostasy from the Catholic faith. Anthony was among the number of these blind persons. He had forgotten all. The poor young man also attended the Protestant services several times; once he even went to the Lord's Supper. But soon he had enough of this new faith. He continued to fall more deeply, until finally he lost all faith. "There is no heaven, no hell, no God; everything ends with death" was henceforth his gospel.

However, God's grace did not abandon this poor sinner. A severe illness struck him down. In his feverish dreams he saw his good mother. She was weeping bitter tears and was complaining: "Anthony! what did you promise me upon my death bed? What have you done?" "O mother!" the lost son cried out. Suddenly he awoke. It was also an awakening from a life of sin. At once he called for a priest and confessed his grievous guilt. And when he received Jesus in the Blessed Sacrament, he became very happy and prayed aloud: "O my Jesus! I firmly believe all that Thy holy Church teaches. In this faith I will live and die." Only a few days more remained for this young man in which to repent. But as he was dying he prayed again so beautifully and in such a Christian manner: "O God! I have deserved death. Gladly will I die as penance for my sins. Lord, be merciful to me a sinner!"

EXPLANATION. 1. *Dangers.* There you see how a person can gradually, step by step, sink into the mire of infidelity and approach the very edge of destruction. That young man was brought up piously and in a truly Christian manner by a good mother. How then did he come into evil ways? His wicked companions were to blame for this. If a good apple is placed among rotten ones, what happens? Is it not true, that soon the good apple becomes affected by the decay? That very thing happened to our young friend. His heart was as yet unspotted and pure; but soon in the company of bad companions it became tainted with the corruption of unbelief. What did these seducers do?—Of course at first Anthony did not want to listen to these godless conversations; he even defended his religion. What else ought he to have done?— The voice of his conscience, too, admonished and warned him: Flee away from these poisonous snakes, or they will surely destroy you! But he did not listen to the voice of God and was unwilling to leave his friends. That was already a mortal sin. For it is a serious danger to listen to impious language.

Soon there came a second danger—bad books. What is found in such books? In these writings appear false teachings about the Christian faith. Such books, which defend a false Christian faith or irreligion, are called heretical books. In other books there is to be found much ridicule about God and religion; the Church and the priests and the sacraments are bespattered with the poison of ridicule and scorn. Such books, which preach and praise unbelief or infidelity, are called godless and impious books. You can easily imagine what an impression the reading of such heretical and impious books made upon the inexperienced young man of our story. Drop by drop the poison of infidelity made its way into this young man's heart; he was in danger of losing his faith. Yes, the reading of heretical and impious books is also a great danger to faith and is, therefore, a grievous sin against faith.

2. *Doubts.* What then were the fruits, which resulted from the keeping of company with wicked friends and from the reading of bad books?—Soon doubts against faith began to make themselves felt. What did the young man think to himself?—Perhaps what my friends are saying is really true! What if that which is printed in these books is really true? Then one needs no longer to live as a Christian. Therefore a free life! That is what would have pleased him very much. What ought he to have done with those doubts?—He ought to have driven them away from his mind at once; then they would not have been sins at all. However, he entertained himself with those doubts as with dear friends. That was indeed a serious sin. For wilful doubts against faith are a serious sin against faith. Our faith must be firm. For what we believe comes from God; but God is eternal, infallible truth.

3. *Indifference.* But Anthony did not stop at doubts against faith. Soon a new and wicked fruit began to show itself. The young man became careless and indifferent towards his holy religion. He thought to himself that every religion is true in God's sight. Therefore it is all the same whether a person be Catholic or Protestant. It does not matter so much what one believes, provided only that one lives a good life. To be sure, many a fallen away Catholic talks like that; but God judges otherwise. Indifference in matters of faith is a serious sin against faith.

A person, that thinks in that way generally too, lives in accordance with that belief. Was not that the case with Anthony?—Very soon he found no pleasure any more in prayers and in assisting at divine service and in the reception of the sacraments. Gradually he grew colder and more indifferent in the practice of his religion.

(In a similar fashion by means of examples the catechist can explain: 4. denial of faith, 5. heresy, 6. atheism.)

Write on the blackboard:

You sin against faith — against the first Commandment

a. by neglecting to study what God has taught,

by neglecting to know some Christian doctrine,
b. by neglecting to practise your faith
by failing to acknowledge the true Church
by believing that you can be saved in a state of apostasy.

APPLICATION. a. *Danger to faith.* "Resist the beginning", says an old proverb. If that young man had done that, he would not have gone so far astray. Wicked friends sowed the poisonous seeds in his heart. Beware of persons who ridicule the faith! Just as wicked is the reading of bad books. Nowadays there is a regular deluge of bad books and newspapers. In them the devil preaches the finest sermon every day. And he has many zealous hearers, many more than the priest in the Church. But he only chloroforms their consciences, in order that he may make them poor and weak in the faith. What must one do? Cast aside all such writings! They poison the heart. You, too, can lose your faith, this most precious jewel.
b. *Doubts about faith.* Doubts against faith can come to anyone. In itself that is not a misfortune. If a bee alights upon your face, what do you do? Do you not chase it away at once? Otherwise it may sting you. Act in the same way when doubts come to you against your holy faith. Chase away the doubt from your heart, otherwise it might wound your soul. Pray at once as that young man did on his death-bed: "O my God! I believe all that the Church teaches. In this faith will I live and die. O Lord! increase my faith." Often awaken the virtue of faith by such acts, so that it may not go to sleep in your hearts. Many people do not believe, because they are poorly instructed in the faith. Inform yourselves thoroughly in the faith by studying your Christian doctrine well; and if you do not understand some doctrine, ask for instruction.
c. *Denial of faith.* Queen Christina of Sweden became a Catholic.But she wanted to keep it a secret and asked the Holy Father to give her permission to attend a Protestant service once a year at Easter and to receive the bread and wine in that church. The Pope refused. Why? Because allowing her request would have been tantamount to a denial of faith. The Queen accepted his decision and gave up her throne. Her faith was dearer to her than her crown.—May Catholics attend Protestant services? No. May they attend a Protestant funeral? Yes.
d. *Infidelity.* Who is an infidel? Infidelity is a great misfortune; for without faith there is no heaven. But surely many heathens have gone to heaven. How can that be?—The heathens, too, hear God's voice in their hearts. If they obey that voice, they can obtain salvation. No one is lost except through one's own fault.—There are infidels even among Christians. Whence comes unbelief? Surely not from being wise and learned, but rather from being proud or from being wicked.

e. *Heresy*. Who is a heretic? Are you allowed to attend a Protestant church?—No. May you, without denying your faith, be present at the funeral or marriage of a Protestant?—Yes. Protestants are heretics, but to be a Protestant is not of itself a sin. Most of them are in error through no fault of their own and believe that they are in the right. But whoever knows the truth and refuses to believe it, cannot obtain heaven. But to be a Catholic is a great blessing. Thank God for that every day and be a really good Catholic! "Thanks be to God, that I am a Catholic!"

For about a decade the Munich Method was under fire.[13] Dogmatic difficulties were raised against it. It was said that the method offends against the Catholic rule of faith. Dogmas cannot be derived from stories even if the stories are taken from the Bible. These dogmas must be received reverently from the Church and then imparted to the children. However, the Church presents these dogmas to us in the catechism, consequently the text of the catechism could only be explained to the children according to the traditional "authoritative" (text-explanatory) method. In answer we may say that the Church is not content with giving the children a book, she sends them a catechist. The catechist is obliged to speak to the children in such a way that they are able to understand him. He must begin with visible facts, which is what a child's mind requires. The children should then find the results of his catechesis summarized in the answers of the catechism. In such a procedure the Catholic rule of faith remains safeguarded, the new method simply preparing the children to receive from the Church not merely words but also their content and meaning.

[13] Cf. Pfliegler, Vol. III, pp. 210–214.—A selection of the most important reactions to the method, emanating from one of the most important reviews of pastoral theology, is given by W. Pichler, *Unser Religionsunterricht* (Vienna, 1907), p. 130. One of the more severe attacks on the Munich Method was delivered by W. H. Meunier, *Die Lehrmethode im Katechismus-Unterricht* (Cologne, 1905). Cf. also R. Bandas, *op. cit.*, especially pp. 206-210; J. T. McMahon, *Some Methods of Teaching Religion* (London: Burns, Oates, 1928), pp. 106–118.

Akin to this objection was the criticism that the Munich Method simply took over the Herbart-Ziller system of steps. This objection is hardly worth considering. Some connections certainly existed even though prominent catechists had not realized it.[14] This connection was due to the catechesis given in schools and to the resulting contacts between catechists and teachers of secular subjects. We can only deplore the fact that many years had to pass before the experiences gained in secular education could be applied also to the teaching of the Catholic faith.

Of more importance were the objections raised against the method from the standpoint of didactics. These were not so formidable as to dislocate the method entirely, but they did lead to certain limitations. Such limitations were:

1. There are subjects which the Munich Method does not cover: hymns, prayers and doctrinal tests. With these subjects it is better to use the text-explanatory method. Often when the catechist has to cover ground rapidly he will content himself with explanations of the text. He will then, especially with his younger pupils, stress the perceptible elements and whenever possible place these at the beginning of his instruction.[15] Indeed, he will, when explaining a hymn, first develop its basic idea or situation and then proceed to explanation.

2. It is not always necessary to tell a story. A description of real events or of what the children themselves have experienced personally, or a wall picture, may be equally satisfactory.

[14] In J. Baier, *Methodik der religiösen Unterweisung* (Würzburg, 1897), p. VII (Preface) and *passim,* it is evident that the Herbart-Ziller didactic was not unknown in catechetical circles in Bavaria even before the turn of the century.

[15] If, for example, the catechist has to explain the hymn, "I adore Thee humbly", he must anticipate his explanation by giving the meaning of the word, "light": "a human being errs because he is in darkness, God is light."

3. It is not necessary that the presentation should contain all points of doctrine.[16] This would severely overtax the skill of the catechist. In many instances, especially if several dogmas have to be dealt with in the same period, this cannot be done without artificiality. It is sufficient to give some of the children an understanding of the subject by means of a presentation which appeals to their senses; more precise details can be added later on, or, if necessary, by means of a shortened, new presentation.

4. The text-developing method will remain the rule for the older children. An abridged form of it may be used, particularly when the more advanced children have already acquired some knowledge of the subject. This will be the case particularly when a topic has already been dealt with in class and on the basis of sensible data. For this reason, the text-developing method can gradually be dispensed with in the case of children of the intermediate grades in secondary schools.

5. The Munich Method deals only with the problems connected with the psychological form of the catechesis, but the synthesis presented in the catechism as well as the material of each single catechesis have their own logical structure which must be fully expressed.[17] For this reason the perceptible presentation will sometimes be replaced by the logic of the content or, in the step of explanation, certain details of the presentation might be used or applications be anticipated.

6. The logical structure of instruction should never be lost sight of. In the Catechetical Movement, Otto Willmann emphatically insisted on this in the face of a misleading terminology. Theorists often used terms like "synthesis" and "synthetic method" as opposed to "analysis" and "analytical method" which was said to have prevailed up to that time, for in the new

[16] As is often the case in the catecheses of Stieglitz; see what was said in the passage which we have quoted above, p. 97.

[17] Cf. Eggersdorfer, p. 351.

method the catechism text was "to be pieced together" (synthesized) from the perceptible elements. It was not realized, however, that notions like "synthesis" and "analysis" belong to the logical order and have the opposite meaning, so much so that the new method should have been called "analytical". Actually, from the logical point of view, the catechist, in the instruction, analyzes the concrete event, the concrete image that has been previously presented. In the step of explanation he omits the special characteristics and by abstraction arrives at the concept, at the general law, at the concisely phrased doctrine, of the catechism answer. He then proceeds to the synthesis: the catechism answer, the doctrine, the principle must again be "pieced together" from the concrete characteristics and must be applied to life. This happens in the step of application. The "text-developing" method thus embraces both procedures, analysis and synthesis.[18]

7. Lastly, one final restriction must be made. The "text-developing" method is the classical form of catechesis, or at least the normal form. The young catechist must school himself in this procedure, until its basic outlines become self-evident for him. He may then gradually permit himself more and more latitude in applying it, provided that he remembers clearly his proper task and the psychological laws of the children in his care. In place of the strict order of the steps system the catechist may sometimes substitute "free or original structural elements in various numbers and orders according to the stage of the instruction".[19] In fact, circumstances may often dictate that

[18] This misunderstanding can be avoided, if we speak of a "text-synthetic" as opposed to a "text-analytic" method as has frequently been done: J. M. Wolfe, "The Processes of Analysis and Synthesis in Relation to the Teaching of Religion" in *The Educational Review,* Vol. 22 (1924), pp. 463–472.

[19] G. Götzel, *KBl,* Vol. 75 (1950), p. 210, together with A. Heuser – J. Solzbacher, *Katholischer Religionsunterricht* (Hannover, 1949) who

such an "arbitrary treatment" of the method actually be used. The superficiality and the carelessness of the children may, perhaps, compel the catechist to offer new concrete material to enable the children to grasp some part of the instruction that is being given to them; he may be forced to have recourse to some homely incident, or to devote more time to some chance question of the children, to some momentary interest, to achieve his educational aim. In this way the strict succession of steps which the classical form of the method prescribes may scarcely be recognized any longer.

With such clarifications the text-developing method has finally attained universal recognition. This method has also exercised some influence in other countries and has contributed to the solution of problems in much the same fashion.[20] Only recently a change has taken place in the method of catechesis

deviates from the strict order of the steps to a large extent.—Similarly Eggersdorfer, p. 350: the steps "do not tell us *how* the constitutive elements of the instruction must be arranged in every instance, but they do tell us *what* are the elements which we must take into consideration during the act of instructing, if we are to satisfy the psychological laws which regulate all formation"; cf. the survey in Eggersdorfer "Die Kurve katechetischer Bewegung in Deutschland in einem halben Jahrhundert" in *KBl,* Vol. 76 (1951), pp. 10–19. One sentence which summarizes his essay runs as follows: "For the catechist the scheme of the steps should be much like an examination of conscience."

[20] A. Boyer, *Pédagogie chrétienne* I (Paris, 1947), p. 196, says on one occasion when discussing the Munich Method in connection with his appraisal of American methods: *"Son rayonnement fut universel"*.—The Spanish Bishop, D. Llorente, in his very learned *Tratado elemental de Pedagogia Catequística* (6th ed.; Valladolid, 1948), p. 165, begins his methodological directives with a chapter dedicated to: *Método psicológico de Munich*. See also F. Bürkli, *Methode und Methoden im Religionsunterricht* (Zur Methodik des Religionsunterrichts. Referate der 4. schweiz. Seelsorgetagung [Lucerne 1945], pp. 75–86); A. E. Meyer, *The Development of Education in the Twentieth Century* (New York: Prentice-Hall, 1939), pp. 1–124.

in missionary countries where the need for a psychological approach was equally urgent.[21]

So much having been attained, the discussions on basic catechetical method did not end, new suggestions were and are being made. Although the basic outlines were not affected by them, further elaboration was achieved. It was necessary to advance further in the direction of making the catechesis both vital and effective for the lives of the children since they now understood what they were being taught. At this juncture a valuable contribution was discovered in two new pedagogical currents which became known as the "Learn by doing" and the "Principle of personal experience" methods. The purpose of both these principles was to give to children something more than instruction, which they absorbed more or less passively. The intention of the former was to stimulate the children's own powers and to utilize to the full their experiences. According to the latter, the teacher should not only aim at their understanding but, by appealing to their emotions, should attempt to instil into them the values inherent in the subject being taught.

2. Vitalizing the Method

The "Learn by Doing" Principle

The catchword "learn by doing" or "the work school" is taken from secular teaching, from which the formal steps were also drawn. It denotes that method of instruction in which the

[21] J. Thauren, *Die religiöse Unterweisung in den Heidenländern* (Vienna, 1935) in which he establishes on the basis of questionnaires, that, at that time, in the majority of the missions all instructions began with the catechism and that these instructions consisted simply in explaining it word for word in the traditional *(sic)* way—an exception was the biblico-genetical method employed by the White Fathers in Uganda.—An attempt to arouse and to encourage better methods was made in the *Blätter für die Missionskatechese und katechetische Zusammenarbeit der Länder* which were

children learn "by doing", or "by working", that is through their own activity. The Munich educationalist, Georg Kerschensteiner (d. 1932), used the term for the first time in 1908. He received the stimulus for it in the course of a journey through the United States where he became acquainted with the American technical schools. The idea caught on quickly everywhere. The term, however, soon began to be understood in different senses: on the one hand manual activity was stressed, as if the aim of the school actually was to prepare children to become good craftsmen; on the other hand, the intellectual cooperation of the pupils with the teacher, and the forms which corresponded to this cooperation both inside and outside the school, was meant.

The new principle was relevant to catechesis only insofar as it signified the intellectual cooperation of the children with the catechist. Consequently we speak of the "active school" in connection with catechesis but not as if it offered an entirely revolutionary method or represented a methodological innovation. In general its sense would be better understood if instead of "activity method" we used the term "activity principle".[22]

published in Vienna, 1935–1938; F. F. Ewing (ed.), "The Training of Converts" in *Proceedings of the Fordham University Conference of Mission Specialists,* First Annual Meeting, Jan. 24–25, 1953 (New York: Fordham University Press, 1953), pp. 29—37 in which E. G. Mommaerts offers his views on "World Survey of Contemporary Training Systems for Converts".

[22] S. G. Noble, *A History of American Education* (New York: Rinehart & Co., 1953), pp. 397–403; J. Dewey, *The School and Society* (Chicago: University Press, 1913); *The Thirty-third Yearbook of the National Society for the Study of Education,* Part. II, *The Activity Movement* (Bloomington, Ill.: Public School Publ. Co., 1934) in which such phrases as "activity movement", "child-centered school", "activity curriculum", "creative youth", or "center of interest" are all used as synonyms for activity. Active Committee, *"Creative Schools", The National Elementary Principal,* Twenty-third Yearbook, July 1944, Vol. XXIII, No. 6; E. J. Power, "Progressive Education and Bishop Spalding" in *The Catholic Edu-*

In its essentials, this method had already been embodied in the three steps. By means of the activity principle, however, they receive the more definite directive that the children should cooperate as much as they possibly can. For a long time it had become increasingly evident that that instruction, to which they merely listened passively, had no lasting results in the children, even though the catechist had taken care to make the subject matter understandable. Children must not be lectured at. The instruction makes a much deeper impression when the children are able to collaborate in acquiring new knowledge.[23] This cooperation should not, however, be limited only to the understanding, but should enlist as far as possible all the faculties of the children and should use all forms of expression. In this way the catechist can lighten the burden of apperception, that is, the spontaneous reception and assimilation of the subject matter. Such a course will be all the more important the greater the expected educative result, as is the case in religious education. If the life of the child is to be formed in a Christian fashion, this formation must begin in catechesis in as many ways as possible. Thus Göttler said at the first Catechetical Congress, 1912: "The demand for 'an active school' must therefore be met by religion more than by the other secular subjects."[24] For this

cational Review, Vol. 51 (1953), pp. 671–679; J. A. Hardon, "John Dewey, Prophet of American Naturalism" in *The Catholic Educational Review,* Vol. 50 (1952), pp. 433–445; 505–517; 577–588.

[23] This idea can be found in St. Thomas, *De veritate,* q. 11 *(= De magistro)* a. 1.; cf. St. Thomas (J. V. McGlynn, trans.), *Truth* (Chicago: Regnery), Vol. II (1953), pp. 77–87. In the educational process the teacher has the same role as that of a doctor toward his patient; the patient is cured chiefly by nature which knows how to take care of itself. The doctor is only a servant of nature *(minister naturae);* he is called in to lend his assistance to nature. It is, however, nature which is active and effects the cure *(principaliter operatur);* cf. O. Willmann, *Aus Hörsaal und Schulstube* (Freiburg: Herder, 1904), pp. 4–45.

[24] *Referate des Kongresses für Katechetik* (Vienna, 1912), I, 4.

reason in German catechetical circles the "Arbeitsschule" (work-school) was also called "Tatschule" (the school of action).[25]

In order to understand the various forms of collaboration, we must examine them as they were developed in the secular subjects. The teacher attempts to incorporate as much variety as possible into the curriculum: school trips, inspection tours, assistance at festivals, to be followed-up by an oral or written report by the children. In the school itself, drawing, painting, and singing take on a new meaning. Various forms of handicraft are added: modelling, carving, carpentry. In the actual instruction, greater use is made of question and answer. The teacher no longer simply presents the subject matter in the form of a lecture. The children learn by means of "informative discussions" which are carried on between teacher and pupils.

Among the more radical forms of the active school, the traditional roles of the teacher and pupil within the class are interchanged. The children ask the questions, not the teacher. Whenever possible, the children give the answers. From this there emerge the pupil-initiated discussions in which the teacher acts only as chairman and guide. If a problem is posed, the children, unasked, consider its implications and express their opinions, their views, and their solutions, but always in the form of a well-disciplined discussion, so that only one pupil at a time stands up and only one speaks. It is hoped that a school

[25] Cf. the two volumes *Religion und Leben, Arbeiten des Münchener Katechetenvereins, gesammelt von G. Götzel (Religionspädagogische Zeitfragen* 4/5*)* (Munich: Kösel und Pustet, 1920).—At the second catechetical congress in Munich (1928) the activity principle was one of the chief topics of discussion; cf. "Der Bericht" *op. cit.,* pp. 69ff.—A new orientation to it was given by F. Kopp, "Grundformen der Arbeitsschule" in *KBl,* Vol. 75 (1950), pp. 49–57 and also pp. 163 ff.; cf. also R. Dunigan, "New York's Activity School" in *The Catholic Educational Review,* Vol. 41 (1943), pp. 408–415; Sr. M. Raymond Carter, "A Catholic Activity Program" in *The Catholic Educational Review,* Vol. 44 (1946), pp. 259–271.

conducted in such a way might contribute considerably to social education. The teacher may be asked unusual questions by the children, yet only in this way can he become acquainted with their true interests in order to build upon them. The direct exchange of ideas among the children, even mutual help in class, is not proscribed by the active school. Restlessness in the classroom that is due to work need not, however, be discouraged.

It is clear that in such a method only a teacher of genius can ensure orderly progress in the work of instruction. But it is true of some schools in the U.S.A., for example, that the teaching personnel is specially trained in such an instructional method (among other things, "panel discussions"), and that the children are prepared for life by an education in which mutual assistance, well-ordered community cooperation, and social living are self-evident principles.

A special type of the active school cultivated in the U.S.A. promotes "group work".[26] The class is divided into groups of about four children each. Each group is given a problem to solve. They all contribute to its solution. If the subject matter permits, the problem assigned differs with each group, but it forms a part of a larger whole. They may be told to look up some point in a book, to make an observation, to perform a calculation, to draw up plans for a dramatic play, et cetera. The group leader reports his results which are then pooled and fully discussed in common.[27] These are methods which have been

[26] J. U. Michaelis and P. R. Grim, *The Student Teacher in the Elementary School* (New York: Prentice-Hall, 1953), pp. 192–209; A. G. Melvin, *General Methods of Teaching* (New York: McGraw-Hill, 1953), pp. 173 to 197.

[27] A. Witak, *Moderne Gruppenarbeit* (Vienna, 1950). In opposition to the praise poured out on "group work", we should examine the objections which have been raised against it; thus by G. Wössner, *Lernen und Lehren auf der Stufe der Volksschule* (Stuttgart, 1948), pp. 135f; cf. also G. Johnson, "The Activity Principle in the Light of Catholic Principles" in

derived from science and which are especially suitable in the case of advanced pupils enabling them to develop latent abilities. They are, however, employed and are recommended for use also in other subjects and at the elementary school level.

Extremist supporters of the active school would like to assign the task of teaching to the pupils and not to the teacher. The pupils, organized into school communities, are to determine the matter of the instruction as well as the details of the school discipline, because it is thought that the creative powers of the children can thus be developed. These people, however, overlook a basic principle of all teaching, namely, that in most instances the content of the instruction cannot be acquired by private work, but must be accepted from others; they negate a cardinal principle of all education, namely, that through their class work the children should learn to fit themselves for life in an ordered society. On the basis of his own personal experience, Michael Pfliegler pronounces his judgement on the children who were the supposed beneficiaries of such instruction in the Vienna schools, from the elementary grades to the university level: "Frequently, all powers of reflection are lost. The pupils are livelier, and cleverer than before, but also more superficial, more disrespectful, more glib, less capable of being taught. They are impertinent and forward, incapable of deep feeling, thin and worn out. . . . They have forgotten how to listen, as well as to obey."[28]

For some time now, thoughtful educators have circumscribed the scope of the active school, even in secular subjects.[29] Their

The Catholic Educational Review, Vol. 39 (1941), pp. 65–72; R. E. Kahrhoff, "Traditional Objectives and Progressive Methods" in *The Catholic Educational Review,* Vol. 49 (1951), pp. 434–445 and pp. 601–615; Sr. M. Callixta, "Activity and Intellectual Discipline" in *The Catholic Educational Review,* Vol. 39 (1941), pp. 547–556.

[28] Pfliegler, Vol. III (1935), pp. 270f.

[29] T. J. Quigley, "The Implications of Religious Education" in *The*

strictures are even more relevant for catechesis which deals with revealed truth. Although approving in principle the method of the active school and its objectives, the German Bishops' Conference at Fulda emphatically stressed its limitations as early as 1924.[30] It is the duty of the catechist as the ambassador of God to instill into the children the riches of faith; it is not the duty of the children to acquire these truths solely by their own unaided efforts. It is true that truths of the natural order, for example, many precepts of the moral law, may be arrived at by class discussion. It is also true that one truth of faith may be illuminated and clarified by another with which the children are already familiar, for example, the full powers of the Church which are deduced from the threefold office of Christ, or the value of the sacrament of Penance derived from a consideration of sin on the one hand, and of grace on the other. By reviewing subject matter that has been treated in class, the children may with the help of the catechist be able to solve new problems, such as those suggested in the new catechisms at the end of the lessons. Biblical events and the mysteries of faith, however, can not be acquired by the personal efforts of the children. A further stricture is the fact that the content of Christian doctrine is not only meant for the mind, but also for the heart. In those instances in which the subject matter is designed to touch the heart the religious instruction period should not be spent in idle discussion, rather the catechist should speak and the children should listen in silence.

Within these limits the principles of the active school can be of value to catechists. The text-developing method can receive

Catholic Educational Review, Vol. 40 (1942), pp. 264–273; Eggersdorfer, pp. 151–163; J. T. McMahon, "A Trinity of Disciples—Body, Intellect, Will" in *The Catholic Educational Review,* Vol. 39 (1941), pp. 133–140.

[30] The text of the agreement may be seen in Göttler, *Religions- und Moralpädagogik,* pp. 203–205.

both support and development from it, because this activity principle does aim to affect the lives of the children. The extent to which it may be employed will in particular cases depend entirely on the fact, how the children of the classes in question are being taught in the other branches. For children who are accustomed to a great deal of personal activity, the catechist must allow as much freedom and liberty of movement as possible and entrust them with more ambitious work. In the case of others, who have been trained only to listen passively, he should not become unduly perturbed about their apparent inertia. For the average case, certain principles may be laid down. The collaboration of the children should be enlisted especially in the preliminary step of preparation, with certain reservations respecting the explanation, and the application.

The beginning is generally a preparation which indicates the purpose of the lesson. It is necessary to build upon the knowledge already acquired by the children and to awaken their interest in the subject matter. The ground has to be ploughed, before it can be sown.[31] The catechist should permit the children to tell what they know of the matter. For example, wishing to treat of Baptism; he may ask the question: " which of you has been at a Baptism?" or, if he wishes to discuss the law for the observance of Sunday: "Why should we go to church on Sunday?" Perhaps, in a previous period, he might have given them home-work to do which in his mind would serve the formal steps of preparation. Once the children have their own knowledge, acquired by their own limited experience, and in this process have given voice to the feeling that there is much unexplored territory still to be covered, especially such as can be of importance for their own lives, the catechist may feel that he has captured their interest and can embark upon the formal step of presentation of his own matter.

[31] Cf. Pfliegler, Vol. II, pp. 174ff.

In the presentation, itself, there is usually no room for a discussion between the teacher and the class unless the catechist should utilize experiences which the children have already made, or should deal with examples which are sufficiently well-known to his pupils.

In the explanation, there is room for the activity of the children. Helped by the questions of the catechist, the children may, from examples, from actual events, learn the essential facts, the general law, the rule, and so arrive at a knowledge of the doctrine. But the definitive formulation, at least when dealing with the statements of the catechism, must not be left to the children, but should be reserved to the catechist.

Finally, another opportunity for collaboration is afforded in the step of application. This can be done, first of all, by permitting the children to draw conclusions, to offer solutions for particular cases, to judge examples and by applying what they have already learned: prayer, song, and confession. We intend to come back to this point later.

From what has already been said, it is clear that the most important means at the disposal of the catechist in the "active method" is the question. For centuries the sole means by which catechesis was differentiated from preaching was by questioning. Undoubtedly the word itself frequently suggests an investigation, a test of sorts; the teacher asks questions about the instruction. The "active school" demands in addition that the catechist employ "the exploratory question" and the "thought-provoking question". From these derive the instructive, the informative discussion.

In the era of Enlightenment, these different types of questions were generously employed in catechesis. In fact the ideal of catechesis was thought to consist of their unlimited utilization, of asking what the pupils knew, of following the Socratic method. Precisely because of this preoccupation with the question, questioning itself fell into desuetude. It is clear, however, that the "exploratory question" can be valuable for catechesis. When the catechist, for example, in the step of explanation, has explained a difficult part of the subject matter, he may by means of questions be able to determine whether the children have understood what he has told them, and can repeat it in their own words. Of even greater importance is the "thought-provoking" question which may impel the children to think for themselves. They will be encouraged by the catechist to draw their own conclusions from the premises which have already been presented, to derive the doctrine from a story, to apply from a principle to a given case.

As we have already indicated, questioning should not be employed indiscriminately. Much less may the time for catechesis be spent simply in asking questions. Especially during the presentation, the catechist alone should be speaking. The question should be phrased correctly; it should not be couched in too general terms. "What is man?" "What can the priest do?" are too general. The question should not cover several different points under one heading ("when and why should we pray"); it must be worded in such a way, that only one precise answer can be given to it.

The question should be asked with tact. Reverence for the saints and the guileless faith of the children should not suffer because of it; for example, a catechist should never introduce a topic by a question which voices a doubt. Saint Thomas might begin a question: "It would seem as if God did not exist", but children are not yet able to distinguish between a methodical and genuine doubt.

The question should be addressed to the entire class. The children should be induced to show modestly when they are ready to answer. One of the children is usually called upon to give the answer. This procedure has the advantage of compelling all the children to be prepared to reply. The catechist should see to it that the less talented children are also occasionally afforded an opportunity of making a contribution. In general, the answer should be given in the form of a complete sentence. Sometimes, it may be defective, perhaps because the child is unable to find the right expressions. In such an emergency the patient love of the catechist should manifest itself, so that "the glimmering spark is not extinguished", but is helped along with kindness and understanding. The catechist who knows how to manipulate the question method is like the conductor of an orchestra. Each child contributes his own particular instrumentation to the whole as drum, piccolo or first violin. The catechist gives the signal to join in and they collaborate.[32]

The other forms of the active school which are utilized in the secular branches may only be sparingly used by the catechist in catechesis—as a rule he does not have an overabundance of time at his disposal. Among the various kinds of manual activity which are employed in the secular subjects, drawing should be given first consideration. But this, as some other types of creative work, should be pressed into service primarily as homework. More recent catechetical treatises and now especially the German "lesson unit catechism" (English translation published 1958) offer a variety of suggestions and hints for such work. In the case of the more mature children, group-work may be attempted at this point but only under certain circumstances. It may be used, for example, when the class are told to gather impressions and observations which they have had, for example, in a church, a cemetery, or a chapel; when the children are required to answer questions about Bible stories that have already been dealt with in class; and especially when they are told to make preparations for a religious assembly in

[32] *KBl,* Vol. 71 (1946), p. 93.

which suitable hymns from the diocesan hymnal should be suggested, or texts, poems, mottos chosen and prepared for delivery.[33] Another occasion for group-work is present when, for instance, a catechist in a one- or two-class school sets one group a task to keep it occupied while he instructs the other.

The catechist will to some extent remain sceptical towards pupil discussion. If he should be assigned to a school in which certain periods are devoted to such discussions, he would for the sake of prudence not forbid them entirely. If he has not yet mastered the art of instructing, he should refrain from making use of the discussion method in lessons devoted to new subject matter, only employing it during the repetition of material taught on a previous occasion.[34]

In his use of the activity principle, the catechist should not forget that the most important activity which he may and must exact from the children is the practical application of what they have learned. Their conduct towards God and their neighbours, their prayer life, Mass attendance and the consistent and zealous practice of all the virtues, should thus be affected.

The Principle of Personal Experience

The principle of personal experience both in instruction and education was first formulated for secular pedagogy at the beginning of the present century. Its roots, however, extend far back into the past; they were evident in the repugnance of many

[33] Among others, weigh the suggestions offered in the *ChPBl,* Vol. 62 (1949), pp. 193–196 (J. Klement), Vol. 64 (1951), pp. 269f. (Ernestine Blach), Vol. 65 (1952), pp. 54–57 (E. J. Korherr).—Heuser-Solzbacher, pp. 28f.; Sr. M. Irene, "Report on Prayer Book Experiment" in *Catholic Educator,* Vol. 24 (1953/54), pp. 331–334; Sr. N. Wilfrid, "Nursery Rhymes and Religion" in *Catholic Educator,* Vol. 19 (1948/49), pp. 213–215.

[34] During the *Österreichische Tagung für Religionsunterricht und religiöse Erziehung* in Vienna 1951 some lay catechists who were experienced in

for the dry intellectualism which found its most radical embodiment in the Romantic movement and later in the philosophy of vitalism. The German "youth movement" made it possible for the principle of personal experience to penetrate into the sphere of education.

It is claimed that not only the intellect but also the sum total of the soul's faculties: senses, imagination, heart, feeling, will, joy, enthusiasm, all sentiments of the soul, should be fostered and developed. By reason of its rejection of intellectualism, the principle of personal experience agrees with the activity principle. Whereas the active school is, however, bent on all-pervading activity and is directed outwardly, the principle of personal experience denotes the faculty of passive reception, involving all the powers of the soul; it is thus directed toward the interior life.

Without doubt it can be useful for catechetics: while adhering to the basic rational structure of catechesis it may receive stimuli from that source which will help it to overcome an exaggerated intellectualism. As we have often stressed in the above, the aim of catechesis is not achieved if the catechetical material is only taught and learned. What matters is that faith

this particular form of instruction, gave two model lessons which were based substantially on pupil discussion. On another occasion, however, doubts were expressed as to the value of the discussion (panel and otherwise) for catechesis. Cf. the report in *Katechetische Besinnung* (Vienna, 1951), pp. 118 f., in which J. Klement adopts a position in regard to it; consult the same author, "Für und wider das Schülergespräch" in *ChPBl,* Vol. 62 (1949), pp. 65–67. He pointed out the danger of its degenerating into senseless prattling carried on by the more uninhibited individuals in the class, of its wasting time, of its lessening reverence for sacred things.—Consult the experiences of a Viennese school inspector, *ChPBl,* Vol. 64 (1951), p. 41, who believes that this type of discussion should be used only for the purpose of repetition; cf. G. J. Schnepp, "Panel Discussion in the Classroom" in *The Catholic Educational Review,* Vol. 46 (1948), pp. 490–496.

and the kingdom of God are grasped by the whole soul as the supreme realities and as ultimate values; as the pearl of great price for which the finder is prepared to sacrifice everything; as the holy law according to which man must fashion his life. True, we can conceive of "religious instruction" which disregards these objectives and imparts only doctrines and facts and strives to make them understood. Even unbelieving parents would surely desire such an instruction for their children. For it is a part of general culture, if not good breeding, that the children would know something of Paradise and the Flood and of incidents in the life of Christ, if for no other reason than that our language and the history of art often refers to them. But, as catechists, we have not been called to impart such a "religious instruction".

More than anything else, religion or better still Christian doctrine should thrill men and should touch them to their very core. But this is exactly what personal experience can do. We must remember, however, that one personal experience differs from another. A personal religious experience, in the wide sense, of being an interior event which can affect a person profoundly, for example, the conversion of St. Paul or St. Augustine, an event which continues to make its repercussions felt for life, such a personal experience is not the stuff of everyday life, and we could never hope to provoke one for ourselves or for someone else. Such an experience is reserved for the extraordinary workings of divine grace. We can, however, and we should, stress and make fertile the values that are contained in the texts of revelation. We can and should arouse the capacities for faith, hope and charity slumbering in the hearts of children and make them fruitful for life and for Christian living. This means that in the course of our ordinary catechesis an elevated and dignified mood should prevail, so that not only the intellect but also our feelings, our hearts, should be touched.

This cannot be done simply by developing the single points of doctrine in accordance with the formal steps beginning with the visual facts, and ending with their application to life; for these steps are of the logical order and, as a result, lack effectiveness.[35] Nor can it be done simply by arousing the active powers of the children, as the "activity principle" prescribes.[36] It is much more decisive to enthrall the hearts of the children by the sublime and holy realities which we are commissioned to teach, to fill them with wonderment at the greatness and goodness of God, to arouse their holy joy in the beauty of a Christian life, in short, to make the children feel that this religion period is concerned with things of profound importance. This is what personal religious experience means and how it should be understood.

We must of course reject a religion that is purely sentimental but it would be an error equally grave to foster a religion entirely devoid of all feeling. Even if we continually stress the fact that in charity, in contrition, and in prayer, it is not feeling that matters, we should not want to say that true love, genuine contrition, and correct prayer are entirely without feeling. What we mean is that the primary element is thought and the resolution of the will. The natural radiations of this hard core will always affect the feelings, if no special obstacles are placed in their way. Conversely a certain compelling power is immanent and peculiar to feeling. This power not only lightens the task of making a resolution, but also eases the burden of acquiring knowledge, especially for children whose reasoning

[35] Cf. Pfliegler, Vol. III, pp. 215–249 and especially pp. 217f.

[36] In any case the activity principle may be employed to help engender a personal religious experience, not indeed merely by prescribing a number of activities or by encouraging a zealous employment of the questioning technique, but by utilizing the experiences which the children may already have acquired; cf. Pfliegler, Vol. III, pp. 297ff.

is never logical. That is why the harmony of feeling is educationally of great importance.

It is entirely in conformity with the nature of religious truth that it stirs our sentiments. The feeling of being a creature corresponds to the knowledge of our complete dependence on the Creator. A feeling of gratitude is awakened when we realize how richly we have been endowed by God both with nature and grace. The feeling of a fear of God is fanned when we perceive the holiness of His law and our own insignificance and frailty. The feeling of proud admiration is stirred when we become aware of the personality of our Saviour, of His mighty achievements and of His compelling goodness. Even feelings which are aroused by a consideration of the natural order can and should be linked with subjects of the religious and moral order. The love of a child for his parents may well serve as a preparation for the love of God; the joy in the clouds sailing majestically across the sky, in the pure beauty of spring blossom, the delight in all that is beautiful and noble, can all be utilized to further the education of the children in chastity.

The question is, what can we as catechists do in this direction? It should go without saying that we should avoid everything that smacks of artificiality and affectation. The emotional response, the atmosphere of fervour, should arise spontaneously as a result of the conception and presentation of the subject matter. The catechist must create within himself the proper conception and presentation, and adopt the right religious attitude. True, this cannot be done in a moment; it is a matter for his entire personality, which should in a sense be awe-inspired by the magnitude of divine revelation. This awe can be acquired only by a genuine and intensive life of prayer. In such a way the catechist will absorb in prayer and reverence, the "good news" of God, transmitting it to the children with holy joy. In this sense every catechesis should be "truly a religious service for children".[37] The catechist need not be afraid during the religion period of permitting his own personal feelings to find expression in the tone of his voice, in the choice of his words, in the expression of his face and in his gestures, just as a mother does when she admonishes or warns her children, or when she has something worthwhile to tell them.[38] A reverent atmosphere is thus almost bound to be created. In order that this atmosphere may unfold, it is necessary that certain conditions be fulfilled.

First of all, externals are of importance. In this respect catechesis in school, and in a secular environment, labours under a disadvantage that was absent from the catechesis formerly given in church.[39] It has been recommended, not without reason, that occasionally when an important catechesis is to be given, for example, on the sacrifice of the Mass, that it be given in a church or a chapel. Under certain circumstances a catechesis on death and the last things could be given in the cemetery or in a mortuary chapel. But a zealous catechist will know how to transform his classroom into a holy place.

Still more important is that the catechist removes entirely or lessens as much as possible whatever disturbs or disrupts the catechesis. Good discipline is indispensable. It is likewise important that a happy, joyful atmosphere prevails in the classroom and that the children feel at ease in the religious instruction

[37] Gatterer, p. 351.

[38] The catecheses of Augustin Gruber can serve as a model of language charged with feeling. See above, p. 30.

[39] Without doubt the church with its imposing nave and its religious impressiveness is not the ideal solution. In France where catechesis has no access to the official State school the ecclesiastical authorities are trying to create a *salle de catéchisme,* a room which would combine the advantages of the church and the classroom. Something similar is the aim of those who promote the pastoral, organized religious instruction. The official Catholic school system in the U.S.A. has no difficulties on this score; in the case of the year round school and vacation schools for children, Fishers and Helpers provide suitable quarters in most instances.

period. In a detailed discussion of the question St. Augustine stressed the importance of *hilaritas* for catechesis.[40] Again it is advisable that the catechist should relate his instruction to everything that fills the lives of the children and to whatever constitutes the content of their interests at home and in school, so that they can feel that their own personal problems are being discussed, and thus become more receptive to the light of doctrine. To this category belongs especially the frequent references to one's native land with its customs, its tradition, its shrines and Christian traditions. The homeland is the epitome of what is cherished and loved by the children. Thus the catechist can combine with advantage the feelings which the children entertain for their own country with the subject matter of the catechesis.

When we have said all this, we have sketched only general assumptions and viewpoints. Can we offer any more detailed suggestions by which the catechesis can incorporate more personal experiences and ensure a reverent atmosphere. We must thus ask ourselves how we can bring these new principles into accord with the already well-established method, or more precisely, with the laws of the formal steps.

At first glance it would seem that a certain incompatibility exists between the two insofar as in the formal steps a certain definite, but essential, logic prevails: the preparation for the abstract by the concrete and then the return again to the concrete. Feeling and sentiment whose cultivation is demanded by personal experience appear to be in complete opposition to the logical steps. In fact, the German teacher Heinrich Kautz who advocates emphasis on personal experience is an opponent of the doctrine of the formal steps.[41] He retained only two

[40] Augustinus, *De catech. rudibus,* c. 10–14; J. P. Christopher, *op. cit.,* pp. 34–51.

[41] Kautz, *Neubau des katholischen Religionsunterrichtes,* 3 vols. (Kevelaer:

main steps, the step of preparation for a personal experience, and that of performing the action. On a closer examination, however, we can detect in his theory the first and third of the traditional formal steps, presentation and application, in a new form.

The step of explanation, namely the work necessary to impart an understanding of the principle, is omitted by Kautz. And concerning this point the methodology developed by him at that time is unacceptable. For as long as catechesis implies the handing on of Christian doctrine, it cannot do without teaching, hence without communicating clear notions. We may add that even the richest personal experience will eventually disappear, insofar as it consists of feeling and of sentiment. That which lasts, which endures, is that solid core which has become a principle; this is the new insight into the truth of a doctrine which continues to exercise its influence as motive—however deep-rooted the insight might first have become as a result of feeling.[42] The exclusion of the step of explanation is therefore unjustifiable. But it is correct to restate more precisely the

Butzon u. Bercker, 1923/26). *Translators' note:* On the basis of correspondence carried on between Fr. J. A. Jungmann and Fr. H. Kautz, the latter today holds that a combination of the pedagogy of personal experience and of a triad of formal steps is not only possible but also necessary, because of the materials (cinema, television, illustrated newspapers, etc.) which flood the child with experiences that are personal but come to him from without.

[42] There is as we know a basic idea in the pedagogy of the will that motives are responsible for decisions; there is also a basic demand that they be associated with sentiments and with joyous experiences; they should, however, also contain a solid core of idealistic elements. J. Lindworsky (A. Steiner and E. A. Fitzpatrick, trans.), *The Training of the Will* (Milwaukee: Bruce, 1929); A. Willwoll, *Denken und Erlebnis: Zur Methodik des Religionsunterrichtes* (*Referate der 4. schweiz. Seelsorgetagung* [Lucerne, 1945]), pp. 60–74; Sisters of Notre Dame, *Aids to Will Training in Christian Education* (New York: F. Pustet, 1943), esp. pp. 41–75; cf. also Pfliegler, Vol. II, pp. 201f.; Vol. III, pp. 225 f.; J. T. McMahon, *Building Character From Within* (Milwaukee: Bruce, 1940).

steps of presentation and of application in the light of these new suggestions.

If the step of presentation should serve to create a visual basis for knowledge, this need not necessarily mean that it should be restricted only to knowledge. Actually it can and should accomplish much more. An event, an example, a picture which we offer the children as a visual starting point of our catechesis should capture their feelings for what is good, for the kingdom of God, for the person of our Lord, as far as it is possible. And if we should here succeed in increasing the impression to the point of a personal experience, so much the better. But what is required to make a personal experience possible?[43]

An experience is achieved when an important object, a reality, in our case a religious reality, is not only grasped by the mind and by all the powers of the soul, but when the very senses themselves are affected, and feelings of endeavour result. If possible all these things should take place simultaneously. The soul is thrilled by an object, it is captured by an ideal, which is suddenly and vividly presented to it. This has the effect of prompting questions to arise in the heart, of compelling the soul to seek help, instruction and direction. Thus the way is paved for further guidance by which the notions are deepened and the possibilities of some kind of activity are pointed out. If such a presentation has succeeded, the explanation will become of interest to the children and they will want to see its application.

Such an awakening of all the powers of the soul can be realized, however, only in those instances in which the children are brought into contact with what is alive; in this case, if they are confronted with the practice of religion. The splendour of

[43] Pfliegler, Vol. II, pp. 58–63; Vol. III, pp. 215–249.

a Solemn Mass, the perfection of a liturgical service, can do this. A meeting with a holy person would also be of this kind. In a deeply religious person a sudden shock, not necessarily religious, could become a personal religious experience. But we are as a rule not able to evoke that in catechesis. As a substitute for it, however, the catechist may find that a vivid description of such happenings may suffice. In such a substitute we are faced with what we originally called the step of presentation; but its task becomes more intensive and extensive. It is clear that we should never choose just any common illustration for the beginning of the catechesis but one that makes the impression of something of extreme value, for example, a heroic figure, a famous religious apparition. And we must not treat the persons whom we have chosen only from the outside but let them become alive in their real selves. This can be done by giving a psychological dimension to their acts, so that the children can really experience their hopes and their fears, their joys and their sorrows, their great resolutions and their miserable failures. Holy Scripture, the history of the missions, the lives of the saints, contain numerous examples of this kind. The life of our Lord is filled with scenes which are most appropriate for this kind of treatment. Rightly used, religious, art, especially biblical pictures, can be a great help in enriching and in enhancing the presentation. This realization has caused leading catechists no longer to refer to the step of presentation but rather to the step of personal experience.[44] As a sample of such a presentation, we offer the introduction of a catechesis written by Edmund Jehle on "a good intention":[45]

"In the preparation, the catechist should point out that many people, even though they work and do much good, do not possess the proper

[44] For example, Jak. Bernbeck, *Katechesen für die Oberstufe,* 3 vols. (Munich, 1941).

[45] E. Jehle, *Katechesen für die Oberstufe,* Vol. II (Freiburg, 1928), p. 185.

intention. This we know from Scripture in the case of the Pharisee, whom our Lord attacked so vigorously.

In the presentation, there should follow the story of the widow's mite. 'It was Tuesday of Holy Week and Jesus had just finished pronouncing his eight "woes" against the Pharisees. He had called them hypocrites, and whited sepulchres. He then went and stood near the collection box. Different people came and dropped money into it. A rich Pharisee appeared on the scene. Showily, he took a goldpiece from his purse, held it between his fingers in such a way that everyone could see it and walked with a swaggering gait to the collection-box (show how this was done). All the people watched him and all heard the clink as his piece disappeared into the mouth of the box. All eyes turned to Jesus, as though wanting to ask him: Isn't he a good and pious man? Does he not give a lot to the Temple? Jesus kept silent. Then an old lady entered. She limped painfully and was dressed in threadbare and patched clothes. She took a little piece of cloth out of her purse and slowly undid it. Two little copper pieces were nestled there. The Pharisees looked at her, turned up their noses and thought: the old hag should keep her coppers. Nothing can be done for the Temple with such a gift. Shamefacedly she put her gift quietly into the box. It represented her entire fortune. Again the people looked to Jesus and awaited an answer from Him. This time He did not keep silent, but said: "This poor widow has put more into the box than all the others. They gave of their plenty. She, however, gave of her poverty, and all that she possessed." ' "

In the step of factual explanation nothing need be changed. In the transition from the explanation to the application the catechist should sometimes summarize briefly the results of his work, incorporate the individual points of the doctrine into the larger synthesis, and attempt to make the children conscious of the importance of these truths for their own lives. The auxiliary step of recapitulation will then serve to deepen the impressions already made. This should nor be a mere intellectual deepening. A profound realization will always affect the whole soul, and this can in many instances be heightened in such a way as to produce an emotional reaction. A further example may also produce the desired effect.[46] If at this point a prayer or a song, is

[46] Cf. E. Jehle, *Katechesen für die Oberstufe*, 3 vols. (Freiburg, 1926 to 1930), in which regularly at the end of the catechesis under the title "For further reading" he refers the reader to an example in the appendix of the book.

interpolated, this will help to root the doctrine to be learned even more firmly in the hearts and sentiments of the children. But such a deepening process can be deferred to a subsequent period in which the subject matter may again be gone through by way of a repetition.

The step of application retains its place, but so many favourable preliminary conditions have been achieved that its task is made easier. If the catechist has succeeded in evoking something like a personal experience in the children he may expect that they will look forward to being told what they can do to make it their own.

We must mention yet another occasion which permits Christian doctrine to become a personal experience within the framework of the school: the religious assembly.

The ancient Christian catechumenate used the religious assembly.[47] The Jesuit schools of the sixteenth and seventeenth century made very copious use of it. Among the various groups of the German Youth Movement the religious assembly in a self-planned setting played a great role. In present day secular instruction such assemblies are employed in a variety of ways—for a school celebration, for example, on Memorial Day. It might also be used occasionally instead of the religious instruction period.[48] For the smaller children such an assembly may serve to prepare for a topic to be treated in the catechesis itself or in to connection with a liturgical season. For the older children it can take the place of the recapitulation as a review or exploration of matter that has already been treated. Traces of God in creation, incidents and mysteries in the childhood of Christ, the mysteries

[47] Cf. above, pp. 6-7.

[48] B. Kammler, *Feierstunden im Religionsunterricht* (Munich, 1930) with a number of topics for these assemblies, graded according to the school year, as well as a variety of projects developed for the benefit of the teacher.

of the Rosary, Christ the King, the sacrament of Baptism, the works of mercy (joined perhaps to the legend of St. Martin) are examples of suitable topics. Such a religious assembly is simply a catechesis that is embellished with artistic devices, with recitations, songs, pictures, dramatic interludes, a period in which learning is relegated entirely to the background and in which the lesson that has been learned is made to appear in a new light.

The religious assembly should in essence be produced by the children themselves. Even in the case of the more mature children, it should be kept as simple as possible. The catechist should draw up the plans, assign the parts, establish the links, and at the psychological moment perhaps, personally develop one or the other thoughts or compose a prayer. The preparatory work done by the children is of decisive importance for such a religious hour. The children must practise and learn their roles by heart and perhaps gather material that may be required (texts from the school Bible, from the catechism, or other sources).

If the treatment of the Old Testament has been concluded before Christmas, a Christmas assembly might be organized in the following way.

A few words of introduction by the catechist.

1. Description by the children of the types of our Lord.
   Display (or project) a picture illustrating this theme.
   Sing a hymn such as *Rorate, caeli, desuper*.
2. Recital of the messianic prophecies, one by each child.
   Display a portrait of one of the prophets.
   Sing an appropriate hymn.
3. The reading, by the children, of the gospel texts on the annunciation and the birth of Christ.
   Display a picture of the nativity.
   Sing a Christmas carol.

Here is a suggestion for Advent, conceived in a stricter fashion.

Introductory hymn.

A dramatic-reading in three scenes depicting the life of John the Bap-

tist. The material to be drawn from Luke 3:1-20. Scene I: his appearance. Scene II: his preaching of penance. Scene III: his testimony. After each reading a team of speakers repeat the plea: "Make ready the way of the Lord!"
Concluding hymn.[49]

Adaptation of the Method to the Subject Matter

We have attempted to clarify the basic laws of catechetical method by dealing with one of its more difficult cases, the catechism-catechesis. A few suggestions will suffice here for their applications to other kinds of subject matter, which are easier to treat. It is chiefly a question of subject matter which in contrast to the dogmatic statements of the catechism has a more visual character, and as a consequence, does not need to be presented by means of concrete examples. Some detailed hints may be useful.

Biblical catechesis is the opposite of catechesis on the catechism because it employs a school Bible or a Bible History.[50] In any case the historical episodes, narratives of Holy Scripture, constitute the chief subject. The narrative presentation is, moreover, much more acceptable to the children. We must, however, make a distinction in regard to the method of treatment: between biblical texts which are studied for their own sake and those which serve rather as an illustration for matter that has been developed elsewhere. Among those portions which are treated solely for their own sake we may list the following dealing with the events of redemptive history. An account of paradise, the fall of our first parents, the call of the patriarchs

[49] Berta Koch, "Feierstunden zur Advents- und Weihnachtszeit" in *KBl*, Vol. 73 (1948), pp. 325–327.

[50] For further details consult Mayer, pp. 113–121.—See also A. Elchinger, "Structure des leçons d'Histoire Sainte" in *Vérité et Vie*, Vol. 17, no. 146; in addition to much scepticism of all methods which place strictures on the catechist, cf. Heuser-Solzbacher, pp. 20–51.

and of the Chosen People, the legislation on Mount Sinai, the birth of Christ and more or less all those passages which deal with the life, passion and glorification of Jesus.[51] With regard to these the steps of presentation and of explanation coincide, the happening itself is what the children should remember. Explanations must, nevertheless, still be given in order to make the happenings understandable, for these are set in a past age and a long-forgotten culture. Even the language itself often forms an obstacle because of its traditional form. Generally the explanation will come at the beginning, and should be brief; for example, when the catechist starts to recount the story of the curing of the man born lame (Matt. 9), he should first describe the plan of a typical Jewish house. He must weave other details into his account as he progresses. Moreover, to enable the children to participate in the narrative more easily, an account of the spiritual stages through which the principal characters had to pass will vivify and enrich the text.[52] By such illustrations we do not falsify the account, but only make its content more comprehensible for the children. It goes without saying that the catechist may not alter the text or attempt what the Protestant writer, Heinrich Scarrelmann, did, namely, modernize it.[53] In any case the catechist himself can narrate

[51] See above, pp. 103 f., 129.

[52] We can satisfy the hunger for knowledge which pupils in the upper grades possess by giving them supplementary details which are both geographical and historical (perhaps even cultural). On this point see M. A. Gramlich, *Gehet hin und lehret* (Freiburg: Herder, 1949), p. 21.

[53] There were, for example, two boys, Jacob and Esau. Both went to school. Esau was a grade ahead of his brother and he always got better report cards and was confirmed a year before him, etc. The whole story is given in the *KBl*, Vol. 45 (1919), pp. 356f. Other examples of the same kind may be found in Gatterer, pp. 508f.—The Bishops at the Fulda conference (1917) cautioned against the use of such a procedure in a pronouncement entitled: *Kirchliche Grundsätze über die Behandlung der Biblischen Geschichte im Religionsunterricht:* "... 3. The historical truth must remain

the event. He should do this with as much warmth and love as he possibly can. It is precisely at this point that he might attempt to develop it into a personal experience. He will find that in many cases a wall-picture or a blackboard sketch is invaluable.[54]

After the catechist has delivered his presentation, the children should repeat the story, and then they should read it from the textbook either immediately or at the end of the catechesis. Everything that follows this in the catechesis, may be considered as the step of application. Frequently it may be necessary to emphasize the dogmatic content of the biblical event, the evolution in the history of salvation. In general, however, the catechist should be concerned only with an interpretation and evaluation. That is to say, he should pause to meditate on one or the other points of the sacred event or should attempt to link it to related matter, to draw conclusions for prayer and life. In treating, for example, the birth of Christ, the catechist will stress the following thought: the divine Child as our brother. He should then take up a prayer or a hymn praising or thanking the Child, or consider the feast of Christmas, the *Gloria in excelsis,* the veneration of the Mother of God or other matters of the same kind.

In other instances, the Bible story should serve more as a framework for an idea than as an independent subject in itself.

untouched. The modernization of Bible History is as a consequence entirely inadmissible; the catechist may not remove it from its context of the biblical scene of the biblical era, of morals and of customs of the East. He may, though, make use of modern conditions for the purposes of comparison and of concreteness, so that the children will be enabled to understand more easily what is actually historical. For didactical reasons this should take place during a discussion, rather than in the preliminary narration of the historical event." The full text is reproduced by Göttler, *Religions- und Moralpädagogik* (2nd ed.), pp. 201–203.

[54] For further information on this score, see below, pp. 226 f.

In the parables of the prodigal son we should learn to treasure the paternal goodness and mercy of God towards penitent sinners. Here the catechist should in fact offer a special explanation. In general it is true of parables—and similarly of Old Testament prototypes—that the presentation should arouse a certain tension in the children and should evoke some question about the deeper meaning to be found in them. The explanation will then provide a solution, which may be offered in a blackboard sketch which deals with the parable step by step.[55]

Many incidents in Bible History, especially those of the Old Testament, are important for catechesis chiefly because of the moral doctrine which they contain. Thus, for example, the story of the Egyptian Joseph should not be developed in all its broad implications simply as a story, but should be used as an example of the virtues and vices in the conduct of the brothers. In this story especially, the catechist should try to give the children some idea of the destructive effect of envy, or, on another occasion, of the providence of God, which rules over our life. From these he should deduce practical applications. In this way the biblical catechesis will approximate the catechism-catechesis both in arrangement and construction.

In liturgical topics, insofar as they are treated in special catecheses and are not used only incidentally with other subjects, the schema of the formal steps should have its own form. In the liturgy we deal for the most part with procedures and institutions which are concrete and visual. In some fashion or another they are already known to the children (the ceremonies, for example) or can be shown to them in a picture or be made understandable to them by means of a description

[55] J. Missliwetz, "Der Bibelunterricht in der Hauptschule" in *ChPBl,* Vol. 66 (1953), pp. 161–165.—On the treatment of doctrinal texts, see above, p. 188.

(for example, the procedure in the case of a sick call). The catechist must then draw the necessary conclusions and evaluate the more profound content. A liturgical text, a sacred song, a hymn can be taken through simply by means of the "text-explanatory" method, but in such a way that, as far as possible, the perceptual element is stressed and placed at the beginning.[56]

[56] Cf. p. 188.

VII

SPECIAL QUESTIONS OF CATECHETICAL METHOD

Up to the present we have studied only the most general laws of method, especially such as are drawn from the psychology of the child and find application in the step procedure of catechesis. A closer examination of the catechetical task will pose further problems and considerations to which we must now apply ourselves. We shall do this by taking the formal steps one by one, and in that connection deal with all the relevant questions. Among the demands which must be fulfilled in the course of the presentation are: (1) the correct use of different visual aids, and especially (2) of correct catechetical language. The explanation, which should result normally in an understanding of what is being presented, must be of a kind that is adapted to the mental capacity of the children, and yet does not falsify the deposit of faith (3), it should not aim merely at sober knowledge but at assent by faith (4) and should tend to form consciences and to build up moral dispositions (5). Then we pass on to practical application, which achieves its noblest expression in education to prayer and prayer itself (6); which assumes a tangible form in home work (7) of which memorization is not the least part (8) and which is continued in practical work (9).

1. *Visual aids*

If concreteness is one of the basic demands for children's catechesis, and if the first formal step is designed to attain it, the catechist will readily avail himself of aids that enable the child not only to grasp an object with the imagination, but also to see it with the bodily eye. That many, indeed most topics in Christian doctrine, permit visual examination is due to the fact that the Word has become flesh and dwelt amongst us, moreover, that Christ founded a visible Church, which carries on the work of redemption with visible means.

Of such important topics of catechesis as the Church, her life and mission, her sacraments and her divine services, the children may indeed learn by direct observation. In the classroom the catechist is for them a visible embodiment of the Church's teaching office. This view is enlarged when they see the priest in the pulpit, or at the altar, or when on Sundays the children form a part of the parish which gathers around him for prayer and for sacrifice. This community is for them a genuine miniature of the Church on earth. And the Church in turn truly impinges on their consciousness, if, for example, the Bishop visits the parish from time to time.

This is the place for liturgical instructions of which we will speak later on. The catechist should afford the children an opportunity of being present at a Baptism. Under favourable circumstances, for example, in the country, he may permit them to accompany him on a sick call, or when the class is to study Extreme Unction, he may allow them to set up a table for a sick room on which all the necessary articles are arranged.[1] Above all, he should take them into church and there explain to them the details of its furnishings and its utensils: the baptismal font with its symbolical representations, the pulpit, the altar (or altars), enriched with their statues, especially the altar stone with its cloth coverings (linens), the care which is taken of the tabernacle (keys, veils, etc.). He should also take them to the sacristy where they can look at the vestments, the liturgical

[1] How a lay catechist did this in the presence of children, see *ChPBl.* Vol. 64 (1951), pp. 41f.; cf. also M. L. and J. Defossa, "Ceremony of Preparation for Baptism" in *Lumen Vitae,* Vol. 9 (1954), pp. 9–16.

books, the sacred vessels. He will take care that reverence for these sacred objects is not only preserved, but also increased by telling them, for example, that as the golden chalice was designed with such great artistry and completed with even greater love because its maker knew that it was destined to hold the Precious Blood so, in like fashion, our hearts should be prepared to receive Holy Communion. Certain vestments must be kissed by the priest, before he puts them on for Mass; he can repeat this when he shows them to children. He may even permit one or the other of the children to do the same. Such a visit to the church should end with a prayer or with a short service.

The Church and her activities are the foundation for the history of redemption. This history can be presented to the children in pictures. We have already spoken of the illustrations in the Bible Histories.[2] Pictures can be useful also for catecheses on the catechism. Those of special value are of a large size, viz., catechetical wall pictures, which can be fastened to the blackboard or elsewhere and are visible to the entire class.[3] It should be evident that such pictures should be the work of true artists, especially when they are intended to be more than a mere delineation of an historical event, that is to say, when they

[2] See above, p. 111, 113.

[3] A. Heilmann, *Bibel-Bilder, Gedanken zur religionspädagogischen Wertung biblischer Kunst* (Kempten: Kösel und Pustet, 1911). In addition to a discussion of principles, this book presents a penetrating study of various series of pictures for catechetical use, which were available at the time.— J. Krones, *Die neuzeitlichen Anschauungsmittel und ihr didaktischer Wert für den Religionsunterricht* (2nd ed.; Rottenburg: Badersche Buchhandlung, 1932).—For a discussion of the other kind of audio-visual aids for biblical uses within the framework of Bible history, consult: *The Catholic School Journal* (Milwaukee: Bruce) which frequently during the year discusses the various audio-visual aids and their practicality for catechetical purposes; and also *The Catholic Educator* (New York: J. F. Wagner) which in every issue carries a special section devoted to audio-visual aids.

purport to interpret the supernatural significance of an event or to express spiritual meanings in a form that the senses can perceive. On the other hand the conditions necessitated by catechetical practice should also be taken into consideration; the picture should help the children to understand and to appreciate the circumstances in which the event portrayed takes place. This can be done by making its composition simple, by paying strict attention to each and every figure and detail. The picture should, moreover, express some noble sentiment, should create some religious impression. In the pictures of holy men and women their otherworldiness should at least be indicated by the nobleness of their bearing and by the sublimity of their attitudes.[4] Of course, this places some restriction upon the artist, but no more than he must expect in any commission.

On the other hand, we should point out that only the content of the picture is important for the children of the lower grades, that only after the age of ten the form too will be noticed; only for the first time in adolescence will its artistry be fully appreciated.[5] Extremely forceful pictures which succeeded in leaving an indelible imprint on their souls in childhood will continue to

[4] It may be permitted us here to express our misgivings about whether pictures of God in human form,—a custom which was introduced in the golden period of the Middle Ages,—represent a salutary development. Up until that time artists (and teachers) had been content to depict God's intervention in the affairs of men by means of a hand stretching out from behind a cloud. Only after the faithful began to interchange the notions of God and Christ more and more (e. g., constantly recurring phrases such as "the corpse of God", "God's feet"), did they begin to transfer the human appearance of Christ to the invisible God. By this, the Christian view of the world began to lose its clarity. The further historical spiritual processes which were implicit in this disfiguration, cf. J. A. Jungmann, "Die Abwehr des germanischen Arianismus und der Umbruch der religiösen Kultur im frühen Mittelalter" in *ZkTh,* Vol. 69 (1947), pp. 36–99, especially p. 82.

[5] Eggersdorfer, pp. 390 f.; B. E. Mellinger, *Children's Interests in Pictures* (New York, N. Y.: Teachers College, Columbia University,

exert a profound influence for their entire lives. "And when all words and admonitions of the catechist have long since been scattered by the whirlwind of youthful fickleness or have been buried under the cares of life, the memory of such a picture continues to live on in the soul."[6] It is inevitable that a certain tension between the demands of the catechist and the personal experience of the artist[7] working for him, will be created, and that only in exceptional cases will it ever be completely resolved.[8]

As illustrations of a purely didactic nature we must mention: wall maps and the pictures (sketches) of liturgical ceremonies. In order that the maps of the holy land may be effective from a catechetical standpoint it is important that historical and biblical

1932); J. G. Morrison, *Children's Preferences for Pictures* (Chicago: University of Chicago Press, 1935).

[6] Heilmann, *op. cit.,* p. 26.

[7] This tension is analyzed in an article written by the artist who drew the illustrations for the new German catechism A. Burkart, "Gedanken zur Katechismusillustration" in *KBl,*Vol. 74 (1949), pp. 346–352.

[8] In the works of Heilmann and Krones we can find a critical appreciation, with an analytical criticism, of catechetical pictures available during the first quarter of this century. Among these there are the 100 biblical pictures of G. Fugel, a new edition of which was published in 1948 (Munich: Isaria); there are also 60 illustrations of Ph. Schumacher (Düsseldorf: Patmos-Verlag). There is a collection of the pictures of Mate Mink-Born, consisting of 150 biblical scenes which has reappeared in a new edition. Concerning these and three other collections of biblical pictures which appeared outside of Germany consult A. de Marneffe, "Bible History Pictures" in *Lumen Vitae,* Vol. 7 (1952), pp. 91–109.—In the U. S. A. there are also collections: *The Nell Series* (four series of fourteen charts) (Geo. M. Nell, Paris-Co-Op.). Fr. Heeg borrows some seventeen of twenty-six of these for his *Jesus and I* booklet (or paste in project); and the *Nelson Collection* (103 for the Life of Christ and 43 for the early years of the Church) (Edinburgh, Scotland: Thomas Nelson & Sons).—Twelve excellent catechetical wall pictures illustrating the fundamental truths of Christianity (knowledge of God, revelation, Christ, the Church) are offered us by J. Klement, *Lehre in Bild und Gleichnis* (Vienna: Herder, 1952).

events in miniature form be inserted on them at those places where they actually happened.[9] This lends credibility to the historical nature of these events; they are thus seen to have taken place in our own world and among men such as we are.

In State schools where it is frequently impossible for the catechist to bring children in a body to assist at Mass, at which they might all receive similar impressions, he will have to use pictures which depict liturgical ceremonies. The concrete character of this data is enhanced, if the wall picture which, let us say, represents the altar, is provided with movable figures which can be inserted into slots provided for them.[10]

In larger schools projectors are available for showing pictures and frequently there are also special projection rooms. The

[9] *KBl,* Vol. 74 (1949), p. 219, gives us a report on the *Lebensweg Jesu* of W. Harwerth; cf. maps of this kind may be procured from Geo. A. Pflaum, Dayton, Ohio; Dennoyer - Geppert, *Story Map of the Life of Jesus* (Chicago: Dennoyer - Geppert); I. S. Hunner, *The Life of Christ* (The John Day Co.). We cannot miss the opportunity of recommending the new L. H. Grollenberg (J. M. H. Reid and H. H. Rowley, trans.), *Atlas of the Bible* (New York and Edinburgh: Thomas Nelson and Sons, 1956). The spelling of names, biblical place names is that of the *Revised Standard Version* of the Bible (Protestant).

[10] A great deal of this material can be procured from Belgium where it was produced at the instigation of G. Lefèbvre: on this subject, see G. Lefèbvre, "La formation liturgique a l'école primaire" in *Lumen Vitae,* Vol. 1 (1946), pp. 73–90. L. P. Goldin, *The Catholic Liturgy in Visual Lessons,* 2 parts, produced by the Visual Text and Equipment Co., Los Angeles, and distributed by the *Society for Visual Education* (SVE) (Chicago, Illinois); Catechetical Guild, *The Perpetual Church Calendar* (St. Paul, Minnesota). This calendar is made of metal with moveable circles and segments by means of which the liturgical year, its seasons, and its feasts are computed and made visual for the pupil. Sr. Mary Ambrose, *The Mass* (Chicago: Lawdale Publishing House); Catechetical Guild, *Miniature Altar* (St. Paul, Minn.: Catechetical Guild, 1935); D. B. Hansen and Sons, *Steel Mass Chart* (Chicago, Illinois); E. M. Lohmann, *Mass Chart* (St. Paul, Minn.); F. Pustet, *The Child's Mass Chart* (New York: F. Pustet).

catechist may also be able to use projection equipment which can be carried into the classroom and, without any special preparation—apart from darkening the room—can be set up there for instant use. As types of projection material from which the catechist may choose, we can mention the following: the photograph diapositive in the narrow sense, hence individual pictures or slides (glass or cardboard frames); the roll film (picturol) which contains a series of pictures on a film strip; these can often be purchased singly as slides.[11] In addition to these kinds of "still" pictures, the catechist can also rent, lease or purchase miniature movies, the 16 mm. or 35 mm. editions of feature films, with or without sound.

Of these various possibilities the one most feasible for normal

[11] On this subject see: "Das Bildband praktisch angewendet" in *ChPBl,* Vol. 63 (1950), pp. 118–121, with an index of films which can be obtained from Austrian firms. On p. 212, he gives a report of the founding of an *"Arbeitskreis für Katechetisches Lichtbild und Unterrichtsfilm"* in Vienna (I, Stephansplatz 3) which makes it possible for catechists in Austria to procure copies of pictures and of films (and also to borrow projection apparatus from the district officers) by means of the state *"Hauptstelle für Lichtbild und Unterrichtsfilm",* and which is also empowered to receive any suggestions for the production of catechetical film series.—For Germany: consult E. Raudisch, "Neue Bilder und Filme für den Religionsunterricht" in *KBl,* Vol. 75 (1950), pp. 66–70; further material in *KBl,* Vol. 77 (1952), pp. 249f.; and also P. Wesemann, "Das Lichtbild im katechetischen Unterricht der Volksschule" in *KBl,* Vol. 76 (1951) pp. 296–300, who wants the catechists to select single pictures from various films and to put them under glass and in this way form the basis of a collection of glass slides.—For the U.S.A it would be impossible to give an inventory of all the material that is available on this subject. At most it can be suggested that those interested use *The Catholic Educator* (which publishes news pertinent to *CAVE*), *The Catholic School Journal* and *The Catholic Educational Review* where articles on this and kindred subjects are unusual only when they are missing. For France and Belgium: A. de Marneffe, "Appendice" to the book of P. Ranwez, *Aspects contemporains . . .,* pp. 319–325; A. Léonard, "Filmothèque du professeur de religion" in *Lumen Vitae,* Vol. 9 (1954), pp. 139–144.

catechesis is the "still", that is, glass or cardboard slides, because a single picture contemplated silently will best serve to deepen the impression already made on the children. A number of pictures shown in rapid succession would only cause confusion. This would be justified only during a religious assembly or for the sake of extensive recapitulation.[12] But although a wide range of these filmstrips (picturols) made up of masterpieces of Christian art are available for adult lectures, a comparable catechetical series is still needed.[13]

In any case the catechist cannot expect salvation or indeed a lightening of his real task from these technical aids. Fully justified is a warning which was voiced some years ago that whereas formerly we had to reproach the older school for their intellectualism, today we must warn against visual aids and technical apparatus which are not one whit less dangerous.

In what way should the picture be linked to catechetical method? The natural place is in presentation, which should

[12] U. H. Fleege, "Movies as an Influence in the Life of the Modern Adolescent" in *The Catholic Educational Review,* Vol. 43 (1945), pp. 336–352; L. J. McCormick, "Classroom Value of Films" in *The Catholic Educational Review,* Vol. 45 (1947), pp. 387–393; V. C. Arnspiger, "The Contribution of the Film in Today's Education" in *NCEA Proceedings and Addresses,* Vol. 42/43 (1945/46), pp. 392–401; Sr. M. C. Kavanaugh, "Evaluation of Educational Film" in *The Catholic Educator,* Vol. 24 (1953/54), pp. 342–347, and also *The Catholic Educator,* Vol. 23 (1952/1953), pp. 535–539. For Germany: A. Otteny, "Das Bildband als Anschauungsmittel" in *ChPBl,* Vol. 62 (1949), pp. 147–149; F. Hubalek, "Unterrichtsfilm und Lichtbild" in *ChPBl,* Vol. 64 (1951), pp. 242f.—For a very optimistic evaluation of the use of films see H. Böhner, "Arten und Stufen des Lichtbildes in der Katechese" in *KBl,* Vol. 68 (1942), pp. 44–50.

[13] Perhaps the need for catechetical slides, and especially for catechetical films (for which liturgical subjects almost alone are suitable) is less than it is for films on other subjects. These other subjects have to do with the external world (geography, natural sciences and work projects) and of them there is an adequate supply already on hand.

receive visual support. The picture should be shown, when the story, perhaps of a biblical event, has reached that precise point which the artist depicts. In this respect a printed wall picture that can quickly be unrolled or uncovered without difficulty has a great advantage over projection material which requires a darkened room.

If the catechist should wish to use such a picture or if he should ask the children to open their religion-textbook and look at a picture in it, he will do so only when the oral presentation has been completed, and before he has asked them to repeat it. After a short time spent in examining the picture, the children, guided by the catechist, should enumerate the details which they found in the picture. In this way the picture will be more deeply imprinted on their memories and on their hearts. If he should show it only at the end of the catechesis, it would lose its value for catechesis proper and would serve only as an independent repetition or supplement.

A very simple means of visualization, but one that can practically always be used in the religion period is drawing and especially the drawing on the blackboard by the catechist. By this we do not mean an artistic sketch, and still less a finished picture which might have to be drawn on the blackboard beforehand. While speaking to the children, he might sketch roughly with chalk, one of those simple objects which symbolize for us the mysteries of God:[14] a road, a door, a key, a flower, stars, running water, a burning light, a crown, etc. For the works of mercy he could sketch the symbols: bread, jug, etc. To represent God and the Divine Persons he may use the eye of God, to symbolize Jesus the crib and the cross, and tongues of fire.

[14] R. Guardini, *Sacred Signs* (St. Louis: Pio Decimo Presses, 1956); D. Winzen, *Symbols of Christ* (New York: P. J. Kenedy, 1955) Sr. M. A. Justina Knapp, *Christian Symbols* (Milwaukee: Bruce, 1938).

The use of a "symbol shorthand" is less suited to the step of presentation, where the picture is much more appropriate. The shorthand method should rather be used for the purpose of explanation or for recapitulation. A few points suitably distributed would enrich or complete the survey. It is wrong—or rather only a special prerogative of the artist—to think that entire scenes, complete with human figures, need to be drawn. That would be a waste of time and would also be superfluous. To strengthen the impression that has been created by a story the catechist should have a variety of artistic wall pictures at his disposal. To make his instruction more lively and to anchor it more firmly in the memory, simple symbols suffice. Children are only too happy to use their own imagination.[15]

Akin to drawing is the graphic outline which will frequently be used in conjunction with the drawing itself. This consists in writing the key words of a catechesis in relevant order on the blackboard. The various elements of a concept (for example, the qualities of true contrition, the effects of the sacraments, the contrast between the Old and the New Testament) which are developed during the course of the catechesis and are to be found more precisely formulated in the catechism, can thus be

[15] Look up the suggestions, brief but excellent, and the models for sketches and drawings (with the note, "the first line") of J. Reder, "Zeichnen im Religionsunterricht" "for those who think that they cannot draw" in *ChPBl*, Vol. 64 (1951), pp. 207–210; cf. also J. F. O'Connor and W. Hayden, *Chalk Talks, or Teaching the Catechism Graphically*, 3 vols. (St. Louis: The Queen's Work, 1928). Similarly simple and pertinent are the wall pictures (symbols with brief explanations appended) by J. Goldbrunner, *Sakramentenunterricht mit dem Werkheft* (Munich: Kösel, 1950). (These appeared for the first time in the *KBl*, 1946–1949). To be recommended are those drawings with which Alfred Riedel illustrated the *"workbook"* of Oderisia Knechtle, *Mit dem Kind durchs Kirchenjahr* (3rd ed.; Freiburg: Herder, 1954). Joh. M. Pemsel, *Der Katechet zeichnet mit der Jugend* (Regensburg: Pustet, 1956) similar to Goldbrunner and worthwhile.

established in the catechesis itself. In this way the survey and memory work can be lightened for the children.

A final way to obtain concrete visualization, which we should not discard, but use with certain reservations, is dramatization. Its value is to be found in the fact that it is a repetition, in sublimated form, of biblical events (for example, the flight into Egypt, the wedding feast at Cana, the parable of the ten wise and ten foolish virgins), and also of events in parish life (for example, an infant to be baptized). The personal skill and the tact of the catechist will condition the value of such experiments for the children. Properly carried out such plays can, thanks to the imaginative powers of the children, and despite the simplicity of their presentation, be productive of results similar to those achieved by the primitive medieval dramas of Easter and Christmas. These did not contain much beyond simple dialogue; nevertheless, they exerted a great influence over the people.[16]

For more advanced pupils there is the sketch, which applies a religious theme to everyday life, clarifies a problem in monologue or dialogue form, answers difficulties, and encourages inner resolution. The proper time, however, for such a sketch would be during after-school activities.[17]

[16] Suggestions more in detail may be found in Mayer, pp. 83, 89, 206.—Dramatization is practised on a grand scale in the Catholic schools of England where the catechist has, it is true, a great number of religion periods at his disposal. F. H. Drinkwater, "La religion enseignée par le drame" in *Lumen Vitae,* Vol. 3 (1948), pp. 154–172. In *The Sower* it is unusual when a play adapted for children does not appear in its pages. F. H. Drinkwater has himself written plays, cf. his works which were cited below, p. 408. On similar endeavours in France (Françoise Derkenne Lentner reports (above, pp. 37 ff), pp. 64f. For the end of the religious plays cf. H. C. Gardiner, *Mysteries' End* (New Haven: Yale University, 1946).

[17] On this subject consult: Kl. Tilmann, "Kurzspiele beim Gemeinschaftstag" in *KBl,* Vol. 75 (1950), pp. 514–516; idem, "Über religiöse Kurzspiele und Religionsgespräche" in *KBl,* Vol. 76 (1951), pp. 92–99.

The first introduction to a dramatic presentation, feasible in most instances, can be given, for example, when the catechist, after assigning various roles, permits suitable biblical episodes to be read or to be re-enacted in the classroom—similar in fashion to what takes places in the liturgy during the reading of the Passion.

In all this the catechist must not forget that he himself is the most powerful means of making Christian doctrine visual to the children. In him the children are brought face to face with the Church and so with Christ. His manner of greeting, of speaking, of praying, the reverence with which he talks of sacred matters, the self-mastery which he exercises when dealing with them, the conscientious justice which he practises, and the love he manifests for them are for the children the most vivid instructions, and the most effective illustration of his doctrine.

This is also true of the children's Christian environment, the local church and its services, the school, which not only during the religious period, but also in its entire curriculum and in all its external features and activities, should possess a thoroughly Catholic character, to say nothing of the family. In such surroundings the child is enabled, step by step, to observe the most varied examples of Christian life, which not only support what he has heard and been taught, but also stimulate the desire to lead one himself.

2. *Catechetical Language*

It is not always easy for the young priest catechist, who takes up his work after a long course of studies, to employ language that the children easily understand. Not only the technical theological terms, but also the language used in lecturing to adults or in preaching sermons are so many stones, and not bread, for the children. Catechetical language must be childlike. As we have pointed out, a step is taken in this direction when the subject matter is offered to younger children in a narrative form and even to older children is explained at the end of a story. A basic requirement for catechetical language is that it be visual; stories are always visual. In the first place there are Bible stories which are characterized in their original form by concreteness and clarity. The catechist, however, needs other narrative material in addition to the Bible, less for the formal step of presentation for which the "lesson unit" catechism as a rule offers the outline of a biblical story, than for later on, in the step of deepening, in repetition. The ideal would be for him to draw upon his own personal experiences. The most insignificant details, minute personal experiences drawn from everyday life, have a special attraction because of their personal character. There are printed collections of such story material, but these are unequal in value and uneven in quality.[18] The catechist should avoid fictitious stories as much as possible; at all times he should be the messenger of truth. On the other hand, there is nothing to prevent him from using a

[18] F. Spirago and J. J. Baxter, *Anecdotes and Examples* (New York: Benziger, 1904); D. Chisholm, *The Catechism in Examples,* 5 vols. (London: R. T. Washbourne, 1908); H. Rolfus (with F. Girardey), *Illustrated Explanations of the Commandments;*—Vol. II, *of the Creed;* Vol. III, *of the Sacraments* (New York: Benziger Bros., 1897); F. H. Drinkwater, *Catechism Stories* (London: Burns, Oates, 1941). This volume first appeared in the form of five distinct booklets; idem, *More Catechism Stories* (Westminster: Newman, 1948); idem, *Third Book of Catechism Stories* (Westminster: Newman, 1957).—See also J. Minichthaler, *Heiligenlegenden katechetisch ausgewertet* (2nd ed.; Munich, 1935); P. A. Budik, *Leuchten auf dem Lebensweg. Das Heiligenleben in Beispielen* (Mödling, 1948); J. Fattinger, *Der Katechet erzählt,* 3 vols. (Ried, 1934ff.) (only the first volume is outstanding and it has appeared in several editions). Additional material may be found in First Communion literature that has already appeared, as well in the reports from missionaries in pagan lands. Various works on catechesis also contain appendices which are filled with examples.

situation taken from the lives of the children themselves, and then embroidering it with concrete details, in order to make a certain doctrine or moral teaching more real for them.

The story must always, however, remain subordinate. On occasion it may perhaps be necessary to use it simply to hold the attention of an especially unruly class. But it may never become a mere instrument of amusement. Gustav Mey warned catechists very clearly against an excessive use of such stories. He waxed especially vehement against catechists who encouraged in this way a certain "spiritual love of dainties" among the children. With justice he criticized the opinions that "catechesis provides for variety rather than for unity, for ornamentation rather than for content, and pleasant conversation deserves priority over an instruction that is clear, correct and thorough."[19]

If we have demanded that catechetical language be concrete, we did not mean that it must be rich in images. Figures of speech have value for children only when they can be fully developed. The catechist should not say, "many people streamed by", but, "many people came, so many in fact that the crowd appeared to be like a mighty stream". If the children are to understand parables they must first know something about the objects with which the comparisons are being made. "Similarly this is true of people like us. . . ." Abstract expressions should be avoided as much as possible in the lower grades. The catechist should not say, "Jesus has the power to forgive sins", but, "Jesus can forgive sins", not, "It is our duty. . .", but, "we must . . .", not, "A good child enjoys prayer", but, "he likes to pray", "he likes to talk to God".[20]

[19] G. Mey, *Vollständige Katechesen* (4th ed.; Freiburg: Herder, 1879), p. 34; J. Millot, *Trésor d'Histoires,* 8 vols. (Paris: Lethielleux, 1941).

[20] For other pertinent observations, see Raab, pp. 196f. He maintains that "children speak the language of action and not that of notions".

Catechetical language also demands simple sentence structure. Long sentences and those with involved subordinate clauses are impossible for children to understand. Expressions which are used should, moreover, be adapted to the vocabulary of the children. In American schools precise lists have been drawn up for the teacher. In these the average word mastery of children in different age-groups is noted. Equipped with such aids theorists are beginning to revise textbooks for children. This does not mean that the catechist may not use a word with which the children are not familiar. Many ideas are clarified by an added paraphrase; others, by the content itself. The language of the catechist need not be simply a reproduction of the child's word list; in the mouth of the catechist it may sound not child-like but childish. The catechist may keep a step ahead of the children, but not so far that they are unable to follow him.

Basically the catechist should use language as it is written. The environment of the classroom, and also the dignity of the subject matter demands this. This again does not mean bookish language. It should be taken for granted that to make himself understood the catechist may make use of paraphrase, couched in the idiom of the children. He may even encourage the smaller children who are still clumsy in the use of words and whose stock of phrases is limited, by saying to them "Say it as you would at home". In general, however, his language should not be the language of the printed page, but the colloquial language of educated people.[21]

Any mother can teach us the correct way to speak to children. Without having taken any courses in pedagogy, solely by means of her love and of her feeling for the thought processes of the children, she has discovered the correct solutions. She speaks in one way to a three-year old, in another to a six-year

[21] In the same sense see also G. Mey, *op. cit.,* p. 36; F. H. Drinkwater, "The Use of Words", in Sloyan, *op. cit.,* pp. 263-280.

old, and in still another to the teen-ager. An excellent way of learning correct catechetical language is to listen to catecheses given by able catechists or by proficient teachers. Printed catecheses also offer valuable hints.[22] Especially beginners must, in their preparation of their catecheses, devote some time to the choice of the right language and prepare also verbally all the more important chapters of the catechism.

In addition to its adaptation, catechetical language ought to fulfill two other conditions. It should strike the note of genuineness as well as preserve the ring of reverence. The language in which the truths of our religion are couched contains a number of expressions and certain technical phrases which today sound rather strange and may create the impression that we are treating of an unreal world, to which our everyday earthly world bears no relation. In the life of Jesus we come across such terms as disciple, publican, thief. Jesus Himself is described as Redeemer, Only-begotten.[23] Without avoiding these or similar expressions, which have been given a definite meaning by constant usage, the catechist will sometimes paraphrase them, use other terms, out of a feeling for language. In so doing the catechist must guard against everything that is uncouth or trivial; he must remain conscious of the fact that sacred objects should be touched only with holy hands.

[22] As examples of good style for children, cf. D. L. Greenstock, *Christopher's Talks to Catholic Children,* 2 vols. (London: Burns, Oates, 1947); M. Sheehan, *A Simple Course of Religion* (London: M. H. Gill, 1938); Maud and Miska Petersham, *Stories from the Old Testament* (New York: J. C. Winston, 1938); Mary Perkins, *Your Catholic Language* (New York: Sheed & Ward, 1942).

[23] For this word we have the Latin term used in the *Apostolicum "unicus": "the only".* He is the only Son, in Greek the *Only-Begotten.* In reality we could paraphrase this by saying "the eternal Son of God".

3. Christian Doctrine and the Child's Intellectual Capacity

No matter how far the catechist may actually go in his attempt to adapt his teaching procedure and his language to the children, and no matter how great the capacity bestowed upon them at Baptism to absorb the doctrine taught, it is evident that children are able to grasp Christian doctrine only in a childlike way. On the other hand, we must never distort or adulterate what we teach them, nor for their sake present as small what is large, or what is firm as weak and unsure. Whatever we teach the children must be capable of supporting the superstructure of Christian living.

For this reason we ought to mention some points which can be a source of temptation to the catechist to present the content of Catholic doctrine in unsuitable forms. There is above all the idea of God. In the idea of God which we impart to the children, there must indeed be included from the very beginning eternal love. Indeed, the catechist should consider himself to be a messenger of the love of God, who calls all men to Himself. But this does not mean that should he pass over in silence or render obscure the majesty and the dominion of God. The holy fear of God always remains "the beginning of wisdom" (Ps. 110, 10).

In order to convey some idea of the love which God bears for us, we should never lose sight of the fact that He who draws us so graciously to Himself is the eternal, holy God, the holy God of creation to whom we belong, body and soul. Consequently, it is not fitting continually to speak of "our dear Lord" or "our dear God", we should rather say, "God" or "the Lord". Neither in Sacred Scripture nor in the whole of ancient tradition can we find God referred to with terms of endearment. Only during the Age of Enlightenment was it fashionable to use such language; the deism of that time was very questionable.

It seemed that God's task was merely to adorn human life. The creator, having, with all wisdom and fatherly care, equipped the world for men's use, had withdrawn Himself, allowing them to pursue their own pleasures. This kind of thinking has had its effect also on Catholic apologetics.

It is significant that at that time Augustine Gruber (d. 1835), the Austrian opponent of rationalism in catechesis, entered the lists against such a method of presentation. He pointed out that it was contrary to divine revelation "to represent God (something that man frequently does and has wished to do in religious instruction for several decades) as an over-indulgent father who permits sin to go unnoticed, and does not demand a change of heart but forgives those that remain obdurate in their wickedness; attempting to justify himself by saying that to do otherwise might cause the faithful too much distress by picturing divine justice as it is, and thus make their hearts leaden."[24] This is in essence the same complaint which a little later on Beda Weber raised somewhat more sarcastically against the then current Protestant instruction on confirmation and on the idea of God. "The dear God whom they sometimes mentioned and repeatedly taught thus becomes a friendly Oriental potentate from whose beard tears of emotion constantly fall, who is pictured with a shepherd's crook of green reeds, lest anybody might be hurt by it."[25]

We cannot deny that the expressions "the dear God", and "our dear Saviour", especially if they are used carelessly, smack of levity, and that through them our idea of God might suffer. In ordinary conversation we may sometimes employ them as a kind of disguise, and in the teaching of little ones we

[24] A. Gruber, *Des hl. Augustinus Theorie der Katechetik* (3rd ed.; Salzburg, 1844), p. 63.

[25] B. Weber, *Cartons aus dem Deutschen Kirchenleben* (Mainz, 1858), p. 475.

may even tolerate them—although we could equally well employ the phrase, "our Father in heaven", and be as readily understood (Matt. 5, 16). In all other respects they should be dropped completely from catechetical language.[26]

A similar temptation, originating in a similar source, is the teaching of divine providence. This doctrine means that all creatures and all events are in the hand of God and are governed by Him. At the same time we know that God permits man great latitude in his activities and that often He does not prevent the beneficent forces of nature from harming us. God can do this or allow this to happen because in everything His is the ultimate will; all the more since He has bestowed upon us gifts of the supernatural order and Christ has preceded us into glory by way of the Cross. Here we might be tempted to spare the faithful and especially the children such a harsh picture of reality and to deceive them with pious platitudes concerning the burdens which God may ask them to bear—with the result that when they are brought face to face with reality, their faith will be shattered all the more brutally. Many prefer to forget that every hair on their head is numbered and that in every situation there is always a way that will lead them to God

[26] Compare this to what is in Gatterer, pp. 445f. The same things might be said of that other expression that is so frequently heard: "the loving Jesus". The present writer is well aware that the criticism which R. Firneis in *ChPBl,* Vol. 62 (1949), p. 12, expressed on this point (that it was "too sentimental") was not well received by the Viennese Catechists, both men and women, *ibid.,* p. 122. It is indeed true that the native genius of a people has the right to determine the language which it uses. Compare further, *ibid.,* p. 90, where it is remarked, that this and other expressions of the same kind should serve, "to restore the harmony between the intellect and the heart in our spiritual life, which has been withered by rationalist thought". This should indicate to us sufficiently the origin of such turns of expression. We should consequently endeavour to prevent such rationalism from appearing in our catecheses. —On the question of names for Christ, see above, footnote no. 69 p. 144.

and to eternal salvation, with the consequence that everything that befalls them redounds to their own advantage, if only they love God (Rom. 8, 28). Instead they prefer to imagine that everything that happens is for the best and that there is a happy solution to every problem. In every collection of stories and anecdotes, we can always find a great number that have happy endings; these might tempt us to draw the conclusion that these are the rule rather than the exception, and that in other instances the happy ending is not so apparent to the naked eye. No one is helped by such over-simplifications of reality.[27] We should, however, be grateful that God has provided for the manifold needs of our life in the natural order (see Matt. 6, 25 ff.). We should point out that a life based on Christian principles offers us the best guarantee that the order of things, in this life, will best promote our eternal salvation, and further, that God is often ready to help in extraordinary ways. We ought also to accustom the younger generation to the idea that God does not spare even His beloved children the hardships of life, but through them tests their strength.

On what we have already said depends also the correct treatment of prayer. We should never permit the children to believe that we should pray only when we stand in need, that prayer is limited only to the prayer of petition, and that the petitions themselves are restricted to the goods of this earth. This could only result in the conviction that prayer does not help us in any way and should, therefore, be abandoned.

Besides the prayer "for something" and "for somebody" which are the usual themes, we should attempt to teach the children prayers of praise and thanksgiving. Catechesis in school

[27] St. Schmidt, "Überfromme Redensarten" in *Benedikt. Monatschrift,* Vol. 23 (1947), pp. 369 ff.—It is an error to say that God could not have created a better world, cf. Chr. Pesch, *Praelectiones dogmaticae,* Vol. III (4th ed.; Freiburg: Herder, 1914), pp. 31 f.

supplies us with many opportunities for doing this. Each newly acquired piece of knowledge should awaken some expression of gratitude, just as in the liturgy, after a lesson from Holy Scripture, a hymn of praise follows in the form of a *Responsorium,* and, only then, the prayer of petition. We need, moreover, only to examine the perfect model of Christian prayer, the Our Father, and make the children conversant with the thoughts it contains. It begins with adoration: "Hallowed be Thy name",[28] and only in the second half is it turned into a petition. Seen in this light an introduction to active participation in the liturgy also assumes a new importance.

Another tendency to simplify a truth unduly is encountered in the doctrine of the Eucharist. The catechist may think—but erroneously—that he is making the mystery easier for the child as well as doing justice to the sublimity of his subject, when he says: "God is in the Sacred Host. You may receive God (or the 'dear Lord')." Gustav Mey passes the following judgement. "By mentioning the presence of the Godhead in the beginning, the dogma is inverted and distorted; the mystery becomes a monstrosity."[29] Such an orientation directs the child to draw false conclusions—the Eucharist has not been given to us that God might be present in our midst—God is omnipresent—but that Christ might dwell in our midst, and still more precisely in order that we might have his Body and Blood to offer, a perfect victim, to God, and as nourishment for our souls.

[28] We can paraphrase this formula, which is difficult for the children to understand, because of the Hebrewism it contains, in the following way. The angels in heaven "sanctify" God or the name of God by chanting the triple *Sanctus,* by adoring: or, the angels are not the only ones who act in this way, men and all creatures ought "to sanctify" God and to adore Him in this way.

[29] G. Mey, *Vollständige Katechesen* (4th ed.), p. 364. Mey advocates that we should as a rule use the terms: The Body, the Blood of the Saviour.

It should go without saying that regarding the other mysteries of faith we must never tone down anything in order to adapt it to the mental capacities of the child. The danger today, however, is not as great as it was during the Age of the Enlightenment, when it was widely held that all truths had to be tailored to the measurements of human reason as well as to the child's intelligence; when doctrines concerning the Trinity, original sin, actual grace, were either omitted or falsified. When teaching these mysteries it is not necessary for the children to understand everything—mysteries can never be "understood"—nor is it required that every concept should be fully clear to them.

Especially in the lower grades a figurative expression may have to suffice and it is possible that it actually will, especially if it is taken from Scripture. The "washing away of sin", "the wedding garment of the soul", "the light of heaven which is enkindled in the soul at Baptism", are telling images to justify this. A sense of wonder which is awakened in this way is much more in conformity with the mystery and is much richer in religious significance than a premature and consequently unsuccessful attempt at rational explanation.

The catechist, when addressing children in the lower grades, for whom picture and concept are identical, may, when he deals with the judgement of conscience or with the impulses of grace, sometimes speak of the "voice of God"[30] without much further explanation being needed. The more mature children

[30] The expression, "the voice of the Guardian Angel" can be justified: we cannot limit and still less exclude the activity of our Guardian Angels. We could in fact invoke the liturgy to corroborate the correctness of the phrase. On the 29th of September we praise St. Michael in the fifth Response of Matins: "may he conduct the souls of the faithful into the paradise of joy", and immediately this phrase is repeated as the substance of our petition, that God might send us the Holy Spirit.

will understand if in explaining its meaning he says that what is meant is conscience enlightened by faith.[31]

In a similar fashion the catechist should present the first chapters of the Bible in the traditional form as given in Genesis. Only in the upper grades will it be possible for him with due reverence and restraint to add those limitations and classifications by which the harmony between our present knowledge of nature and human history is established.

In other points, too, it will be necessary as the children grow older to correct in their minds many childish ideas, especially in those instances in which everyday language supports the primitive notions. This, for example, is the case with the idea of heaven. Our increased astronomical knowledge has exploded the earlier picture of a "real" world, not infrequently endowed with the characteristics of fairyland.[32] Precisely from this perspective of a progressive development of religious thought it becomes imperative to prolong catechesis beyond the years of childhood.

4. Faith and its Basis

When in catechesis we try to advance from the visual presentation to clear notions and in this way initiate the children in Christian doctrine, we shall have to remember that it is not merely a question of increasing knowledge but faith.[33] The catechesis must have a definite aim: the children should

[31] J. I. Schade, *Catholic Morality* (Paterson, N.J.: St. Anthony Guild Press, 1943), pp. 39–44.

[32] R. Firneis, "Der Himmel in der katechetischen Unterweisung" in *Der Seelsorger,* Vol. 18 (Vienna, 1947/48). Firneis teaches the children that "to be in heaven" means: "to be with God". Now God is truly everywhere; but just as we cannot hear radio programmes unless we have a set, so God remains hidden to us in this life.

[33] Garrett Pierse, *Virtues and Vices* (Dublin: Browne and Nolan, 1935), pp. 130–152.

understand the new truths not only with their intellects, but with that faith which is due to the Word of God.

In catechesis we are dealing with baptized children. At Baptism along with the life of grace there is also infused into their hearts the virtue of faith. It has only to be unfolded, and in that respect our catechesis is for the children always mystagogical; it is an introduction to what they already possess subconsciously. The subconscious possession must be extended into the realm of the conscious—by opening up the content, but also by leading towards the act of faith by which this content is embraced.

The child who has been raised in Christian surroundings has become acquainted, through his parents, with many details of Christian doctrine. If he should have realized that this content stems not only from his parents, but also from God, he will already have made an act of faith. The catechesis offered by the Church must now lead on from here. Devout acceptance to which we try to guide the children means more than merely holding something to be true. What is at stake from the beginning is their devout attitude which will affect the whole man and in which man wholly subjects himself to God and makes God the ultimate purpose of his life. In other words it is a question of faith unfolded in love.[34] Such a faith alone counts and only such a faith can be expected to withstand the threats and dangers to which today even children are exposed.

Yet this faith must also and especially include an acceptance of truth, an acceptance based on the authority of God Himself. The catechist stands before the children not simply as a teacher of a branch of knowledge called "religion", but as the holder of a commission from God, as a "catechist", who transmits the

[34] For a development of the phrase: *fides qua creditur,* cf. F. X. Arnold, "Glaubensverkündigung in der Gegenwart" in *Gloria Dei,* Vol. 5 (1950/51), pp. 38–55.

"echo" of the Word of God to the children. He will thus make it his aim that all new knowledge which he imparts is received by the children as befits the Word of God.

How can he achieve this? One condition is that he be fully conscious at all times that he comes to the children as the ambassador of God. Augustin Gruber put this thought at the very beginning of his teaching:

"The subject matter of our instruction must be, and is exclusively, divine revelation. Only as ambassador of God, and not as his teacher or as a purveyor of any other kind of human knowledge, does he stand before his pupils. Thus every imagined distinction between natural and revealed religion disappears entirely. Everything that he teaches must be taught as a gracious revelation of God to man—of Creator to creature. Consequently, in the form of his instruction, in the tone of his voice, in the attitude of his body the catechist must give the impression that he speaks as the ambassador of God. Any carelessness in his demeanour, any frivolity in his voice, and any facetiousness in his expression must be avoided. In order to convey to the children the dignity of being an ambassador of God the catechist himself should be fully imbued by the greatness of divine revelation. When he proceeds to give an instruction he should recall as vividly as possible the sublimity of Him whose ambassador he is, the greatness of the message which he as ambassador must impart, and the love of our Lord for those to whom he as ambassador must speak. In this way he will acquire that spiritual disposition which befits the ambassador of God among men."[35]

In this way the catechist naturally will awaken and foster in the children the consciousness that in his words (the more mature soon make the necessary distinction: not in every single word) is being imparted a message from God. The younger children, who from psychological necessity, accept with complete confidence the words of adults—those of the catechist as well as those of the parents—will thus naturally be led to faith,[36] in a

[35] A. Gruber, *Praktisches Handbuch der Katechetik* (7th ed.; *Katechetische Vorlesungen II*) (Salzburg, 1853), pp. 3f.

[36] For this reason Hirscher maintains in his *Katechetik* (3rd ad.) with justice: If catechists rebuff their catechumens and lose their love and their confidence, they have for all practical purposes cut off their right hand as far as practical results are concerned.

manner adapted to their capacity without their having been given any insight into reasons.[37]

Among the older children, the act of faith ought to have that foundation which its nature requires. This can be given, provided the catechist gradually introduces them to the twofold recognition that, firstly, what he teaches is the doctrine of the Church, and secondly, that we must believe what the Church teaches, because God speaks through her.

The knowledge that the doctrine which is propounded stems from the Catholic Church creates no difficulties for the children. Through the catechist the Church, in effect, does speak to them; for the catechist is her living instrument. Especially if the catechist is a priest, his very presence, his external appearance, offers a much more cogent proof than if he were to demonstrate the agreement between what he teaches and the dogmatic definitions of the Church by means of logical arguments or by recourse to documents or to Scripture.[38] The book, too, which they use in

[37] There is also another theological opinion which holds that it is impossible to awaken an act of fact without an insight into the *praeambula fidei,* cf. Chr. Pesch, *Praelectiones dogmaticae,* Vol. VIII (5th ed.; Freiburg: Herder, 1922), pp. 141 f. These theologians must as a consequence assume that even the child who at the tender age of six or seven is being prepared for the reception of first Confession and first Holy Communion (and for this an act of faith is certainly necessary) has acquired a certitude concerning the fact of revelation with corresponds to his age, if for no other reason than that many persons who are gathered in the church (and along with them the entire Church) profess the same doctrines.—Concerning the state of the question cf. R. Aubert, *Le problème de l'acte de foi* (Louvain, 1950).

[38] On the secondary level we are able to appeal to reason on the basis of a personal experience gained in a technical school for young girls, J. Adrian, *Weisheit aus des Höchsten Mund,* 3 vols. (Mergentheim, 1926–1929), places special stress on the proof based on the agreement between dogma and the sources of our faith.—The agreement of doctrines with passages from Sacred Scriptures is suggested in the catechism itself by the number of citations made from them; cf. F. J. Connell, *Dogmatic*

the classroom and outside it has been given to them by the Church, be it a school Bible or a catechism, but especially the catechism, in which doctrine is presented in a form sanctioned by the Church in the course of the centuries.

It is a somewhat more difficult task gradually to make clear to the children that, in those things which the Church teaches, the Word of God is being communicated to them and that for this reason they must accept it with their whole heart. We ought to obtain from the children that spontaneous and simple assent which they have already given to the words and teaching of other adults and which is based on relative certitude.[39]

The catechist must gradually base this assent upon a valid and perfectly sound certitude or at least prepare for the transition to it. Though the need for such a real corroboration of the faith does not make its presence felt before the onset of adolescence, it will, however, become an urgent need for which it is better to be prepared.

The children should be aware that in the Church we are not required to believe anything blindly; rather, that we believe because we perceive that the teaching presented to us by the

and Scriptural Foundations for Catechists (Notes on Baltimore, No. 3) (Paterson, N.J.: Confraternity Publications, 1955); G. H. Guyot, *Scriptural References for the Baltimore Catechism* (New York: J. F. Wagner, 1946).

[39] For their entire lives a majority of the faithful possesses a certitude that is apparently unshakeable but for reasons which objectively are not sufficient from a logical point of view. It is clear, however, that in the face of the many dangers to which faith is exposed today, such a certitude is inadequate. A kind of substitute for it is the consciousness of the faithful that within the Church (among priests, theologians and educated laity) the objective certitude they lack certainly exists, cf. L. Kösters, *Zeitgemäße Glaubensbegründung, Lebendige Seelsorge,* edited by W. Meyer and P. Neyer (Freiburg: Herder, 1937), pp. 78–90; this may be found in English, W. Meyer *et al.* (A. Green, trans.), *The Pastoral Care of Souls* (St. Louis: Herder, 1944), pp. 80–93.

Church comes from God. For those to whom historical studies will always remain a closed book, the natural way by which they can know that God has spoken is to look to the Church which stands before them as a miracle of God.[40]

It all depends, therefore, on making visible to the children the beauty, the compactness, the indestructibility of the Catholic Church, its authority in proclaiming doctrines, its wealth of heroic virtue and holiness. Just as St. Thomas the Apostle recognized the risen Saviour by the five wounds in His transfigured body, the children should recognize in the marvellous works performed by the Church, the Mystical Body of Christ, that it is truly the work of God.[41] We ought also to recall what Augustine told his catechumens, namely, that in this our time and world, much cockle and tares are mixed among the wheat lying on God's threshing floor.[42] This does not, however, affect the taste of the wheat.

For those unfamiliar with historical thinking it will be difficult to provide historical proofs for the fact that God has spoken in history. These proofs have only been developed in the controversies with Protestantism and with unbelief during the last few centuries. It is argued that there are reports about the life and miracles of Christ which also as human testimonies deserve the fullest consideration. From these testimonies it follows that Jesus received a mission from God which was authenticated by miracles, and that he entrusted His teachings to a Church which is known to us today as the Roman Catholic Church.

This approach is possible at best only for adolescents, and then

[40] *Concilium Vaticanum, De fide cath.,* c. 3 (Denzinger *et al.,* n. 1794), The Church as *signum levatum in nationes,* Kösters, among others, p. 91 (English edition).

[41] D. Wolkenau, *KBl,* Vol. 48 (1922), pp. 197ff.; P. P. McKenna, *The Theology of Faith* (Dublin: Browne & Nolan, 1914), pp. 45–49.

[42] Augustinus, *De catech. rud.,* c. 7; J. P. Christopher, *op. cit.,* pp. 27–29.

only if we transpose it into the present. This is not impossible, for Christ is not only an historical, but also a contemporary figure. The echo of His footsteps on this earth can still be heard today. In numerous works of charity, art, customs, language, in our calendar which is based upon the year of our Lord's birth, and not least in the organization of the Church, can we detect traces of his coming. These are ripples of the waves which had their source in him.

For a graduating class of children of fourteen, who had asked whether Christ actually lived, the following argument was proposed by Klemens Tilmann.

"Who are the most famous men in the world today? Churchill, Eisenhower and Krushchev are the names we hear most frequently repeated. Let us compare Christ with them, let us ask the men in the streets of any important city whether they can tell us about these personalities, and then enquire whether they know the place of Christ's birth, details of His life, sermons that He had preached. The test will probably result in Christ's favour. We may thus conclude that his birthday, his death and resurrection are celebrated throughout the whole world. Not twenty or fifty, but literally millions speak to Him daily".[43]

Thus, in broad outline, Christ is shown to the children as the miracle of history.[44]

If, towards the end of childhood, it should be possible to lay the foundations for a proper theological basis of the faith, the value of such an attempt at this stage will only be in the suggestion that such a foundation is possible and that, there-

[43] Kl. Tilmann, "Zur Glaubensbegründung in der Entlassklasse" in *KBl,* Vol. 74 (1949), pp. 77–79.

[44] Tilmann also attempts to make clear to the children the genuineness of the biblical accounts which have been spread throughout the world. To do this he cites an example of a road-accident which has been witnessed by twelve different witnesses. They disperse after seeing it, but recount it to others with whom they come into contact. Later a claims agent or police officer questions each one of them alone. If one of them in order to help one of the drivers should give a different account he would at once be found out.

fore, our faith is not a blind one. The psychological moment for a more extensive treatment of this subject is reached only in adolescence, but even then we must expect the less talented children to understand the questions but not the answers.[45]

In any case, and especially wherever the limits have to be fixed between faith and unbelief, the catechist should avoid offering rationally convincing arguments in a manner of light-hearted triumph, or by pouring scorn upon the opponents. Because we are here dealing with that form of moral certitude, termed voluntary certitude, no compelling proofs can be given at all in this field. Reason recognizes the necessity of assenting, but it is the will that has the final word, but there will always be further obscurities behind which those who want to can hide. We must remember that faith is a gift of grace, a gift of divine goodness. Faith is the door through which we have access to the gifts of the supernatural order. Intellectual pride and obdurate self-will, which would dictate to God the manner in which His revelation should be made, will never be able to pass through this gate.

Consequently, in the elementary school, the task of the catechist in laying the groundwork for the faith can amount to no more than an attempt to keep alive the children's factual believing, to nourish the joy in what faith contains, and to develop a humble attitude towards God in every possible way, so that when the time comes to supply the rational structure of faith, a receptive attitude will have been prepared.

Practice of the faith will keep alive factual believing. When an important truth is being considered, the catechist, together with the children, should conclude the lesson by making, in the form of a prayer, an act of faith. St. Francis Xavier used to

[45] All that concerns instruction on the secondary-level we leave to one side; in the upper grades of such schools the catechist can count on more favourable conditions existing.

do this when teaching the ignorant Christians whom he discovered in the coast lands of Malabar.

In his book on Saint Francis Xavier[46] Father James Brodrick quotes the saint as saying:

"On Sundays I assemble all the people, men and women, young and old, and get them to repeat the prayers in their language. They take much pleasure in doing so and come to the meetings gladly. We begin with a profession of faith in the unity and trinity of God, I first saying the Creed in stentorian tones and then they all together in mighty chorus. That done, I go through the Creed article by article.... As they confess themselves to be Christians, I require them to tell me whether they firmly belive each and every one of the articles, and they reply in loud chorus, with their arms folded in their breasts in the form of a cross, that they do. I make them repeat the Creed more often than anything else because only a man who believes in the twelve articles has a right to call himself a Christian."

Francis then described a similar procedure regarding the Ten Commandments.

"I give out the First Commandment which they repeat, and then we say all together, Jesus Christ, Son of God, grant us grace to love thee above all things. When we have asked for this grace we recite the Pater Noster together, and then cry with one accord, Holy Mary, Mother of Jesus Christ, obtain for us grace from thy Son to enable us to keep the First Commandment. Next we say an Ave Maria, and proceed in the same manner through each of the remaining nine Commandments. And just as we said twelve Paters and Aves in honour of the twelve articles of the Creed, so we say ten Paters and Aves in honour of the Ten Commandments, asking God to give us grace to keep them well...."

It is of decisive importance that the children should realize ever more and more acutely that their faith is a precious thing and that they should embrace it with holy joy. The catechist, therefore, ought to be aware that he is not only imparting knowledge to the children but also unfolding to them the beauties

[46] This is taken from J. Brodrick, *St. Francis Xavier* (New York: Wicklow Press, 1952), pp. 141–142. The original of his text is taken from G. Schurhammer and J. Wicki, Vol. I (*Monumenta hist. S. J.,* 67 vols.; Rome 1944), pp. 161f. See also J. Hofinger, "Das katechetische Apostolat des hl. Franz Xaver" in *KBl,* Vol. 79 (1954), pp. 56–62.

that are implicit in it, so that their faith may be transformed into love and love into holy enthusiasm. In other words, he must proclaim "good news of great joy". This has been the concern of the catechetical revival during the last two decades, and is what chiefly concerns us in this book. Indeed, simply proclaiming the "good news" is, in itself, not sufficient; the children will also have to be given the opportunity of explaining the gladdening riches of Christianity, the liturgy, sacred customs, pious and joyful devotions; all the more so if such a beneficient atmosphere is lacking in their homes.

It is a frequent experience of teachers that however zealous the catechist he will achieve little in a large number of young people. Towards the end of their school education, many pupils adopt the following attitude: "What we were taught in the religion period may be true but why should I concern myself with it?" True to the spirit of our world they would like to leave religious problems to take care of themselves and to be satisfied with what is offered here on earth. Indifference, therefore, not only affects actual dogma but also the basis of religion itself, and every kind of religious practice, especially the institutional and sacramental life of the church. What can be done about it?

Catechists and priests may be tempted to offset such an attitude by the argument of need: that without faith and without the help of the sacraments it is impossible to check the passions and to lead a good life. And indeed, it is natural that young people at this stage in their development, when their attitude to life is involved, should be guided above all by their needs and thus be most easily approached from this direction.

But in what sense is such a procedure justified? How far may we build upon needs, upon youth's yearning for happiness, and so construct a bridge to the sacramental life, and to the gifts of the supernatural order? At this point we are confronted by a great difficulty. The supernatural life is by its very name that for which there is no need in human nature, not even a positive receptiveness but rather that which God gives freely out of his goodness. The only thing which can serve as a foundation for the grace which God grants us is that as creatures endowed with reason we can respond to His call when He wills to raise us to the dignity of His children. This is what theology calls the *potentia oboedientialis*.[47] We cannot, however, deduce a need for the goods of the supernatural order from it. But we can demonstrate a need for subordinating our entire life to God and to His divine order. Man without God (and mankind without God) sooner or later necessarily falls prey to chaos, as the experience of individuals and nations has amply proved. This divine order, we might add, is nowhere observed so completely and nowhere followed so constantly as in Catholic Christianity. In other creeds the notion of God has been diluted by Deism or debased by Pantheism. In this sense we may say that man "needs" the Catholic faith and should accept it in its totality. Experienced priests know that acquaintance with the New Testament, and with Christ as He appears in its pages, often makes such an overwhelming impression upon the young that all difficulties concerning faith disappear. This does not mean that all resistance has been overcome. Why, they may ask, are other things "added" in the Catholic Church?

We must divide this thought into its component parts.

[47] In a conference report *Übernatur und erziehender Religionsunterricht* (ed. by L. Bocks, Hildesheim, 1937) we should examine the paper read by Th. Soiron, which refers to this basis. True the attempt is made here to derive a certain need from this *potentia oboedientialis;* see also J. A. Jungmann, "Der Zugang zur Übernatur in der religiösen Jugendunterweisung" in *KBl,* Vol. 75 (1950), pp. 225–227; cf. W. R. O'Connor, *The Eternal Quest* (New York: Longmans, Green, 1947) in which the author takes up the teaching of St. Thomas Aquinas on man's natural desire of God, especially pp. 181–185.

Firstly, our need for God is clearly established. Unless we recognize God and His laws, inscribed in the very nature of things, human order must disintegrate. God can be known by every man (Rom. 1, 10). Few people today actually want to be godless, although many offer a very questionable interpretation of the idea of God. Secondly, we must proceed by saying that if God exists and if He is a personal being, we must expect this God to want to communicate with us, His creatures. For our part we must listen if He speaks.[48] He speaks, and when He shows us the path along which we should travel, we must follow it. He has spoken through Christ. It is surprising that He does not place upon us an intolerable burden, but He makes known to us "good news of great joy", inviting us to share in His own blessed life. Two things are thus required if we wish to facilitate for young people not only faith, but also willing and joyful participation in the Church's sacramental life. To lead them from their need for a well-ordered life and guide them to a personal God. It is from God, however, that the glad tidings in their entire glory should be made resplendent.

All faith rests on knowledge of God, ultimately on the natural knowledge of God derived from creation by the use of reason.[49] Today, this ultimate basis of faith, too, has been destroyed to a large extent, and not a few children who have received Baptism and attended our catecheses come to us from an environment which is more or less unbelieving. Of the rest we can say that sooner or later the majority will find itself exposed to the influence of a world estranged from God.

Should we then begin our catechesis with proofs for the existence of God? Even in unfavourable circumstances, we assume as normal the child who believes in God, since the know-

[48] J. C. Fenton, *We Stand With Christ* (Milwaukee: Bruce, 1942), pp. 429–433.

[49] *Concilium Vaticanum, De revel.* (Denzinger *et al.*, n. 1785).

ledge of God is natural to the child's psychological development. Belief in God is simply presumed to be present and is taken as a matter of course.[50] In connection, however, with the doctrines of faith, the catechist should pay some attention to a consideration of the ways by which we arrive at a knowledge of God. Answering the question: How do men arrive at knowledge of God? proof of His existence will also be determined and constructed. But this, too, should not be left to cold presentation in syllogistic form. Rather, when an opportunity arises, be it a text of Sacred Scripture or an example drawn from life or an observation in nature, the catechist, united with the children in devotion, should attempt the ascent from creature to Creator, and to the joyful praise of His wisdom, power and goodness.

5. Formation of Conscience and Moral Sense

The knowledge acquired by the children is to become faith, but should penetrate their lives. At this point we approach the problem with which catechetical method deals under the heading of deepening and application. Every catechesis begins, in some fashion or other, with real life and later returns again to it, to the life of the children and their own environment. We must learn to see reality and everyday life afresh and correctly, as it is in the light of conscience; the law of God must become the law of life. For a formed conscience is not that which arrives at a decision by itself and by some vague feeling, but that which has made the law of God its own.

[50] Hirscher, p. 326, remarks rightly in regard to the question (which was to be found in the catechisms during the era of Enlightenment): Is there a God? "This offends the innate, habitual and unopposed belief in God which young people possess." Concerning present day reactions to the problem, cf. F. Schreibmayr, "Thesen zur Glaubensverkündigung" in *KBl,* Vol. 74 (1949), pp. 198f.

Formation of conscience belongs especially, but not exclusively, to subjects treating of moral questions, as in the catechism or Bible History. When dealing with the different commandments we teach the children how to distinguish between good and evil, practising the application in detail, with examples drawn from their own lives; negatively by teaching them to distinguish correctly between major and minor transgressions; positively, by proposing model solutions and inspiring examples of virtuous actions and making them aware of the blessings which come from the divine order. The children should be made conscious that the will of God consists not only of a series of commandments and prohibitions, of precepts, the transgression of which must be confessed, but that there is an immense field in which one can choose between what is good and what is better, where the Christian can try to advance spiritually. In all these matters their judgement must be exercised, especially by means of discussions. These discussions may have as their subject matter any small episode from daily life, any simple experiences, encountered by the catechist or by the children. These may be joined to a story, for instance, in such a way that at the decisive moment the catechist may pause to ask what shall this particular child, man or woman, in the example, do now? In this way consciences can be formed so that at a future occasion the child may be able to judge quickly and decisively.

It goes without saying that the theoretical judgement of the children should always be translated into practical resolutions and concrete tasks. This includes also the examination of conscience. We should, therefore, encourage the children to examine their conscience every night. This self-examination can and should be introduced into the catechesis whenever the catechist treats of subject matter which lends itself to this purpose. For instance, the children might cover their faces with their hands while the catechist questions them, say, on the topic of charity. How have I acted toward smaller children? Do I refuse to let them play with me? Did I make fun of them? Did I help any of my playmates last week? Does any child needing help live in my neighbourhood? What can I do to help him in the future?[51]

The formation of conscience, however, will be effective and successful only when it develops the moral sense: conscience tells us what we should do; our moral sense furnishes the motives which should compel us to do good. But the motives are decisive for our actual conduct insofar as it is not influenced by mere habit. Motives are the compass by which we plot our life's course. A touching story with a happy ending may momentarily stir the hearts of the children but only when some firm thought, something of lasting value is enshrined in it, will its message be fruitful in the later decisions, because only in such a way are moral attitudes formed.

The formation of conscience linked to the teaching of moral theology also fosters, at least partially, the acquisition of motives and of moral sense; for in moral theology we do not teach arbitrary dogmas which must simply be accepted, but rather the proper evaluation of all in conformity with the God-given order. Here we have already achieved a portion of God-fearing sense, but beyond this the whole of Christian doctrine also serves to further the formation of a Christian attitude. All revelations of God with which we deal in the course of our instructions, biblical or catechism, demonstrate the marvellous achievement of His paternal love: "Yes, we must love God, He gave us His love first" (1 John 4, 19). For each step by which we advance in the knowledge of the mysteries of redemption, of the Church, of the sacraments, and consequently in the mystery of divine love, we must awaken a corresponding love in the hearts of

[51] These questions were suggested by Kl. Tilmann; cf. W. H. Russell, *Teaching the Christian Virtues* (Milwaukee: Bruce, 1952), pp. 60–64.

the children, a desire to thank God and to glorify Him all their lives. Knowledge of the "good news" which has come from God should impel us to seek for the kingdom of God and His justice before all other things. This knowledge ought to become the focal point of all those motives which give life a definite purpose and bold impetus. We have already stressed sufficiently that mere knowledge is not enough but that the hearts of the children must be made receptive for the content of this knowledge.[52]

In particular, what has to be done respecting deepening and application is to translate the concepts of faith into terms of everyday life and to anchor them in the hearts of the children, so that they will always meet them there again. Especially the habitual forms of the religious life must be filled with new life by demonstrating the truths of faith actually contained in them; in the feasts of the ecclesiastical year, in the forms of the liturgy, in various types of churches, in daily prayers, in religious customs and practices. Although our social life has been threatened by secularization, it still continues to incorporate numerous religious features and usages. Churches and chapels rise in our midst; religious pictures are still to be seen in many homes; certain religious greetings still continue to be employed; Sunday is still kept as the day of rest; and there are holy seasons. In forming the children's moral sense we can make use of the concept of home and country. This is where the children have their roots and to which their hearts are tied by a thousand ties; it could be the means of leading them to God. Pious sayings, statues in church and monuments in cemeteries, and in Catholic lands, the wayside crucifix, in fact everything that has at any time become a personal experience for them can thence be made a double treasure for their spiritual life.[53]

[52] See above, pp. 92ff.

[53] See the suggestions for this in M. A. Gramlich, *Gehet hin und lehret*

Nor should we forget that nature is also revelation of God. The children should be made conscious of it not merely when the doctrine of creation or the attributes of God are discussed. Yet all generalizations which quickly become monotonous for the children should be avoided. It is better to use concrete details by means of which God's wisdom and His loving providence can be illustrated. For example, let the children consider the many uses to which the human hand may be put—from a table to a hammer and pincers. The eye may be compared to a camera, or a swallow or mosquito to an aeroplane.[54] If in doing this we and the children should arrive at the conclusion that there is evidence of careful planning, of thought, we would not only help them to become aware of the presence of God, but would supply them with a proof for the existence of a personal God. In the country especially, the catechist can make use of the children's contact with nature and bring them to a realization of God's proximity.

The ascent to God, which nature suggests, is frequently threatened today by the advance of modern science, the servants of which are something filled with false pride or estranged from the totally different world of faith. We ought to attempt, therefore, to link science to the divine creator, a task which acquires special urgency when we deal with adolescents. In

(Freiburg: Herder, 1949), pp. 37–39; A. N. Fuerst, *op. cit.,* Vol. II (1946), pp. 204–207.

[54] In addition to works on the natural sciences we can find much material in T. Tóth (S. Chapovich, trans.), *God's Amazing World* (New York: P. J. Kenedy, 1935); R. J. Southard, *Almighty Magic* (St. Paul: Catechetical Guild, 1943); T. A. Lahey, *God's Amazing World* (Notre Dame, Ind.: Ave Maria Press, n. d.) in twenty little pamphlets; Sr. M. Francesca, *Our Lady's Garlande* (London: Philip Allan, 1931); C. S. Cobb, *God's Wonder World* (Boston: Beacon Press, 1918), the work of a Protestant author, containing material that can be used to good advantage.

principle this is not difficult. The desire to harness the world and its forces "in its roots and in its essence not evil, rather a divine urge implanted in man by the Creator Himself . . . to permit him to experience personally and actively the divine joy in creation."[55] It may be more difficult to find a way to bring this home to the children. There are two different ways to integrate science into the Christian concept of the world: (1) it is God who endows nature with those powers which men are beginning to discover only today: chemical processes, various rays, atomic power. It is truly marvellous that man has made all these discoveries, but greater still is He who has constructed the world; (2) it is God who has implanted in man the mental powers, the desire to search and to investigate, the ability to find syntheses and to employ them for his own purposes. God has willed that man should exert his mental powers in order to make creation subservient to himself, to give his earthly existence a dignity commensurate with his human nature and thus to exercise his kingship over creation. "Thou hast put all under his dominion" (Ps. 8, 7). If science continues to advance, it will help us to realize God's plans for the world more perfectly.

In this way the values of the natural world, too, placed in their proper context, can help greatly to re-enforce basic Christian attitudes: the consciousness of the presence of God, gratitude to God, finally love of God.

6. Prayer and Training in Prayer

That prayer has its part in catechesis is an old tradition, at least in the sense that the religious instruction period begins with a prayer and also ends with one. This practice is of course not unusual, for in the Austrian state schools, for example, a prayer

[55] D. Thalhammer, *ZkTh,* Vol. 74 (1952), p. 89.

is prescribed for the beginning and for the end of each period. Such prayers are not without value. Apart from the value of every genuine prayer, the necessity of religion in education is stressed by it. If perhaps the catechist can suggest variations from time to time, such prayers will contribute greatly to teaching children how to pray.

In catechesis proper prayer will have quite a different place. Catechesis should lead children to God. This guidance to God must always culminate in prayer. At different stages, therefore, prayer forms an important topic for catechesis. It is evident that the principal prayers, such as the Lord's Prayer, will be treated in special catecheses. The supreme form of prayer and of the liturgy, Holy Mass, will occupy the attention of the catechist repeatedly and for long periods of time. As in the catechism, a definite place will be allotted to lessons on prayer, in which the qualities of prayer are treated, including its possible forms from oral prayer to the more simple kinds of meditation.

The catechist's task, however, is not thereby exhausted. Much more important than these details of the training in prayer is that every catechesis ought somehow to be transformed into a prayer. Prayer should not only be taught theoretically, but also exercised in practice. In prayer (as in a religious hymn) we find a form of evaluation and application in which we link up with life not only in thought (as we are accustomed to do when we compare moral and practice in an attempt to form the children's moral sense), but also in actual practice. This is, indeed, also the object of the secular subjects, for it represents the most desirable form of application. A mathematical rule, for example, will be explained and then an example will illustrate the rule; a rule of syntax will be expounded and followed up immediately by practical examples.

If in catechesis we advance from teaching to prayer, we shall have accomplished the task for which we were appointed. We shall have done what St. Augustine wanted us to do—to teach in such a way as to guide the listener from hearing to believing, from believing to hope, and from hope to charity. Faith, hope and charity are not so much special topics of catechesis, but aims towards which every catechesis should strive to attain. They represent spiritual attitudes which ought to result from the sum of our catechetical efforts. But faith, hope and charity are exercised in prayer, regardless of whether or not these theological virtues are expressly named as such.

In the ancient Christian catechumenate each catechist ended with a prayer and with an imposition of hands by the catechist.[56] Training in prayer is, therefore, not a mere point in a programme of religious education which is inserted somewhere in the teaching plan, one of many subjects to be dealt with, but a necessary element of any subject whatever it may be.

The most favourable place to make this transition to prayer will, as a rule, be at the point at which the explanation has been completed and before entering upon the practical problems, which may indeed involve certain distractions, and perhaps before taking up the more prosaic formulation and discussion of the text to be learned by heart.[57] We may describe prayer as the principal form of deepening in catechesis.

Prayer may be freely voiced in the catechist's own words, or it may be formal. It is important that the children experience how to speak to God freely, in their own words, in any given

[56] Hippolytus of Rome (d. 235), *Apostolic Tradition* (Dix, pp. 29f.). The imposition of the hand signified a blessing. Even today many priest catechists conclude their instruction with a priestly blessing. Whether this can be done with the proper reverence after every class depends to a great extent on circumstances.

[57] In France where the new catechetical movement equally emphasizes the importance of prayer, it is frequently used in a subsequent lesson as a conclusion to the repetition of the topic, and before embarking on the, usually very brief, new lesson. A. Elchinger, "Moderne katholische Erziehung in Frankreich" in *KBl,* Vol. 75 (1950), p. 288.

circumstances, and to learn to pray in this way. Children from Christian homes may sometimes come to us imagining that prayer is to repeat pious phrases. They have probably learned certain prayers by heart, but have not realized that one might also think about them, and be able to understand the words. The catechist should, therefore, never begin the practice of formal morning and evening prayers, nor even of saying the Lord's Prayer. Neither should he first start with the obligation to pray, but rather allow the most simple prayers to grow spontaneously from his catechesis.[58] He may, for instance, have just finished telling the children about the creation of the world. God's omnipotence having been considered the following prayer might result: "O great and almighty God, we praise Thee for having created the world." Or he might have told his class about the healing of a sick man by Jesus and pointed out that our Lord still restores health to sick souls. Such a prayer might result: "Lord, make our souls more healthy and sound."

Little children, who have, as yet, no inhibitions, might themselves be encouraged to compose simple prayers, simply by being asked: "What have we learned about God? About our Lord Jesus Christ? How could we say this to Him?"[59] At other times he himself may, somewhat more extensively, formulate the prayers. The children should stand up, fold their hands, and remain silent for some moments—for prayer should spring

[58] Kl. Tilmann, "Gebetserziehung" in *Lumen Vitae,* Vol. 4 (1949), pp. 529–551; *idem,* "Die Aufgabengebiete der Gebetserziehung" in *KBl,* Vol. 75 (1950), pp. 314–323; Sr. M. Oliva, "Sister, Teach Us to Pray" in *The Catholic Educator,* Vol. 19 (1948/49), pp. 34–36; Sr. L. Agnes, "God Becomes Someone to Sally" in *The Catholic Educator,* Vol. 21 (1950/51), pp. 11–13.

[59] Tilmann, "Gebetserziehung" in *Lumen Vitae,* Vol. 4 (1949), pp. 533f.; F. H. Drinkwater, *Educational Essays* (London: Burns, Oates, 1951), pp. 374–377.

from the realization that one is in the presence of God.[60] The catechist should then recite the prayer. When praying he should not stand facing the children, nor should he lose sight of them. He might stand at the side of the room or in the middle of the class. When praying the children should be given an opportunity to participate, as in the liturgy, if only by a simple "Amen". A prayer in the form of a litany is very suitable, or, better still, a responsorial prayer, because it need not always be a prayer of petition. The catechist first recites the prayer, developing its thoughts in short paragraphs. The children then repeat it.[61] Thus in connection with a catechesis on divine providence, the catechist can compose a hymn to praise God for His benefits. Country children may have come to school through fields, or pass gardens filled with flowers. The catechist may recall briefly some of the blessings of springtime which God has sent us. He might begin: "O God, who has clothed the flowers with beauty, who has taught the birds to sing . . . ." and the children could answer his every invocation with an eulogy: "We praise and glorify Thee for this gift." Praise-passages in the Bible (for example, Dan. 3, 51–84) will thus take on a new significance.

In a similar way the catechist can translate into prayer the themes of a great feast, or in the form of a repetition, the con-

[60] Under favourable circumstances the pause may last even a little longer. The practice of silence and exercises practised in silence were esteemed highly by Maria Montessori especially for religious education. The same holds true of the gestures and the postures of prayer; they should be carried out with reverence; cf. H. Lubienska de Lenval, "Das Gebet der Kinder" in *KBl,* Vol. 76 (1951), pp. 100–105; M. Montessori (A. E. George, trans.), *The Montessori Method* (New York: F. A. Stokes, 1912), pp. 209–214. Father Gavan Duffy, the great Irish missionary, favoured such silences.

[61] Consult in the above the manner of teaching which St. Francis Xavier employed with the Paravas, pp. 252; Sr. M. Rosalia, *The Adaptive Way* (St. Paul: Catechetical Guild, 1955), pp. 162–164.

tent of a section of the catechism. Again, we may translate into prayer form those parts of the catechism which are to be memorized, and which have to be explained. The prayer may be a simple expression of faith: "We firmly believe, O God, all Thou hast revealed to us, especially . . .", or it may be a plea: "O God, who hast revealed to us Thy commandment . . . help us to avoid all sins which are contrary to it." The children may also be led to translate into the "Thou" form portions from the new "lesson-unit" catechism, and in this way to create prayers for their own use.[62]

Original prayers in the classroom presuppose that the catechism has captured the attention of the children and has created something like an atmosphere of fervour, in any case a disposition for prayer; otherwise such prayers would appear to be artificial and could possibly do more harm than good.

A prayer expressed in a set formula may be introduced more easily into the catechesis. Its very formula acts like a suit of armour, protecting prayer from desecration even though all the children do not participate with the desired reverence.

The catechist will use in the relevant context prayers with which the children are more or less familiar, or which are known to them from Mass or liturgy. As a rule these prayers need not, in fact should not, be prayers which are intended only for children. When using these set texts the catechist should not require the children simply to learn them by heart. Insofar as an atmosphere of devotion has not already been created in the catechesis some short preparation will be desirable. As a rule the

[62] It is not recommended that the catechist permit the children to compose long prayers of their own and then to recite them before the whole class, because such compositions may easily become affected if made in the knowledge that they are to be held up to public criticism; cf. J. Gatz, *Kinder reden mit Gott* (Dülmen, 1938); A. N. Fuerst, *op. cit.*, Vol. I (1939), pp. 455–456.

catechist should use only a part of a prayer: one petition from the Lord's Prayer, a sentence or two from the Gloria, the Sanctus, the Angelus, or one verse from a hymn. These few words can be properly explained within the context in which they appear; they will become meaningful later. In any case, prayer texts which the children repeat from memory as a matter of habit (for example, a much used school prayer; a prayer drawn from the liturgy) should again and again be explained by singling out particular phrases. The thoughtless repetition of the Lord's Prayer and the Hail Mary in rapid succession can be stopped by letting the children say the Lord's Prayer by itself, and even that should not be recited in its entirety, but sentence by sentence, in such a way that the catechist introduces each article with a few words of explanation, much in the manner of the sentence spoken before the Pater Noster in the Mass.[63] Dignity of bearing and clear enunciation of the words are important. Such a schooling in prayer should naturally be continued during the children's Mass and, when possible, also in special devotions for children. An hour in church, devoted to the children's pastoral care, is especially useful.[64] The forms of teaching bigger children, at the early stage of adolescence, how to pray, will have to be more restrained. The essential elements of Christian prayer and the prac-

[63] Concerning a personal experience of this kind, consult F. Dörfler, *KBl,* Vol. 75 (1950), p. 175; Sr. M. Rosalia, *Child Psychology and Religion* (New York: P. J. Kenedy, 1937), pp. 12–22.

[64] Within the catechesis itself we can choose any one of several ways of confiding to the children certain responsibilities in connection with prayer. We can, for example, in the month of October organize the *"Living Rosary":* each day as catechists we assign to each one of five volunteers a decade of the Rosary to be recited that day. A special intention may be decided upon. Fathers Callan and McHugh, *Our Lady's Rosary* (New York: P. J. Kenedy, 1939), pp. 145–148, 157; Sr. M. Josephine, "A Rosary Rally" in *The Catholic School Journal,* Vol. 53 (1953), pp. 249–250.

tice of daily prayer will now have to be secured. The method of the "first five minutes" is recommended.[65] This is a loosely conducted special course which is intended to preserve, in spite of the storms and stress of later life, the link with God through prayer.

Akin to prayer is the hymn. Indeed, it is only a freer form of prayer; free insofar as it is not so much concerned with man's direct relationship to God but with a poetical or musical meditation upon divine realities, and in an artistically elevated form, so that it is less dependent upon the spiritual preparation of the individual than prayer. It can, therefore, be placed either at the beginning or at the end of the religion period; but sometimes it may take the place of the actual prayer.

In another aspect the hymn has values all its own. A hymn that is sung by all the children in common denotes a high degree of self-activity on their part. Because of its musical and poetical sound structure, and because it represents an achievement of their own, it is something which the children greatly enjoy. The devout sentiments which it expresses, and also the thoughts when they have been explained, will affect the singers. Indeed, these sentiments will be imprinted upon the memory more easily than by texts which have to be learnt by heart.

The first objective which the catechist should have in mind when teaching a new hymn, is to give the children an introduction to its principal thoughts. He may do this either by talking about its origin and connection with personal experience, or by taking up a meaningful phrase contained in it. He should not, however, venture upon an explanation of details that would pluck the text to pieces.[66]

[65] Tilmann, "Gebetserziehung" in *Lumen Vitae,* Vol. 4 (1949), pp. 538 f. More developed suggestions may be found in the work of the same author written especially for children: *Kleine Schule des Gebetes* (Freiburg: Herder, 1949).

[66] For the method to be employed, see pp. 189 f. More detailed

Insofar as music practice is concerned, it is natural that hymns should have an important place in the school curriculum. In Catholic schools this will be self-evident, but it presupposes a previous agreement between the catechist and the music teacher.[67] But whatever the circumstances, the catechist should not forego fostering church music and hymns. If their time in school is fully taken up, those children who have a liking for music will gladly attend special practice sessions after school, especially if they are made attractive by distractions of various kinds, a story or something similar. These children will then have quite a considerable influence on the others in the religious period. Something might also be achieved by some regular pastoral hour and it is never a waste of time to do some singing even during the catechesis. The catechist might, during a free period, write out the text on the blackboard (which can afterwards be turned around); or he might distribute copies of the text. He might then sing the first verse alone — a piano or organ accompaniment is not necessary—and once more repeat half a verse. At the third attempt he will find that some of the more musical children will join in and at the fourth will have the whole class with him.

For his choice of hymns the catechist should limit himself

instructions may be found in Bopp, pp. 231f.; Mayer, pp. 150f.; J. J. Baierl, R. G. Bandas, *et al., Religious Instruction and Education* (New York: J. F. Wagner, 1938), pp. 82–88.

[67] The *Confraternity of Christian Doctrine* began to collect material for a uniform hymnal at the Buffalo Congress, 1956. The majority of the dioceses have hymnals of their own choice. Training for singing is done within the standard course of study of the individual dioceses: G. Corrigan, "A Method of Teaching Music Reading" in *The Catholic School Journal,* Vol. 54 (1954), p. 238; Sr. Cecilia, "The Boy Choir in the Grade School" in *The Catholic School Journal,* Vol. 54 (1954), pp. 249–250; Sr. M. Evangeline, "Music in Christian Education" in *The Catholic School Journal,* Vol. 55 (1955), pp. 331–334, to which a bibliography on the subject is appended.

to the diocesan hymnal, and, in certain instances, to the directives which have been given either by the school superintendents, or are contained in the course of studies.[68] Because of the great fluctuations in population at the present time the children should be taught songs which are popular beyond the boundaries of their own parish or diocese.[69]

Thus in catechesis, children ought to be brought closer to God, if not through formal prayer, then at least through singing, and if possible, by both. Truly justifiable is the admonition given to catechists: "A supernatural truth which does not lead to a response of the heart, to prayer, or to action, has in a certain sense lost its sacred character for the children. The message of salvation will then have become simply a knowledge of material facts and will have lost its genuine religious value."[70]

7. *Homework and the Work Book*

Application, reference back to life, is always the last step in catechesis. During the catechesis itself this reference to life can, it is true, only consist of various hints by which the catechist might outline the factors embodying his teaching, enumerating the occasions in which it should be followed; or lists exercises

[68] For the U. S. A. see also: *Our Parish Prays and Sings.* The Complete Parish Hymnal, edited by a committee of the National Catholic Music Educators Association of America (Collegeville, Minn.: Liturgical Press, 1959).

[69] In Germany: a few years ago due to an accord reached by diocesan delegates 73 hymns (texts and melodies) were prescribed for all the dioceses; in it are also contained all the important texts of the country; cf. *Einheitslieder der deutschen Bistümer* (with Notes) (Freiburg: Christophorus-Verlag, 1947); *Die einheitlichen Gebete der deutschen Bistümer und die Einheitslieder* (Cologne: Bachem, 1950).—In Austria there is the volume: *Die Einheitslieder der österreichischen Bistümer* (Salzburg: Institutum Liturgicum, 1952). Apart from the *Singmessen* there are 119 Church hymns and songs contained in it. Of these 37 agree with the songs selected for the German dioceses.

[70] Kl. Tilmann, *KBl,* Vol. 76 (1951), p. 294.

in which one or other feature might be realized. An intimate contact between religion and life is, nevertheless, of extreme importance for the children. It is therefore important that application be extended whenever possible, by means of tasks which the children can finish at home. The modern "lesson unit" catechism offers many valuable suggestions for every lesson. For example, the children are directed to gather examples of a principle, or of a rule, from books which are on the bookshelves at home, or from their everyday environment. They might have to answer a question or to draw a picture; or to copy some sentences to be memorized. In such a way the children are encouraged—frequently they will do these things of their own accord—or at least stimulated to take an interest in their religion period even at home. If the tasks chosen are adapted to the children's mentality, and to their natural way of thinking, the content will be more indelibly impressed upon their memories. An excellent help for such homework is the work book.[71] By this we mean a note book which the children plan under the guidance of the catechist, and into which they might enter short summaries, noteworthy sayings and especially drawings. The work book is an aid which was adopted by educationalists during the last few decades, first in the secular subjects and, later on, in the religion period, because it was felt that the children, at least in big cities, were rapidly losing

[71] V. M. Schumann, "Is Homework on the Decline?" in *The Catholic Educational Review,* Vol. 51 (1953), pp. 88–89; K. Fröhlich, "Das Werkheft im Religionsunterricht" in *KBl,* Vol. 66 (1940), pp. 217–223; B. Brück, "Hausaufgaben im Religionsunterricht" in *KBl,* Vol. 73 (1948), pp. 342f. In several of the National Congresses of the Confraternity of Christian Doctrine work done by the children was put on display. The use of work books is recommended and it appears to be gaining adherents. F. H. Drinkwater, "Home Made Catechisms" in *Lumen Vitae,* Vol. 5 (1950), pp. 417–425; F. J. Connell, "The Problem of Home Work" in *The Catholic Educational Review,* Vol. 45 (1947), pp. 605–610.

their ability to concentrate and especially their capacity to retain anything they have acquired simply by listening. The thousand and one impressions to which they are exposed on the streets and in their homes explain this phenomenon. More frequently than formerly children need to be given visual aids. These aids are all the more valuable if they come into being before the eyes of the children, and most effective when the children themselves have collaborated in their making, in the sense of the activity principle. This is the purpose of the work book. We have already mentioned that during the course of the catechesis the catechist would be well-advised to give a survey of the subject matter by means of some key words which he writes on the blackboard. Often this would be a forceful phrase or command, a resolution, a prayer; he may even offer a simple drawing.

So far the children were obliged simply to be attentive, to listen, watch and to cooperate in the discussion with the catechist. Now, at the end of the lesson, they will have five to ten minutes to spare during which they may copy what is on the blackboard. They can do this quickly on rough paper or in a note book. Later they are given the task of carefully transferring these jottings into their work books.[72] They are free to add details and to use coloured pencils. Texts may be copied as artistically as possible or be printed in block letters. A single page is devoted to each catechesis.

On some other occassion the catechist might propose a question for homework. Its answer will also be entered into the work book.[73] These books will then be collected at the

[72] Because of sketches to be made the work book should not be too small and for the same reason the paper should be checked.

[73] A few examples are suggested in *KBl,* Vol. 72 (1947), p. 123; My night prayers? How do I observe Sundays? Why do I go to church every Sunday? How can I, a child, fulfill my obligation of love of neighbour at the present time?

next lesson and briefly examined by the catechist. Work that has been particularly well done will receive praise.

This method has the advantage that the children perform their tasks with more enthusiasm, and show pride in preparing beautiful work for the religious class. In doing this they will, at the same time, have learned the content of the lesson, and this much more thoroughly than by mere memorizing. Since in such books symbols express concisely the most central truths of religion, the children will thereby also become acquainted with the symbolic language of ecclesiastical art, of church vestments, etc. The symbols for Christ which recur so frequently will help to strengthen the Christ-centred nature of the catechesis, and the knowledge that all salvation is from Christ. Moreover, as the experience of many catechists has confirmed, the work book has the further advantage that the parents will often be interested to see it. Sometimes they will ask their children to explain to them not only the meaning of the sayings and of the phrases, but also the significance of the drawings. In homes deprived of religion the children will thus infrequently play the role of apostles to their own parents. In more favourable circumstances the parents might help their children and in this way they cooperate with the catechist and become his helpers; they take up again, as it were unwittingly, that catechetical duty of which they should never have lost sight. Such work books, moreover, will be guarded as precious treasures long after the children have left school. A supporter of the work book method has given the following example from his experience.[74]

As basis for a catechesis on the living Church the words of Peter were used: "You, too, must be built up on him, stones that live and

[74] Fröhlich, *op. cit.,* in footnote No 71; as model consult the work of J. Goldbrunner, *Der Sakramentenunterricht mit dem Werkheft* (Munich: Kösel, 1950).

breathe, into a spiritual fabric" (1 Pet. 2, 5). After a presentation in which he described the construction of a church from strong and durable stone blocks—in the course of which he drew a portion of a wall built up of bricks laid one upon the other—the catechist drew a parallel application between such an edifice and the living Church, and he utilized the image contained in Peter's words. To the following question: What do these stones drawn on the blackboard mean for the living Church? the ten year old children replied: "These are us." The catechist then wrote the Christian names of each child on the stones, which the children greatly enjoyed.

The incidental story of a cathedral into whose sandstone foundations well-water had soaked, thereby threatening the entire structure, evoked as answer to the question: What does this water denote? This is sin. How the eyes of the youngsters shone as they made the resolution in common: we will always be healthy and useful stones in the living Church of Jesus Christ. The subsequent religion period began with the question: "Children where must I go to be able to see the living Church?" And with disarming pride they showed their work book with the drawing they had completed at home in which the various stones bore the name "Father" and "Mother" and the names of brothers and sisters, as well as those of their school friends. (Their own first names occupied the most important places.) The exhortation addressed to the children to show on the following Sunday that they were living stones brought more than a fifty percent response in assistance at the parish Mass and in the reception of Holy Communion. Only those who saw the children could know how much this recognition had been deepened by the use of the work book.

8. Memorizing

Despising, as we might, any mere memory exercise method, we cannot entirely dispense the children from learning a certain number of texts by heart. Learning by heart was at one time the only homework which the children were called upon to perform; even now it must not be the least important thing they should be requested to do. It certainly must not be allowed to disappear entirely.

Catholic Christianity is not a matter of mere emotional experience, but is in its essence an unequivocal message, an objectively valid doctrine, presented in clear notions. For this reason the Church of the early centuries demanded from each candidate for Baptism a definite profession of faith in the content of Christian teachings, as well as the acquisition, in terms of memory, of the most important dogmas which are contained in the Apostles' Creed. On the subject of the extent and the choice of catechetical material to be learned by heart there are, it is true, several different viewpoints. These should, however, be reconcilable by adopting a middle course, if some distinctions are made.

We must, first of all, determine what is really necessary. In certain subjects, for example, biblical catechesis, it is sufficient if the children understand the matter without being required to retain them in a definite word formula. This applies especially to the narrative parts of the Bible. The children should be able to recount what happened. It may even be enough, for instance, when dealing with enumerations, to remember certain key words; but were it a question of explaining certain simple concepts, for example, the attributes of God, it is more important to clarify the matter itself and bring it closer to the hearts of the children (God's omnipotence, omnipresence, eternity) than to instil definitions into them. In any case, if known by heart, a verse from a hymn, a passage from the Bible or liturgy, in which the same idea is expressed in terms of praise, is a satisfactory substitute for an important text to be learned from the catechism.

The catechist will demand literal renderings of certain statements or formulas which are important for the understanding of a dogma, as for example, Christ both God and man, Joseph, the foster-father of Jesus, the assumption of Mary into heaven, body and soul, conditions for Papal infallibility, and kindred subject matter. In any case, the old basic formulas of the catechism: the Apostles' Creed, the Lord's Prayer, the Ten

Commandments, the Seven Sacraments, must be made the lasting possession of the children.[75] In order to assure himself that the children have not learned them parrot-fashion, but that they also understand their meaning, the catechist should from time to time call upon the children to write them down as they have learned them—there will almost always be surprises.

We have thus fixed the minimum limit of what is to be memorized. In favourable, and also in normal circumstances, much more should be required. The questions and answers printed in bold type in the English translation of the German catechism serve this purpose: not so much is demanded today as formerly. In addition, texts taken from the Bible, verses from the Psalms, messianic prophecies, the words of Christ, especially verses from the Sermon on the Mount, should be given to the children at least as voluntary tasks. The same applies to certain well-known hymns which, once committed to memory, remain a valued possession for life. Learning by heart of well-formulated texts will also promote clarity of knowledge, and help the children to be more serious. It is not too much of a burden for the less gifted ones.

If possible the catechist should do everything to facilitate memory work. Whatever the method used, the questions and answers to be learned by heart should be previously worked through, and some of the words noted on the blackboard. The finished sentence should be recited first of all by the catechist, then repeated by a child, and finally, perhaps by the whole class. Such a chorus is a useful and lively method, at least in the case of the smaller children.

Again, especially when dealing with lengthy excerpts to be memorized, the catechist will let the children open their books and read the text; anything that may be outside the present

[75] Cf. above, pp. 165f. the remarks which were made about the fundamental catechism.

instruction can be explained briefly.[76] The catechist should never expect the children to learn by heart texts that have not been sufficiently explained to them, and have not, therefore, been understood.

Repetition gives the children mental help to retain the essentials. This should take place at least once in a subsequent lesson. It should not consist simply in asking questions which have been put previously nor should it be restricted scrupulously to the matter that has been treated in the previous period. From time to time general repetition will be desirable, but this should not be a mere repetition of words, but always also of the matter. This can be accomplished by not adhering too slavishly to the order of questions and answers as arranged in the textbook, by presenting a new point of view, by formulating the questions differently, and by proposing new questions. A new example, a fuller explanation or application will also serve the same purpose. In the later classes the repetition may occasionally take the form of an essay, to be set either as homework or in class.[77]

Of especial importance is the so-called immanent repetition, where the catechist repeats the subject matter without the children being aware of it. He can do this by recalling related topics which he has treated previously and by adding to them. In the course of the catechism instruction he will thus recall biblical events as these are suggested by the catechism lesson. In biblical catechesis the opposite procedure will be adopted. Episodes from the Old Testament illustrate the attributes of God, the miracles of Jesus symbolize the effects of the sacraments.

[76] Cf. Mayer, pp. 101f.; K. Cronin, *Teaching the Religion Lesson* (London: Paternoster Publications, 1952), p. 30.

[77] V. Keller, "Die Methodik, X. Die Übungs- und Repetitionskatechese" in *Grundfragen der Katechetik,* Vol. I (Wien, 1912), pp. 43–48.

A special form of repetition are religious tests which, according to accepted usage, are held more or less formally at the end of the term. In Continental countries such examinations serve as an opportunity for the Bishop's representative or for the inspector to observe the progress made in catechetical work. On account of the dignity of the subject matter the test ought not to range over too many points or to display feats of memorizing on the part of certain children, but rather deal with related points and aim at some deeper insight that will add to the children's enjoyment, and reduce the examination fever. At the same time the catechist has a chance of proving his own sincerity by not just asking for outwardly brilliant performances, and of showing his sense of justice by letting the more backward children also make their modest contribution. In all this the catechist should, however, guard against the self-deception that successful examinations also mean that he himself has thereby fulfilled his essential task, which, ultimately, is religious education.

An unpleasant duty of the catechist in our school instructions is the giving of marks for religious doctrine. Religious knowledge alone can be judged and measured; religious conduct should be considered only in border-line cases. The catechist should, in his assessment, be inclined to leniency, especially in the case of the less talented, but zealous pupils.

9. The Pastoral Hour for Children

An important means of extending the step of application and of bringing religion and life into the closest possible union, is the so-called "Pastoral Hour" for children. This corresponds, in the case of the older children and of adolescents, to the "Hour of Faith". Both originated in Germany and Austria during the persecution of Christianity under the Third Reich, when catechesis in the schools was frequently obstructed or stopped altogether, or imparted by teachers not having the approval of the Church. In this emergency, some priests transferred catechesis to the churches and fostered there what had become impossible: the introduction to religious practice and religious practice itself; preparation for the feasts of the Church and for the reception of the sacraments, active assistance at Mass, the "Community Mass", practice in singing, explanations of prayers, devotional exercises, and so forth.[78]

The experiences which were thereby gained were so favourable, that the weekly "Pastoral Hour" and the "Faith Hour" were continued in most places after the restoration of catechetical instruction in schools, and frequently also prescribed by the ecclesiastical authorities. Although school catechesis will also be concerned with pastoral work for children, these new "Hours" can concentrate on purely pastoral matters, since the imparting of knowledge is catered for elsewhere.

In the larger cities where the school district and the parish boundaries never coincide, this arrangement has the advantage of restoring and strengthening the links with the parish. Of course, it is never possible to get all the children together at any one time,[79] but it is already an advantage to gather a fairly large core, and to guide it to a deeper religious practice. There will always be the hope that this group may influence the more inert majority.

The addition of this practical course to school catechesis is especially important wherever the number of religion periods is

[78] An elaborate programme for this practical course in religion with concrete details and suggestions may be found in H. Hörle, "Die Kinderseelsorgestunde" in *Seelsorge im Aufbau,* Vol. 3 (1941), pp. 71–84.

[79] In the cities of Austria 25% is vouched for as average attendance. See the statistics that were compiled by L. Lentner, *ChPBl,* Vol. 65 (1952), pp. 99f. On the other hand such a flourishing parish as St. Canisius in Vienna reports an average of 73%: 800 children divided into 19 groups and into 3 sections for servers.

strictly limited, as it is, for example, in Austria, and where these periods must be held in the rarefied atmosphere of the "neutral" school.

The favourable results produced by the "Pastoral Hour" are not least conditioned by the fact that it is attended on a voluntary basis. In the eyes of the children this adds to the attraction; on the other hand, the undesirable element stays away of its own accord. This does not mean, however, that the priest need not undertake extensive canvassing for it, by announcements from the pulpit, handbills, family visits (a task for lay helpers), and especially by arranging meetings for the parents with children of school age.[80] The religion hour should, of course, be its own best advertisement. The parish should provide a suitable room, that is, one combining a friendly and religious atmosphere. If possible, it should be reminiscent of home. Religious pictures on the walls might commemorate the different seasons of the year.

The attractiveness of this practical course is also enhanced by the fact that it need not be concerned with actual instruction and with the laborious task of learning the catechism. Its domain is life itself, liturgical life in the widest sense, perhaps also the consideration of biblical topics, but not as in school but rather in connection with the liturgy of Sundays and holy days. For instance, the gospel of the Sunday just past might be examined. Visual aids will be frequently used. What is to be learned will actually be learned and practised immediately on the spot. The lives of the saints, incidents in the history of the Church, examples of everyday life, religious practices, acquaintance with the religious history of one's own country, besides prayers and hymns, can provide ample variety.

[80] J. Franzl, *ChPBl,* Vol. 64 (1951), p. 205. "The monthly meetings of parents are the best means of encouraging the growth of this practical course in religion."

It should be evident that this "Pastoral Hour" need not be conducted by the priest or by the catechist who normally teaches the children. Indeed it offers a wide field for lay catechists and other helpers in the parish. In all this it is still possible and to a certain extent desirable that those in charge might coordinate this religious hour with the compulsory catechesis in school in as natural a fashion as possible, so that what the latter can only initiate in the step of application, the former can extend in reality.[81]

10. Conditions for Successful Catechesis. Discipline

The best catechetical method is, in order to achieve its true purpose, tied to the condition that the children are receptive and that their acceptance of the word of God is not marred by any disorder. Receptivity will largely be conditioned by the kind of place in which the catechesis is given and by the choice of time. The children should, above all, be comfortable. In general, the classrooms used for catechesis fulfil the spatial and physical requirements but their bareness makes an unfavourable impression in other respects. If, as is the case in some countries, the last period of a rather full day is devoted to catechesis, when the children will already be tired, there should be a suitable break allowed.

Another condition is that the catechist by his general manner shall have succeeded in winning the confidence and the love of the children. A careless and indifferent attitude or, at the opposite extreme, a blustering manner, from the start precludes any genuine results. The catechist should try hard to avoid displays of depression or fatigue, as we have already pointed out.[82]

[81] Such a coordination by grace of which, for example, catechesis on the Bible may be inserted into the context of the ecclesiastical or liturgical year, is provided for in *Syllabus for the Diocese of Paderborn;* for a survey, consult O. Hilker, *KBl,* Vol. 75 (1950), pp. 233–239.

[82] See above, pp. 71f.

It is, moreover, necessary to prevent any likely disturbance during the instruction. Children are full of life and even a fly on the wall can distract them. The best way to ensure attention is a lesson so interesting that it will hold them spellbound. If his choice of words is uncertain and his language colourless, or he degenerates into generalities which are meaningless for the children, they will quickly turn their attention to other matters and disorder will ensue. This will be no more than the children's self-defence against the failure of the catechist. A careful preparation for each catechesis is, therefore, the best guarantee of attention and order.

Yet even the most zealous and skilled catechist will not be able to keep the attention of children always at a high pitch, especially if, as is often the case, in catechism-catechesis they cannot be spared some strenuous mental work. Moreover, among the children, there are always some thoughtless and fickle elements, and perhaps others who, as a result of difficult conditions at home, over-exertion or undernourishment, cannot give their undivided attention. The catechist should know how to maintain discipline in his class. The first few periods of catechesis at the beginning of the school year may often be decisive for good order in the classroom during the entire year. The catechist should choose a place in the classroom from which he can watch all the children constantly, he should not move about too much. He should speak clearly and distinctly, without haste and nervousness. If there is disorder, he should try to control it by exercising, only sparingly, the authority at his disposal, especially for the sake of the sacred topics with which he is dealing. If one look or a meaningful pause in the course of the instruction is enough, he should refrain from using words. If a word, an exclamation or the mentioning of a name suffices, he should refrain from admonition. To make the offender stand up for a time or send him to another seat in the classroom should, as a rule, be regarded as extreme measures. The catechist should exclude any kind of corporal punishment; in the case of girls there should be absolutely no exception from this rule. In cases of severe lapses in discipline the catechist should see to it that the parents are informed. With older children a private talk will often suffice to bring the offender to see the light.

If punishments are to be administered sparingly, rewards should not be wasted either. Not every good effort deserves to be recompensed, for in the classroom as in later life, doing our duties to God and man should be considered a matter of course. A satisfied glance, sometimes a word of praise, should be sufficient. In exceptional cases, chiefly with smaller children or on some special occasion, the catechist may award a holy picture or other prize.[83] If in certain places it is a custom to bestow a devotional book or a fitting object at the end of the school year, or at graduation, this should be considered rather as a continuation of the catechesis than as a reward, and will, of course be looked upon with approval.

[83] On this subject of discipline, look up the practical recommendations which are made in K. Buerschaper, "Nebensächlichkeiten" in *KBl*, Vol. 74 (1949), pp. 243–245; F. J. Sheed, *Are We Really Teaching Religion?* (New York: Sheed & Ward, 1953), p. 7; J. B. Collins, *op. cit.*, pp. 72–86.

VIII

SPECIAL TASKS PROPER TO VARIOUS AGE-LEVELS

1. The Religious Guidance of Small Children

THE religious care of small children who are not old enough to attend school is, it is true, not the concern of the catechist, but the person entrusted with the care of souls should see to it whether and how the parents fulfill their obligations of religious education.[1]

The baptized child is indeed a Christian. The life of grace which was bestowed upon him at Baptism cannot as yet be lost, but in order to develop properly and to strengthen the forces which protect it no less care is needed than for the physical life. Such care need not await the time when the mental faculties of the child are first in evidence; his early years are extremely important for the formation of his character and indirectly

[1] Archconfraternity of Confraternity of Christian Mothers, *Manual of Directors and Officers* (rev. 5th ed.; Pittsburgh: National Office, 1952). This Archconfraternity has its own organ: *The Catholic Home* (Pittsburgh: National Office). Consult the articles which are in Part II, *Lumen Vitae,* Vol. 7 (1952), pp. 239–282. There is also the Parent-Educator group, a segment of the Archconfraternity of Christian Doctrine, which from time to time issues material through Confraternity Publications (Paterson, N. J.). There are several fair-sized pamphlets written for preschool children, to which reference has already been made, cf. above, p. 44, note 87. Further material may be consulted: K. B. Byles, *Religion in the Home* (For Elementary School Children) and idem, *Religion in the Home* (For the Pre-School Child), both published by the Paulist Press, New York; D. A. Lord, *The Guidance of Parents* (St. Louis: Queen's Work, 1944); C. Burns, *Your Modern Children* (London: Burns, Oates & Washbourne, n.d.); E. G. Geissler, *You and Your Children* (Chicago: Fides, 1956).

also for his future attitude to religion.[2] For at this stage certain attitudes are formed which later can be the basis of some lack of restraint, obstinacy, and selfishness, or of a good and orderly life, and also of the right attitude towards God in reverence and loving obedience.[3] Though the child is dependent upon the warmth of a mother's love in order to develop soundly, yet he should learn early on that he is part of an established order and should not be spoiled by the satisfaction of unreasonable wishes.

The first steps in religious education too, will be taken much less by words than by the influence of a well-integrated environment, by the whole atmosphere of a Christian family. The mother will talk to the child in any case, pray with him, answer his questions and also tell him about God who created everything, about the Child Jesus and Mary, his Mother, and about the Guardian Angels. Knowing her child she will treat him accordingly, correct him firmly but without severity when he has misbehaved, and accustom him to obedience, modesty and sincerity from the very beginning.

But of much greater importance in these years is the education which he receives from the environment in which he grows up, and from the impressions which he gathers every day. Thus the style of the house and the living conditions are of the utmost importance. If cleanliness and order prevail there, these will strike a corresponding note in his own soul. It matters a great deal in the religious education of the child whether the decorations in the home include anything of a religious nature, perhaps a little altar, or a holy water stoup on the bedroom wall.

[2] R. Allers (Abridgement of Vera Barclay), *Practical Psychology in Character Development* (New York: Sheed & Ward, 1934), especially pp. 40–45.

[3] M. Pfliegler, *Der rechte Augenblick* (5th ed.; Vienna: Herder, 1948), pp. 27–57.—A. Wallenstein, *Kindheit und Jugend als Erziehungsaufgabe* (Freiburg: Herder, 1951). In this we can find a chapter on the prenatal formation of children.

In addition it will be relevant whether the day to day life of the family includes prayer in common, if not in the morning at least at table and in the evening. It is important that the mother should pray with the little child when he gets up and when he goes to bed. The children should become acquainted with the holy days as well as with Sundays. Something of the rhythm of the sacred year should find its way from the church into the home: the crib at Christmas, the palms on Palm Sunday, the easter egg. All this presupposes that the household and the parents are pervaded by a Christian spirit, that parents should be aware of their responsibilities for the religious education of the children; they are their first catechists.

Thus the pastoral care of the small child is essentially linked with the pastoral care of the whole family and especially of the mother. If the child grows up in a truly Christian family, and from the very beginning adapts himself to a Christian order of life; if from the very beginning he understands as a matter of course that man has not been created to enjoy life but to serve God, he will not indeed be dispensed from making a definite decision later on but he will have been helped considerably, and will have been given a precious religious investment for life.

Today a great majority of the children in big cities may spend the years before starting school in a kindergarten. From what we have just said it should be evident that it is not a matter of indifference what kind of an atmosphere prevails in such pre-school institutions.

The Catholic kindergarten should achieve in a more conscious and orderly fashion what the Catholic parents have given the child hitherto. But religion in the kindergarten should not become formal instruction.[4] Such instruction would not

[4] In the *ChPBl*, Vol. 63 (1950), pp. 18–20, there was published a "Vorschlag zu einem religiösen Arbeitsplan im Kindergarten" with an

correspond to the mental development of the three to five-year-old child. It would be as premature as reading and writing and would as a rule be more harmful than useful. At this sensitive age religion would be looked upon as something contrary to their nature. Even Bible stories in narrative form would not be suitable. The child should become acquainted with his religion and with the forms of the Catholic faith as he would with life in his environment. All teaching should be given incidentally and without compulsion. There need not as yet be a well-rounded idea of the world. He need not understand that Jesus is the Son of God or that the Saviour has redeemed us on the cross.[5] But he should be taught to fold his hands reverently before the crucifix. He ought to sense something of the rhythm of religious life, greeting our heavenly Father at the beginning of the day, know what Sunday is and that throughout the year there are many holy days. But over-saturation with religion should be avoided. The small child should first be allowed to grow into the natural order which surrounds him, rejoice in grass and flowers, light, water, animals and birds, and all the figures of fairyland. Only then, and as a complement to our

outline of definite topics (simple prayers and hymns, the most important events in the Bible) which kindergartens should teach their children in the form of impromptu talks gradually, week after week, on notable feast days, e. g., Christmas, Epiphany. This caused some after-thoughts to be voiced (O. Etl, *loc. cit.*, pp. 86f., and Johanna Huber, *loc. cit.*, p. 150). Kindergarten Committee, *The Catholic Kindergarten:* A Curriculum Guide (New York: W. H. Sadlier, 1948), pp. 19–58, deals with religion. Controversial points are avoided. In France, C. Boyer in his article in *Pédagogie chrétienne,* Vol. I (1947), p. 177, objected strenuously to several points in this programme, *Formation chrétienne des tout-petits,* because in it the natural teacher of the child was encouraged to speak to these young children of sin, confession and Holy Communion as well as the Mass. The articles in *Parent Educator,* above p. 44, avoid some of these pitfalls.

[5] The parents should not tell the child—as happened in the past—that the "heavenly Father" hung on the cross, because such an idea is erroneous.

colourful world, should he be told about God who has made all things and loves us very much.

If the priest makes a personal appearance in the kindergarten or if some pastoral occasion should bring him there—perhaps the blessing of homes on the feast of the Epiphany—he should remember that this meeting may have for most of the children the significance of an important event.

The child enters school normally about the age of six. This is an important stage in his life. For many children it may be the first time that they have been away from the family. In any case a new world opens for them. The age of play has ended, the time for serious work has begun. It has, therefore, been suggested by a German catechist, Linus Bopp[6] that their first day should be celebrated with a children's Mass, similar to that Mass which is already frequently offered on the day when they leave school. This Mass might be given a special form; the children accompanied by their mothers could form a procession in which the godparents might also assist. In place of the Communion Prayer at the end of Mass the celebrant could give the liturgical blessing for children, or this blessing alone could be the focal point of a more simple celebration. Soon after the beginning of school the catechist makes, for the first time, his appearance before the beginners. In some country districts, where the priest generally is the religious teacher, the children will already know him. In any case, he should seek, from the beginning, to gain their confidence, beginning his instruction with that stock of religious truth which they have known from their homes and thus lighten the difficult transition from the family circle to life in school.[7]

It is evident that during the years of the catechesis which are

[6] Bopp, pp. 286f.

[7] About the subject matter of catechesis in the first and subsequent years, see pp. 158f.

now beginning the religious warmth of the home will continue to form their basic support. Even if parents cannot follow the course of the catechesis step by step, the children should be made to feel that their further religious training is a matter of deep concern to the parents. If occasionally father or mother would discuss with the child any topic from the Bible, or a catechism question, and talk about it, or at least show some interest in the homework, they would contribute towards this accord.[8] For Catholic children the normal order of school life should be one which benefits a baptized child, and which con-

[8] Mother M. Bolton, *God's Hour in the Nursery:* I. *Guidance Book* and II. *Activity Book* (Paterson: St. Anthony Guild Press, 1946); Sister Mary, *et al., The Catholic Mother's Helper* (Paterson, N. J.: St. Anthony Guild Press, 1948); Sr. M. Marguerite, *Their Hearts Are His Garden* (Paterson, N. J.: St. Anthony Guild Press, 1946); M. L. Coakley, *Our Child . . . God's Child* (Milwaukee: Bruce, 1953).—In Germany: Marie Schlumpf, *Religionsbüchlein* (6th ed.; Freiburg: Herder, 1942) (instructions in very simple form on how to teach children); Elisabeth Kötter, *Weg des Kindes zu Gott* (3rd ed.; Freiburg: Herder, 1949) (with many practical examples culled from attempts to educate children in the family); Fr. Schneider, *Katholische Familienerziehung* (6th ed.; Freiburg: Herder, 1957), especially the chapter on the religious education of the child (pp. 172–198). For the very young there are the many religious picture books for children: These are abundant in the U.S.A. and only a few can be mentioned: Sr. M. Juliana, *Listen to God* (St. Paul: Catechetical Guild, 1953); D. A. Lord, *The Friends of Jesus* (New York: Devotional Publishing Co., 1943); J. Bedier, *Jesus Comes For Everybody* (New York: Garden City, 1948); Bishop Morrow, *My Jesus and I* (Kenosha, Wis.: My Mission House, 1949); G. A. Hogarth, *A Bible ABC* (New York: F. C. Stokes, 1941); C. Beebe, *The Story of Mary: The Mother of Jesus* (Milwaukee: Bruce, 1950); Father Brennan, *Tales for Tiny Tots* (Milwaukee: Bruce, 1954); G. M. Dennerle and Sr. M. Magdala, *Jesus Shows Me the Way* (Milwaukee: Bruce, 1955); F. McGrade, *The Rosary* (St. Paul: Catechetical Guild, 1952); Father Gales, *A First Book of Saints* (St. Paul: Catechetical Guild, 1953).—In Germany: Mittelstedt-Kabelka, *Wort Gottes für die Kleinen* (Wien: 1948); Weigl-Zinkl, *Bilderbuch vom lieben Gott; Bilderbuch von Gottes Heiligen; Bilderbuch vom göttlichen Heiland* (all from Freiburg: Herder, 1939–1956).

tinues uninterruptedly the religious education that was begun in the home. It is wrong, therefore, when Catholic children are forced to attend neutral schools where the divorce between religion and life has become an unholy principle.[9] The disadvantage for the child is all the greater when the family looks upon such a state of affairs as normal because religion has become a dead letter to it. The task of the catechist in such circumstances is made infinitely difficult.

2. The Age for First Communion

Having discussed the subject matter of catechesis in the various stages of the school as well as the biblical and catechism-catechesis methods, we need not deal with the general catechetical treatment of the various age levels within the school year. But the preparation for the sacraments and the sacramental and iturgical life has to be considered specially. In fact we might ask whether this is not the chief task of the catechist and whether our disregard of it hitherto could not be regarded as an indication of intellectualism not as yet overcome. Actually in the section of Canon Law devoted to *De catechetica institutione* (can. 1329–1336) catechesis on the sacraments is accorded the most prominent place. Besides the question, who is competent to impart catechesis, and the question regarding Christian teaching for adults, canons 1330 and 1331 only concern the catechesis for children. Of these, the first deals with the preparation for the reception of the sacraments; the second reminds the priest to extend his catechesis for the children after their first Communion. The decree of Pope St. Pius X[10] has created

[9] American Council on Education, *The Function of the Public School in Dealing With Religion* (Washington: American Council on Education, 1953); F. E. Johnson, *American Education and Religion* (New York: Harper Bros., 1952).

[10] The decree *Quam singulari* (August 10, 1910), *AAS,* Vol. II

an entirely new attitude, the catechetical effects of which have not as yet been everywhere fully considered.

In order to understand the problem which it poses, it would be useful to look at history and consider the many possible solutions.[11] In the early Church it was customary for the children to receive Communion with the same naturalness and unaffectedness with which all the faithful received the sacrament, if not every day then at least every time when they attended Mass.

Even at Baptism the child received Communion under the species of wine. Communion at Baptism lasted in the Western Church until well into the twelfth century.[12] In the East the practice continues to this day, also in some Uniate communities.[13] It followed from this practice that children were

(1910), pp. 577–582. A commentary on this decree was written by the then Secretary of the Congregation of the Sacraments, D. Jorio, *Il decreto "Quam singulari" sull'età richiesta per la prima communione* (Roma: Marietti, 1928); J. T. McNicholas, "The First Communion Decree" in *American Ecclesiastical Review,* Vol. 44 (Jan., 1911), p. 77; F. M. de Zulueta, *Early First Communion* (London: Burns, Oates & Washbourne, 1911).

[11] L. Andrieux, *La première communion. Histoire et discipline* (Paris: Beauchesne, 1911); J. Baumgärtler, *Die Erstkommunion der Kinder* (Munich: Kösel und Pustet, 1929). A good conspectus is offered by M. Waldmann, "Neue Forschungsergebnisse zur Geschichte der Kinderkommunion" in *Theologie und Glaube,* Vol. 22 (1930), pp. 273–290. Furthermore, the chapter, rich in content, in P. Browe, *Die Pflichtkommunion im Mittelalter* (Münster, 1940), pp. 128–184; idem, *Die häufige Kommunion im Mittelalter* (Münster, 1938).

[12] To answer Baumgärtler's doubts whether Holy Communion at Baptism was customary before the time of St. Augustine, cf. J. A. Jungmann, *ZkTh,* Vol. 54 (1930), pp. 627f. Remnants of Communion at Baptism have been preserved down to our day: the popular custom which is connected with it, namely, immediately after Baptism to pour a drop of wine into the child's mouth is in vogue among the Slovenians in Carinthia and in Champagne even today; see references to this in J. A. Jungmann, *The Mass of the Roman Rite,* 2 vols. (New York: Benziger Bros.), Vol. II (1955), pp. 413-414, footnote 47.

[13] H. A. Heiser, *Die Kinderkommunion im Geiste der Kirche,* Vol. I

given Holy Communion occasionally at other times also,[14] at least when they were older.[15] If after the celebration of Mass many consecrated Hosts were left over, the celebrant called the children and gave them the Sacrament, as accounts from the East as well as from Gaul inform us.[16]

Towards the end of Christian antiquity the practice of receiving Communion underwent a change. At the Synod of Agde (506) the faithful had to be urged to receive Communion at least three times each year. The emphasis on receiving the Sacrament with the greatest reverence, which began about the eleventh century, gradually influenced the Communion of children. It was beginning to be thought better to wait until the children could understand what they received. The Fourth Lateran Council (1215) was the decisive landmark, for it laid down that the obligation to go to Confession at least once a

(4th ed.; Wiesbaden: Hermann Rauch, 1931), pp. 25–31. In 1741 a Capuchin father attempted quietly to drop the custom which he had encountered among the Coptic Christians, but he was warned and prohibited from continuing to do so by the Holy Office. This decision has been in force ever since; cf. Andrieux, *op. cit.,* pp. 73–77.

[14] Cyprian, *De lapsis,* c. 25 (*CSEL* 31, p. 255); cf. F. J. Dölger, *Ichthys,* Vol. II (Münster, 1922), pp. 524ff.

[15] In the 12th century, scholars defended the theory that Communion at Baptism satisfied the obligation of children for two to four years (hence, not for any longer time); cf. A. Landgraf, in *ZkTh,* Vol. 66 (1942), p. 127. Examples of Communion received by children without first going to Confession, cf. P. Browe, *Die Pflichtkommunion im Mittelalter,* pp. 143f. L. Eisenhofer, *Handbuch der katholischen Liturgik,* 2 vols. (Freiburg: Herder, 1933), Vol. II, pp. 301f. For practices among the Orientals, cf. Baumgärtler, *op. cit.,* pp. 94–100. Heiser, *op. cit.,* Vol. I, pp. 28–30. Among the Non-Uniate Copts the children form today at least half of those who receive Holy Communion. They go to Communion until the years of discretion without first going to Confession; cf. Cl. Kopp, *Glaube und Sakramente der koptischen Kirche* (Rom, 1932), p. 145; compare p. 158.

[16] J. A. Jungmann, *The Mass of the Roman Rite,* Vol. II (1955), pp. 407f. and also footnote No. 7.

year and to receive Communion at Easter, should begin with the "years of discretion" *(anni discretionis)*.[17]

What was meant by the "years of discretion"? This question has received its definitive answer only in recent times.[18] At the time of the Lateran Council theologians meant the age at which the child was able to decide between good and bad in moral and intellectual matters to the extent of being *doli capax*, "capable of deceit".

This was understood at the time as the capacity to commit a mortal sin. According to our notions it would suggest a rather advanced age. Theologians and canonists of that era, which knew so little about psychology, almost unanimously—a certain Gandulph (c. 1170) appears to be the only exception—held the view that this capacity for deceit was already present with the seventh year. For this reason they took the decree of the Council to mean that the obligation to go to confession begun at that time,[19]

[17] Can. 21 (Denzinger *et al.*, n. 437): *Omnis utriusque sexus fidelis, postquam ad annos discretionis pervenerit, omnia sua solus peccata saltem semel in anno fideliter confiteatur proprio sacerdoti . . . suscipiens reverenter ad minus in Pascha Eucharistiae sacramentum.*

[18] Consult the conspectus of the controversy in Waldmann, *loc. cit.*, pp. 275ff.—The definitive presentation was made in substance in the work of F. Gillmann, "Die *anni discretionis* im Canon *Omnis utriusque sexus*" in *Archiv für kath. Kirchenrecht,* Vol. 108 (1928), pp. 556–617; see the epilogue to this (after the objections of J. Ernest had been raised), idem, *loc. cit.*, Vol. 110 (1930), pp. 187–192.

[19] In another context—when dealing with the judicial oath or with the contract of marriage—the *anni discretionis* were understood to be the years which dated the advent of adolescence (14 for boys and 12 for girls). This elasticity in the interpretation of the expression was due to the fact that the young were grouped in accordance with a septenary division which is still customary in Canon Law, and so in round figures considered the seventh year of age as the first, and, 12–14, as the second stage of development. Penal prescriptions which were directed against those who failed to receive both sacraments at the times designated were designed to cover only the fourteen year old; cf. Baumgärtler, *op. cit.*, pp. 193f.

and logically the duty to receive Holy Communion was also fixed to begin with this age.[20]

In practice, however, the reception of Holy Communion began to be viewed in a different light. It is a fact that throughout the whole of the late Middle Ages there are references to the confession of seven year olds[21] but never of Communion for children of this age. In this matter St. Thomas appears to have become authoritative. He laid down as requisite for the reception of Communion the presence of true devotion *(actualis devotio)* in the recipient, but that this could be expected only with the tenth or eleventh year.[22] This view was quite a frequent one in later times. Henceforth the years ten to eleven were generally recognized as the earliest date at which Holy Communion could be administered for the first time. During the late Middle Ages, however, an obligation, to go to Confession and to receive Holy Communion once a year was assumed to exist only at the fourteenth year (in the case of girls sometimes at the age of twelve),[23] and this represented the general practice. Other considerations, besides solicitude for the required devotion and reverence, were responsible for the late term set for the reception of first Holy Communion. At the reception of Communion it became customary to make contributions in money and kind to the parish priest and sometimes also to the secular authorities.[24]

As early as the thirteenth century frequently, and later almost universally, an earlier age limit was set for first Confession, and a later one for first Holy Communion. The age for first Com-

[20] Gillmann, *loc. cit.,* Vol. 110 (1930), pp. 189f.

[21] Baumgärtler, *op. cit.,* pp. 189f.

[22] St. Thomas, *In IV Sent.,* d. 9, a. 5, sol. 4.—Cf. Baumgärtler, *op. cit.,* pp. 140–174.

[23] Browe, *Die Pflichtkommunion im Mittelalter* (Münster, 1940), pp. 166–168.

[24] *Idem,* pp. 162–165.

munion fluctuated between the tenth and fourteenth, and sometimes even fifteenth, years.[25] First Confession was fixed some time, mostly some years, before first Communion.[26] Only since the eighteenth century has there been opposition from theologians and individual synods to the late first Communion date insofar as they thought that this should not be a hard-and-fast rule without exception, and without attention being paid to the meaning of the condition "years of discretion".[27] The revival of historical studies also contributed to a new interest in the practice of the early Church, accelerating the return to tradition.[28]

[25] Baumgärtler, *op. cit.,* pp. 186f.; Andrieux, *op. cit.,* pp. 143–166.—When universal compulsory schooling was introduced in the 18th century, the reception of first Holy Communion was frequently put off until the end of school; Heiser, *op. cit.,* Vol. I, p. 42. From the diocese of Strassburg, as Pope St. Pius X reports it in his decree on first Communion, the question was asked in Rome (1910), whether children of twelve or fourteen years of age could be permitted to approach the Holy Table for the first time.

[26] This point of view was commonly defended, even by theologians of note, e. g., Suárez and de Lugo, on the grounds that Confession is more necessary, and that for the sacrament of the Eucharist *maior discretio* must be demanded; cf. Browe, *Die Pflichtkommunion,* pp. 174f.—Even Hirscher gives, as his opinion for the average age for first Confession, the completed eighth year, for first Holy Communion the completed 12th or 13th year; *Katechetik,* pp. 609, 627.—The practice from the thirteenth to the middle of the nineteenth century corresponds to the opinions that were proposed, cf. Andrieux, *op. cit.,* pp. 106ff. and 143ff.; also P. Browe, "Die Kinderbeichte im Mittelalter" in *Theologie und Glaube,* Vol. 25 (1933), pp. 689–701, especially pp. 697ff.

[27] Andrieux, *op. cit.,* pp. 177–179. On a practice of early first Communion which was suppressed during the era of Enlightenment in Southern Germany, consult J. Grötsch, "Ist die Frühkommunion etwas Neues?" in *KBl,* Vol. 79 (1954), pp. 89–96.

[28] W. Trapp, *Vorgeschichte und Ursprung der liturgischen Bewegung* (Regensburg: Pustet, 1940), p. 303.—Heiser, *op. cit.,* Vol. I, pp. 46–51. Toward the end of the nineteenth century in a majority of dioceses in Austria and in many German dioceses children were permitted to go to

A complete reorientation was begun by Pope St. Pius X who, in 1905, issued the decree on frequent Communion and in 1910 the decree on the first Communion of children.

The decree on frequent Communion expressly criticized the excessive emphasis placed on reverence for the sacrament in the previous era, by declaring that it was not the primary purpose of the sacrament "that through it the honour and reverence due to our Lord should above all be safeguarded, or that it should serve as a reward for virtue in the recipients".[29]

The decree on the first Holy Communion of children[30] refers to "not a few errors and deplorable abuses" which have entered into the fixing of the age of discretion,[31] especially of different ages for the reception of the sacrament of Penance and for that of the Eucharist before the tenth and twelfth or even fourteenth year. The obligation to receive Communion should coincide with the age at which the child begins to use his reason, "that is about the seventh year or a little later or even sooner". Then it sets out the detailed conditions to which we shall return later.

The law that is in force at the present time, which only

first Confession when they were nine or ten years of age, and the next year to first Holy Communion (in the diocese of Brixen they were permitted to receive Holy Communion the same year, in fact immediately after their first Confession); J. E. Pichler and W. Pichler, *Lehrplan für den katholischen Religionsunterricht* (Vienna, 1904), pp. 44–46.

[29] *ASS,* Vol. 38 (1905), p. 401.

[30] *AAS,* Vol. 2 (1910), pp. 577–583; English translation: Pastoral Letter of the Bishops of the Province of Cincinnati, *The First Communion of Children* (Cincinnati, Ohio: Diocesan Chancery Office, 1910): A sixteen page pamphlet containing an English translation of the decree *Quam singulari* as well as the pastoral letter of the bishops of the province.

[31] *AAS, loc. cit.,* p. 579: *haud pauci errores plorandique abusus.* By these words the abuse that had become almost universal in the previous centuries is characterized patently as the result of a deviation in practice rather than as the outgrowth of an error in a matter of faith.

summarizes the prescriptions issued by St. Pius, is to be found in the Code of Canon Law of 1917. It achieved a middle course between the excessive simplicity of Christian antiquity and the all too severe restraint of the later period. Holy Communion is declared to be both the right and the duty of every Catholic. The dignity of the sacrament is safeguarded insofar as it is to be administered to the children only when they are able to receive it with some understanding. In particular there are the following regulations:

1. "It should not be given to children who, by reason of their tender age, are unable to know and desire this sacrament" (can. 854, para. 1). The Communion of small infants which had been permitted for twelve centuries is thereby excluded. The benefits which they would gain from the Sacrament are not judged to be so great as to compensate for the inevitable lack of reverence inherent in its unconscious reception. Integration into the Mystical Body of Christ, which was formerly associated with the Communion of infants, is in any case brought about by Baptism.

2. As soon as the consciousness of the children has matured to some extent, the duty of Easter Communion should be fulfilled. This is laid down in essentially the same words as those of the fourth Lateran Council (can. 859, para. 1). "Every Catholic of either sex, who has reached the age of discretion, that is, attained to the use of reason, must receive the Holy Eucharist once a year, at least during the Easter period, unless his own priest should, for a reasonable cause, advise him to abstain from it for a time." The law regulating Easter Communion by giving the age when the obligation is to begin, thus also constitutes the law for first Holy Communion. The phrase, "that is, attained to the use of reason *(id est ad usum rationis)*", which was added to the famous canon of the Lateran Council, is obviously intended in the sense of meaning an earlier

age. The age fixed by Pope St. Pius X in the phrase "about the seventh year" was, it is true, not repeated, but in another section of the Code these two phrases occur together and are seen there to possess an identical meaning.[32] In this way a certain latitude, which takes into consideration the stage of development actually reached by the child, is possible. Precisely the same expression is also employed for the time when the obligation to receive the sacrament of Penance is to begin (can. 906).

The opinion has been held that this somewhat loose manner of expression is a sign that the first Communion law is not an ecclesiastical but a divine law, the ecclesiastical precept being only another way of expressing our Lord's own precept: "Unless you eat the flesh of the Son of Man and drink his blood you can have no life in you" (John 6, 53).[33] This view cannot be maintained, however, if we do not give the Code a wider interpretation, but simply regard it as fixing the age around the seventh year. This would certainly be the case if we would argue that the child who has reached the age of reason is already in danger of falling into sin; for the danger of venial sin does not imply the necessity of the fortifying sacrament, at least not as a strict duty.[34] There could be the danger of serious sin,[35] but in the case of a seven-year-old child this is

[32] Canon 88: *expleto autem septennio (puer) usum rationis habere praesumitur*. The expression, "use of reason", is in the language of Canon Law not used in a psychological sense—for a two year old who has learned how to talk uses his reason to some extent—but in a moral and theological sense, as a use of reason that is already developed.

[33] Gatterer, pp. 136f.

[34] M. Conte a Coronata, *Institutiones Iuris Canonici,* "De Sacramentis", Vol. I (Turin: Marietti, 1943), p. 291.

[35] *Concilium Tridentinum,* sess. XXI, c. 4 (Denzinger *et al.,* n. 933) (Schroeder, *op. cit.,* p. 34) in which the reason why children are not required to go to Holy Communion before they have reached the age of reason is simply: they cannot lose the grace which they received at Baptism.

not as yet likely.[36] Nor is it to be supposed, that for centuries a divine precept had been grossly neglected throughout the Church, and that this had been supported by countless ecclesiastical regulations or at least by custom. On the contrary, there is no doubt that this new regulation corresponds much more closely with the meaning of the divine precept.

3. What dispositions are expected from the children? The Code makes several distinctions (can. 854, para. 2f.):

a. If the child is in danger of death, it is required only that he should be "able to distinguish the sacred Host from common bread, and to adore it reverently". Evidently it suffices to say to him (especially if he has seen adults genuflecting before the Host): "The Child Jesus (that is, He whom the child knows as the 'Child Jesus') is present in this piece of bread", and then devoutly folds his hands. This can obviously be done by a four or five-year-old.

b. More is asked of children who are well. They ought, at least, to know "those mysteries of the faith which are absolutely necessary for salvation *(necessitate medii)* and approach the Holy Eucharist devoutly, according to the capacity of their age". Very little is thus required, certainly not more than two affirmations: that God exists, and that He rewards what is good and punishes what is wicked. No certain theological justification exists for demanding also a knowledge of the three divine Persons and a knowledge of Jesus Christ as God-Man. In any case the Code's requirements are qualified by "according to their capacity" *(pro suo captu)*.

4. Who will decide whether a child possesses the disposition thus required, whether it is not too early to receive first Com-

[36] Actually on February 2, 1920, in response to the question: whether the "use of reason" of the "Decree of First Communion" meant the ability to commit sin, a negative reply was given: *Archiv für kath. Kirchenrecht,* Vol. 110 (1930), pp. 152f.

munion? The Code of Canon Law answers (can. 854, para. 4): "It is for the confessor and the parents or guardians to judge." It is assumed that the child will have seen a confessor before his first Communion.[37] The confessor should put some questions to him, but it is nowhere indicated that in each case absolution has to be received. The child need not have sinned in order to be admitted to his first Holy Communion.

Also relevant is canon 860, which deals with those entrusted with the responsibility of seeing that the child fulfills his obligations, that is by receiving Holy Communion at the right time and not too late. The list of persons named includes parents, guardians, confessors, directors of schools and pastors, in that order. The parents are accorded the first place; in this respect at least they are to prove themselves the child's first catechists.

5. It is the pastor's task to see that these regulations are properly observed. Two duties are especially incumbent upon him (can. 854, para. 4). He must take care that children are not admitted to Holy Communion before they have attained the age of reason or without sufficient preparation. If necessary he will submit them to an examination. He will also have to see that those who have attained to the use of reason are admitted to the sacrament as soon as possible. Moreover, it is his duty to provide the necessary instruction for the children. More will be said about this later.

3. First Confession

In present-day practice first Holy Communion is as a rule preceded by Confession. The necessity of preparing the children for the sacrament of Penance is perhaps the chief obstacle

[37] This prescription reflects the ancient practice of taking the child to Confession several times a year before the time of first Communion. According to the *Catechismus Romanus* (II, 4, 63) those who are entrusted with the task of deciding the exact time for the first Communion of

why many pastors find it hard to accept the idea of early first Communion. For it is certainly much more difficult to prepare the children to receive correctly the sacrament of Penance—in which the penitent's positive attitude is of the essence of the sacrament—than it is to prepare them for Holy Communion, in which it is really only a question of reception. A seven-year-old child can readily receive the Eucharist with devotion, but to confess his sins contritely is more difficult for him.[38] The difficulty grows if the pastor believes that he ought to acquaint the child with all the details of a good technique for confession or if he attempts to give him the complete teaching on penance. Such demands, however, cannot be reconciled with the sense of the Church's regulations. If anywhere, then surely here ought to be applied the principle of the old Christian mystagogical teaching, that the sacrament should first of all be actually received and only then explained in its essence and in the details concerning its fulfilment.

Instruction on the sacrament of Penance—and similarly also on the sacrament of the Eucharist—should be given essentially in two stages, before first Confession, only insofar as it is necessary for its valid and fruitful reception, and at the catechism stage with that completeness desirable for later life. In the meantime the ordinary course of catechesis and the continual reception of the sacraments will afford sufficient opportunities for the gradual development of what has been begun.

But we should establish, first of all, whether and to what extent the law of the Church actually demands Confession

children are: "the father and the priest to whom the children confess their sins".

[38] The Middle Ages entertained a contrary view, but only because they demanded that the children should possess an extensive knowledge and a fervent devotion to be able to receive Holy Communion.

from the seven-year-old child. As a general rule this is undoubtedly the case. Admittance to first Communion requires, as we have seen, the cooperation of the confessor. This does not as yet, strictly speaking, presuppose Confession; but it requires only that the child should see a priest who might also be the child's confessor. The priest could draw no conclusions for the external guidance of the child on the basis of an actual confession,[39] but a second passage in Canon Law is quite clear. When fixing the age at which the obligation to go to confession begins for the faithful, canon 906 uses precisely the same expression employed in connection with the duty of first Communion, namely, "as soon as they have reached the age of discretion, that is, the age of reason". Hence confession is required even for children of about seven. On the other hand, it is today a generally accepted opinion of moralists that the obligation to confess once during the year binds only those who are conscious of a great sin.[40] This interpretation, however, has not always found acceptance in the Church. When in eighth-century France the obligation to confess once a year was introduced, all the faithful had to go to confession. If some had nothing to confess they were referred to the sins of thought and to the seven (or eight) capital sins, because "a man can scarcely live without committing one of these". Even in the first half of the thirteenth century the prescription of the Fourth Lateran Council was still understood in the sense of an obligation binding also those who were conscious only

[39] This is because of the concept, which actually prevails today, of the distinction between the *forum internum* and the *forum externum*. In any case the declining years of the Middle Ages, whose usage appears to have inspired the present canon, conceived this distinction less strictly than we do at present.

[40] Noldin - Schmitt - Heinzel, *Summa theol. moralis,* 3 vols. (30th ed.; Innsbruck: F. Rauch, 1954), Vol. II, § 669, p. 583; Vol. III, § 410, p. 352.

of venial sins. St. Thomas was the first to effect a change in this interpretation.[41]

Since this more liberal interpretation justifiably prevails today, we ought also to understand the prescription for children in the sense not of actual obligation to confess venial sins, but as a directive which ought to be respected so long as there is no reasonable ground for a departure from the rule. It must be assumed that on account of insufficient insight grave sins are as a rule not possible before the tenth or eleventh year.[42] The confessions of seven to eight-year-olds are certainly only "confessions of devotion", but even such confessions have their value. It is meaningful that small lapses, too, should be confessed, and that pardon for them should be received in the sacrament. Thus the basic link with the Redeemer will be ever reaffirmed anew. Moreover, the general practice of secret confession for venial sins too will facilitate the approach to the confessional also for those who need to confess because of grave sins and even for individual penitents generally if later they should have occasion to confess grave sins.

[41] J. A. Jungmann, *Die lateinischen Bussriten* (Innsbruck: F. Rauch, 1932), pp. 175f.

[42] This is the opinion of authors who have investigated the psychological aspect of children's sins. It is clear that children, especially when they have been under bad influence, can perform actions which objectively are grave sins. But taking into consideration their thoughtlessness and their dependence on the feelings of the moment, it is evident that the malice of even a very wicked action is not sufficiently grasped to make it a grave sin. Th. Müncker, *Die psychologischen Grundlagen der katholischen Sittenlehre (Handbuch der katholischen Sittenlehre II)* (Düsseldorf, 1934), pp. 113f. In fact Müncker says of the years preceding adolescence ("around the tenth to the twelfth year"): "Considering the psychological state of the child at this age, we may ask whether or not at this age the child is capable of committing a grave sin" (p. 114).—J. Engert, *Psychologie und Pädagogik der Erstbeicht und Erstkommunion* (Donauwörth, 1918), p. 31: "A grave sin accompanied by the consciousness of a serious offence against God is probably never encountered before the age of eleven."

It is especially valuable also for the child to confess his own childish sins. It is salutary for him to examine his past faults and to be sorry for them. Through his contrite confession before God he will turn from the evil which he has committed. He will be open to a sincere admonition and an encouraging word from the confessor. In this way the child will be the recipient of the priest's beneficial individual guidance. Finally it is of great educational value for the child to recover in the sacrament of penance full purity of soul and to become conscious of it. This gives him courage to start anew, and spurs him on to a greater zeal and conscientiousness—just as a person who wears new clothes is always more careful of them than he is of old, worn-out garments.

From what has been said, we can draw certain conclusions concerning the preparation of children for first Confession. If we must be satisfied with minimum requirements (and under the circumstances we frequently must), preparation will not take many days.[43] In fact, the Code of Canon Law requires only that "the pastor is obliged, each year, to prepare the children for the proper reception of the sacraments of Penance and Confirmation by a continuous course of instruction lasting

[43] "Of extreme importance not only for his own day but also for many subsequent centuries is the famous canon 45 of the Council of Laodicea (c. 381) which was wrongly understood and as a consequence incorrectly translated by Martin of Bracara (d. 580), the Apostle to the Suevians (*PL,* Vol. 84, c. 49, col. 581). In his translation he failed to distinguish between simple catechumens and the *competentes*. As a consequence the instruction of four weeks (the days of Lent) which in the early Church had been prescribed for the *competentes* was shortened to three weeks; and this shortened period was then made mandatory for the simple catechumens. The strange error was often repeated during the succeeding centuries and has even found acceptance (with the weeks of Lent restored) in the Code of Canon Law: L. Kilger, "Zur Entwicklung der Katechumenatspraxis vom 5. bis 18. Jahrhundert" in *Zeitschrift für Missionswissenschaft,* Vol. 15 (1925), pp. 168–169.

several days *(per plures dies),* to be held at stated times". This canon, as the context reveals, deals with children who have never received or are not receiving a regular course of instruction. It is, therefore, only necessary that, apart from the knowledge of the basic truths of religion which they must know for first Communion,[44] they should be able to recognize certain of the faults which they commit as sins, to detest them before God and to confess them to the priest. No instruction on the Ten Commandments, on the distinction between grave and venial sin, on perfect and imperfect contrition, on the necessity and duty of confession, is required. It is enough to point to some of the ordinary sins of children. More important than detailed teaching in the sense of the catechism is the knowledge that God is displeased with lying, disobedience, and stubbornness, and that we should humbly ask His pardon. To this we might add a simple explanation of how we should ask God's forgiveness, that is, how to awaken sorrow, and how to tell about one's sins.

In this way the child will be led to make his first Confession. This does not imply that he should receive absolution. There are two reasons which might cause the priest to dismiss the child without absolution, simply with his priestly blessing. Firstly, because he has realized that the child is not guilty of any sin, but secondly, because he may discover that although the child may have sinned he does not possess, due to his immaturity, that degree of inner concentration that would enable him to awaken true contrition for what he has done.

Such a procedure, making so few demands, and corresponding roughly to that which good priests would have used in the Middle Ages,[45] must not be the rule today when there are con-

[44] See above, p. 299f.

[45] In his *Instructiones Pastorum* St. Charles Borromeo says: "It is a beautiful custom to introduce the children of five or six years of age to

ditions of proper pastoral care and regular catechesis in school. That is why episcopal ordinances have been added to the universal Code of Canon Law. But from what we have said, we may better appreciate the points upon which our attention should be focused, and that Confession need not be an obstacle to the early first Communion of children.

Proper preparation for first Confession—and likewise for first Communion—may already be included within the normal school-catechesis, without special instructions being necessary for Confession and Communion. At the beginning of the second year most of the children will have reached the age of seven. They are thus subject, in the sense we have already explained, to the rule of annual confession and of making their Easter duty. If they are to be admitted to the sacraments at the end of this second year, they will have received two years of religious instruction.[46] Without the even course of catechesis being in any way disturbed and turning into formal sacramental catechesis, the children will have received, in these two years, a well-rounded and sufficient, in fact excellent, preparation. If in the first year

their confessor, so that they can gradually be instructed and then be brought to a knowledge and reception of the sacrament. In any case priests ought to guard themselves against giving sacramental absolution until they have ascertained whether or not sufficient matter is present, and whether or not the children have reached a sufficient use of reason."—The introduction to the confessor means here that instruction is necessary. In general, however, throughout the preceding centuries we can find no trace of a preparatory instruction; those in authority were satisfied if the child could repeat the most important prayers by heart (especially the Lord's Prayer and the Creed); these the children learned from their parents, and when they had memorized them the parents saw to it that sooner or later after they had reached the age of seven, they were brought to Confession. P. Browe, "Der Beichtunterricht im Mittelalter" in *Theologie und Glaube,* Vol. 26 (1934), pp. 427–442.

[46] In the U.S.A. it is customary for the children to receive their first Holy Communion sometime after Easter in their second year in school.

they have learned only some basic notions and a few simple prayers, the second year will provide an introduction to the history of salvation as perhaps contained in their religious textbooks, and ample opportunity to cover the ground necessary for an understanding of the sacrament of Penance. The sin of our first parents and their punishment, as well as the story of the flood, will offer occasions to speak to them of sin and of the purpose of amendment. The promulgation of the Ten Commandments on Mount Sinai offers the catechist an opportunity to consider in detail the various kinds of sin and to prepare the children for the examination of conscience. The Saviour who forgave the woman caught in adultery or who gave the Apostles the power to forgive sins are suitable starting points for his treatment of the sacrament of Penance.[47] It will then only be necessary in the weeks immediately preceding the reception of the sacrament of Penance to summarize what has already been taught and to speak about the actual procedure.

In the case of well-organized schools, in which each school year is represented by a class, preparations within the normal catecheses are the most natural solution. It has even special advantages because the whole of religious training and character guidance can become more unified. It will be worth retaining unless the time available is so limited that special extension periods become desirable, or that, for other reasons, instructions on first Confession and first Holy Communion are required by the parish. On the other hand, it is clear that this preparation would be more thorough, if it is given in special classes designed for this purpose, as this is the rule in many dioceses or necessary in less organized schools. The preparation will then

[47] The *Religionsbüchlein* of W. Pichler has instructions for more detailed Confession catechesis. Similarly Raab, *Gotteslehrbüchlein,* which (in an appendix) gives among other matters a complete catechesis for Confession and Communion.

still less have the character of a series of religious instructions and still more that of edification and of religious guidance. It would not do simply to begin with instructions on Confession and then to proceed to Communion; he should not begin with the statement that we ought to confess our sins. From the very beginning Confession should only be part of the preparation for first Communion. The catechist should consequently turn the attention of the children to the heavenly banquet to which they have been invited, or even better, to the truth that God is good to us and wants us to be with him. Indeed, at this point he has his first opportunity to announce the good news of the love of God to the children, who will be filled with awe and devotion. Only against this background will he begin to teach about sin, penance and Confession.[48]

Concerning the details in our teaching on the sacrament of Penance, we should not set our goal too high even under

[48] Some guides for the instruction of the children of this age level (7–8): G. M. Dennerle, *Leading the Little Ones to Christ* (Milwaukee: Bruce, 1932), very detailed, complete and good instructions, adapted from Gruber-Gatterer, *Katechesen;* W. R. Kelly, *Our First Communion* (New York: Benziger, 1937) for the children themselves; D. Lynch *et al., The Holy Eucharist* (St. Paul: Catechetical Guild, 1952); Catholic Teachers Association, *Little Lessons for Little Catholics* (New York: Paulist Press, 1937); H. Freese, *First Steps to God* (St. Paul: Catechetical Guild, 1941); Mother M. Loyola, *A Simple First Confession Book* (Brooklyn: ITS, n. d.); Sr. Annunziata, *First Communion Catechism* (New York: Benziger Bros., 1946), this is a "Lesson Unit" catechism; J. V. Brownson, *Feed My Lambs* (Detroit: Diocesan Press, 1938); J. J. Baierl, *A Method of Confession and Communion for Children* (Rochester: Seminary Press, 1937); A. J. Heeg, *A Little Child's Confession Book* (St. Louis: The Queen's Work, 1941); E. Horan, *My First Communion Catechism,* and also a Teacher's Manual (New York: W. H. Sadlier, 1942); L. L. Morrow, *My First Communion* (New York: E. O'Toole, 1941); F. McGrade, *My Confession* (St. Paul: Catechetical Guild, 1953); Our Lady's Catechists, *Happy Half-Hours for Sixes and Sevens* (Miss Devitt, Tenth House, Oxted, Surrey); Mother M. Bolton, *A Little Child's First Communion,* 6 pamphlets or booklets (Paterson, N. J.: St. Anthony Guild Press, 1935).

favourable conditions. Fortunately we need not expect an actual conversion at this age; at most there might be a first conscious turning towards God. But the psychological state of the child must not be lost sight of. He is not yet mature enough to make momentous decisions independently. At his stage of mental development he may be able to acquire knowledge of various kinds and delight in it, but he must have adults to teach him what to do. "The morality of children in the elementary schools is a morality of obedience; it is a time devoted to learning and acquiring knowledge and forming habits. The primary objective of instruction for first Confession is training in the correct performance of external actions."[49]

Having described the goal, the catechist will enter upon what is to be done. There are the "five fingers", the five stages which belong to the sacrament of Penance: conscience, contrition, resolution, confession, penance. These, however, only refer to what the penitent has to do, the elements essential to the sacrament; the absolution of the priest is not mentioned. For this reason Father Joseph Goldbrunner prefers the order: examination of conscience, contrition and resolution, confession of sins, absolution, penance.[50]

If there is sufficient time, as will be the case in special instruction on first Confession, the catechist should deal at greater length with the examination of conscience which can also become conscience formation. As we have already mentioned, a systematic approach is not indispensible for first Confession. It will be necessary later and should be prepared

[49] J. Goldbrunner, *Sakramentenunterricht,* p. 12.—Müncker, *op. cit.,* p. 113 (Footnote in the above No. 42) says: "Even up to the age of eleven, the motive of authority dominates all others"; cf. also Leo Kunz, "Das Schuldbewußtsein des Kindes und seine Seelsorge" in *Anima,* Vol. 7 (1952), pp. 62-68.

[50] Goldbrunner, *op. cit.,* p. 15.

during these instructions. The basis are the Ten Commandments taught in such a way that each is linked with some key-word indicating the sins which most frequently occur at this age, or better, with some positive act which God expects of us. A great obstacle to such teaching is the ninth and tenth commandments. It has been a useful suggestion to speak of ten points rather than of ten commandments upon which the children should examine their consciences. These points would naturally be connected with the Ten Commandments, but in such a way that in the ninth place "school" (later to be substituted by "trade" or "profession") and in the tenth something like "self-education" might be included; the latter perhaps immediately to be connected with self-examination in connection with the seven capital sins.[51]

The catechist should not give the children a complete table of sins with perhaps even stereotyped formulas for confession. (A printed list would anyhow be entirely unsuitable for this age.) Many children would only repeat such a list more or less verbatim and lose any personal character and, indeed, the

[51] *Id.*, p. 39, and also p. 36. Goldbrunner also offers the following division: Prayers—Honour of God—Sunday—Parents—Neighbours—Modesty—Property—Truth—School—Self-Education. See also Al. Barth, *Meine Erstbeicht und Erstkommunion.* Gedanken und Merksät[illegible] (Freiburg: Herder, 1951), pp. 6f., who puts the Friday law of fast and a[illegible]stinence and the seven capital sins in the ninth and tenth place.—Diff[illegible]ently A. Kirchgässner, "Der Gewissensspiegel im Erstbeichtunterrich[illegible] in *KBl,* Vol. 76 (1951), pp. 201f., who for the younger children reco[illegible]mends the schema: 1. In the Service of God, 2. At Home, 3. In Scho[illegible] 4. In Free Time, 5. In Secret. Cf. also W. J. Smith, *Preparation for F[illegible] Confession* (St. Louis: Queen's Work, n. d.) who simply asks the ch[illegible] ten questions without using any headings; A. Heeg, *A Little Chi[illegible] Confession Book* (St. Louis: Queen's Work, 1941) uses the followi[illegible] 1. God, 2. Name, 3. Day, 4. Parents, 5. Be Kind, 6. Be Pure, 7. Be Hon[illegible] 8. Be Truthful; Catholic Teachers, *Little Lessons for Little Catholics* (N[illegible] York: Paulist Press, n. d.) content themselves with making fift[illegible] statements (short, concise) as starting points.

sincerity of confession. Abuses are possible even when such formulas are put in question-and-answer form. The catechist might discuss some pertinent examples based on key-words taken from the lives of the children followed by such questions as: What is it such a child ought to remember when examining his conscience? How should he say this in the confessional? The catechist should encourage a varied expression and stimulate the child's confession to be both individual and concrete.[52]

The main emphasis in the instruction on Confession, though not that necessarily demanding the greatest amount of time, should be on contrition. Its purpose and necessity will become evident to the children through the use of biblical examples. Precise distinctions are not necessary for the children. The worthless, "bad" act of contrition, which only springs from worldly motives, should be distinguished from the "good" act of contrition, which is fixed on God. Leading the children straight on to the practice of perfect contrition (sorrow springing from love) by overlooking the immediate and more understandable motives, should also be avoided, even in the later, more thorough, teaching. In by-passing these there is danger that even "sorrow springing from love" might remain a matter of mere words. Shame in the sight of God, who sees all things, ingratitude towards our Father in Heaven who has bestowed marvellous gifts upon us, are motives of genuine contrition.[53]

[52] Gatterer, pp. 251 ff., criticizes the use of a table of sins (confessional mirror—examination of conscience). Examine the cautions which B. Nisters, *KBl,* Vol. 74 (1949), has to offer. The danger that the children simply repeat mechanically what is contained in a confessional mirror was realized as early as the late Middle Ages. They tried to meet it by inserting, at intervals, some evidently impossible crime, e. g., "I killed the emperor with my battle ax"; cf. F. Falk, *Drei Beichtbüchlein* (Münster, 1907), pp. 18 f.

[53] For the small child who can grasp the idea of guilt only by means

And is the suffering of Jesus also to be offered as a motive of contrition? Yes, in the sense that our Lord wished to suffer so much in order to atone for our sins. But it is surely not necessary to exhaust all possible motives? If the presentation is not felicitous thoughtful children (and also adults) will find it difficult to imagine how the sins we commit now could have caused the sufferings of Jesus such a long time ago. There is also the danger of mistaking natural compassion for true contrition. We should rather use the idea of the sufferings of Christ to make the children realize why it is that sins are forgiven in confession, and so to awaken their trust and gratitude.

It should be understood that a definition of contrition is superfluous for children going to confession for the first time. More important is a simple formula for the act of contrition.[54]

The natural result of true repentance is, also for the small children, a firm resolution. The actual confession will create no special difficulty if examination of conscience has been prepared in the way which we have suggested. The confession of sins is much easier for children than for adults, especially when they have learned that the priest must keep silent about what he has heard.

The sacred character of the sacrament requires that even in the

of a mental picture of loss, this idea must be made more concrete: the stained garment of the soul; the Heavenly Father who will no longer love such a child as he did before cf. H. Spaemann, "Das Moment des Verlustes in der Reue" in *KBl,* Vol. 75 (1950), pp. 279–284.

[54] In Austria the formula contained in the *Religionsbüchlein* of W. Pichler has caught on without, however, silencing its critics; see for example: *ChPBl,* Vol. 62 (1949), pp. 174–178; Vol. 63 (1950), pp. 16f., 277–279; *Der Seelsorger,* Vol. 18 (1947/48), pp. 249–255; *Theol.-prakt. Quartalschrift,* Vol. 99 (1951), pp. 348ff. In the U.S.A. a variety of formulas is in use; it is very likely that the revised Baltimore catechism will in the end effect some one formula that will be universally adopted.

case of the very young some attention should be paid to the words which frame the actual confession, for if once learned the formula will not be changed again. For many centuries — even today in many countries — the *Confiteor* was used, the first half serving as an introduction to, the second as a conclusion of, confession.[55] In practice, during the past few decades shorter formulas have been introduced either to save time or for some other pastoral reason. For many a poor sinner making his confession after many years, a failure to remember the "confession prayers" has proved the final obstacle.

As introduction it is enough to say: "Humbly and sorrowfully I confess my sins." At the end: "For these and all my other sins I am heartily sorry and beg pardon and absolution," would suffice. Sometimes it is customary to say finally: "My Jesus, mercy", but this would appear to be less appropriate because it might often sound affected. If a diocesan prayer book or the catechism offers definite formulas, the catechist should keep to these.

It is desirable that the penance given should have an educational effect,[56] but this cannot generally be realized because the home circumstances are rarely known. Where it is merely a matter of devotional confession it is justifiable, for other reasons, to impose a penance of some simple prayers.

The procedure we have recommended presupposes that we are dealing with children of seven to eight years of age. It is important to realize that this is quite a different system than the one formerly prescribed for children of ten to twelve years of age.

[55] For this reason, the formulae of the *Confiteor* are among the oldest linguistic features both in Old High German and in Old Slavonic.

[56] J. C. Heenan, *Priest and Penitent* (London: Douglas Organ, 1946), pp. 39–47; F. D. Joret, *The Eucharist and the Confessional* (Westminster: Newman Press, 1955), pp. 84–110.

That is why such preliminary instructions for those going to confession for the first time need to be correspondingly developed in subsequent years. This will largely be done incidently since the various elements of penance and of confessional procedure will come up in the different stage of catechesis. Later occasions fixed for the confession of children and linked with preparations in common in church or school will provide new opportunities for dealing in greater detail with individual points.

The upper grades above all will provide opportunities for systematic instructions on the sacrament of Penance. They will be more thorough and take into consideration some of the circumstances of adult life.

The matter of examination of conscience has been sufficiently dealt with in the main section on moral law. What is now important is to bring out the difference between venial and mortal sins. Mortal sin is something more than an aggravated venial sin. Mortal sin is committed when the sinner knows that if he commits a certain action he breaks with God. The subjective element of acting knowingly will thus have to be taken into account.

On the other hand, the catechist must not convey the impression, even to the older children, that it is a matter of course to commit mortal sins from time to time. Grave mistakes have been made, not only in catechesis but also in many of the older catechisms, by enumerating mortal sins in the old language of moral theology and by speaking, in the instruction for first Confession, in a matter of fact tone about the kind and the number of sins which the penitent must confess, or about the way in which invalid confessions, due to the omission of mortal sins, could be repaired when it was assumed — in order to awaken deep sorrow — that everyone is going to hell.[57]

[57] H. Mayer, *Religionspädagogische Reformbewegung* (Paderborn: Schöningh, 1922), p. 149, has called attention to unhappy efforts in this

Certainly, mortal sin must be treated in the upper grades, both frequently and with all due earnestness. But it should only be done in such a way that the terrible and unnatural character of such conduct is realized, otherwise the impression may be created that mortal sins are not to be taken too seriously, or looked upon as unavoidable, or — and this is or was frequently the case — children are encouraged to search their consciences for mortal sins which they have never committed. This results in confusing their conscience and creates states of anxiety due to supposedly invalid confessions, sometimes with disastrous results.

The importance of interior sorrow in the sacrament of Penance will have to be increasingly emphasized when teaching older children. They will have to realize that when the five points have been memorized and understood, more remains to be done. Especially in the case of a grave sin what really matters is a turning back to God. The parable of the prodigal son may be used to illustrate this interior process. The fairly widespread notion that it is sufficient to confess one's sins from time to time, even when there is no serious intention to improve and to live in conformity with the laws of God, must be opposed. Indeed, the idea that to be a Christian consists solely in the observance of the commandments must be banished. The state to which one should be converted through penance is the joyful service of God.[58]

A vital point for later and wider catechesis on penance is a

direction; T. E. Bridgett, *Blunders and Forgeries* (London: Kegan Paul, 1891), pp. 149–151.

[58] In this sense consult the directives on *Führung zu Busse und Busssakrament,* which were issued by the German bishops primarily for the pastoral care of youth, and are printed in *KBl,* Vol. 72 (1947), pp. 25–29, 84–92.—For the guidance of older children, see what Tilmann has in his "Unsere Kinderbeichtpraxis im Lichte des Neuen Testamentes" in *KBl,* Vol. 71 (1946), pp. 17 ff. (with several other numbers up to page 150).

proper evaluation of the sacrament of Penance itself. The catechist should anticipate the objection that it is meaningless to confess one's sins to a mere man, that we ourselves can come to some agreement with God without such mediation. These arguments suggest a complete misunderstanding of the Christian order of redemption. It is, therefore, not necessary to deal with them in the form of special apologetics. The best defence s by means of a general catechesis in which the children have become clearly conscious of Christ as the sole redeemer and mediator between God and man. Thus it will have been made apparent that it is not we who decide how to reach God, but God Himself. There is only One who can lead us, especially when we have sinned, to God and who can reconcile us to Him. That is the Good Shepherd in whose name the priest in the confessional speaks the words of absolution.

4. First Communion

In our planning for a catechesis on first Communion, we must be clear in our minds that it is important to draw the correct conclusions from a given premise. As the history of the Church shows, two systems are possible apart from the Communion of infants just baptized. A system of late first Communion and one of early first Communion. The system of late first Communion presupposes more mature children and can be applied with care.[59] But since the introduction of compulsory education,

[59] In the Middle Ages there was no question of any special instruction for children in preparation for first Holy Communion. After the thirteenth century it became customary on solemn days of Communion to preach a sermon during the Mass of Communion itself, to which children no doubt were permitted to listen. P. Browe, "Mittelalterliche Kommunionriten" in *Jahrbuch für Liturgiewissenschaft,* Vol. 15 (1941). At the close of the Middle Ages in many dioceses specific formularies were prescribed for such occasions or for similar preparations for the Sacrament on Palm Sundays. These centred on the Blessed Sacrament and were

and especially in the course of the nineteenth century, it was developed into an instructional and ascetical preparation which sometimes lasted the whole year. It was bound to awaken a disposition of great zeal and expectancy, such as would have been impossible in the case of younger children. Much had to be learned and much was learned. The children were given ascetical tasks in the form of particular examinations, and special devotions were held with them.[60] They were given religious books. Catechetical magazines especially addressed to first communicants were published. As a result the day of first Communion was "the most beautiful day of my life".

This system had much to recommend it; it had much the same effects as a good retreat. These advantages, however, were dearly purchased, apart from the great spiritual demands made upon the children and their subsequent fatigue.[61] In order to

doctrinal or exhortatory in character. E. Martène, *De antiquis Ecclesiae ritibus* IV, 25, 29 (Antwerp, 1737: Vol. III, 490ff.); A. Dold, *Die Konstanzer Ritualientexte* (Münster, 1923), p. 52, Footnote 15. After the Council of Trent different synods came to require for the first Communion of children a special examination on the principal catechetical formulas and on the Sacrament of the Altar. A brief preparatory instruction appears to have been prescribed for the first time by St. Charles Borromeo in 1564.—P. Browe, *Die Pflichtkommunion im Mittelalter* (Münster, 1940), pp. 179–184.

[60] In Germany there were at least eight. As late as 1951 there were still six, and one in Austria. These papers are, as a rule, published monthly, one for each month of the year in which first Communion is administered. They are illustrated and intended to appeal to the emotions of the children. F. Bauer, "Erstkommunionzeitschriften" in *KBl,* Vol. 76 (1951), pp. 477–479; J. Solzbacher, "Zeitschriften für Erstkommunikanten?" *loc. cit.,* pp. 489–492. Solzbacher recognizes how valuable these papers have been, but rightly anticipates their eventual disappearance. Both *The Catholic Messenger* and *Mine* serve this purpose in the U.S.A.

[61] Memories of infancy are recalled by A. Adam, *Spannungen und Harmonie* (Kevelaer: Butzon & Bercker, 1940), pp. 176f.—Also Hofmann

increase their cooperation as much as possible, the children, who had been ready for a long time and able to receive the sacrament worthily, were held back from it for years. Thus the order of Christian life, to which the sacrament belongs as its regular nourishment, was altered in a questionable manner.[62]

Now we have a system of early first Communion or more precisely, the system of a relatively early first Communion which coincides with the awakening of childhood. This system has distinct advantages, but there are also disadvantages with which we have to put up. It is, for example, a fact that many children receive their first Communion in a certain twilight of semi-consciousness and of matter only half understood. There need not have been a false Communion, as many had feared; even the former Communion of children just baptized is not a false Communion. True, the human contribution, the *opus operantis,* can amount only to a bare minimum. The main emphasis is on the divine action which takes place in the administration of the sacrament *(opus operatum).* The child, sanctified and incorporated into the Mystical Body of Christ through Baptism, is finally also to be strengthened and nourished by the sacramental Body of the Lord. It is impossible to ask of seven year old children what can be expected only of twelve year olds.

"Auf was bereiten wir die Kinder im Kommunionunterricht vor?" in *KBl,* Vol. 67 (1941), pp. 4–6, points to the danger of a specific kind of "Low Sunday piety": "Precisely because of this rapid acceleration the fruits which are derived from it are short-lived and ephemeral": P. F. Klenke, "First Communion Notes" in *NCEA, Proceedings and Addresses,* Vol. 47 (1950/51), pp. 512–515; Sr. M. Philothea, "The Age for First Communion" in *The Catholic Educational Review,* Vol. 48 (1950), pp. 606–611.

[62] Early in his life the author discovered a prayerbook for children published in 1906; it was entitled, *Die betende Unschuld* (Prayerful Innocence). It contained prayers for Confession, but none for Holy Communion.

First Communion literature of the last century is no longer of any use. Several kinds of methods are possible today.

Under certain circumstances, even before he attends school or before he is given any pastoral ecclesiastical instruction on first Communion, a child may receive Holy Communion. In such cases he must be prepared either by the parents or by their representatives.[63] The preparation is not likely, as far as knowledge is concerned, to differ too much from that minimum set down in the Church's laws for first Holy Communion.[64] More important, however, than instruction, is that the child should be surrounded by the religious atmosphere of a Christian family, that he should know how to pray, however simply, and that he should be held to the practice of virtues befitting a child. Systematic training is not necessary.[65]

The immediate preparation during the last few days before the reception of the sacrament should attempt to awaken devotion to the Saviour in the Blessed Sacrament and to teach the children how to conduct themselves when they receive the sacrament. Such preparation might be encouraged and fostered on a larger scale. Many pastors have used it successfully by giving special instructions to mothers. Voluntary helpers, or catechists too, could cooperate in the immediate preparation, which also includes confession. They could be useful in the case

[63] B. Nisters, "Die rechtzeitige Kinderkommunion" in *KBl,* Vol. 74 (1949), pp. 301–307.

[64] See above, pp.

[65] Nisters, *op. cit.,* p. 304, suggests to mothers: "During the course of a walk, she may speak of God and of His care for everything in the world; during a visit in church, she can recall the Saviour; when seeing a crucifix she may talk about death. In this way, she can combine teaching with practice, since in the case of these small children knowledge of objects outside themselves is always connected with action"; D. L. Greenstock, *Christopher's Talks to Catholic Parents* (London: Burns, Oates & Washbourne, 1951), pp. 95–103.

of the less zealous families and thus extend the number of early communicants.[66]

They should take only a few children at a time and the smaller the children are the fewer. It should also be assured that in every case of such early Communion the child's religious care and guidance will be continued without overzealousness or excess, and in as simple a manner as possible. Briefly, the child will continue to be surrounded by a religious atmosphere.[67]

The cooperation of the family is a factor that will naturally always remain indispensible even in the case of the other method of preparation for first Communion which, for the time being, will remain the one most widely used, namely systematic first Communion catechesis. This may be the catechesis ordinarily

[66] Read the suggestions offered by J. Pascher, "Die Frühkommunion der Kinder" in *KBl,* Vol. 75 (1950), pp. 489-497, especially p. 496f.; K. Sudbrack, "Eucharistische Familienerziehung" in *KBl,* Vol. 73 (1948), pp. 266-268. Concerning experiences with the equivalent of *Parent-Teacher* groups in Germany consult B. E. Krahl, "Zur Vorbereitung auf die Erstkommunion" in *Theol.-prakt. Quartalschrift,* Vol. 100 (1952), pp. 160-164. Extensive suggestions for the less immediate preparation of the child, see Helene Helming, *Die häusliche Vorbereitung der Kinder auf die heilige Eucharistie* (Freiburg: Herder, 1952). Spiritually akin, but more dependent upon natural factors and objects, is the book of Hilger (author) and Al. Burkart (artist), *Büchlein vom lieben Brot* (Freiburg: Herder, 1952). In English: Sr. Mary *et al., The Catholic Mother's Helper* (Paterson: St. Anthony Guild Press, 1948), in lesson form for the most part, and remote preparation. Sister M. Marguerite, *op. cit.,* the whole book on remote preparation; Sister J. Patrice, *Your Family Circle* (Milwaukee: Bruce, 1952), pp. 49-61, pp. 104-114; M. L. Coakley, *op. cit.,* pp. 64-81, remote preparation.

[67] The support and the guidance of helpers or catechists will be especially needed for children from homes in which religion is absent, if they are to receive the sacraments at the normal age, having been prepared for this with the other children. They should not be put off to a later date, because the situation is not thereby improved, and because the parents will only be annoyed.

given in school. Without doubt the training imparted in the first year might suffice, but we might also avail ourselves of the advantages to be derived from the catechesis of the second year.

Bible stories taken from the New Testament are the most natural means of leading the little ones to Christ and to the Blessed Sacrament.[68] Such incidents as the visit of the shepherds to the crib, the coming of the wise Men from the East, the changing of the water into wine, the marvellous multiplication of the loaves and the fishes. Christ, the friend of children, will serve as introduction. A few suggestions from the catechist, some children's verses, will serve to provide the link with the sacrament and stimulate a holy desire in the children. The Last Supper affords an opportunity for final instructions which can be extended by special acts of devotion and the last preparation.

As this is envisaged in Canon Law as the normal procedure, a special catechesis lasting several weeks, which prepares for first Communion outside school hours, will not be very different.[69] It will concentrate more fully on the essential elements,

[68] Among others these might serve as examples: W. R. Kelly, *Our First Communion* (New York: Benziger, 1937) and A. J. Heeg, *Jesus and I* (Chicago: Loyola Univ. Press, 1933).

[69] Canon 1330, 2: The pastor is obliged "to instruct the children with special zeal, especially if there are no obstacles during Lent, in order that they may worthily receive first Holy Communion for the first time from the altar".—Christian antiquity knew of a rather extensive and enriched catechesis on the Eucharist for those who had been recently baptized. The catechist explained the nature and the effects of the mystery, and devoted a great deal of time to Christ's presence in the sacrament and to an attempt to demonstrate to the baptized its sublime importance. Symbols for the Old Testament (the loaves of proposition, manna, water gushing from the rock, Melchisedech) as well as the Psalms (22 33 42 49) were used. J. Daniélou, "La catéchèse eucharistique chez les Pères de l'Église" in *La Messe et sa Catéchèse* (*Lex orandi* 7) (Paris, 1947), pp. 33–72.

make the teaching seem less like school and instruction, and stress and develop rather all that is religious and educative. The child on his way to God; the Saviour who comes to us; stories from His life; the bread from heaven with which He will nourish us, not only once but again and again, so that we should never grow tired. This might be the dominant idea.[70]

Thus a certain wide perspective should be the rule. It is not merely a matter of doctrine on the sacrament of the altar to be offered, or some complicated Communion ceremonial to be exercised and explained.[71] The sacrament must not be isolated, it should lead the children to Christ and to love of Him, and to develop a healthy piety so that from the beginning it will have its rightful place.

Is Communion to be explained to the children as a sacrificial meal, a participation in the sacrifice of the Mass, the "first complete participation", as some zealous exponents of the liturgical revival would sometimes desire? No matter how important it is to work gradually towards this knowledge, it would be premature and an unnecessary burden for a seven or eight year old child. We must proceed step by step. Just as it is sufficient for a sick child to know the difference between the Eucharist and ordinary bread, so it also suffices for the normal case of early first Communion that the child should know he is

[70] See footnote N. 48.—Demanding more of a mental effort, with the sacrifice of the Cross and the sacrifice of the Mass as chief topics, and also methodologically very informative: J. Goldbrunner, *Sakramentenunterricht mit dem Werkheft* (Munich: Kösel, 1950). Similarly W. Ziehrer, *Zum heiligen Mahle. Ausgeführte Katechesen zur Einführung in die volle Mitfeier der hl. Geheimnisse* (Stuttgart, 1949).

[71] The custom of expressing devotion to the Eucharist in accordance with acts of virtues was developed only in the seventeenth century. This form of devotion was unknown to Canisius and Bellarmine and the *Catechismus Romanus*. A. Schwarzmann, *Die Eucharistie in den Katechismen bis zum Einbruch der Aufklärung* (Innsbruck, 1951), unpublished dissertation, p. 81.

receiving the Body of our Lord. As a matter of fact, he has already received the Lord spiritually during the sacrifice in which he actually participates. But the point which matters and must matter to him is that the Communion, which he is receiving for the first time, is a holy gift. Thus, to begin with, this point only needs explaining. In the words of our Lord Himself, preserved for us in the Gospel, it is almost this aspect of the Eucharist alone that is emphasized. And if it is meaningful to speak about the banquet character of the Mass it is at least justifiable to let the child find the approach towards it from this angle.

Later it will become clear to him that the banquet is a sacrificial meal and that the whole feast is the offering up of a sacrifice. For first Communion catechesis should be given in such a way that what has been said can be expanded later, but also that nothing need be retracted. If, for example, we may say that the Lord is coming we should explain that it is not the Child in the manger that is meant, but Christ in His heavenly glory, disguised under the shape of bread.[72] But this idea, too, should be subordinated to that of the Body of Christ. Our Lord calls us to Himself and feeds us with the bread from heaven, which is His Body.[73]

In general, the aim should not as yet be to instil a great deal of knowledge into the first communicants. The catechist would do better to spend the ample time available for communion instruction in developing the piety of the children, as well as a holy joy in the practice of their religion, in prayer and in being good. Besides Bible stories, edifying examples taken from the lives of holy men and women and pious children are of special importance at this age level. Occasionally he might end his

[72] F. Weber, "Jesus kommt" in *KBl,* Vol. 67 (1941), pp. 8–10.
[73] See above, p. 240ff.

instruction by taking the children into the church, or by making a trip to some shrine in the neighbourhood.

These years of awakening, when, for the first time and with a sense of marvel, the children hear about God's prodigies of power and love, are also the first opportunity for them to take their religion seriously. They now have fewer inhibitions than later on, and are also capable of a childish heroism. Regarding outward actions, however, the catechist should not make too many demands upon them. The most valuable fruit will be the impression that he has made upon their souls.[74]

Also, as far as the Blessed Sacrament is concerned, his aim will be deep reverence rather than a precise knowledge. When at benediction of the Blessed Sacrament the sacred Host appears like a shining star in the golden monstrance, when clouds of incense are seen rising towards it, and the priest taking the monstrance, only after the precious veil has been placed upon his shoulders, gives the benediction, while the congregation bows low—all this is much more valuable than many words about the Real Presence.[75] And if he succeeds in inculcating this inner reverence, he will not find it difficult to guide the children in external devotion and in proper conduct at the moment of Communion.

The celebration of children's first Communion in common was unknown until the seventeenth century. Earlier, children took Communion for the first time accompanied only by their parents. The celebration in common developed only since there was a systematic church catechesis for children. In Germany the first evidence of such a celebration was in 1661,

[74] Kl. Tilmann, "Die Gebetserziehung während der Erstkommunion-vorbereitung und darüber hinaus" in *KBl,* Vol. 65 (1939), pp. 322–329, and especially 329.

[75] M. Gatterer, *op. cit.,* pp. 148f.

in the diocese of Münster, in France a little earlier.[76] Subsequently, in many places the Jesuits advocated special instructions for first Communion, as well as a solemnization of first Communion. This was soon organized dramatically with candles, the children dressed like angels, with solemn procession, sermon and, not infrequently, with a play based on the catechism. Later, following French example, there was added the renewal of baptismal vows. This, however, met with considerable opposition in Germany, even as late as 1800, because it seemed reminiscent of Protestant confirmation.[77] In the nineteenth century Low Sunday came to be almost universally the day on which Holy Communion was administered to the children for the first time.

The situation is now somewhat different owing to the change to early first Communion. In the case of older children it is possible to arrange external solemnities, but with children of seven or eight it is more difficult. We have, moreover, come to realize that the phrase "the most beautiful day of our life" has also its questionable aspects, even if we disregard the outward displays and sometimes exaggerated festivities within the circle of friends and relatives, which have become customary in many Catholic countries. Is it right for Christians to extol first Communion day as something extraordinary? Communion is not a sacrament received only once in a lifetime, like Holy Orders or Matrimony. It is, after all, our "daily bread". Nor is first Communion the child's first encounter with Christ; at

[76] F. X. Bauer, "Zur Geschichte der feierlichen Kindererstkommunion" in *Theologie und Glaube,* Vol. 25 (1933), pp. 562–590; H. J. Thurston, "First Communion: Studies in Old French Rituals" in *Amer. Ecclesiastical Review,* Vol. 44 (1911), pp. 125–141; Bishop Dupanloup, *The Ministery of Catechising* (London: Griffith, Farran, Okeden Welsh, 1890), pp. 422–452.

[77] J. Grötsch, *Die Erstkommunion in der Diözese Regensburg* (Regensburg: Pustet, 1933), pp. 59f.

Baptism he has already been incorporated into the Mystical Body and filled with His life.

On the other hand, a preparation in common calls for a first Communion in common, just as a private preparation should have as its counterpart a private communion of the children accompanied only by their parents. A first Communion in common must somehow be organized as such, but the form which it takes should be much more simple than the traditional Low Sunday festivities.[78] It is not at all necessary for the children to wear new clothes, even less for the girls to wear white dresses. The procession into the church need not be in rank and file and to the accompaniment of music. The choir need not be trained to sing special numbers nor need there be a long sermon. The Community Mass, adapted to the simplicity of the Children's Mass with songs and prayers suitable for the occasion, would be the correct basic form. There might be an offertory procession, perhaps with candles or with hosts as actual offerings.[79]

Should the renewal of baptismal vows be retained? The reception of any sacrament, thus also the reception of Communion, is in itself a confession of man's basic union with God, by grace, into which all have been assumed through Baptism, as well as of the obligations which we have taken upon ourselves through it. This confession can be renewed on many occasions,

[78] A. Kirchgässner, "Die Erstkommunionfeier" in *KBl,* Vol. 73 (1948), pp. 52–55; A. N. Fuerst, *op. cit.,* Vol. I (1939), pp. 308–309.

[79] In favour of this last solution is Kl. Tilmann, "Zwei Opfergangformen bei der Erstkommunionfeier" in *KBl,* Vol. 73 (1948), pp. 262–265. Each child receives a host in his hand which has been covered with a white linen cloth. This they give to the priest. The Offertory procession with candles is very suitable, if the custom is retained that the sacristan should place the candles to burn somewhere close to the altar. But we may wonder whether the use of the Communion candle is not too much of a distraction for small children in any case.

as, for example, is envisaged by the liturgy of the restored Easter Vigil at the climax of the liturgical year. Such an express renewal is also appropriate when the young people reach that age when they begin to understand the implications of their union with God, and when there might be some solemn occasion for such a renewal.[80] The first Communion day of the seven or eight-year-old children is not as yet the right moment. At this age it would seem preferable to follow the suggestions that before the beginning of the celebration Mass there should, in the presence of pastor and catechist, be an examination devised in some liturgical form, to determine how well the children are prepared to receive the Sacrament.[81]

More important than to celebrate this first Communion with external pomp is the need to develop what has already been taught for first Communion. Even when the catechist has been afforded the opportunity of holding special catecheses on Communion, these should not be concluded once the first Communion day is past.[82] Also in the case of the normal catechesis

[80] The day of Confirmation or graduation exercises could be such an occasion. In France it is the day of the *communion solennelle* of the twelve year old; consult above, pp. 38-39. On the meaning and the way in which such an occasion is to be organized, many papers have been written and speeches given, at various Congresses, in addition to articles in magazines and periodicals; see the special number of *La Maison-Dieu,* IV, No. 28 (1951): "Le problème pastoral de la Communion Solennelle." On this subject see also what Rome has said about private first Communion: SC Council, July 21, 1888, quotes in A. Lehmkuhl, *Theologia Moralis,* 2 vols. (12th ed.; Freiburg: Herder, 1914), Vol. II, No. 1, p. 201.

[81] K. Glückert, "Zur Gestaltung der Erstkommunionfeier" in *KBl,* Vol. 75 (1950), pp. 41f.

[82] In the book of H. Gatzweiler and E. Gerhards, *Die Erstkommunion in Vorbereitung und Nacharbeit* (Mainz, n. d. [1942]) are presented twelve catecheses which are to be given immediately after Low Sunday and which could actually be called a practical exercise in Christian fidelity. These catecheses are intended for first communicants who will shortly after Low Sunday transfer to a secondary school of some kind. They

in school, continuation should be equivalent to expanding previous instructions. Now is the time to demonstrate the elements of a life of Christian virtue such as is fitting for those who have been guests at the Lord's table.

After first Communion day the catechist should help the children to go to Communion regularly and to receive it worthily. It is clear that henceforth Confession and Communion are not to be insolubly linked. Holy Communion must always come first. Under the circumstances children are permitted to go to Communion frequently, even daily. But this presupposes, if it is not to degenerate into an external habit, that the education which children receive at home aids them in their religious and moral efforts. This will only be possible in a truly Christian family. An instruction of the Sacred Congregation of Sacramental Discipline (1938) has stipulated that great prudence must be exercised in Catholic colleges and boarding schools where daily Communion may be the rule.[83]

There are some unenlightened parents and teachers who seemingly want to make up for their poor educational efforts by urging the children to go to daily Communion, since, they say, Christ is the best of all teachers. They forget, however, that this sacrament was not instituted for such a purpose. The children are not likely to remain enthusiastic for long; with the advent of adolescence the habit will, in most cases, be discarded

are therefore children of about then years of age.—The "Paderborn Lehrplan" itself (1946) which proposes to "avoid placing undue emphasis on asceticism in the course of preparation for the sacrament" recommends for the period after Low Sunday "a strong emphasis on the moral formation of the children" (p. 25).

[83] "Instruction of the Congregation of the Discipline of the Sacraments", December 8, 1938, in *Periodica de re morali canonica et liturgica*, Vol. 28 (1939), pp. 317–324. According to this we must avoid everything that might appear to be pressure put on the pupil in what concerns the regular reception of the sacrament (frequent communion).

once and for all. The rule which Father Goldbrunner tells his children to enter into their workbooks is a good one: 1. I must go at least once a year (commandment of the Church), 2. I should go every Sunday and on Feast Days, 3. I may go every day.[84]

To prevent the practice of frequent Holy Communion from leading to undesirable abuses, it is necessary for the children to have easy access to the confessional. Specified times should be designated for children's confessions, either by the pastor or by the priest giving catechesis in school, provided he can make the necessary arrangements. These occasions might be preceded by a special preparation and would not only contribute to a worthy reception, but would also deepen the understanding of the sacraments. In addition, zealous pastors will invite the children to go to monthly confession so as to prevent crowds turning up all at the same time. If there are large numbers the children can be divided according to classes, districts or streets, each group to come on a special day. In this way the sacrament of Penance and the sacrament of the Eucharist can become an evermore effective weapon to protect the living union with Christ in the hearts of the young.

5. Introduction to Holy Mass

If children are to fit organically into Christian life, their preparation for Holy Communion ought to lead gradually to an understanding of the Mass and to proper participation in it; for the life of the Eucharist will remain healthy only if it is rooted in a genuinely liturgical life. This is the principal objective of our catechesis. If we succeed in making the children feel at

[84] J. Goldbrunner, *Sakramentenunterricht mit dem Werkheft,* p. 89. The children themselves add the two conditions to what is suggested in the above text.

home at Holy Mass we shall have created a spiritual home for their entire lives as Christians. The Mass will enter their lives at least every Sunday. In it they will discover all the basic truths of Christian doctrine and all the decisive requirements for Christian living. They will find the whole of life ordered towards God and the renunciation of selfishness. They will discover faithful attachment to Christ on His way of the cross and in His resurrection, the Christian community of brethren, the sacramental life of the Church.

The practice of early first Communion necessarily entails that the young children can have only a sketchy knowledge of the Mass. But the child may already have realized that the priest at the altar performs an action similar to that which our Saviour himself performed at the Last Supper, and that this is why the small white host becomes, after the consecration, the Body of Christ.

This notion, which even the first communicant can understand, that much of what takes place in the Mass took place at the Last Supper, should be the first to be expanded. Then there was a large room, a laid table, bread, and a chalice of wine; now the solemn atmosphere of the church, the altar covered with white linen, hosts of bread, and wine. Instead of our Saviour there is the priest, instead of the apostles the congregation. The priest prays both aloud and silently and finally distributes the Body of Christ to the faithful.[85] In order

[85] Maria Montessori, *La santa Messa spiegata ai bambini* (1932; 2nd ed.: 1949); idem, *The Mass Explained to Children* (New York: Sheed & Ward, 1932). This small book, sad to say, takes for granted a Mass that has not been influenced in any way by the liturgical movement. The precious recommendations which are made by the great pedagogue for the use of the liturgy in education are further developed by Hélène Lubienska de Lenval, *L'éducation du sens religieux* (1946); *L'éducation du sens liturgique* (1953); synopsized very briefly in *Lumen Vitae,* Vol. 1 (1946), pp. 331–347; Vol. 3 (1948), pp. 382–392.

to hold their attention the children might be given occasional tasks, such as observing the number of candles, the colour of the vestments, the moments at which the servers hand the cruets to the priest, and when the priest genuflects.

Here the training proceeds by means of occasional teaching and systematic instruction. From the Old Testament we learn of the sacrifices offered by Abel, Noë, and Abraham. Next it will be pointed out that Christians, too, have a sacrifice, the sacrifice of the Mass.

When dealing with the creation of the angels, the "Sanctus" could be mentioned, with the birth of Christ, the "Gloria". These are hymns with which the children will be acquainted in the Mass.

A systematic and planned instruction on the Mass should also have its place even in the lower grades. It should be limited, as far as possible, to what the children can see and hear of the outward actions; it need not be a thorough instruction on the essence and the effects of the divine sacrifice, or a complete doctrine of the Eucharist. Since children at this age can memorize only with difficulty the exact sequence of the ceremonies, it is advisable to show them pictures of the different parts of the Mass. These could be either wall pictures or illustrations in a book which the children have open before them.[86] At first,

[86] Examine the study which P. Ranwez has made of the principal prayerbooks and missals for children in *Lumen Vitae,* Vol. 7 (1952) under the title, "Teaching the Mass to Children" (pp. 494–499); Anonymous, *Know Your Mass* (St. Paul: Catechetical Guild, 1954); Joseph P. Hedderman, *We Go to Mass* (Milwaukee: Bruce, 1954); J. Hoever, *St. Joseph Children's Missal* (New York: Catholic Book Publishers, 1954); Mary Irwin, and Brogan, Edward, *Missal for the Children's Mass* (New York: William Sadlier, 1949); Sylvester Juergens, *Marian Sunday Missal* (New York: Regina Press, 1956); Daniel A. Lord, *Children's Missal* (New York: William Hirten Co., 1954); Lawrence Lovasik, *The Mass for Children* (New York: Catholic Book Publishers, 1954); Demetrius Manousos, *My Mass Book* (St. Paul: Catechetical

however, they will have to be acquainted with the essential happenings of the Mass and with its structure. The consecration will already be known to the children on account of its impressive ceremonial. It must now be made clear that there is not only a change in the bread and wine, but that a sacrifice is being offered. This is signified by the elevation of the Sacred Host by the priest. Thus seizing upon the already acquired notion of sacrifice we explain that this implies giving something to God in order to show Him that we love Him and that we wish to obey Him. The sacrifice of the Mass should now be explained from two angles, firstly, as a sacrifice which Christ offers, and secondly, as a sacrifice which we offer with Him.

The catechist may develop this thought in perhaps the following fashion. Christ, the Lord, first offered His sacrifice on the Cross. He gave His own life, His own flesh and blood to the Heavenly Father, thereby showing the immensity of His love for Him; but He did this not for Himself but for mankind. But only a few people were present at this sacrifice. That is why our Lord instituted the Sacrament of the Altar in which this, His sacrifice, is continued. This sacrifice must be renewed by the priest wherever there are Catholics and at all times. It is, however, no longer Christ Himself who speaks the words of consecration, but He asks the priest: "Lend me your tongue, pronounce the words for Me. Offer, with Me and for Me, My Body to the Heavenly Father. Distribute It to the faithful in the shape of bread."

This is one sequence which leads to the sacrifice of Christ with which also the memory of His sufferings is linked. But in order to make it possible for the children to participate actively in the Mass—which is the aim of our efforts—it is of decisive importance to proceed further and explain the Mass as the

Guild, 1954); Francis Turmezei, *My Little Missal* (St. Paul: Catechetical Guild, 1950).

sacrifice of the Church, as that sacrifice at which we are not merely allowed to assist, but which we ourselves may also offer up. In the Old Testament mankind offered God many different gifts; but what Christ offered was much more precious. Now we may give to God what Christ gave Him. It is true that at first we offer only bread and wine—this happens at the Offertory. This is a first sign that we love God and that everything belongs to Him. But that is not enough, that is only the beginning. The priest must consecrate these gifts of ours in order that they might become the same gift that our Lord offered.

Only upon such a basis will it be possible to explain the structure of the Mass. For this structure can only be understood when we concentrate upon the sacrifice of the Church in which the sacrifice of Christ is, as it were, wrapped. Now it is important to show the sequence of the Mass as the natural development of the sacrifice of the Church. This is not too difficult for adults. The Offertory and the solemn prayer of thanksgiving are like a presentation to a well-deserving person. We organize a party at which a speech is made praising the achievements of the honoured one. The speech corresponds to the prayer of thanksgiving in which all are invited to join by the *Gratias agamus*. The previous preparation of the gifts to be presented corresponds to the Offertory. And because it is a sacred action we anticipate it by readings which set the tone for the occasion. This parallel can be translated into a form the children can understand; for example, the birthday of one of their parents. On this day, besides offering their congratulations, the children will also have an appropriate gift to offer. Perhaps some flowers or some small article that they have made themselves. The presentation, however, does not take place in silence. The children may recite a little piece of poetry and then thank their parents for all the good things they have received from them.

That is precisely what we do in the case of God who is our greatest benefactor. This may also serve as a starting point for an explanation of Holy Communion.

Sometimes the children may give their mother something to eat, perhaps an apple which they have received. A good mother accepts it but does not keep it for herself. She divides it among her children.[87]

In such an outline the structure of the Mass is explained in all essentials. We have almost arrived at the division which Dom Pius Parsch recommended many years ago as the key to a fuller understanding of the Mass and which we can paraphrase much as follows: 1. We (come in order to) pray; 2. we listen; 3. we prepare our gift; 4. we offer it; 5. we receive it back again.

In the upper grades this basic material must be expanded. For more systematic instructions on the Mass we can follow the relevant sections of the catechism, with its parts to be memorized and the appended liturgical explanations. But as always the occasional teaching is of great importance. Again and again in the course of the catechesis, especially in the step of application, this or that point of the Mass can be illuminated, this text or

[87] Even more striking is the picture which J. Hofinger, S.J., a former missionary in China, has drawn from the Chinese celebration of New Year "at which the children of the family under the guidance of the eldest brother reverence their parents for their multiple benefactions by the customary deep bow. Then the children are invited by the parents to partake of the family meal"; J. Hofinger, "Die Messe in der missionarischen Verkündigung" in *Die Messe in der Glaubensverkündigung,* edited by F. X. Arnold and Balth. Fischer (Freiburg: Herder, 1950, pp. 208–238), pp. 228f.; Kl. Tilmann, "Kindermessfeier und liturgische Erneuerung", in the same volume (pp. 329–336) on p. 331 recommends that the family meal of the children of God with the customary grace before and after be used as the basic image with which to express this notion. But the idea of the sacrifice has then to be introduced into the presentation to complement it.

that ceremonial correctly interpreted. The "first five minutes" method might be used to take up some details of the Mass and to discuss it with the children. In this way the whole of the Mass liturgy will gradually come to life: the prayers at the foot of the altar, preceded by the use of holy water as a sign of purification, the joyous praise of God in the *Gloria,* the special sublimity of the Gospel, the symbolism of bread and wine, the constant thanksgiving, the Our Father as a prayer in preparation for Holy Communion, etc. Each of the purposes of the sacrifice has its own concrete expression and concrete terms. Thanksgiving finds its outlet in the Preface; adoration, in the *Sanctus;* asking for favours, in many different prayers; reparation, in the *Memento* for the dead. In this way it will be possible to explain to the children the most important Latin phrases used in the *Ordo Missae,* at least those that are said in a loud voice during the Mass. It is only fitting that they should know the meaning of the *Kyrie eleison, Sursum corda* and *Agnus Dei* and similar formulas which they hear Sunday after Sunday throughout their whole life particularly since every children's prayerbook has a translation of these phrases from the Latin. It will also be possible, gradually, according to their capacity, to give them an explanation of certain difficult thoughts, for example, the *Per Dominum nostrum* at the end of the *Oratio:* in praying we do not approach our heavenly Father entirely alone, but Christ accepts our prayers and makes them His own, because we are His brothers and sisters and belong to Him. He prays with us, just as does our mother when she prays with us and enfolds our tiny hands into her own.

But all instruction during the religion period or pastoral "hour" is only a part of the introduction to Holy Mass. To these must be added practice, real participation in a well-celebrated service. A special children's Mass on Sunday has today become widely accepted in many parishes as part of their catechetical work.[88]

In order to avoid giving the impression that Sunday Mass is a duty, like going to school, which ends once school days are over, it is better that, whenever possible, the children's Mass should be organized by the parish, especially because schools are rarely connected with any one church.[89] Both the form of this children's Mass and the sermon accompanying it should be designed for their understanding.

The basic form of assistance at Mass, at least on Sundays, is the Community Mass with chant (*Betsingmesse,* a form widely used in Germany today in which parts are alternatively recited in the vernacular by the congregation). A children's Mass should also be provided at least on one other weekday, when simpler forms of the Community Mass, the *missa recitata,* may be used.[90] In any case its form should be simplified omitting the

[88] Today it might be a matter of wonder to us that a special Mass for children became customary only toward the end of the nineteenth century. In the previous centuries the most that had been done for the children was to devote a special sermon to them, especially at the time of first Communion. F. Zoepfl, "Kinderpredigt und Kindergottesdienst in ihrer geschichtlichen Entwicklung" in *Bonner Zeitschrift f. Theologie u. Seelsorge,* Vol. 2 (1925), pp. 126–154, especially pp. 151f. (consult footnote No. 59).

[89] Without doubt it is difficult to obtain reliable information on the percentage of attendance. We should, furthermore, not prevent the children from going to Mass with their parents. We cannot dispense with all control of attendance, if for no other reason than to impress upon the children the seriousness of the precept of assistance at Mass on Sunday. To check, the catechist may call on the children to give an analysis of the sermon or to report on the kind of announcements made on the previous Sunday. By questioning the children directly, he must proceed with caution; he should not embarrass those children who have been prevented from assisting at Mass by their parents.

[90] Consult Kl. Tilmann, "Grundsätze zur Gestaltung von Kindermessen" in *KBl,* Vol. 73 (1948), pp. 201–208, and the continuation in the subsequent papers, *KBl,* Vol. 74 (1949), pp. 104–107, 177–183.—Examine

singing of the Proper. A difficult epistle may be replaced by another one. During the Canon some of the essential ideas may be expressed in short sentences which are said aloud, but loud prayers should not be recited all the time. Before Communion, while the priest recites his own silent prayers, a suitable form of preparation might be said aloud unless there is a hymn which fulfills the same function. Some hymns at Mass may sometimes be spoken instead of sung. In the hymns at the beginning and end of Mass the theme of the liturgical year should be expressed.

Even freer forms of assistance at Mass which may resemble Mass devotions are permissible provided that there are no changes in the basic outline of the liturgy. If the type of Mass is used which features hymns in the vernacular, the Gospel and the Apostles' Creed, as well as the Lord's Prayer, should at least be recited in common.[91] It is, on the other hand, inadvisable to expect children to participate in the silent Low Mass.[92]

Also regarding bodily attitudes and deportment at Mass, young children should not be expected to do what can only be asked of adolescents. The children should sit during the epistle and sermon, stand up at the Preface and *Sanctus,* and kneel at all other parts.[93] To kneel during the presence of the sacrament upon the altar, that is, from the Consecration to the

the remarks which were made by F. Mahr, *KBl,* Vol. 74 (1949), pp. 211f.—See also E. Horan, "Toward a More Active Participation in the Mass" in *The Catholic Educator,* Vol. 24 (1953-54), pp. 375–377; R. A. de Sauveboeuf, *Our Children and the Mass* (Chicago: Fides Publ., 1955), pp. 39–45; Mother Emmanuel, C. S. A., *Teaching Liturgy in the Schools* (Chicago: Fides Publ., 1958).

[91] F. Mittelstedt, *ChPBl,* Vol. 62 (1949), p. 140.

[92] Certainly the children ought to know how to occupy themselves during a Low Mass or during a Mass that is not arranged for them especially. Prayerbooks of recent years as well as Missals have been written with this in mind. (See above in Footnote No. 86).

[93] Kl. Tilmann, "Die äussere Ordnung bei der Kindermesse" in *KBl,* Vol. 74 (1949), pp. 260–264.

Communion will not merely prove meaningful for the children but can also be justified by the rules laid down for choirs.

All the more attention should be paid to teaching the children to observe these attitudes and to perform these "holy signs" (Guardini) with respect and care: from their entry into the church and the blessing with holy water to the kneeling at the Consecration.[94] The servers at the altar should be so well instructed that they can be examples to the others.

A Mass thus organized will not be an object of boredom for the children or risk becoming routine. Klemens Tilmann has spoken of "a kind of catechetical paradise" opened to us since the liturgical revival has taught us again to understand in their own right individual elements in the structure of the Mass liturgy and to perceive their well-planned inner harmony and cohesion. It has made possible, both for adults and children, divers forms of participation. Today they can sing, listen, respond, profess their faith, hold Offertory processions and, not least, share in the holy meal.[95]

It is a disadvantage of conditions in the cities that, owing to the large number of children, many will be compelled to sit a

[94] It should be clear that at the consecration the children should not be compelled to perform a number of complicated movements. All they should be taught is to look reverently at the Host and Chalice when they are elevated, and to make a simple sign of the cross. If these simple actions are to be accompanied by a formula of any kind, it should be to greet the sacred body and the precious Blood, unless it is thought necessary to make an act of self-offering to the heavenly Father; in this sense, compare the text in the new German catechism: English translation, *A Catholic Catechism* (New York: Herder and Herder, 1958), p. 429.

[95] Kl. Tilmann, "Kindermessfeier und liturgische Erneuerung", p. 330 (see above footnote, No. 87); G. Ellard, *Lest They Assist Passively* (St. Louis: The Queen's Work, c. 1943); idem, *Men At Work At Worship* (New York: Longmans, Green, 1940); idem, *The Dialog Mass* (New York: Longmans, Green, 1942), especially pp. 1–33; idem, *The Mass of the Future* (Milwaukee: Bruce, 1948).

long way from the altar with the consequence that they will see little of what is taking place there. Thus the teaching will be deprived of its visual and concrete basis. In this case we would suggest that during the time the various classes receive their instructions on the Mass—and this they will at least twice during their years in school—a special Mass might be celebrated for them alone. The children gather around the altar; while the priest celebrates the Mass, the catechist explains what is happening, formulating a suitable prayer at all the important stages so that the children will be led to a real participation.[96]

Circumstances will be different in the country. In the smaller communities there will be no ground for departing from the parochial Mass at which the children also assist. But in many such places the parochial Mass will be generally or predominately a *missa cantata,* the Latin High Mass, which children can follow only with difficulty. Even if the responses of the faithful have not yet been introduced there should be at least a hymn before the sermon or a Communion hymn or a song at the end of Mass.[97] Sometimes, in order to give all, including the children, an opportunity to participate, children may come to Mass on week-days, perhaps regularly and as a group. In such

[96] This procedure is recommended by G. Götzel, *Religion und Leben* (see above p. 195f.), Vol. II, pp. 83ff.—In France this Mass is called the *Messe commentée* and is used frequently in the pastoral care of souls. Actually it does not represent a complete innovation. In the West Syrian liturgy, for example, the deacon turns frequently to the faithful assisting at Mass not only to intone the prayers, but also to teach and to admonish them.

[97] The practice of permitting the children to sing hymns in the vernacular at various times during the Mass, in place of the Latin sung by the regular choir, was authorized by a letter from the Cardinal Secretariate of State, dated December 24, 1943, addressed to the German bishops. Since then, the Instruction of the Sacred Congregation of Rites on Sacred Music and Liturgy, Sept. 3, 1958 (paragraphs 14b and 33) has approved the practice for all. For full text, see *Worship,* Vol. 32 (November, 1958).

circumstances it would be intolerable if the children, who might be the majority of those attending, would always have to assist at a High Mass, or even a Mass for the dead with dubious musical accompaniment, to which they would have to listen patiently and in which they could take no active part. It might be possible to hold Community Mass in an acceptable form or, better still, to allow them to have the major share of the singing, either in Latin or in the vernacular. Even a Mass in Gregorian chant, disregarding, of course, the Proper, is not, as experience has shown, beyond their powers.

6. Confirmation

Catechetical preparation for the sacrament of Confirmation suffers to a certain extent from the fact that in its theology complete clarity is lacking.[98]

Should we, for instance, emphasize the profession of faith which characterizes Confirmation as the sacrament of the apostolate of public life: our investiture, as it were, with the knighthood of Catholic Action? Without doubt, such elements are among the effects of Confirmation,[99] but it seems that, according to the sense of the older tradition, for which there is much evidence in patristic writings, its real essence is to form the "completion of Baptism" *(complementum baptismatis).* The life of grace has been kindled in the soul of the child at Baptism, through which the child is incorporated into the

[98] D. Koster, *Die Firmung im Glaubenssinn der Kirche* (Münster, 1948). Analyze the critique of H. Zeller, *ZkTh,* Vol. 71 (1949), pp. 358–360; cf. also B. Leeming, *Principles of Sacramental Theology* (Westminster, Md.: Newman Press, 1956), pp. 206–216.

[99] The Council of Florence in its *Decretum pro Armenis* (Denzinger *et al.,* n. 697): "In this sacrament the Holy Spirit is given for strength just as He was given to the Apostles on Pentecost so that the Christian may courageously confess the name of Christ": see J. F. Clarkson, *et al., The Church Teaches* (St. Louis: Herder, 1955), p. 274.

Body of Christ which is the Church. But the "fullness of the spirit" will be imparted at Confirmation. In Confirmation the reception into the Church and the bestowal of full rights as a member of the people of God are confirmed and sacramentally completed by the bishop himself, the actual pastor in the Church.[100]

Besides the lack of clarity in the determination of its essence, there is also some uncertainty as to the most suitable time when confirmation should be administered. When it is a question of dealing with adults, as was most frequently the case in the early Church, Confirmation followed naturally after Baptism. The newly baptized left the *baptisterium* and entered the *consignatorium* where the bishop confirmed them. Together with the rest of the faithful they were then led into the basilica where they participated for the first time at the Eucharistic feast and received Communion. In the Eastern Church the custom of conferring Confirmation immediately after Baptism—the priest being allowed also to confirm the former—was also applied to children. There was, during the Middle Ages, a tendency in the West, for example, in England, towards early Confirmation, whereas elsewhere it was customary to wait until the years of discretion were reached. This latter practice became the general rule.

The modern practice allows wider scope. The Roman Catechism suggests that it is desirable to defer it to the twelfth year.[101] The present Canon Law of the Church sets a lower age-limit when it introduces the possibility of an earlier date, for sick children or *ob iustas et graves causas,* with the words: ". . . although the administration of the sacrament of Con-

[100] This thought is developed by L. Bouyer, "Que signifie la Confirmation?" in *Paroisse et Liturgie,* Vol. 34 (1952), pp. 3–12; cf. also B. Leeming, *op. cit.,* pp. 201–206.

[101] Callan and McHugh, *op. cit.,* p. 208 (II, 3, 18): "If it does not seem well to defer (Confirmation) to the age of twelve, it is most proper to postpone this sacrament at least to that of seven years."

firmation is, in the Latin Church, deferred fittingly until about the seventh year of age." (Can. 788) Present day practice moves between these two limits. Two schools of opinion are opposed to one another, as was shown by the Munich Catechetical Congress of 1928.[102]

One school of thought argued that Confirmation, as "the completion of Baptism", should follow as soon as possible upon the reception of Baptism, and that for the child's religious development the grace of the sacrament should be secured early on.[103] The other school would defer the administration of this sacrament to the time when childhood, and religious instruction, come to an end, and the child goes out to confront the world for the first time, so that this important transition might have the religious blessing of the sacrament. And this for two further reasons, firstly because Confirmation is not necessary for salvation and hence essentially of lesser urgency; secondly because as an "anointing", a strengthening,

[102] In both the papers of O. Etl, who favoured the administration of the sacrament the year following first Communion (in the third grade of school) and J. Göttler, who sought to have it placed during the last year of school (the compulsory school attendance). The discussion which followed inclined in favour of the last-mentioned solution; *Zweiter Katechetischer Kongress München,* 1928 (Donauwörth: L. Auer, 1928), pp. 159–195; see F. H. Drinkwater, "Confirmation at Eleven Plus" in *The Sower,* No. 198 (Jan., 1956), pp. 5–6; J. Rickaby, "Why Confirm Before Fourteen?" in *Month,* Vol. 94 (1929), pp. 308–313; Studies and Conferences, "Instruction on the Age of Confirmation" in *The American Ecclesiastical Review,* Vol. 87 (1932), pp. 513–515.

[103] This thought is expressed by G. Delcuve, "A Necessity for the Normal Efficacy of Religious Education; Confirmation at the Age of Reason" in *Lumen Vitae,* Vol. 5 (⁴1950), pp. 305–332. Delcuve asks whether or not Russian spirituality and the mystical strain in Spain cannot be explained at least in part by early Confirmation (pp. 324–325). But is the perceptible increase of psychic powers purposed by this sacrament? And is the defection of so many recently confirmed simply the result of a delayed reception of this sacrament? Delcuve augments his historical argument considerably in Sloyan, *op. cit.,* pp. 281–314.

an equipment with the weapons of the Holy Ghost, it fits in well with this stage of the youthful development.

The decisions of the Church would appear to leave the door open for such an approach because they require thorough catechetical instructions to precede the conferring of the sacrament.[104] The notion of Confirmation as completion of

[104] The Commission for the Interpretation of the Code was asked: Whether can. 788 must be understood in the sense that Confirmation could not be administered in the Latin Church before approximately the seventh year, other than in cases which were cited. The Commission gave the reply: "It is quite proper to begin the reception of the sacrament at about the seventh year" (June 16, 1931), *AAS,* Vol. 23 (1931), p. 353; cf. T. L. Bouscaren, *Canon Law Digest* (Milwaukee: Bruce), Vol. I (1931), p. 348, but in this answer emphasized the words: *ob iustas et graves causas.* Following this pronouncement another question was put to the Congregation of the Sacraments by the episcopates of Spain and South America, where there existed the custom of confirming children before the use of reason, in fact immediately after Baptism: Whether this custom could be retained? On March 30, 1932, they received the answer: This custom may be retained, but the faithful should be taught the meaning of the universal law: Confirmation is to be preceded by a catechesis which has proved to be so salutary: *praemissa sacrae Confirmationis administrationi illa catechesis instructione, quae tantum iuvat ad animos puerorum excolendos et in doctrina catholica solidandos, prout experientia docet; AAS,* Vol. 24 (1932), p. 271; cf. T. L. Bouscaren, *op. cit.,* p. 349.—By this reply it is evident that there is taken for granted a catechesis which goes far beyond what is demanded for first Communion (see p. 299).—Confirmation could be "the culmination and the consecration of religious training", by which the children would be strengthened far beyond what would be possible through a first Communion catechesis, be it short or long, cf. P. Galtier, "L' âge de la confirmation" in *Nouvelle Revue Théologique,* Vol. 60 (1933), pp. 675–686, especially p. 685. In the decree of the Congregation of the Sacraments on the right of a priest to confirm sick children, all are reminded that in normal cases there is required: *aequa praemissa catechesis instructione; AAS,* Vol. 38 (1946), p. 350; T. L. Bouscaren, *op. cit.,* Vol. III (1954), p. 314; cf. A. N. Fuerst, *op. cit.,* Vol. I (1939), pp. 231–233; C. Zerba, *Commentarius in Decretum "Spiritus Sancti Munera"* (Rome: Libreria Editrice Vaticana, 1947).

Baptism gives, indeed, no indication when this completion is supposed to take place.[105] It is, therefore, for the bishop to determine the time more precisely. In rural areas a later limit will probably be the rule for the majority of children, since the bishop has to visit his entire diocese only once every five years (can. 343). But even in the cities, where Confirmation is administered every year, it should not be permitted to follow immediately after first Communion. There should be an interval for the development of catechesis.[106] If Confirmation then forms another climax this would certainly add to the value of the catechesis and of the sacrament for which a more thorough preparation would at least not be worthless.[107]

The special preparation for the sacrament should be given according to circumstances either as part of the regular catechesis or in some special lessons, and in this latter case, in the parish church, as some episcopal directives have prescribed. If Confirmation is to be conferred around Pentecost, the teaching on the very mystery of Pentecost will prove an excellent preparation. The Apostles received, as it were, their "Confirmation" at Pentecost; they became visible expressions of the power of the Holy Spirit. Soon they themselves passed on Confirmation to the faithful.[108] Further material for instruction is supplied by the ceremonies of Confirmation themselves: the

[105] In any case the Congregation of the Sacraments in its decree of June 30, 1932 (*op. cit.*, pp. 271 f.) remarks that it is more in accordance *(conformius)* with the nature of Confirmation as the *complementum baptismatis,* if it precedes Holy Communion. To carry this out in practice is, however, difficult to reconcile with the demands enumerated in the preceding footnote.

[106] See above, footnote 104.

[107] At the Second Catechetical Congress in connection with a resolution accepted by a majority of the participants the wish was expressed that Confirmation "be conferred within a span of one or two years after first Communion", *op. cit.,* p. 195.

[108] For this reason the Roman Catechism (II, 33, 22) (Callan and

prayer of the bishop for the seven gifts, the anointing with oil, the sign of the cross on the forehead.

But such a detailed preparation should not remain isolated in the religious instruction of the children. Upon it should be centred everything that the children have already heard of the workings of the Holy Spirit in us, of that divine life which begins in Baptism and, as it were, is a spark from the heart of the God-Man. Now this spark is to be fanned into a flame; the the fire is to gain in intensity. Examples of those who upheld their faith in adversity, especially the lives of youthful saints, should be given. Thus Confirmation catechesis will go over the great themes of catechesis in general, just as the preceding catechesis will already have prepared the way for it.[109] The work of the catechist after Confirmation will, above all, be to awaken in the children, the more closely they approach the years of maturity, a consciousness of their calling as citizens in the kingdom of God, and as soldiers of Christ.

Since the early Middle Ages a godparent has been required for Confirmation as well as for Baptism. At the present time his presence is still deemed desirable (can. 793), as a reserve for the parents. The godparent is to be the guarantor for the Christian education of the godchild. In many cases, and not merely in

McHugh, p. 210) directs the pastor to explain the efficacy of this sacrament through the wonderful changes experienced by the Apostles themselves at Pentecost.

[109] Such a procedure can be found in L. Kammerlander, *Firmlehre* (Innsbruck: Rauch, 1947) and also in the *Werkheft* of J. Goldbrunner (see above footnote No. 70); G. M. Dennerle, *I Receive the Holy Ghost* (St. Paul: Catechetical Guild, 1936); Bishop Butt, *A Confirmation Book for Boys* (London: CTS, 1924); D. M. Dougherty, *Confirmation for Children* (New York: Paulist Press, 1934); J. Overend, *Preparation for Confirmation* (New York: Paulist Press, 1936); J. J. Morris, *A Catechism of Confirmation* (Forest Park, Ill.: D. Farrell Co., 1955); R. E. Power, *The Seal of the Spirit* (Collegeville, Minn.: Liturgical Press, 1950), a text of the ceremonies of the sacrament with necessary explanations.

the case of orphans, such a reserve is obviously necessary also today. The godparent at all events symbolizes the importance of the sacrament. By accepting him the parents express their concern for the spiritual welfare of their child. In some Catholic countries there exists a time-honoured custom for the children to visit their godparents on certain important Feast Days. This can strengthen the religious concept of godparentship. In fact, one of the most important tasks in the pastoral care of children is to fight against those worldly aspects by which the office of godparent is being threatened.

7. *Training in Chastity*

The age at which compulsory school attendance usually ends marks the beginning of sexual maturity. Youth about to go out into the world finds itself, at the same time, confronted by the dark forces of instinct eager to force it beyond the barriers set by God's commandments. There is the danger that the work which the catechist has built up through the years might collapse at this point. Training in chastity is, consequently, a subject which catechesis cannot afford to neglect if it is to be truly a part of the true spiritual care of children.

This does not imply that in catechesis the catechist must devote much of his time to discussions of the virtue of chastity and similar matters. On this point educationalists are in agreement. The best teaching on sex is a sane, all round, education. Up to the last year of compulsory schooling it is indeed possible only by concentrating upon an all round education that any results might be achieved in this field. The children should certainly be told about modesty and what is meant by it: that some parts of the body should always be covered in the presence of others, that they are not to be looked at unnecessarily, etc. The story of the sons of Noë may provide a suitable background. The catechist may also use the term chastity, but he will not be able to explain, to the younger children, the precise difference between modesty and chastity.

He will have to content himself with fostering the all round education of the child and, in this respect, he should make a decisive contribution. If he succeeds in impressing upon the children that in all matters they must be guided by the will of God, that God is witness of all our acts and omissions; and especially if the children can be brought to enjoy their religion, their prayers, their attendance at Mass, he will have done the best thing he can for their training in chastity.

When dealing with the sacraments, the catechist will point out that God honours our bodies for it is with them that we receive the sacraments of Baptism, Confirmation and Holy Communion. Our body is as sacred as a church which must never be desecrated. Also the natural forces in the formation of character should not be neglected. Everything we do to train the children in the practice of self-mortification, neatness, cleanliness, obedience and truthfulness is also the best kind of sex education. It is particularly important to develop their sense of enjoyment in little things—songs, stories, healthy games, natural beauty, walking, mental pursuits—so that their pleasure-seeking be confined to less perilous paths.

More, however, will have to be done for the upper grades when the years of adolescence have begun. But even now considerable restraint is required of the catechist standing before his class. In the catechesis on chastity he will have to explain the sixth commandment. He must now clearly explain in what the sin of impurity consists: that there is an evil desire dormant in man which may awaken of its own accord, and that we must not consent to it. We must also take care not to arouse it by immodest acts, must guard against wicked company and conversation. Those who deliberately seek to gratify these evil desires or consent to them commit a grievous sin because they desecrate the temple of God.[110] The phrase "evil desire"[111] may be open to objections since sexual desire is permissible in marriage, is designed for it, and is evil only insofar as it incites many to abuses outside marriage, but in the case of young people it is the abuses that will have to be considered. The expression will, however, be immediately understood by those who have had such experiences: others it will not deprive of their innocence. There is another still bolder course which the German catechism develops, and which is justified by present-day conditions. This catechism begins by a precise formulation of the sixth commandment: "Thou shalt not commit adultery", and immediately continues to explain the purpose of marriage, the procreation of children, and by this route arrives at a discussion of those powers which are dormant in a child, which awaken later but must be preserved by the young in purity and with discipline.[112]

In neither case should descriptions of physical details or sex education be given in catechesis to a whole class of children. In the case of children in the last year of school the catechist may speak in such a way as to presuppose an understanding of the essence of motherhood, and explain other matters connected with it, without arousing an unhealthy interest in the subject.

[110] Here the catechist should mention mortal sin. On the other hand, he should be careful not to describe every sin against modesty or "against the sixth commandment" in general as a grievous sin; cf. Th. Mönnichs. *Zur Katechese über das* 6. (9.) *Gebot* (5th/6th ed.; Munich: Kösel, 1928), G. Kelly, *Modern Youth and Chastity* (St. Louis: Queen's Work, 1941), pp. 88–89; S. J. Juergens, *Fundamental Talks on Purity* (Milwaukee: Bruce, 1941), p. 25.

[111] The German catechism hitherto used the phrase "unchaste pleasure".

[112] Look up the Commentary of Kl. Tilmann, *KBl,* Vol. 75 (1950), pp. 401–405; J. L. King, *Sex Enlightenment and the Catholic* (London: Burns, Oates, 1944), p. 6.

When, for example, discussing the article of the Creed "conceived by the Holy Ghost", he may say quietly that the Child Jesus took up His dwelling under the heart of Mary and remained there for nine months until He was born. Similarly, when he has to use the words "Blessed is the fruit of thy womb", he may explain that Mary was the tabernacle for the divine Child and every expectant mother is her counterpart. Such thoughts will elucidate the mystery of motherhood in a dignified fashion. In this connection it will scarcely be possible, in the course of the ordinary catechesis, to deal with the detailed plan of God because the levels of education vary greatly, even among children in the same year of school. What might be of help for one child might scandalize another. But it is even more widely recognized that even for a child of twelve years, some sex instructions are necessary. This is due to the fact that, owing to the influences exerted by our technological age, sexual maturity starts considerably earlier today; also to the fact that greater dangers threaten the child from without.

The parents are generally considered to be those primarily responsible for giving this instruction, but it is a proved fact (it almost seems to be a law of nature) that parents having to face their own children show almost insurmountable inhibitions.[113] Only a very small percentage is able to overcome these. All that the parents can actually be asked to do is to take care that some responsible person relieves them of the task. To whom should they turn if, indeed, they have the

[113] F. Schneider, *Katholische Familienerziehung* (4th ed.; Freiburg: Herder, 1941), p. 295. "I hold that it is both utopian and senseless to demand of the parents that they impart the necessary sex knowledge to their children, adjusted to their individual differences and their capacity." To explain the apparently insurmountable difficulty he refers to "a natural diffidence", the "incest barrier" (the diffidence engrained by fear of incest) which is also opposed to sexual relations among blood relatives even though strong emotional ties might exist (p. 294).

courage to take such a step? Only rarely will they be sufficiently acquainted with an experienced teacher or conscientious physician to ask him to oblige. As a matter of fact, having considered the problem they will probably conclude that it is the priest who must help them.[114] The young people themselves expect above all to be helped by the priest.[115] But there are many who are opposed to this opinion and see in it a very definite risk.[116] The priest must be no source of scandal. He must not expose his calling to evil gossip. His sphere of activity is the spiritual realm.

In any case, not every priest would consider himself capable of assuming such a task; he must feel sure of himself and have

[114] Cl. Pereira, "Über Aufklärung" in *KBl,* Vol. 75 (1950), pp. 415–420, and as well as W. Smet, "A propos de l'initiation des enfants" in *Nouvelle Revue Théol.,* Vol. 68 (1946), pp. 44–60, and especially 50ff., who arrives at the same conclusion; J. L. King, *op. cit.,* pp. 25–27, p. 40, who does not think that it should be the priest in the confessional who should give this instruction.

[115] Kl. Tilmann, *Vor der Reife* (see below in footnote No. 117[a]), pp. 35f., reproduces the result of a questionnaire in which some thousand boys between fourteen and seventeen were asked whether the religion teacher should deal with these problems. An affirmative answer was given by 954. Cf. Kl. Tilmann, "Not und Aufgabe der geschlechtlichen Erziehung" in *KBl.,* Vol. 78 (1953), pp. 285–289; F. J. Connell, "Sex Instruction in High School" in *The Catholic Educational Review,* Vol. 47 (1949), pp. 442–447, who points out some of the difficulties implicit in it.

[116] H. Mayer, *Katechetik,* agrees (pp. 129f.) According to *Der Seelsorger,* Vol. 22 (Vienna, 1951/1952), pp. 334f., the French bishops after their Conference (March, 1952) admonished the clergy "that in this question they should confine themselves to their spiritual office and to forming the conscience above all, leaving parents and physician to explain the facts and give the necessary details". The Bishops of England and Wales in their *Joint Pastoral* maintain: "In such cases (where some parents neglect their duty) the teacher or experienced youth-leader, animated by Christian charity and having the necessary competence, may be the best person to make up the deficiency" (J. L. King, *op. cit.,* p. 56).

the confidence of the children. The task should, if at all possible, be solved individually. The moment has to be chosen when there is a real need and when the happy period of ignorance must be ended. Furthermore, the priest should assume the task only after having been asked to do so by the parents.

These may be conditions to be realized only in a good educational institution of one kind or another, but scarcely in the case of the many who every year enter the danger zone. But should these be left to their fate? There must be some practical way out of the difficulty if we are to believe a German curate who reported that in his parish a "good sixty per cent" of the youngsters were told about the mystery of life by a priest, and this in the instructions before graduation.[117] This, however, appeared to him to be too late.

If this, then, has been the experience with a wide circle of children, even more so should it be possible to take a carefully selected group of children who are considered to be in need of such instructions and to bring them together in the parish hall or presbytery. There they should be told a few things they ought to know because soon they will be children no longer.[117a] But they should be warned not to speak about these matters among themselves. In any case it is advisable first to

[117] J. Erbach, "Die Gestalt des Religionsunterrichts in der Berufsschule" in *KBl,* Vol. 75 (1950), pp. 244–253; Sr. M. A. Wagner, "Sex Education and the Catholic Girl" in *The Catholic Educator,* Vol. 20 (1950), pp. 250–253.

[117a] Help to impart instruction in such a procedure is given by Kl. Tilmann, *Vor der Reife. Eine geschlechtliche Unterweisung der Jugend für den Gebrauch des Erziehers* (6th ed.; Recklinghausen, 1952). A counterpart (opposite number) of this was composed by Ottilie Mosshamer, *Dem Leben entgegen. Eine geschlechtliche Unterweisung der Mädchen für die Hand der Mütter und Erzieher* (5th ed.; Recklinghausen, 1952); S. J. Juergens, *op. cit.,* offers a practical way of instruction for the use of priests and sisters; C. C. Martindale, *The Difficult Commandment* (London: Burns, Oates & Washbourne, 1941), especially for boys.

obtain the parents' permission, just in case they might want to take care of the matter in some other way.

Instruction about the mystery of life should not be given all at once, but, if possible, in stages. The first stage should deal with the question of motherhood. The adolescent boy should also be told that the emissions which he may now experience during sleep are not signs of sickness but evidence that he is becoming a man. Only at a later stage should the boys be told about the mystery of fatherhood. Parallels drawn from plant-life, where the pollen must fertilize the pistil in order that the fruit may grow, will furnish the catechist with a suitable starting point. More important, however, than a wealth of physical details is to show the processes connected with the handing on of life "in the light of faith",[118] in the plans of the Creator, and thus simultaneously with the essentials to arouse a sense of wonder and holy respect. Such an explanation will have a liberating effect upon the children, and the admonition not to waste these precious powers by which man may share in God's creative might will surely fall upon good ground.[119] If the sacrament of Matrimony is seen as a consecration bestowing upon the parents the right to employ these powers, it will come to resemble the splendour of Holy Orders by which the priest is equipped for his vocation.[120]

If such oral instructions are not thought feasible there is the possibility of finding suitable books and pamphlets which have been written with this purpose in mind.[121] A specially chosen

[118] *Im Glaubenslicht* was the title of a later edition of *Erziehung zur Keuschheit* by M. Gatterer (Innsbruck: Felizian Rauch, 1910); (C. Van Der Dockt, trans.), *Educating to Purity* (New York: F. Pustet Co., 1913).

[119] A. Shamon, "Sex and Seniors" in *The Catholic Educator,* Vol. 21 (1950), pp. 199–201; cf. H. Schilgen, *Im Dienst des Schöpfers* (Kevelaer: Bercker, 1922), esp. pp. 9–12.

[120] Gatterer, pp. 646f.

[121] Here is a list of books that may be found helpful: *For the Children:*

book might be lent to the children, who should be asked to return it after some time. When it is returned there will be an opportunity to say a few words which will relieve any embarrassment, as well as to give any advice that might be needed.

A timely teaching about the mystery of life in a truly Christian manner will prevent or lessen some of the dangers threatening the purity of the children, especially those dangers which result from the kind of gross and brutal enlightenment that can be found elsewhere.

The positive side of training for chastity may be found in the fact that the beauty of a pure life and, beyond that, the richness of truly Christian conduct, can inspire enthusiasm in the young.

Anonymous, *Growing Up* (New York: Benziger Brothers, 1946); Anonymous, *Into Their Company* (New York: Kenedy & Sons, 1931); Paul Edwards, *Sex and the Teen-Ager* (New York: Paulist Press, 1951); C. C. Martindale, *The Difficult Commandment* (New York: Kenedy & Sons, 1925); Mary E. McGill, *Into a Man's World* (Huntington: Our Sunday Visitor, 1938); Fulgence Meyer, *Safeguards of Chastity* (Cincinnati: Mountel Press, 1929); idem, *Helps to Purity* (Cincinnati: Mountel Press, 1956); Lionel E. Pire, *The Heart of a Young Man* (New York: Pustet, 1931).—*For the Teacher:* Eugene Boylan, *What Is Chastity? How to Give the Instructions* (Dublin: Clonmore, 1954); Joseph Buckley, *Christian Design for Sex* (Chicago: Fides, 1952); Maryse Choisy, *Problèmes Sexuels de l'Adolescence* (Paris: Aubier, 1954); Baron Frederick von Gagern, (Meyrick Booth, trans.), *Difficulties in Sex Education* (Cork: Mercier, 1953); Thomas Gilby, *Morals and Marriage: the Catholic Background to Sex* (New York: Longmans, 1952); M. S. Gillet (I. E. Ross, trans.), *Innocence and Ignorance* (New York: Devin-Adair, 1917); Luisa Guarnero, *L'educazione sessuale* (Milano: La Casa, 1951); Joseph Haley, *Accent on Purity* (South Bend: Fides, 1948); Kilian Hennrich, *Watchful Elders* (2nd ed.; Milwaukee: Bruce, 1954); J. Leycester King, *Sex Enlightenment and the Catholic* (London: Burns, Oates, 1944); John A. O'Brien, *Sex-Character Education* (New York: Macmillan, 1952); Jerome O'Hea, *Sex and Innocence* (Cork: Mercier, 1950); Aidan Pickering, *Sex Instruction in the Home* (London: CTS, 1950); Henry Sattler, *Parents, Children and the Facts of Life* (Paterson: St. Anthony Guild Press, 1952); Edgar J. Schmiedeler (ed.), *The Child and Problems of Today* (St. Meinrad: Grail Press, 1954).

It is also to be found in a joyous imitation of Christ and an active preparation in the liturgical and sacramental life of the Church. The sacrament of Penance will necessarily be of special importance in these dangerous years.

8. Leaving School

For all those youngsters who do not attend secondary schools the period of intensive religious instruction by means of regular catechesis ends about the fourteenth year. The young people then start earning their own living.

For youth in the country, who may remain under the parental roof, this transition is likely to be less abrupt. But the young people in the city who will be starting work in factories, shops or officies enter, for the most part, into an entirely different world. If hitherto they have been well protected in school and home, they are now suddenly confronted by various forms of evil such as pleasure seeking and loose morals. If this age-level involves a sudden great change merely on account of its physical and mental development the transition from school to wage earning will, in most cases, amount to a complete revolution. The young people ought at least to meet this transition with open eyes. Catechesis has thus to play a decisive role.

It has been traditional in certain countries to invest the last religious instructions with a special character. Prizes are distributed and special consideration is given to those who are leaving school; these might receive a suitable present such as a prayerbook or other token of their religion. But even this is not sufficient to prepare them for the new phase of their lives which is confronting them. In the nineteenth century it was customary in many Continental dioceses to hold the first Communion ceremonies simultaneously with the dismissal of school leavers. This was an impressive and religious climax owing to long and thorough preparation. Subsequent attempts to give similar importance to Confirmation have not been successful.

Yet something had to be done and all the more so because since the beginning of this century a secular consecration rite modelled upon Protestant confirmation had been developed in agnostic circles on the Continent. Thus, since the end of the First World War, special instructions for those leaving school have been introduced. These concluded with a festive celebration. In some German dioceses special regulations were issued to cover these instructions, for example, at Trier, Osnabrück (1920) and Freiburg (1933).[122]

How should the school leaving instructions be organized? Some weeks or even months before the actual end of the school-year the treatment of the subject should be completed. Catechesis can then be given a different emphasis; all school-like aspects will be relegated to the background. Some general outlines, which will serve as guiding principles for Christian living, can be derived from what has been learned during the past years. This can be done by a special series of summarized catecheses.[123] But the impression should be avoided that this is mere fatiguing repetition. It has therefore been suggested[124] to use two basic formulas for this recapitulation which ought to

[122] F. Weiler and M. Weis, *Schulentlassung—Lebensweihe* (Düsseldorf, 1935), pp. 8f.—This book contains a theoretical introduction to the problem (pp. 7–26), a number of catecheses as well as an outline for conducting a solemnity for school leavers (graduates).

[123] Weiler und Weis treat in twenty-one catecheses: the plan of God, the existence of God as well as the chief points in the doctrine of the Ten Commandments and of the Sacraments. Perhaps twenty-one catecheses might be found to be too numerous.—More practically organized are the sixteen catecheses of F. Gabriel, *Schulentlassungsunterricht nebst Exerzitienvorträgen und Ansprachen* (2nd ed.; Paderborn: Schöningh, 1927).

[124] Bopp, *Katechetik,* pp. 302f.

accompany the Catholic throughout his life: the Apostles' Creed and the Lord's Prayer. In the former an outline of Christianity is formulated, in the latter the practical attitude of the individual Christian is drawn up. Something of a map for the future is to emerge.[125] According to the circumstances of the children some form of warning against the dangers facing them might here be appropriate.

On some suitable occasion before the children leave school a day of recollection or, even better, a triduum, might be held to mark, in a religious form, the end of childhood and the new beginning. In the early days retreats for school leavers (graduates) were frequently proposed and many books and pamphlets were published for such retreats.[126] It was soon recognized—and anyone who has tried the experiment will confirm it—that children lack the maturity for making retreats even when given in a simple form. If the children are of good will, they will use a good deal of their energy simply in trying to remain silent. They cannot stand being lectured at and meditation is not intended for them. Relaxation, games, songs and recreation are preferable, although the sense of recollection and the practice of self-examination need not be dispensed with.[127] There might be periods of silence, perhaps between two lectures. Lay helpers,

[125] The catechist tells the boys to look up passages in the School Bible which could be used as memory tests. Having checked them, he will ask individual pupils to write the text in artistic lettering, perhaps on a piece of polished wood which can be given out on the last day at school and kept to decorate the wall. K. Gutmann, *KBl,* Vol. 71 (1946), pp. 157f.

[126] Especially stressed by J. Sträter, *Die Heilung der Kinderwelt. Anleitung zur Abhaltung von Exerzitien für Kinder* (3rd ed.; Dülmen, 1922); D. Egan, "Try an Eighth Grade Retreat" in *The Catholic Educator,* Vol. 23 (1953), pp. 345–346; Sr. M. St. Angela, "The Retreat Movement" in *The Catholic Educator,* Vol. 24 (1954), pp. 493–494.

[127] A complete plan as well as complete instructions for three days, J. Wisdorf, *Entscheidung, Jungentage zur Schulentlassung* (Haus Alten-

youth leaders, a suitable teacher or, in the case of girls, women parish helpers, should take care of the external arrangements. The priest should always be available for the youngsters. Above all a good Confession should free them from past mishaps and serve as a basis for a fresh start.

If several days of recollection cannot be held,[128] a single such day might be possible; otherwise the topics to be dealt with might be distributed over the last few weeks at school, endowing these with a more religious and practical character. A pilgrimage to some shrine with the recitation of the rosary, group songs, and games on the way, would be remembered for a long time to come.

The conclusion should be the school leaving ceremony itself. If this is sponsored by the school care should be taken that the religious note is assured. Some German dioceses have issued regulation for such a day of graduation.[129] It is to be held in church in the presence of the congregation, preferably in connection with Sunday Mass. The boys and girls who are about to leave school enter together, to the accompaniment of

berg, 1950); idem, *Weg und Weisung. Mädchentage zur Schulentlassung* (Haus Altenberg, 1951).—Of the same type cf. Chr. Allroggen, *Tage der Entscheidung, Einkehrtage für Jungen zur Zeit der Schulentlassung* (Düsseldorf, 1940); F. G. Meyer, *Jesus and His Pets* (Cincinnati, Ohio: St. Anthony Monastery, 1925).

[128] Schools in rural communities, which usually produce only a few who will leave each year might, as Wisdorf suggests, group together on a deanery basis for the purpose of holding three days of recollection in any one of the various ways that have been recommended.

[129] In the German diocese of Münster a diocesan synod laid down the regulation in 1924: "The closing of the school year is marked by a graduation ceremony consisting of a renewal of baptismal vows, Holy Communion in a body, benediction and sermon" Weiler-Weis, *op. cit.*, p. 10.—In other places, e. g., the dioceses of Freiburg and Würzburg, a precise ritual for such celebrations is contained in the diocesan Hymnal and Prayerbook. In Innsbruck-Feldkirch (and in unison, Salzburg) these ceremonies were incorporated into the *Collectio rituum* (1951).

a hymn, and are seated in the front pews. A short talk by the priest is followed by a renewal of baptismal vows,[130] or, in a slightly different form, a promise of fidelity is recited and followed by prayers for the school leavers from the congregation. If those who are leaving are permitted to make an Offertory procession and to be the first to receive Holy Communion the seriousness of the occasion will not be lost upon them, especially if parents and teachers also join them. Details of the celebration, for example, the allocation of seats or the use of candles, could best be discussed with the children themselves.

9. Learning a Trade

It is generally recognized that the young people who will continue their studies for many years need special religious guidance. It is equally obvious that young artisans, too, should not be abandoned in these years of adolescence.[131] Some have suggested that these young people need a religious "closed season". The repudiation of what has gone before may, indeed, appear to be a repudiation of all religious influences, but, in reality, it suggests the struggle and the search for a new direction.[132]

[130] If school should close before Easter, this graduation exercise could be joined to the celebration of the Restored Easter Vigil: the graduating class is seated together in a place of honour in church.

[131] The course of study and the methodology of religious instruction on the secondary school level and beyond are not included in the planning of this book. Assumptions and goals are so very diverse that they cannot be treated suitably in a short compass. For those interested, consult Mayer, pp. 173–192. Only the cardinal points will be treated in the following chapter of this, the second edition of this book.—J. A. Coyne, "What is Vocational Education?" in *The Catholic School Journal,* Vol. 53 (1953), pp. 7–9.

[132] R. Allers, *Character Education in Adolescence* (New York: J. F. Wagner, 1940), pp. 16–20; T. J. Vittoria, *Adolescent Conflicts* (Youngstown, Ohio: Society of St. Paul, 1951), pp. 23–30.

Monsignor Pfliegler, an Austrian priest, understands this when he says that "not only do these adolescents *not* need a 'closed season' in religious instruction but, on the contrary, this is the age having the greatest religious problems. What they require is not protection from religion but protection of their sensitiveness".[133] They can be helped on their way by a sympathetic understanding of their spiritual situation in which childish reasoning is now being left behind. The catechist ought to help in the transformation of their faith from the childish forms in which it has been assimilated into adult ideas, and to find the answers to the questions which now concern young workers more directly than, for example, university students.[134] Especially in regard to religious training, it is true to say that a young man has to absorb the subject matter of instruction on three different occasions during the course of his development. First, in the lower grades of the elementary school, by way of images and pictures; then, in the upper grades, through a sober recognition of facts; and finally through intellectual understanding with an eye to practice.[135] To dispense with this third stage of training would be tantamount to building a house without a roof.

[133] Pfliegler, Vol. II, p. 129. Pfliegler quotes a passage from A. Fischer who characterizes adolescence as that phrase of development in which there is a "psychological optimum" for questions of ideology.—Pfliegler, *Der rechte Augenblick* (5th ed.; Vienna: Herder, 1948), pp. 79f.

[134] J. W. Binder, "Der Religionsunterricht an den Berufsschulen" in *ChPBl.,* Vol. 63 (1950), pp. 221–224. In the U.S.A. some of these problems are handled by the Junior Newman Clubs because the number of purely Catholic industrial schools is not over-great. See J. A. Coyne, "Teachers and Curriculum for Shop Courses" in *The Catholic School Journal,* Vol. 53 (1953), pp. 119–120, who allots three periods of religion for the Freshman, Sophomore and Junior years, and three periods for Catholic Sociology in the Senior year (p. 120).

[135] Eggersdorfer, p. 111.—Similarly G. Delcuve, "Le problème de la formation religieuse dans le monde moderne" in *Lumen Vitae,* Vol. 4

Participation in some youth organization or regular attendance at a course of religious instruction held within the parish can certainly produce the same results.[136] In both cases, however, as experience has shown, only a small section of young people is reached. In some Catholic areas religious traditions are still so much alive that public opinion insists on attendance at regular post-graduation instruction.[137] In general, however, the great majority of the less zealous, and therefore, the more endangered, can be reached only within the framework of an institution specially designed to attract modern youth, but which includes in its programme either lectures on certain days

(1949), pp. 209–232. The three degrees are named: early infancy, adolescence, advent of maturity. The exceptional importance accorded to this third period is manifestly the reason why the dioceses of Holland instituted a special course of instruction for young people of eighteen years of age. This course ends with an examination. If it is successful, the young people are dispensed from the obligation of taking catechetical courses in preparation for marriage.—See also the reports of the Diocese of Utrecht, in *Lumen Vitae,* Vol. 4 (1949), p. 359; of the diocese of Roermond, in *Der Seelsorger,* Vol. 22 (Vienna, 1952), pp. 335f.

[136] When catechetical instructions are not given in these technical schools, as is largely the case in Britain and the United States, they might be provided by means of regular parish meetings, such as the so-called "hours of faith" which have become so popular in some Continental countries. For conditions in Vienna: F. Steiner, "Zur Glaubensstunde der Jugend" in *ChPBl,* Vol. 62 (1949), pp. 23f. In the U.S.A.: in general the CYO, the Sodality *(Prima Primaria),* and the Legion of Mary try to give their members religious instruction and a religious formation, both directly and indirectly. See, for example, Catholic Youth Council, *Youth Department Manual,* Diocese of Buffalo (Buffalo: Chancery, Catholic Youth Council), pp. 58–60.

[137] Cf. above, p. 25f.—Concerning conditions in Switzerland and the possibilities of a more extensive programme, cf. F. Bürkli, *Handbuch der Katechetik* (Einsiedeln: Benziger, 1943), pp. 257–260. In the U.S.A., Confraternity Classes are the only (or practically the only) means that we have of reaching the neglected youth in such schools. The Reports of the various *Proceedings* (National Congresses) contain informational material on this score.

or on half-days during the working week, or specific courses lasting weeks, as in continuation,[138] technical or trade schools.

If the technical or vocational school has as its objective something more than a mere increase in the technical knowledge of the pupil, if it is to form men and women, religion, as an element of formation, must be included in its make-up.[139] It ought to be a part of the syllabus of every vocational school.[140]

Under no circumstances should the lack of suitable teachers serve as an excuse for ecclesiastical authorities not to avail themselves of this opportunity of preaching the Gospel. It should be generally possible to take the able catechists who understand adolescents away from the instruction of small chil-

[138] I. L. Kandel, *Comparative Education* (New York: Houghton, Mifflin, 1933), p. 144; H. N. Rivlin and H. Schueler, *Encyclopedia of Modern Education* (New York: Philosophical Library, 1943): "Since 1933, compulsory continuation schools are no longer common (i. e. in the U.S.A.) because the minimum entrance age in most industrial states has been raised for workers in industry to sixteen or eighteen years. The New York State's *Regent Inquiry into the Character and Cost of Public Education* recommended in 1938 the complete abandonment of continuation schools" (p. 183—"Continuation School"); idem, "Vocational Education", pp. 882–883, for pertinent material on types, etc.

[139] On the development of the legal position in Germany, cf. P. Westhoff, "Der Religionsunterricht an Berufsschulen" in *Die Kirche in der Welt* (Loseblatt-Lexikon), Vol. I (1947/1948), pp. 211–214; W. Vospohl, "Berufsschule und Religionsunterricht" in *Lexikon der Pädagogik,* Vol. I (1952), pp. 413–415. Consult *KBl,* Vol. 77 (1952), p. 47. In Austria, Tyrol and Upper Austria only have prescribed religion periods for the Vocational Schools; cf. J. A. Coyne, *loc. cit.,* in Footnote No. 134; cf. also idem, "Vocational Education: A Case History" in *The Catholic School Journal,* Vol. 53 (1953), pp. 180–181.

[140] There should be, at least, in order to emphasize the voluntary character of such instructions, the possibility of non-attendance. Permission should be granted, however, not only at the request of the pupil, but with the consent of the parents; though not perhaps in the first year. It is of course assumed that religion will not to be relegated to those inconvenient late hours which create the impression that these instructions are no more than disagreeable prolongations of school.

dren, especially in the lower grades, by replacing them by lay teachers as has already been done in many dioceses.

The choice of catechesis material for these schools has been the subject of much discussion, although some agreement has already been reached. Whereas formerly the main parts of the catechism were simply taken up again, though in presentation some consideration was shown for the spiritual problems of the pupils,[141] it is now recognized that the need is not so much for a logical and systematic presentation but for an understanding of the psychological state of these young people, their problems and questions. There should be no systematic repetition of instruction but the young people's problems should be dealt with in the light of the faith, that faith which inspires the catechist himself. The catechist should not begin with God and then treat of Christ, the Church, the sacraments and the moral law. He should begin rather with the sacramental life, discuss our attitudes towards it and the frustrations we experience, and only then delve into those matters which cast light and clarity on Christian living.[142]

All instructions will thus inevitably converge upon the person

[141] As samples of the kind of instruction to be given, consult the three small volumes of H. Stieglitz in which the former head of the Munich Catechetical Movement attempted to adapt to the mentality of the students of the continuation schools, dogma, the moral law, and the doctrine of grace: *Ein glaubensstarker Christ; Ein willensstarker Christ; Ein ganzer Christ* (Kempten: Kösel und Pustet, 1921/22).

[142] W. Vospohl – J. Solzbacher, *Die werktätige Jugend in der Entscheidung für das grössere Leben. Grundsätze und Anregungen für den Religionsunterricht an den Berufsschulen* (Freiburg: Herder, 1950).—Cf. Sr. M. Amadeus, "I Am the Way" in *The Catholic Educator,* Vol. 20 (1950), pp. 303–306; Raoul Plus, *Radiating Christ* (London: Burns, Oates & Washbourne, 1936); G. Delcuve, "What is the Point of Contact Between Religion and Modern Youth?" with two other papers bearing on the same theme, in *The Journal of Religious Instruction,* Vol. 10 (1940), pp. 11–22, 103–126, 196–215: "How Shall We Present Religious Values to the Children and Adolescents of Today?", pp. 320–334.

of Christ. A greater understanding of the different mysteries of the faith will result from His being seen as the God-Man. His impressive appearance, the testimony which He gives of Himself, His invitation to follow Him, His kingship as the transfigured head of the Church, will do more to inspire the young to believe in Him and practice His teaching than philosophical or theological arguments which are, of necessity, abstract, and outside their sphere of interests.[143] Naturally, an introduction to the theological understanding of Christ's person should be given at some suitable point, but it is not necessary to produce elaborate proofs for the existence of God, the possibility and necessity of revelation, etc. In this respect it will suffice to recall the means of arriving at a natural knowledge of God and in so doing to guard against the attraction of pantheism.

An important task on the level of post-school catechesis will be to run over the principal points of Christian doctrine. Obviously the catechist must touch upon topical problems and marginal difficulties arising from the natural sciences and history, but this should be done by stressing the basic harmony which exists between faith and science, rather than by a too apologetic approach.

Other problems troubling the young people, such as those concerning their work or their professions, also sexual and family problems, should also be discussed in the light of faith.

The life of the young is now filled by their jobs and by earning their own living. The work they have to do may be depressing. There is the danger that they may show little interest in it, regarding the job as an unpleasant way of earning a living. It

[143] J. Backes, "Ein Beitrag zur wissenschaftlichen Grundlage einer christozentrischen Glaubensverkündigung an die reifende Jugend" in *Pastor bonus,* Vol. 52 (Trier, 1941), pp. 167–168. For the contrary viewpoint, see Br. A. Victor, "Apologetics" in *La Salle Catechist* (Autumn, 1952), pp. 237–251.

should, therefore, be shown that work fits in with the plan of God as sharing in his creative act, as a sound exercise of the powers of mind and body, as a way of harmonious cooperation in the myriad divisions of labour. The words "vocation" and "calling" point to God, who in His providence has called men to fill different posts in the great workshop of the world. Thus young people can be made to understand their daily work in terms of service to God, to be consecrated and elevated in the divine service on Sunday. The ethics of workers and professional people can thus be given new basis and meaning. Naturally it would be an advantage if the catechist knows something of working conditions in the particular industry in which his students are employed. He will then appreciate their difficulties more easily and also gain their respect.

The second group of vital problems arises from the crisis of puberty. As we have said before, the catechist may take it for granted that at this age level the young people possess the relevant knowledge, or perhaps by presupposing that, he may add to it. If there are arrangements for a three years course of studies some experienced priests have recommended that the relevant theme should be treated twice thoroughly. The first time, as a series of problems concerning the preservation of chastity, from the standpoint of personal morality; the second time, as a problem concerning marriage and the family, more from the standpoint of the community.[144] The catechist should unfold the divine order, telling of the blessings which are contained in its observance. The young people, hungry as they are for life, should be made to realize that here, as elsewhere, the Christian commandment is not against life but seeks to subject man's lower faculties to his higher ones.

In the case of the technical school it is very difficult to draw

[144] L. Wolker, *Der Religionsunterricht in der Fortbildungsschule* (Freiburg: Herder, 1926). In this sense is conceived a series of catecheses on this

up precise plans for the choice of topics, because such a catechesis should be linked in some way with concrete experience which here will vary greatly.[145] Also there will not always be the same amount of time available.[146] That is why generally the teacher-pupil discussions will be more important than the lecture or even the formal steps of catechesis. The young people should feel able to speak out openly and feel that their difficulties, simple as they may be, are being taken seriously. Home work is no longer the order of the day. Written work will be undertaken only in order to help elucidate the matter.[147]

At the end of their training these boys should have imprinted firmly on their minds the ideal of a young Christian, whose feet are firmly planted on this earth, but who looks to Him who preceded us triumphantly through the darkness of this world, and whose name he bears. Religious education need not, however, end with this catechesis. Adults, too, need to continue to receive spiritual nourishment and inspiration through reading, hearing suitable sermons and possibly through courses on Christian doctrine,[148] and, above all, by means of a Sunday Mass that has been suitably adapted to their needs.

subject for the first and for the third year by J. Decking, *Katechesen für reifende Jugend* (4th ed.; Freiburg: Herder, 1949), pp. 90–123, 273–326.

[145] It is significant that Vospohl-Solzbacher (see Footnote No. 142)—have proposed two entirely different teaching plans for the young men and women, because they rightly recognized the guiding principles for each will have to be different. That is why these authors in their plan concentrated on the most acute problems: sequence and the inner connexion of topics and questions are the teacher's responsibility.

[146] Whereas Decking (see above) envisaged 100 religion periods in a three years' course. L. Kammerlander proposed only sixteen in the first of two courses. J. A. Coyne apportions three hours a week for one year of Catholic sociology (in the above Footnote No. 134).

[147] *Briefe an junge Menschen,* which appeared in *Haus Altenberg* in 1953, is a welcome help for the catechist.

[148] For the revival of interest in Christian Doctrine see J. Peitzmeier "Christenlehre" in *Theologie und Glaube,* Vol. 41 (1951), pp. 495–498.

10. Secondary Schools

The years spent at a secondary school are a period marked by the greatest inward transitions. It is obvious that religious instruction at this time has a special task to fulfill. It should serve as a signpost for these boys and girls. It should supply them with the answers to the doubts and difficulties which are typical of their age and development; it should help them to make correct judgements in matters of faith and, indeed, bring about the possible contact between faith and their ordinary thinking. They should make up their minds concerning all kinds of problems, arising either from their instruction in secular subjects,[149] or from current ideas. A further task for religious instruction at this level will be not only to strengthen personal convictions in matters of faith, but also to instil a sense of responsibility for others and a readiness to help, in a truly Christian spirit, those who might be in need.[150] This is all the more important because many of those who attend these schools are likely, later on, to occupy important positions in the community.

The premises for reaching this objective are relatively favourable.[151] The number of class hours is not limited to an absolute

[149] Many branches of knowledge challenge the viewpoint of theology, so that religious instruction must lay that foundation upon which all individual branches of science must rest. See K. Schümmer and J. Schippenkötter, *Christliche Höhere Schule als Unterrichtsgestalt* (Cologne, 1949).

[150] For the ends of education and what follows from them, see: H. Rösseler, *Geist und Gehalt des katholischen Religionsunterrichtes der Höheren Schule* (Cologne, 1910); W. J. McGucken, *The Philosophy of Catholic Education* (New York: America Press, n. d.), pp. 22–31; Sr. M. Janet, *Catholic Secondary Education—A National Survey* (Washington: NCWC, 1949), pp. 68–71.

[151] By this we do not mean to say that religious instructions alone suffice. It always remains true that those who are studying should participate in some kind of outside activity or youth group. Within the school

minimum as in technical schools. In most European secondary schools two hours a week are allotted to religious instruction, and, since the schooling lasts, on an average, for eight or nine years,[152] the students are open to religious influence for a comparatively long time.[153] Moreover, they are likely to be drawn from all classes of society, even those estranged from their religion, so that contacts are possible with many who would not normally be reached. Their mental equipment, too, is, on the whole, promising. Their spiritual development occurs more quietly than in the case of those who have gone to work. Provided there are stable conditions in the family the difficulties which they have to meet are fewer than is the case

it will be advisable to get the pupils to take up some kind of religious or social activity. The religion teacher might also choose from among the more zealous students one or several "associates" who are respected by their fellows and may be able to have some good influence on them. From them the teacher can learn most quickly what problems are actualy troubling the class.Naturally he should guard against the "informer type". S. Stapleton, "How the Catholic School Prepares the Students for Parish Activities" in *NCEA Proceedings and Addresses,* Vol. 49 (1952/53), pp. 287–291.

[152] In many places it has become possible to introduce a so-called "core course". In addition to the ordinary two periods (the core) a week, two additional hours have been added. In these the students who are willing to join can discuss some particular subject in the form of a "working group" under the guidance of the teacher. On this subject see J. Weiss, "Religionsunterricht im Kern-Kurssystem" in *Religion und Weltanschauung* (= *RW*), Vol 7. (1952), pp. 190ff.

[153] In the U.S.A. the division of schooling differs from the European that is being discussed here. The earliest years are spent in *grammar* schools (elementary) with the usual eight years, then come four years of *high school* (secondary schools), although there is sometimes a further sub-division introduced, viz., *junior high* 7, 8 and 9, and *senior high* 10, 11 and 12; *college* (four years) and *university* (generally from 2–4 years depending on the type of subject in which the student majors and the type of degree he aims to achieve, as well as his capacities). F. Cassidy, "The Reorganization of the Catholic School System of Education" in *The Catholic Educational Review,* Vol. 45 (1947), pp. 265–271.

with those who earn their own living. Generally, they show a much greater interest in religious instruction than they will often admit.[154] They expect much from it because they feel that it deals with questions which affect them deeply, though generally they will be less concerned with truth, as such, than with other vital problems. Religious instruction will have to take this into consideration and deliberately attempt to answer some of the questions and difficulties, different as they will be in all phases of development. While interests are mainly objective during the early years, the beginning of puberty is accompanied by a subjective phase. Now there are sexual difficulties for which solutions are sought; other problems too, connected with character formation, caused perhaps by conflicts with family or society, take precedence. Later on there will be questions concerning a future job and the first love affair. At this age, too, interest awakens in problems of a philosophical and ideological nature. It is for the teacher of religion to find the right word at the right time for all. Then, and only then, will his instructions succeed in that chief concern of all religious training, the formation of Christian personality.

This consciously pastoral goal of religious instruction will necessarily also largely influence its form. It is today widely recognized that secondary schools should not be mere institu-

[154] By means of a questionnaire submitted to the students of an Austrian trade school, 173 from a total of 306 acknowledged the necessity of religious instruction; practically all said that they liked going to the religion classes and had listened with interest to the instruction, but the topics that had been discussed and evidently officially prescribed did not find universal acceptance, *Orbis Catholicus,* Vol. 1 (1948), p. 489. E. Havemann and P. S. West, *They Went To College* (New York: Harcourt, Brace, 1952); although an empirical investigation (non-Catholic source) of college graduates, it is informative and startling: 89 per cent. of Catholic women who had attended such colleges were church-goers, and 79 per cent. of the Catholic men.

tions of scholarship, and that religious instruction, above all, should be free from intellectualism.[155] It is justly required that the choice of topics should be confined to these matters which are really important for Christian practice, the truths of faith and morality. These should form the essential core of the instruction and everything else will be in addition. It would, therefore, be laughable, indeed irresponsible, to overtax the memories of these young people with extensive knowledge of ecclesiastical, artistic and liturgical matters. In fact, not even the study of scripture should be conducted on academic lines, for this would result in the accumulation of a mass of knowledge which could not, anyhow, be utilized in later life. This is not to suggest that such matter should be entirely dispensed with. It has its place in the instruction on the secondary level, in fact a very important place, but we must appreciate its function clearly. The content of religious instruction is important only in so far as it serves to elucidate, as vividly as possible, the leading truths of Christian doctrine and morality. Their understanding and realization is more important.

Structure and arrangement of the subject-matter will also, for the sake of the pastoral objective, have to be designed to express the value and character of the deposit of faith. To

[155] Concerning the attempts being made to give a new form to religious instruction on the secondary level, see Rösseler, *loc. cit.* Supporters of the work of reform were especially the religion teachers who belonged to teachers' groups, especially those who were associated with the "Nordwestdeutsche Religionsverband" which in many discussion and working groups and, last but not least, through their review, *Religion und Weltanschauung,* paved the way for a new form of religious instruction in Germany. In the diocese of Cleveland a new method of approach to religious instruction on this level was made in the four volume series, C. E. Elwell, *et al., Quest for Happiness* (Chicago: Mentzer-Bush). For an evaluation of this series, see A. Léonard, "Textbooks in the United States of America" in *Lumen Vitae,* Vol. 6 (1951), pp. 521–525. See also: V. Monty, "Un manuel de religion" in *Relations* (Sept., 1956), pp. 244–245.

accomplish this it will be necessary to depart both from the old system of dividing the catechism text into separate sections on faith, the sacraments, and morals, and from the methods of systematic theology. Both are too rigid and one-sided to be useful for vivid instructions. Revelation, which, after all, is a unity, is too much torn apart into different sections. It would also be necessary to assign individual sections to different classes, although they might contain problems which are without interest for the children of that level, whereas other problems, which would be highly topical for them, would have to be relegated to another stage. Finally the scientific approach of theology is also too abstract in form to appeal to young people.

An arrangement of the subject matter will therefore have to be chosen which, while not dispensing with the systematic approach, will permit divisions more closely related to life.[156] It is again to our advantage that revelation in its original form was imparted to us not in abstract terms but most concretely as the history of salvation. God has revealed himself by His first dealings with man. Revelation is, above all, history; history which reached its culmination in Christ, and has been continued, down to the present day, in the Church with her sacramental life and ups and downs of her existence in the world. If religious instructions are to remain alive they must fall back upon the original form of revelation. Bible, liturgy, and Church History will be the point of departure for the presentation so that

[156] So-called "topical" religious instruction which deals only with current problems and news without any attempt at synthesis have been widely rejected; see, for example, the present course of study for religious instruction for the secondary schools in the province of the Archdiocese of Freiburg (n. d.), p. 6. R. Bandas, *Vital Problems* (St. Paul: Archdiocesan Confraternity, 1954), achieves interest without forsaking synthesis.

from them the real teaching matter, the truths of faith and morals may be derived.

Contacts with scripture, above all, should not be confined to one or two years at the secondary school level. Recourse to the Bible will always be necessary either to find an answer to the problems posed by life, or to enliven with its help the mysteries of faith and the moral commandments. In the first year of the secondary level it will be best to make use of the already mentioned catechism in lesson form. In the intermediate and upper classes, however, many topics will be treated more advantageously after a cursory reading of Holy Scripture.[157] Even for many questions of apologetics scripture readings will be a good starting point. In this way the whole teaching will become more alive and yet there need be no loss of system. It is certainly no longer the system of theology, but an arrangement according to individual topics. The reading of the Bible, however, will become more attractive for the students through this treatment according to topics. Deeper connections will become apparent, and the individual narratives of Sacred Scripture will rather be safeguarded from being considered mere episodes without specific significance.

The Bible, as well as the liturgy, will constantly have to be drawn upon. Since it is not necessary to give the children a thorough grounding in liturgical history, it will not be necessary to set aside a special year for dealing with the liturgy. It will be much better to link the teaching material of the year as far as possible with the liturgical seasons, occasionally to add special lessons about the principal ecclesiastical feasts, and, above all, to

[157] The doctrine on the Church, for example, can scarcely be treated more concretely and easily than in connection with the Acts of the Apostles. What is essential in the Church, the community of the Holy Spirit is here emphasized. Similarly the mystery of the Blessed Trinity can be learned from the parting words of Jesus.

take the relevant factors of divine worship in connection with the Church's teaching on faith and morals.[158] In this the unity of dogma, liturgy and life can be discerned more readily, and an active participation achieved in divine worship, which ought to be the exclusive aim of all liturgical instructions.

The history of the Church will finally also serve to reveal in the right way the mystery of the Church. The historical method facilitates recognition of basic Christian principles and opens the mind to present-day features in the life of the Church. Let the students recognize that the members of the Church too are only human beings; but they should, at the same time, learn to appreciate that the entire history of the Church has been but a single struggle for freedom, for the integrity of faith and morals and for her own sanctity. Of course the dividing line between the *civitas Dei* and the *civitas terrena* cuts right through the Church; but this is evidence only of the bitter struggle and the way of the cross that is her earthly lot. Church History should, therefore, not be presented, like secular history, in the form of historical narratives, but with a genuinely theological nterpretation.[159] At the higher school level it should become history of ideas.

[158] H. v. Lassaulx, "Ein Beitrag zur Didaktik des liturgischen Unterrichtes" in *RW,* Vol. 7 (1952), pp. 101 ff. Balth. Fischer offers many worthwhile suggestions as to how the liturgical material may be apportioned over the single years and can be correlated with the topic of the year. See also Dom D. Rutledge, *Catechism Through the Liturgy* (London: Douglas Organ, 1949).

[159] A solution envisaged in the French study plans that Church History should be taught by the same teacher who teaches secular history might possibly be justified only if secular history is also taught by a priest; *RW,* Vol. 7 (1952), p. 20. See also J. Burschid, "Zur kirchengeschichtlichen Situation im Religionsunterricht an Höheren Schulen" *loc. cit.,* pp. 97 ff.; C. J. Ryan, "Teaching Church History in High School" in *Journal of Religious Instruction,* Vol. 17 (1946/47); "The Facts", pp. 718 ff.—"Why", p. 797–805;—"What to Teach", p. 877–888.

How this material is to be assigned to the various school years can be settled only by a teaching plan. A good plan will first of all take into consideration the psychological make-up of the pupils in the various stages of their development. The old plans did not fulfill this condition satisfactorily.

If, for example, morals are to be taught in their entirety in the second year, and not at all in the decisive years of adolescence, this can hardly be regarded as a happy arrangement.[160] The reason for these mistakes is ultimately that such teaching plans still cling too slavishly to the traditional division of the catechism in its old, theology textbook, form. But as we have already said, neither the catechism formula, Creed-Commandments, nor the scientifically written theological treatises, represent the only valid summary of revelation. The commandments contain only the natural moral law, and it is questionable whether the supernatural morality of Christianity should be mixed up indiscriminately with, or added to, it. It would seem to be more correct to distinguish clearly the typical Christian commands from the merely natural morality, and to deduce these from the new state of man effected by Christ. That is, man raised by grace to be child of God. But rather will this be attained by dividing the moral law into different sections and when dealing with these by starting perhaps with the Sermon on the Mount or a Pauline Epistle.

Even less open to hard and fast systems is the teaching of Christian doctrine. After all it is no mere summary of abstract truths, but essentially history. The various dogmas can of course be linked with one another, but the best link is that of the Person of Jesus Christ in whom all the truths of revelation have been made accessible to us. We thus need to have the

[160] The present practice in Austrian secondary schools and in Germany: in secondary schools in Bavaria morals are taught for a second time in the fifth class (and not as in Austria in the seventh).

courage to drop the traditional systems and to deal with the teaching on faith and morals as based upon the scriptures. Many new study plans have already taken this step.[161] All require cursory readings from the Bible, at least in the intermediate and upper grades.[162] Sacred Scripture, liturgy, and Church History are sometimes well distributed over the various years, and in such a way that the selected passages subserve the year's teaching matter on dogma and morals. Even the children's own problems are sufficiently taken into consideration in these new study plans.[163] Questions concerning self-education and sexual

[161] In this context we may regard the plan of studies adopted in the Rhineland-Pfalz schools since 1951 as a perfect model. As its basis were used the regulations drawn up at the Fulda Bishops' Conference in 1938. But later work, especially the recommendations of H. E. Wetzel, *Lebensgestaltung in Christus* (Paderborn: Schöningh, 1947), the work of the Saar schools, the studies of the committee of the North-West German union of religious teachers appointed were made use of in *RW,* Vol. 6 (1951), pp. 73–80, 89.

[162] The Austrian teaching plan (September 25, 1948) requires Bible readings in all classes on the upper level, if possible to be linked to the other matter, cf. *Verordnungsblatt für den Dienstbereich des Bundesministeriums für Unterricht,* Jahrgang 1949, Nr. 4.

[163] The *Lehrplan* for Rhineland-Pfalz considers as educationally appropriate for the first two years the fellowship with the Father, who is God, and with the Christ, because it meets with the, as yet, childish mental attitude at this age. But in the third year, when growing adolescence requires matter that is as interesting as possible, the workings of the Holy Spirit in the Church and in the world are suggested as appropriate topics. The intermediate years treat of the preparation, in Old Testament times, that Christ made for His coming (fourth year), His personality (fifth year), His continued life in the Church (sixth year). In the final year a summary view of the faith is aimed at, because they are now ready to come to grips with religious problems as a whole. The French study plan, which was developed by the *Commission Nationale du Catéchisme* and has been in force since 1949, is also adapted to the psychological growth of the students; *RW,* Vol. 7 (1952), p. 19. In the U.S.A. there is no uniform plan for the whole of the nation, the choice is left to the individual diocese. Some of these have worked out their own plans, for example, Cleveland, Pittsburgh.

morality are generally reserved for the fourth year; apologetics for the fifth to the eighth year of secondary schools. In the treatment of apologetics, too, there is a departure from the customary system adopted from theology, which begins with proofs for the existence of God, then enquires into the probability of revelation, in order to demonstrate finally, when the sources of Christian revelation had been proved as genuine, the truth of Christianity and the Catholic Church. The justification for this division appears to be its systematic and scientific approach. It demands too much from the mental powers of the students, however, so that it merely tires without convincing them. Also we shall have to bear in mind that no apologetic proof, however neatly presented, can, of itself, generate faith. The various apologetic problems which, anyhow, are relatively independent of one another, may, therefore, very well be treated separately. It is sufficient to provide the scholars in one of the upper forms with a survey of the whole subject which ought not be too difficult since the individual pieces of the mosaic are already known. In the German study plans special emphasis is given to the sixth year after the completion of which many pupils leave the secondary schools to take up jobs. This year is therefore designed as a kind of final graduation instruction.[164]

Regarding forms and methods, the particular psychological development of the scholar will have to be recognized. In the lower classes we can plan the religion period as in the upper classes of the elementary school according to the method of formal steps. In the intermediate and upper classes it is better to be free of them, for it is now no longer a question of learning

[164] G. Frank, "Der Religionsunterricht in der 6. Klasse" in *RW*, Vol. 8 (1953), pp. 2ff. The same importance is not attached to the sixth form in Austrian schools. Some pupils might leave Austrian secondary schools after the fourth form (especially in the *Realschule*) but mainly in order to transfer to another school and not to take up jobs.

single truths, but of the different realms of life. For this reason the teaching method which is based on a given text is preferable. The problem having been stated, a discussion follows in which all can join. Afterwards the catechist will give his talk which is not to be interrupted, seeking to settle the previously voiced questions and doubts. The practical conclusions will then emerge as a matter of course and should be entered in brief sentences into a notebook. If the pupils are not sufficiently alive to this developing form of instruction, which will require some mental effort, the visual developing method might be used. The difference is that the instructions will be enlivened and loosened up by means of visual presentations which facilitate the thinking process. This method will have particular importance for the intermediate years, but for the final year, too; the principle holds that we can never dispense with the universal psychological law, according to which all thinking begins with what is visual and concrete.

APPENDIX I

The Apostles' Creed

THE origin of the Apostles' Creed, the "symbolum", has been the object of extensive researches during the last century, the results of which are understandably of great importance also for catechesis. A fairly recent account of these researches, by Joseph de Ghellinck, S. J.,[1] fills a volume of 321 pages, twenty-seven of which are devoted to a bibliography of works consulted by the author. Origins, as well as structure, of the "symbolum" have given rise to an entirely new perspective.

The Middle Ages offered a very simple explanation for the origin of the "symbolum". As the name, "Apostles' Creed" suggested, it was thought that they alone could have been its authors and that in particular each of the apostles phrased one article at their last gathering before their separation. There are not a few old churches with pictures of the twelve apostles and a text underneath ascribing to each a particular article. This naive hypothesis was first questioned at the end of the Middle Ages. The Italian humanist, Lorenzo Valla, heard a Fransiscan friar in 1443 telling this ancient legend to a group of children in Naples, and feeling annoyed challenged him to a public disputation. This was forbidden to be held by the King of Naples, but the case caused a considerable sensation.

There was no scholary investigation of the problem until about 1842, when the relevant texts were systematically collected

[1] J. de Ghellinck, *Les recherches sur les origines du Symbole des Apôtres* (2nd ed.; Paris, 1949); J. Quasten, *Patrology,* 2 vols. (Westminster: The Newman Press), Vol. I (1950), pp. 23–27. J. N. D. Kelly, *Early Christian Creeds* (London: Longmans, Green, 1950); idem, *Rufinus. A Commentary on the Apostles' Creed* (Westminster, Md.: Newman, 1955).

and first published by August Hahn in his *Bibliothek der Symbole*. But research was probably started only after 1890, the occasion being the ever-dwindling faith within Protestant Christianity in Germany. The Protestant ecclesiastical authorities finally required the profession of the content of the Creed as a minimum to be held by any of their pastors. Several members of the clergy, however, refused to accept this ruling. Some Protestant theologians, Adolf Harnack among them, came to their support. The "controversy about the *Apostolicum*", as it was called, also served to intensify scientific research into the origins of the formula. At first it was carried on almost exclusively among Protestants.[2] Catholic theologians were slow in taking it up and then mainly by means of critical assessments of the results.[3] What is important in these findings for catechetics we want to explain briefly.

The beginnings of the Apostles' Creed can indeed be found in the time of the Apostles, but the complete formula did not exist before the third century. At first there were two separate formulas, trinitarian and Christological, which were joined only about the year 200 A.D.

TRINITARIAN FORMULA. Apart from the message of Jesus Christ the Redeemer, faith in one God had to be preached to the heathen. The twofold topic of preaching was, God and Christ: the

[2] Among the works which are still valuable, the most important are: F. Kattenbusch, *Das Apostolische Symbol,* 2 vols. (Leipzig 1894/1900); H. Lietzmann, "Symbolstudien" in *Zeitschrift für die neutestamentliche Wissenschaft* (1922/27). In English, F. J. Badcock, *The History of the Creeds* (New York: Macmillan, 1930), pp. 99–146.

[3] See S. Bäumer, *Das Apostolische Glaubensbekenntnis* (Mainz: Kirchheim, 1893); Cl. Blume, *Das Apostolische Glaubensbekenntnis* (Freiburg: Herder, 1893), and Ghellinck whom we have just mentioned. The texts have been gathered by A. Hahn, *Bibliothek der Symbole* (3rd ed.; Breslau, 1897); a selection of such texts in H. Lietzmann, *Symbole der alten Kirche* (4th ed.; Kleine Texte, 17/18) (Bonn, 1935). An orientation on the subject may be found in the Denzinger, Bannwart *et al., Enchiridion* (28th ed.; Freiburg: Herder, 1952), pp. 1–10, nos. 1–12.

two basic concepts of the Christian faith, then and always. But to this relatively complete statement of Christian doctrine was added a third set of topics, an outline of those things for which the Christian faith is responsible: a new life and a new people of God, the Church and all that the Church contains in power and in institutions.

According to the way in which these last topics are summarized we have three, and sometimes four or five, points of doctrine. In the so-called *Epistola Apostolorum* (about A.D. 150) Christian teaching is likened to the five loaves in the miraculous multiplication of loaves. As there were five loaves of bread, so in Christian doctrine there are five principal points: we believe in "the Father, the Lord of all (παντοκράτωρ), and in Jesus Christ, our Redeemer, in the Holy Spirit the Paraclete, in Holy Church and in the remission of sins". Sometimes only three points were enumerated: God, Christ, the Church (as we are accustomed to today), or God, Christ, Resurrection. But the summary most frequently used was God, Christ, Holy Spirit. It also expressed belief in the three divine persons which was only natural when this formula was used in conjunction with Baptism which is conferred in the name of the Father, Son and Holy Spirit.

Profession of faith in the three divine persons was, moreover, in later times introduced into the "symbolum" in a variety of ways. Creeds have been preserved which place the profession of faith in the Blessed Trinity at the very beginning: "I believe in God the Father and in the Son and in the Holy Spirit, and I believe in Jesus Christ our Lord, who was born . . . ." The Athanasian Creed, for example, is constructed in this way. First, very fully, come the Trinitarian articles of faith, then the Christological profession.[4] But as early as the second century the pro-

[4] The *Te Deum* is constructed in much the same way: first a hymn of praise to the Trinity: *Patrem immensae maiestatis,* etc., then the reference to Christ: *Tu rex gloriae, Christe.*

fession of faith in the Trinity was combined with other articles of faith in such a way that the doctrine of God was joined to the name of the Father, the doctrine of Christ, to the name of the Son as such, and the doctrine of the benefits of redemption to the name of the Holy Ghost. God, Christ, the grace of the Holy Spirit. These continue to be also the main headings for the tracts of theology: *De Deo Uno et Trino—De Christo Redemptore—De gratia et sacramentis*.

Thus, quite early, probably about A.D. 100, there were baptismal creeds consisting of three parts of practically uniform length similar in formulation to our present day Creed, if we except the clause referring to Christ. There were, however, many different versions, none of which has precisely the same wording as that used today. Even the Trinitarian formula of the earliest Roman creed, the Roman "ursymbolum" is different. "I believe in God, the Father, the Almighty, and in Jesus Christ, his only-begotten Son, our Lord, and in the Holy Spirit, Holy Church, remission of sins, resurrection of the body."

The different versions of the creed formulas in the West stem from this Roman original. Another similar creed, also Trinitarian, originated in the East; an example of this type, but in expanded form, is the Creed of the Mass.

PROFESSION OF FAITH IN CHRIST. Besides this Trinitarian basic formula there was another formula or, more correctly, various formulas, in which belief in Christ (or as it has become customary to say, the Christ-kerygma) was expressed. We can sense the beginnings of this formula in St. Paul (1 Cor. 15). The ancient acrostic, ΙΧΘΥΣ (Jesus Christ, God's Son, Saviour), or the sign of the fish, were also professions of faith in Christ. A more developed formula of this kind existed very early in Rome. It was joined to the Trinitarian Creed about 200 A.D., thus becoming the older Roman symbolum apostolicum which scholars describe as "R". This "Christuskerygma" in the Roman version reads[5] "Who was born of the Holy Spirit and of the Virgin Mary, who was crucified under Pontius Pilate and was buried, arose from the dead on the third day, ascended into heaven, sits at the right hand of the Father, whence he shall come to judge the living and the dead."

Comparing it to the modern wording, which scholars describe as "T" *(textus receptus)*, a stylistic variation can be noted first of all, the twofold division of the kerygma through the double use of the relative pronoun "who . . ." (in Greek τὸν γεννηθέντα . . . τὸν ἐπὶ Π. Π. σταυρωθέντα). This corresponds to the two chief mysteries in the dogma of Christ, incarnation and redemptive suffering—in other words, to the two principal feasts of the ecclesiastical year, Christmas and Easter. Hence it is not by accident that these two mysteries are emphasized in any modern baptismal rite. Before Baptism the questions are asked: "Dost thou believe in Jesus Christ, His only-begotten Son, our Lord, who was born and who suffered?" "Born"; the wonderful birth through the Holy Spirit and the Virgin Mary illuminates the mystery of the Person of Christ: He is more than a man. He is also the Son of God. "Suffered": the Passion is the work of redemption, for which He came into the world. It should be noted that suffering is immediately linked with passion and is described in words which are hymnal in character;[6] similarly a greater emphasis is on the glorified than on the suffering Lord at Easter and the celebrations have always been continued for fifty days. This accounts for the fact that the creed contains no chronological reference to the birth as might have

[5] Denzinger, Bannwart *et al.*, no. 2.

[6] Even in the more recent texts the interpolated phrase "He descended into hell" is an expression of triumph. In Byzantine art, pictorial representations of the descent into hell generally, even today, take the place of resurrection pictures. See K. Künstle, *Ikonographie der christlichen Kunst* (Freiburg: Herder, 1928), Vol. I, pp. 494–500.

been provided later (ever since the sixth century the years are counted from the "birth of Christ"), but to the Passion: "Suffered under Pontius Pilate". Thus the coming of Christ is placed into the course of world history. It is not a myth, but a definite and tangible fact: "under Pontius Pilate". At that time (for example, under the Emperor Tiberius, or the consulate of Marcus and Duilius) it was customary to date events from the rulers and the years of their reigns. The fact that the name of a minor governor in Palestine was used in this connection indicates that this reference came into use when Christianity was still confined to the narrow area of the Holy Land.

THE TEACHING OF THE GIFTS OF REDEMPTION. The third part of the Creed, which begins with the Holy Spirit, treats of the gifts of redemption, and could, in the Apostles Creed, be entitled "The Teaching of Grace". Although it sounds somewhat different from the teaching to be found in our catechisms and the theological treatises *De Gratia,* it is, nevertheless, a teaching on grace. The process of thought, here encountered, might be explained as follows. The Holy Ghost is named first of all as the principle of the new life which Christ has brought. It dwells and manifests itself in the Church, which is hallowed by it. It effects everyone through the remission of sins, and finally in the resurrection of the body.

First comes the Holy Spirit, who is the third person of the blessed Trinity, but also the uncreated grace for mankind. The early Church, when treating of grace, always preferred to use the name of the Holy Spirit who dwells within us, and who inspires us to do good. The manner of expression is less precise than that to which we are accustomed in theology, but the essence of grace is surely described just as well. It becomes clear that we mean an inward and also a supernatural gift, for the name alone tells us that we are dealing with something to which we could never lay claim by natural means, that God imparts to us His own Spirit, His life.

The Holy Spirit has His earthly dwelling place in the Church. His holiness is transmitted to her, as it were, like a spark. "I believe in the Holy Ghost, the holy Church." So with the other marks of the Church, one, catholic, apostolic, which we pronounce in the Creed at Mass, were mentioned early on. But "holy" is the earliest concept connected with the Church. The Church is essentially holy. This is implied in the very notion of the Church (ἐκκλησία), as the sum total of those who are called by God. Grace, election and holiness are therein contained.

The later form of the Creed, which we use today, which was used by the Gallican Church (T), and which supplanted the older Roman text (R), even in Rome itself after the tenth century, appends an explanatory phrase, "the communion of saints". The expression "holy Church" or "holy Catholic Church" had become a phrase to which not a great deal of meaning was attached. That is why the old idea of holiness was emphasized again in a definite and new colouring: the holy Church is the community of men sanctified in Baptism. The primary idea was not relationship with the saints in heaven, but with the Church as a communion of saints. In modern times, too, many catechisms, the Roman Catechism among them, accepted this interpretation.[7]

[7] Another translation of this phrase is possible: *sanctorum* could be the genitive which is not dependent upon *sancti* but upon *sancta*: *sancta* = *ta agia* = τὰ ἅγια, holy things; *sanctorum communio* = a society for holy things: faith, hope, the sacraments, powers and privileges which are possessed by the Church, especially the Holy Eucharist as a common possession of all those who belong to the Catholic Church. St. Augustine repeatedly used the expression in this sense. But ultimately it means practically the same. The Church is a holy society, holy because of what is bestowed upon her through grace.

The life of grace was, therefore, considered first of all in its communal, social aspect. At the same time, however, grace was said to have been granted to the individual. The Creed expressly mentions all those sacraments by means of which Christians are included in the life of grace: Baptism and Penance, the sacraments instituted for the remission of sins. "The remission of sins" refers in the first place to Baptism. This is clearly indicated in the Nicene Creed: *Confiteor unum baptisma in remissionem peccatorum.* The other sacraments are also included, especially the Eucharist. They are not, however, named individually. This was not necessary, for anyone who enters into the life of the Church through the doors of Baptism shares in the entire life of the Church.

According to the meaning current in the early Church, the phrase "resurrection of the body" referred, above all, to resurrection of the just. Grace is transfigured into glory, and glory also seizes man's body and transforms it. The words, "and life everlasting", added to the *textus receptus* are no more than a further explanation by which the eternal duration of the state of perfection is expressed.

We can maintain that in the thinking of the early Church all these references to the gifts of the redemption are only developments of the first which named the Holy Spirit. It is the Holy Spirit who fills the Church; He is the soul of the Church. In Baptism He effects the remission of sins. He *is* the remission of sins. So prays the Church at Pentecost. The Holy Ghost is also active in the resurrection: He transforms the natural into a "spiritual" body (1 Cor. 15:44).

But from another point of view we can also say that the culmination, the principal notion, of this third part of the Creed is the Church. Holy Church is all embracing, wherein is contained everything else. That is why there were various formulations of the Creed, such as: "I believe in the Holy Ghost (and the forgiveness of sins) and in the resurrection of the body in the Holy Church." That is to say, the whole process of redemption is being accomplished within the Church.[8]

The parallel lines between the various stages in the life of the Redeemer and those in the life of the redeemed should be noted in our Creed. At the annunciation we have the Holy Ghost and Mary, the Virgin from whom Christ was born. In the life of the redeemed we begin with the Holy Ghost and the Church, which is likewise mother and virgin. In Christ's life there is the descent to suffering, to the grave, followed by the glorious resurrection to eternal glory at the right hand of the Father. The redeemed, also are buried in Baptism, beset by the trials of true Christian living, will likewise experience resurrection which will ultimately embrace the body and will terminate in the glory of the eternal life.

These considerations should help to clarify the natural division of the Creed. The division into twelve articles does not correspond to its original structure; it is a later, artificial division, which disguises rather than illuminates the coherence of the sentences. This division can be found already in Rufinus (d. 410 A.D.); but it is clear how it came about. From the very beginning the Creed was called apostolic because it summarized the belief which the apostles left behind. Because there were twelve apostles, a way was sought to divide the formula into twelve parts. In this way the medieval legend was born. But the Middle Ages knew other divisions besides this one. St. Thomas divided the Creed into fourteen articles, of which seven refer to the mystery of the Trinity and seven to the humanity of Christ.

Finally, the formulation of the act of faith is unusual. *Credo in Deum* . . . (I believe in . . .). No special meaning is attached to

[8] P. Nautin, *Je crois à l'Esprit Saint dans la Sainte Église* (*Unam Sanctam*, 17), Paris, 1947.

this formulation in the most ancient texts of the Fathers. From St. Augustine's time, however, it is held to express a loving inclination as well as a rational assent.[9]

The Apostles' Creed was very highly esteemed in the early Church. That is why it was always designated as σύμβολον : σύμβολον = what has been put together, a sign of recognition; for it was also the password which Christian travellers used when visiting other Christian communities. That is why it had to be kept secret from the heathens. It was never written down; it had to be written into their hearts. Candidates for Baptism had, therefore, to learn it by heart. And lest they might forget it they were admonished to recite it every day, together with the Lord's Prayer which was likewise considered sacred, in the morning immediately upon rising and in the evening immediately before going to bed. St. Augustine, for example, admonished the newly baptized:[10] "Say it daily. When you get up and when you go to bed recite the Creed. Say it before the Lord; memorize it, never grow tired of repeating it." This injunction was obeyed. Christians began their daily morning prayers and ended their evening prayers with the recitation of the Lord's Prayer and the Apostles' Creed. And this practice was continued throughout the Middle Ages.

[9] Christine Mohrmann, "Credere in Deum" in *Mélanges J. de Ghellinck* (*Museum Lessianum,* sect. hist. 13) (Gembloux, 1951), pp. 277–285.

[10] Augustinus, *Serm*. 58, 13 (*PL* 38, 399).

APPENDIX II

The Kerygma in the History of the Pastoral Activity of the Church

By the word kerygma, message, we mean the Christian teaching in so far as it is intended to be proclaimed, that is to be realized through pastoral care as the basis of Christian life.[1] Kerygma is thus to be distinguished from Christian doctrine insofar as Christian doctrine is illuminated in all aspects by theology and presented as a logically coordinated system of knowledge.[2] While the

[1] Kerygma originally referred to the preaching of the Gospel to non-Christians; cf. the historical research undertaken by A. Rétif, "Qu'est-ce que le kérygme?" in *Nouvelle Revue théologique,* Vol. 71 (1949), pp. 910–922; idem, *Foi au Christ et mission d'après les Actes des Apôtres* (Paris, 1953), pp. 11ff.; Kr. Stendahl, "Kerygma und Kerygmatisch" in *Theolog. Literaturzeitung,* Vol. 77 (1952), pp. 715–720. Rétif makes a distinction between kerygma on the one hand and catechesis and didascalics on the other. Whereas kerygma announced the kingdom of God which came in the Person of Christ and seeks primarily to bring all to the true faith, catechesis (or διδαχή) offered an elementary, and chiefly also moral, introduction to the doctrines of Christianity themselves; didascalics (διδασκαλία), frequently mentioned in pastoral letters, is a more advanced form of instructions using both argumentation and Sacred Scripture. Rétif admits, however, that the terminology in the New Testament is fluid. In any case the Greek Fathers used the word, κήρυγμα, in a broader sense, e. g., Basilius, *De Spiritu Sancto,* c. 27 (*PG,* Vol. 32, cols. 185ff. with Annotation No. 64). We, too, would distinguish kerygma from catechesis, insofar as by the former we mean the essential content. Our understanding of the term Christian kerygma is also closer to the original in the sense that the message of salvation, which came in the Person of Christ, must today be preached anew in a de-Christianized world.

[2] See above, p. 96.

growth and the continuous development of individual theological concepts, especially of the dogmas themselves, have long been the object of thorough researches and are made use of in the history of dogma, the history of kerygma and its different elements has up until now attracted little attention.

We shall attempt to give only a brief historical outline of the kerygmatic point of view, confining it to what is of importance for a knowledge of the present position of the problem, especially for catechetics. But it is hoped that even such a brief outline might induce some readers to take up seriously one or other of the particular questions that are raised.

The preaching of the apostles was in the first place a witness to the resurrection of the Lord, of an event which had publicly revealed that Jesus of Nazareth truly was the Messias and that He redeemed the world through His death on the cross. The gospels enlarge upon this theme retrospectively by showing the miraculous power and divine origin of Him who rose from the dead. They also tell of the time in between when the Holy Spirit is poured out upon those who believe in Christ and have been gathered as His Church through Baptism.[3] Christ as the one who brought redemption is thus clearly at the centre of the preaching.

This remained the practice throughout Christian antiquity, as is demonstrated by the sermons of the early teachers and the pictorial language of early Christian art.

There was a certain preference in the early centuries for the Old Testament to be used with the New in preaching the faith; it was also commented upon in long homilies, although these were less concerned with the literal meaning of Deuteronomy or of the psalms, as with some mysterious evidence of the central

[3] H. Schürmann, "Aufbau und Struktur der neutestamentlichen Verkündigung" in *Paderborner Schriften zur Pädagogik und Katechese,* 2 (Paderborn, 1949).

mysteries in the New Testament.[4] In Adam was seen the type of the new Adam, Christ, and in Eve, who was created from Adam's side, the Virgin Mary or Holy Mother Church. The saving wood of the ark of Noë was the wood of the cross, and in the eight people who were saved were discerned a reference to the eighth day, the day of Christ's resurrection and of the new creation. Even the Book of Leviticus, which hardly contains material applicable to the New Testament, served Origen as a quarry for images seemingly foreshadowing the New Law. Aaron and his sons represent Christ and the apostles, the Jewish laws of purification and ritual are seen to be fulfilled in a new manner in Christ and in the moral law which he propounded. The four spirits, in the vision of Ezechiel (Ezech. 1 : 5 et seq.), are regarded by Irenaeus and by many later authors as symbols of Christ; the human face points to his incarnation, the figure of a bull to his sacrificial calling, the lion to the victory of his resurrection, the eagle to his ascension into heaven.[5] We are familiar with the pictorial representation of Old Testament scenes found in the catacombs. They were misunderstood only until it was realized that they represent allusions to the redemption accomplished in the New Testament. Isaac, Jonas and the three young men in the fiery furnace represent the death and the resurrection of Christ and of those who die and rise with Him in Baptism.

The message of salvation preached by the early Church found its first systematic summary in the Apostles' Creed. In it as well as in its kindred formulas the message of Christ is

[4] Consult also: the works of J. Daniélou, especially *Sacramentum futuri* (Paris, 1950); *The Bible and the Liturgie* (Notre Dame, 1958).

[5] Karl Künstle, *Ikonographie der christlichen Kunst,* Vol. I, (Freiburg: Herder, 1928), pp. 611f.; O. Casel, "Älteste christliche Kunst und Christusmysterium" in *Jahrbuch für Liturgiewissenschaft,* Vol. 12 (1934), pp. 1–86.

unfolded more fully; at the same time the Trinitarian structure of the faith is emphasized. In the realm of prayer there were the divine praises or doxologies for which a basic outline gradually became evident in the third century. "Glory be to the Father through Jesus Christ in the Holy Spirit", or, placing the divinity of Christ in the foreground: "Glory be to the Father through the Son in the Holy Ghost."[6]

At this point were felt the first signs of the threat by heresy to the kerygma. Arianism, which menaced the Church from the fourth to the sixth century denied the equality of natures between Father and Son, and hence Christ's divinity. To justify their teaching the Arians used to point to the manner in which the Church prayed addressing the Father through the Son, the Son being thereby subordinated to the Father. The defenders of the faith replied that such references to the Son applied only to his humanity, to Christ Jesus the mediator. But this answer made no impact and failed to prevent confusion among the faithful. Thus it happened that in many parts of the Church, in the East as well as in Spain and Gaul, where the Arian Germanic tribes were particularly powerful, the words "through Christ" in prayers, and the idea of the God-Man as the special mediator in the language of theology, was allowed to recede into the background, even although there was no intention of denying or weakening this truth.

There was all the more emphasis, however, on the divinity of Christ and the divine majesty and general dignity of the Lord. The most effective form of preaching the faith is the celebration of a feast. Besides the feast of Easter, followed by fifty days of celebration which for centuries and throughout Christendom was the only feast of the Church, there now appeared a second festal cycle, Christmas and Epiphany.

[6] J. A. Jungmann, *Die Stellung Christi im liturgischen Gebet* (Münster, 1925), pp. 131 ff.

Both existed before the Arian heresy, but at that time experienced a rapid development. Hitherto the work of redemption accomplished by the passion and death of Christ had been celebrated; in the Christmas cycle the incarnation of the Son of God became the object of special adoration. Besides His work, the Person of the Saviour was also specially honoured. The conception and birth of the Redeemer, and thus the Virgin Mother Mary, assumed particular importance. The great Marian feasts which in the meantime had arisen in the East were adopted by the West after the sixth century: Mary's birth, Annunciation, Purification and Assumption.

It is due to the narrowness of man's mind that what undoubtedly was enrichment and clarification in one respect proved a loss in another. The early Middle Ages saw the rise of the German tribes which soon assumed a leading role also in the Church. They were people without any higher culture, and the missionaries active among them had to content themselves with giving the most elementary religious instruction. On the other hand the age of the great Fathers of the Church had ended. Participation in the liturgical feasts became the chief means of imparting religious education. A certain vulgarism in the average preaching of faith, and in religious notions, was thus inevitable. Moreover, the new peoples having come into the Church from Arianism were animated all the more by hatred of the *perfidia Ariana*.[7] This was especially true of the West Gothic Church in Spain which soon, after the conversion of the people to the Catholic faith in 589, experienced a "golden age"—the only Doctor of the Church in the seventh century was Isidore of Seville, a Spaniard—and thus became a model for the rest of the Western Church. The culture of the eighth and ninth

[7] J. A. Jungmann, "Die Abwehr des germanischen Arianismus und der Umbruch der religiösen Kultur im frühen Mittelalter" in *ZkTh,* Vol. 69 (1947), pp. 36–99, especially pp. 61f.

centuries was based upon these foundations. The *fides Trinitatis* became the leading concept of the Creed. Trinitarian formulas were used at the beginning of documents and of any pious work. Adoration of the most holy Trinity became the central theme of Christian worship. Prefaces for Sunday Mass, which until then had referred to the redemption, resurrection, sanctification of the faithful, admission through Christ to God's glory, were replaced by the Preface of the Trinity. The divinity of Christ was emphasized so much that in the preaching of the gospel the notions of God and Christ were often interchanged. A collection of model catecheses from the Carolingian period which have been ascribed to St. Boniface are phrased in various places in such a manner that it would almost appear as if God was born of the Virgin Mary, who endured insults and outrages, blows and a scourging, and died on the Cross for us.[8] Expressions such as "God's body" for the body of Christ, "the martyrdom of God" for the sufferings of Christ, remained for a very long time current in medieval sermons.

It is clear that these expressions are thoroughly orthodox, since they contain but the *communicatio idiomatum*. It is still the same dogmatic structure which confronts us, but it is another aspect, another side of that structure, which was then preferred in every day instructions and in practical devotions. Only rarely was the talk of a transfigured Christ still referred to, who lives and reigns with the Father, who is the head of the Church, and, logically, it was equally rare to hear that the Church is the Body of Christ, and that Christians are incorporated into it at Baptism, thus bearing the divine life within themselves.[9] Prayers of that time, which have been preserved, refer much more frequently to man's personal misery and sinfulness, than

[8] *Idem,* pp. 78f. Also *Ps.-Bonifatius, Sermones* (*PL,* Vol. 89, cols. 843–872).

[9] J. A. Jungmann, "Die Abwehr . . .", p. 94.

grace and redemption. Apologists from the ninth to the eleventh century provide ample evidence. Liturgical prayers, too, unless they originated in earlier times, were preferably addressed to Christ himself or to the blessed Trinity. Intercessions made by the Mother of God and the saints grew in esteem and importance. The Blessed Sacrament became the object of supreme adoration; indeed, at the turn of the twelfth century we can find traces of a veritable eucharistic movement spreading throughout Christendom. But it was not the closeness of Christ which the faithful sought in a more intimate participation in the Mass and Communion, but rather remoteness from Him, an attitude of adoration towards the holy Persons, but made from afar. The deposit of faith was less a well-rounded whole than so many individual doctrines, incidents from the childhood and the passion of Christ, liturgical devotions with their climax in the sacraments, and among popular customs a growing emphasis on indulgences and the veneration of numerous saints. Moral instruction, including the popular enumerations, dominated the teaching of the faith.[10] Knowledge of the faith, an understanding of its content, was reduced to a minimum in the average instructions, and indeed could be so reduced because and insofar as the practice of the faith made up for it.

On the other hand the clarifications of scholastic theology at the height of the Middle Ages have contributed much towards greater emphasis being given again to the essentials of the faith in popular instructions. The *devotio moderna* and, to some extent, even German mysticism, had already applied themselves to the task of acquainting the laity with the results of that labour. At this point the revolution of Luther and of the reformers occurred which sought to simplify Christian teaching and practice by a

[10] *Ut supra*, p. 15.

single violent stroke, an undertaking in which they sacrificed some essential doctrines of the Christian tradition. As far as the threatened doctrines were concerned, the Council of Trent clarified these with authority and provided in the *Catechismus Romanus,* which it ordered to be drawn up, as well as in late catechisms, a firm example of orthodoxy. It happened also, in this development, that the protection required against strong heretical movements tended to influence also the structure of the defended faith in so far as the doctrines attacked had to be specially accented. Catholic teaching thus came to be dominated by matters such as the hierarchical structure of the Church, the *opus operatum* in the sacraments, the Real Presence, the value of good works. In addition the knowledge increasingly gained from the then revived researches of theologians had to be integrated into the religious instructions. It thus came about that as particular doctrines were made known with greater precision the understanding of the whole hardly increased. The facts of the history of redemption were grasped by the intellect, but not related sufficiently to the sanctifying powers in the Church and in the Sacraments, nor seen as a whole.

Integration in the faith and in the life of the Christian community still provided a sufficient substitute for a more thoughtful understanding of the faith and of its inner cohesion. On the other hand, the new religious revival re-enforced the endeavours which aimed at a Christianity which was more consciously understood and realized. This was the object of the retreats recommended by St. Ignatius and their popularization through missions preached to the faithful.[11] This was the object also of the movement which originated in France in Saint Sulpice, and which made the mystery of the Incarnation of the Son of God

[11] Z. J. Maher, *Under the Seal of the Fisherman* (Los Altos, California: Jesuit House of Retreats, 1948); H. Rahner (F. J. Smith, trans.), *The Spirituality of St. Ignatius Loyola* (Westminster: Newman, 1953).

the focal point of its devotion.[12] And it was also the object of the growth in the veneration of the Sacred Heart of Jesus, by which in symbolic language, such as was then easily understood, the notion of a just God was supplemented by reference to the redemptive love of the God-Man.[13]

But there were attempts once more, in the age of enlightenment, at injecting, by violent means, unity into the concept of the world, this time by rationalist elimination of the mysteries of faith in favour of a purely natural world order, for which the work of the Redeemer and the sacraments of the Church had no more than moral significance. The practice of an age secure in the faith which had emphasized the objective validity of the sacraments was opposed by subjectivism which appeared to recognize the achievements of the natural man alone.[14]

Even though the age of enlightenment in its pretentious form was but a short interlude in the intellectual currents of the modern world, the temptation of an enlightened, rationalist, if not materialist outlook, is still increasing among the masses under the impact of the triumphs of modern science and technology. The pastoral work of the Church had increasingly to meet the intellectual curiosity of modern man in new forms of teaching the faith which promoted understanding and comprehension, and allowed the notes of the "good news" to ring again from among the multitude of doctrines.

Some nineteenth century efforts to restore especially the

[12] Pierre Pourrat (W. S. Reilly, trans.), *Father Olier* (Baltimore: Voice Publ. Co., 1932).

[13] L. Verheylezoon, *Devotion to the Sacred Heart* (Westminster: Newman, 1955); J. Galot (John Chapin, trans.), *The Heart of Christ* (Westminster: Newman, 1955); J. Stierli, *Heart of the Saviour* (New York: Herder and Herder, 1958).

[14] F. X. Arnold, *Grundsätzliches und Geschichtliches zur Theologie der Seelsorge* (*Untersuchungen zur Theologie der Seelsorge*, 2) (Freiburg: Herder, 1949), pp. 58ff. and pp. 88ff.

kingdom of God to its central place (prompted, among others, by the German Catholic writer J. B. Hirscher) were at first unsuccessful because it was difficult to draw clear lines of demarcation between the preaching of the faith and scholarly theology.[15] The manner of presenting the faith remained unchanged in that century. On the basis of the findings of theology, it was sought, above all, to propound clear single concepts, and to build with these as comprehensive a knowledge of the faith as possible.

A new attitude sprang from the developments which gave birth to the liturgical movement. There was an increasing appreciation for history and tradition in the nineteenth century: Christian antiquity, the monuments of the catacombs, the writings of the Fathers and the liturgical sacramental life of the early Church were rediscovered. A first fruit was the gradual return to a fuller understanding of the Church.[16] Decisive steps were taken under St. Pius X, which resulted in a return to the fuller sacramental life of ancient ecclesiastical tradition. It came suddenly to be recognized that the life of the Church can be renewed only by gathering the faithful around the altar and by their direct participation in the Mass. Thus arose the liturgical movement. At first it was only a few who recognized in it the outline of a simple but deep Christian faith, a liberating return to the great truths of faith. A new source of inspiration besides the liturgy was Sacred Scripture, but it was soon recognized that this renewal of religious life in the Church must not be dissipated in partisan movements which in some special way

[15] F. X. Arnold, *Dienst am Glauben* (*Untersuchungen zur Theologie der Seelsorge,* 1) (Freiburg: Herder, 1948), especially pp. 31 ff.

[16] O. Rousseau (Benedictines of Westminster Priory), *The Progress of the Liturgy* (Westminster: Newman, 1951), in which a decisive chapter in the prehistory of the liturgical movement is entitled: "German Ecclesiology in the Nineteenth Century", pp. 51–68. The chapter deals chiefly with the work of Möhler and the Tübingen School.

might be added to already existing pastoral methods and aids, but that the whole of pastoral work ought to be based on some large and uniform programme. A kind of faith such as is illuminated in the Roman liturgy as heir to Christian antiquity ought to be unfolded with equal and greater clarity, in the actual teaching of the faith. Sermon and catechesis, religious art and the organization of services ought to strive jointly to promote a consciousness of the faith upon which the liturgical and sacramental life may be based, and from which a joyful Christian faith can arise. This will be possible only when out of the many accretions of the centuries the one single message, the kerygma of the early Church, is once again allowed to emerge. To accomplish this, Christ must be restored to the centre of the faith.[17] The restoration of the kerygma to its full power and clarity is, therefore, a principal task of modern pastoral work.

[17] Th. Kampmann, "Die Gegenwartsgestalt der Kirche und die christliche Erziehung" in *Paderborner Schriften zur Pädagogik und Katechetik,* 3 (Paderborn, 1951), p. 19: "Within that period of Church History of which we are contemporaries, no other happening has as great significance as the liturgico-kerygmatical, the sacramental-biblical revival." Compare this with the synoptic review of H. Elfers, "Verkündigung heute" in *Die Kirche in der Welt,* Vol. 4 (1951), pp. 9–16, 185–190, 329–338; Vol. 5 (1952), pp. 15–18.

APPENDIX III

Kerygmatic Theology

WHENEVER the renewal of the content of the Christian message is mentioned nowadays, phrases such as "theology of the 'message'" and "kerygmatic theology" are used. What is meant by them?

As we have shown in various places in this book,[1] the efforts to bring about such a renewal do not imply a special kind of theology but a clear and effective presentation of Christ's message itself. The message has to be defined apart from theology and in its own right. No other claim was intended by the author of the book mentioned above,[2] and in the treatises on the subject which followed.[3] In subsequent contributions to this subject, however, the opinion was advanced that the "message" should be differentiated not only from theology proper and should remain much closer to the original presentation of the "good news" in the Bible and in the writings of the Fathers, but also that a special theology for the use of pastors was required, which is the theology of the message.[4] This last thesis, especially, has

[1] *Ut supra*, p. 36, p. 96, p. 137, etc.

[2] J. A. Jungmann, *Die Frohbotschaft und unsere Glaubensverkündigung* (Regensburg: Pustet, 1936).

[3] F. Lakner, "Das Zentralobjekt der Theologie" in *ZkTh,* Vol. 62 (1938), pp. 1–36; idem, "Theorie einer Verkündigungstheologie" in *Theologie der Zeit,* Vol. 3 (Vienna, 1939), pp. 1–63; J. B. Lotz, "Wissenschaft und Verkündigung" in *ZkTh,* Vol. 62 (1938), pp. 465–501; Hugo Rahner, *Eine Theologie der Verkündigung* (2nd ed.; Freiburg: Herder, 1939); F. Dander, *Christus alles und in allen. Gedanken zum Aufbau einer Seelsorgedogmatik* (Innsbruck: Rauch, 1939).

[4] Consult especially the works of F. Lakner and J. B. Lotz in the foregoing footnote.

been the subject of lively discussions in many journals and reviews, at first in German-speaking countries,[5] and later elsewhere.[6] The thesis has now been rejected almost universally.[7] While admitting the urgency of the matter as seen by the kerygmaticists, most critics regarded as unnecessary a special

[5] A survey on the discussion is offered in the first part of the book of E. Kappler, *Die Verkündigungstheologie* (*Studia Friburgensia,* 2) (Fribourg, 1949), pp. 7–110: "Darstellung des kerygmatischen Schrifttums", Kappler's own position in the rest of the book (113–262) cannot be considered to advance the discussion, since he often misunderstands basic thoughts (for example, the distinction between *verum* and *bonum* as being the respective views of theology and of kerygmatics—as if when preaching the message, by emphasizing truth as truth of salvation and as a goal to be attained, we attribute to the will a role that should be played by the intellect) and finally because he fails to see the problem as such. For since a deepening of the life of faith is necessarily conditioned by a more intensive assent to eternal truth, it is self-evident "that a proclamation of the faith developed in the content of faith is not capable *eo ipso* of increasing proportionately its exercise" (pp. 245f. and p. 194); cf. also the critical observations work by W. Croce, *ZkTh,* Vol. 72 (1950), pp. 121f. and M. Nicoláu, *Revista española de Teología,* Vol. 12 (1952), pp. 44f.

[6] Consult G. B. Guzzetti, "Saggio bibliografico sulla teologia della predicazione" in *La Scuola cattolica,* Vol. 78 (Milan, 1950), pp. 350–356. This bibliography is a part of a special number that was dedicated to the kerygmatic problem. Among those works mentioned, a special place must be accorded to the historical survey done by G. B. Guzzetti, "La controversia sulla teologia della predicazione" (pp. 260–282), as well as the penetrating study of G. Corti, "Alla radice della controversia kerigmatica" (pp. 283–301): the facts of salvation are recommended as the starting point also for theology; cf. also the fine piece of work by C. Colombo, *Teologia e evangelizzazione* (pp. 302–324), and others. He refers to kindred thoughts in the development of M. J. Scheeben and E. Mersch.

[7] Worthy of consideration is the judgement of B. Poschmann in *Théol. Revue,* Vol. 39 (1940), p. 122, who thinks it useful if the repetition of dogmatics, such as is often customary at the end of theological studies in seminaries could be given in the way proposed by kerygmatic theology.

theology of the "message"; this task had to be solved, they held, by the theologians themselves. But it was also generally recognized that the traditional school theology could not cope with it and that it had become too far removed from the urgent pastoral problems.

The "school theology" referred to was not, of course, the kind of research that deals with various theological problems in an historical or speculative manner without regard for any practical considerations. What was meant was the summarizing systematic presentation, the doctrine as it is usually propounded in lectures, in manuals of theology, especially in dogmatics. It has been said of it that it should be more closely linked to live issues (Schröteler), that it should be more conscious of its charismatic character, in virtue of which it is "speaking from the Spirit of God" (Stolz), that the faith alone should be "unfolded into fuller and deeper knowledge" in theology (Beumer), that the truths of revelation must be seen as truths of salvation, in short, that theology should be a theology of salvation.[8] The German theologian, Michael Schmaus, in his *Katholische Dogmatik*[9] has shown—even before the controversy began—how this problem should be met. Theology, says Schmaus, must free itself of its lack of life by entering into history, into the history of salvation: "the historical Christ, who died, rose again and was transfigured".[10] Schmaus, therefore, demands a Christocentric point of view also for scientific theology; Christ is part of his definition of theology, the proper

[8] More precise passages, cf. Kappler, *op. cit.*, pp. 22–28.

[9] *Katholische Dogmatik,* 5 vols. (Munich: Hueber Verlag (3rd/4th ed., 1948–1953).

[10] M. Schmaus, "Brauchen wir eine Theologie der Verkündigung?" in *Die Seelsorge,* Vol. 16 (Hildesheim, 1938), pp. 1–12; idem, "Ein Wort zur Verkündigungstheologie" in *Theologie u. Glaube,* Vol. 33 (1941), pp. 312–322, especially pp. 318f.

subject of which is not "God in Himself"[11] but God "insofar as he has revealed Himself in Christ and has preserved this revelation of Himself in the Church and throughout time".[12]

If theology is understood in this sense, then the aims implied in a "theology of the message" have actually been realized in their essentials, and it could be dispensed with altogether. Is there any reason why we should continue to speak of a "theology of the message"? We can justify its use, however, if by it we mean all those theoretical discussions and practical efforts which serve to make manifest and to unfold the kerygma and should lead to a renewal of the content of the message in sermon, catechesis and in the forms of worship. In that case it would be better to use the term kerygmatics, in which catechetics and of homiletics would be contained.

Many studies on this subject have been published, for instance, researches on the rules governing religious language and of the changes which these have undergone in different ages and

[11] The majority of theologians declare that "the subject" of theology is *Deus sub ratione Deitatis,* cf. M. J. Congar, "Théologie" in *Dictionnaire de Théologie Catholique,* Vol. XV (1946), pp. 341–352, especially pp. 456f. This concept is connected with the continued use of the Platonic and Aristotelian concept of science, according to which science can deal only with the general and contingent, not with concrete facts. Compare Lakner, *Theorie einer Verkündigungstheologie,* p. 15, and Schmaus, "Ein Wort . . .", *loc. cit.,* p. 319f. See also C. Journet (R. F. Smith, trans.), *The Wisdom of Faith* (Westminster, Md.: Newman, 1951), pp. 76–77, and 86–88.

[12] M. Schmaus, *op. cit.,* Vol. I (3/4) (1948), pp. 26f.; compare this with Vol. II (3/4) (1949), pp. IXf. (Preface to the first edition). Consult J. C. Murray, "Towards a Theology for the Layman" in *Theological Studies,* Vol. 5 (1944), pp. 43–75 and 340–376, who without directly attacking the current concept of the subject matter of theology, proposes *Christus totus* especially for those theological courses which those laymen who study at various colleges must take in order to prepare themselves for Catholic Action (p. 359ff.).

cultures.[13] Individual religious concepts, such as salvation, grace, mystery, the kingdom of God, heaven, etc., do not of course appear in the origins of our faith in the form of pure concepts; they contain symbolical elements which necessarily have been taken from the surrounding cultures. Although we reject a "de-mythologizing"[14] of the New Testament, which in Protestant theology has been demanded by Rudolf Bultmann, a realization is, nevertheless, required of the part played by imagination and time. The assessment of their significance is a task for exegesis, which should be followed up by a study of the symbols borrowed from Patristic times and the Middle Ages: this study can be of immediate value for a transmission of the message through the elucidation of our own religious terminology and through judgement on present studies.[15]

More important, however, than this analysis of individual terms and concepts with reference to cultural factors, should be the historical study of the principal themes of the Christian message with reference to the continuous task of presenting to mankind "the good news" effectively. This enquiry would be concerned with questions about the themes which in particular instances had been given prominence in the transmission of the message and why this was done in so many different ways.[16] The history of Christian feasts can, to a certain extent, provide the clues.[17] It is evidently not mere chance that the

[13] A work of this kind is P. Bolkovac, *Seelsorge und Sprache* (Nürnberg, 1946).

[14] O. Cullmann, "Rudolf Bultmann's Concept of Myth and the New Testament" in *Theology Digest,* Vol. IV (1956), pp. 140–145.

[15] *Ut supra,* p. 244.

[16] On the importance of historical studies which are able "to show us faulty developments, to make us understand better the present situation and so indicate the way to be taken in the future", cf. H. Elfers, "Verkündigung heute" in *Die Kirche in der Welt,* Vol. 5 (1952), p. 17.

[17] As a very modest attempt in this direction, consult the work of the author, J. A. Jungmann, *Liturgical Worship* (New York: F. Pustet,

resurrection was, in Christian antiquity, considered to be the sum-total of all the benefits of redemption,[18] since Easter was the sole feast celebrated in the Church, and that in that era many books were written on *De resurrectione;* furthermore, that the cross of Christ was seen and symbolically represented as a transfigured paschal cross and as the beginning of salvation rather than as an object-lesson in redemptive sufferings. It is also significant for the early Byzantine Church that Marian themes predominated in sermons, since she had instituted and developed the older feasts of our Lady in answer to the christological controversies. One would also have to enquire into the basic changes in the propagation of the Christian message. What radical transformations, have, for example, occured in the Paschal sermon?[19] How much was the concept of the Church or of the Communion of Saints changed under the influence of intellectual currents in the catechisms?[20] We might enquire into the different views of the Eucharist that have been held through the centuries and how deeply these determined the forms of the Mass. To bring out the fulness which the Christian message attained at some stage, or to realize the decay from which we perhaps are still suffering today is to perform a service of greater value for the kerygmatic renewal.

Much has already been done in this connection in Christian archeology and indeed in internal Church History. We need but recall the researches of Franz Josef Dölger on the images

1941), pp. 30–46 ["Das Christusgeheimnis im Kirchenjahr" in *Gewordene Liturgie* (Innsbruck: Rauch, 1941), pp. 295–321].

[18] See above, p. 381.

[19] Br. Dreher, "Die Osterpredigt" in *Untersuchungen zur Theologie der Seelsorge,* 3 (Freiburg: Herder, 1951).

[20] Consult above, p. 145ff. and p. 383, and also C. E. Elwell, *The Influence of the Enlightenment on the Catholic Theory of Religious Education in France 1750–1850* (Cambridge: Harvard University Press, 1944), especially pp. 203–228.

which the early Christian Church developed for Christ *(sol salutis, sol iustitiae, Ichthus)* or for Baptism *(sphragis)*. These researches have been continued in his school and importan contributions have been made to them by, among others, Hugo Rahner.[21] In France Jean Daniélou has published detailed studies on the role of typology in Christian antiquity, and in particular, on the use of the Old Testament in the presentation of the redemption in the New Testament.[22] Some marginal subjects, such as Christian iconography or the history of devotion[23] and not least the history of literature, can add much to the history of the proclamation of the Christian message. Studies on the history of the content of catechesis and sermons are today in process of preparation.[24]

Finally, the notion of a theology of the message, in the wider

[21] H. Rahner, *Griechische Mythen in christlicher Deutung* (Zürich, 1945). Of the many treatises in the *Zeitschrift für katholische Theologie,* we cite particularly *Mysterium lunae* (*ZkTh,* 1939/40); *Antenna Crucis* (*ZkTh,* 1941/43; 1953).

[22] J. Daniélou, *Bible et Liturgie* (*Lex Orandi,* 11) (Paris: Editions du Cerf, 1951); tr. as *The Bible and the Liturgy* (Notre Dame, Ind.: University of Notre Dame Press, 1956).

[23] Especially important is P. Pourrat (W. H. Mitchell and S. P. Jacques, trans.), *Christian Spirituality,* 3 vols. (New York: P. J. Kenedy, 1922/28) Vol. IV (1954) (in various editions).

[24] Here we must place those famous studies from which we have quoted frequently in the course of this book: *Untersuchungen zur Theologie der Seelsorge* edited by F. X. Arnold. There is a history of catechesis according to various subjects, but from a Protestant standpoint (Baptism, Confession, Last Supper, Confirmation) contained in the first volume of G. v. Zezschwitz, *System der christlich-kirchlichen Katechetik,* 2 vols. (Leipzig, 1864–1872). A partial treatment of the history of catechetics is contained in G. H. Gerberding, *The Lutheran Catechist* (Philadelphia: Lutheran Publ. Society, 1910), pp. 45–88. For a thorough study of catechisms, consult J. Hofinger, *Geschichte des Katechismus,* pp. 129–212; using the Austrian catechism of 1777 he has thrown much light on the changes which the treatment of the content of the more important doctrines have undergone.

sense of the term, ought to include also the practical efforts which aim at presenting the message of salvation as a whole, or in parts, in all its richness and not merely as an object of pure scholarship. It is possible to connect theology proper with the concrete propagation of the message in catechesis and sermon. There have been some attempts, for instance, at presenting theology books for the laity or popular catechisms. It is the task of the official catechisms to achieve in a comprehensive form the true ideal of spreading the Christian message.

APPENDIX IV

Catechesis in England

It will be immediately obvious to the English reader that our catechism is very different from the new national catechisms that are now in use on the continent. In these the arrangement of the material is based on the new emphases in theology and the new pedagogical outlook. For the former, the German Catechism is the best (published by Herder and Herder, New York, and available in Great Britain from Burns, Oates). The section on the Church, for instance, is headed: "The Church and our Sanctification", and the whole material concerning the Church is dealt with under this heading: the foundation, jurisdiction, constitution, the Church's teaching office, infallibility and the Communion of Saints. This is immediately followed by the sections on Baptism and Grace.

In all the continental catechisms we find the material arranged in lesson units that begin with a Scripture passage or a narrative, proceed to an exposition of the material, and conclude with a reference to the liturgy, with some practical work, and a suggestion how the doctrine may be carried over into practical life.

Although in some (e. g. the French), there is an attempt to form, within the official catechism, a graded syllabus, so that the younger children are not required to learn the whole of it, yet since there is a tendency to postpone the learning of catechism answers until after ten (as Father Jungmann observes), this need is not now so acutely felt.

In England, most of this matter of the division of material is provided for by the official diocesan syllabuses and the catechism is used in different ways according to the directives of those syllabuses. Thus those using the Westminster Syllabus are required to teach most of the catechism to children between the ages of eight and eleven. In the Birmingham diocese the teaching of the official text of the catechism is postponed until the age of eleven.

Perhaps the chief difference between the continental outlook and the English is that whereas on the continent there has been a steady concern to improve books (whether for the teacher or the children), the English have put their trust in a better training of teachers. Even so, and no doubt largely owing to their circumstances, these countries have been much more active in training lay-catechists than has been the case in England.

Catechism reform is now on the way in in England and one may be allowed to express the hope that the good work and great experience of continental catechists will be taken into account and, where possible made use of.

Bibliography for England

J. J. Branigan, *The Teaching of Religion in Catholic Schools.* Preface by Bishop A. Beck (Macmillan).

K. Cronin, C. M., *Teaching the Religion Lesson* (Paternoster Publications).

Diocesan Schemes:

Archdiocese of Westminster Syllabus of Religious Instruction for Schools.

A Development of the Syllabus of Religion as used in the Westminster Diocese.

Concise graduated leaflet instruction course for teachers:

Suggestions for Teachers using the Westminster Syllabus.

Birmingham Scheme of Religious Instruction (Obtainable free from 27, Temple Street, Lower Gornal, Dudley, Worcs.).

Birmingham. *Syllabus for Primary Schools.* Recently revised and more detailed.

S.N.D., *Religious Teaching of Young Children* (Sands).

F. H. Drinkwater, *Doctrine for the Juniors.* For those under eleven (B.O.W.)

—, *Short Instructions on the Mass* (B.O.W.).

—, *The Abbreviated Catechism.* For secondary-modern schools in the Archdiocese of Birmingham.

—, *The Abbreviated Catechism with Explanations.* For those over fourteen (B.O.W.).

—, *Teaching the Catechism.* A commentary on the whole catechism (B.O.W.).

—, *Twelve and After.* For secondary-modern or grammar schools (Samuel Walker).

—, *Talks to Teenagers* (B.O.W.).

—, *Catholic Schools Assembly Book.* In two editions, for teachers and for pupils (Univ. of London Press).

—, *Educational Essays.* Here will be found many practical hints on teaching (B.O.W. and Macmillan).

L. Greenstock, *Christopher's Talks to Little Ones* (B.O.W.).

For the Grammar School religious examinations:

W. J. Moore, *Christ, the Church and the Soul.* A textbook for the syllabus of the School Religious Certificate (B.O.W.).

F. J. Shutt, *The Higher Religious Certificate.* Two Parts (B.O.W.).

Canon F. H. Drinkwater

F. H. Drinkwater, *Stories in School* (Farnworth, Lancs.: Catholic Printing Company). Material for children under twelve, from Scripture and the lives of the saints, with an introduction on the art of storytelling.

For use with the Catechism for children over eleven:

F. H. Drinkwater, *Catechism Stories* (B. O.W.).

—, *More Catechism Stories* (Hinckley, Leics.: Samuel Walker).

—, *Third Book of Catechism Stories* (Sands and Co.).

Pictures: there are the well known Nelson series, the S.P.C.K. series, the "cut-out" pictures of Our Lady's Catechists and their Parable Painting Books (Oxted, Surrey: Phenth House); the painting pictures of the Bloomsbury Co. (London); a painting book on the Mass, *My Mass Book* (Faversham, Kent: Carmelite Press) as well as many others.

Of all the activities that have been the most used in England, drama, whether in or out of the classroom, has been perhaps the most popular. To this Canon Drinkwater has made a distinctive contribution. It is largely thanks to him that drama has developed as a means of Christian teaching, and he has understood its possibilities and limitations better than any one else. A general statement of his views will be found in: "Teaching Religion through Drama" in *Sower* No. 168, July, 1948. Points that he makes here and elsewhere are that: (1) it should be clearly realized that dramatization of a simple, naive kind suitable for infants would be out of place with older children; (2) plays need careful preparation if they are to have their effect; (3) there should be a distinction between classroom dramatization and what is suitable for a stage; (4) that not all teachers are gifted with a dramatic sense and these should feel under no obligation to use the method.

A list of plays, mostly by Canon Drinkwater, with contributions by Miss M. E. Moloney, to the *Sower*.
Gabriel's Ave (B.O.W. - out of print).
The Five Joyful Mysteries (Univ. of London Press, 1955). For older children.
Prophets and Kings (Univ. of London Press, 1922). For under-elevens.
Catechism Plays (B.O.W., 1955). For older children.
Domine, Quo Vadis? (The Sower, 1952).
A Love Knows How (the same). For boys.
Our Living Sacrifice (the same). For older children, on the Mass.
Looking Ahead (the same). For older children on Vocation.

INDEX OF PERSONS

INDEX OF SUBJECTS